15 CANADIAN POETS X 3

15 CANADIAN POETS X 3

FOURTH EDITION

EDITED BY

GARY GEDDES

OXFORD
UNIVERSITY PRESS

OXFORD
UNIVERSITY PRESS

70 Wynford Drive, Don Mills, Ontario M3C 1J9
www.oupcan.com

Oxford University Press is a department of the University of Oxford.
It furthers the University's objective of excellence in research, scholarship,
and education by publishing worldwide in

Oxford   New York

*Athens Auckland Bangkok Bogotà Buenos Aires
Cape Town Chennai Dar es Salaam Delhi Florence Hong Kong Istanbul
Karachi Kolkata Kuala Lumpur Madrid Melbourne Mexico City Mumbai
Nairobi Paris São Paulo Singapore Taipei Tokyo Toronto Warsaw*

with associated companies in *Berlin Ibadan*

Oxford is a trade mark of Oxford University Press
in the UK and in certain other countries

Published in Canada
by Oxford University Press

Copyright © Oxford University Press Canada 2001

The moral rights of the author have been asserted

Database right Oxford University Press (maker)

First published 2001

National Library of Canada Cataloguing in Publication Data

Main entry under title:

15 Canadian poets X3

4th ed.
First ed. (1970) published under title: 15 Canadian poets.
Second ed. (1978) published under title: 15 Canadian poets plus 5.
Third ed. (1988) published under title: 15 Canadian poets times 2.
Includes index.
ISBN 0–19–541643–0

1. Canadian poetry (English)—20th century.* I. Geddes, Gary, 1940–   .
II. Title: 15 Canadian poets times 3. III. Fifteen Canadian poets times three.

PS8291.F53 2001   C811'.5408   C2001–930244–4
PR9195.7.F53 2001

Cover and Text design by Joan Dempsey

1 2 3 4 – 04 03 02 01

This book is printed on permanent (acid-free) paper ∞.

Printed in Canada

CONTENTS

PREFACE

No Canadian poet was ever mentioned at King Edward High School in Vancouver. Shelley, of course, and Keats—those darlings of adolescence, with their passions and early deaths—but not Dorothy Livesay, who was less than a mile away arguing with her communist and literary friends at the White Lunch restaurant on Hastings Street. And what about Malcolm Lowry, who lived across the Burrard Inlet at Dollarton, and had written his most important work, *Under the Volcano*, during his years there. His satiric poem, 'Christ Walks in This Infernal District Too', would not only have livened up afternoons in the Grey Zone of 1950s secondary school culture, but also have set a few bells ringing. Things weren't much better at UBC. The English Department employed two poets, but kept their candles well hidden, if not extinguished, under a bushel of foreign content. I studied Milton with one of them, Roy Daniells, and was a guest at his house, but never knew he had written two exceptional sonnet sequences. Only in my final year did 'Canpo' grab me, in a most surprising way.

I was ambling, bear-like, along the third-floor corridor of the Buchanan Building, looking at the bulletin boards for inspiration and possible work, when a door flew open and the narrow space was inundated with shouts and banging noises. As I inched past, fingers closed around my wrist and I was dragged into a maze of cardboard boxes, a veritable Badland of books, textbook hoodoos, leaning towers of reference books, and a glacial scree of unused examination copies. My assailant, a lanky man with a grey beard, pinkish complexion, and shifting, mischievous eyes, released his grip and plopped down in the swivel chair behind his desk. He made a sweeping gesture that took in the hundreds of books stacked, leaning, and scattered wall-to-wall.

'I'm out of here. Paroled at last from this goddam place. Be my guest, take any books you want.' Using the desk for propulsion, he spun himself in his swivel chair, making several gleeful revolutions, then leapt to his feet again, swept past me, and disappeared down the corridor in the direction of the washroom. I don't recall the three books I grabbed without looking. I was too rattled by the experience to realize I'd just encountered one of Canada's finest poets, whose name or work I'd never even heard of. Three years later I would meet Earle Birney again, when he came to the University of Toronto as writer-in-residence.

I wish I could say that graduate school was a strong purveyor of things Canadian. At that time, there were no Canadian Literature courses offered in the Honours Program, so I enrolled in something called American and Canadian Literature, which consisted of nine American novels and one Canadian, Hugh MacLennan's *The Watch that Ends the Night*, which I quickly dubbed The Book that Ends the Course. This was wishful thinking, of course, as the instructor never got around to discussing it. The situation was about to change, however—a terrible beauty was being born.

Blocks away, Coach House Press and House of Anansi, taking courage from Souster and Dudek's Contact Press, were busy cranking out works by Ondaatje, Atwood, and bp Nichol on linotype machines and small presses. Cohen, Layton, and Birney were touring the country, pausing to be photographed with E.J. Pratt. Gwendolyn MacEwen was wowing audiences at the Bohemian Embassy with her spell-binding poems and dramatic performances. Across Canada, the names and idiosyncrasies of a hundred localities were being inscribed in poems, their housewives, factory workers, students, and professionals were being named, taking their place amidst what A.M. Klein had called a 'green inventory in world but scarcely uttered'.

So much was happening on the street that academia could hardly ignore it. The felicitous convergence of three literary figures—Claude Bissell as University of Toronto president, Douglas LePan as principal of University College, and Robertson Davies as master of Massey College—helped to advance the cause of Canlit: after Earle Birney, Margaret Laurence was invited to serve as writer-in-residence. To my surprise and delight, F.W. Watt, who pioneered a graduate course on Canadian poetry, asked if I would like to teach University College's new under-graduate course in Canadian Literature.

This posed a problem, since no major anthologies included Canadian, not to mention recent British and American, poets. As I was also teaching Canadian poetry at Trent University in Peterborough and at Ryerson Polytechnic Institute in Toronto, I felt this lack of a good anthology intensely. I was complaining about this in the staff room at Ryerson when one of my colleagues, Patricia Owen, inter-rupted to say, why don't you edit one, then? I said I'd love to do it, but no one was likely to publish a book by an unknown schmuck from Vancouver, whose only credits were a few published poems, articles, and reviews and a fleeting encounter in a hallway with Earle Birney. Pat said she would talk to her husband, Ivon Owen, who was head of Oxford University Press in Canada. The result of our meeting would be three anthologies: *20th-Century Poetry & Poetics, 15 Canadian Poets,* and *Skookum Wawa: Writings of the Canadian Northwest.*

I wanted, simply, to produce a useful and exciting teaching anthology with enough formal variety to alert readers to the poetic treasures that were out there and enough poems by each poet to make possible an in-depth study. I also wanted to make room for a number of younger writers, including Atwood, Ondaatje, Cohen, Bowering, Newlove, and Webb, even if this meant leaving out a few of the more familiar names. Subsequent editions of the anthology pursued the same goal, though the growing embarrassment of riches made the matter of selection more and more difficult. So, too, did the failure to materialize of those scholarly volumes, which I had anticipated would celebrate the reputations of Jay Macpherson, George Bowering, George Johnston, James Reaney, Milton Acorn, and other established poets. Eventually, I felt compelled to draw more of the older guard—Livesay, Gustafson, Pratt, and F.R. Scott—into subsequent editions, though I never pretended, even then, that I was offering more than one editor's choice, a cross-section of Canadian poetry

2

In the midst of changing classroom expectations, where the study of literary texts within a national context has been, to a considerable extent, supplanted by other interests—including feminism, ethnicity, gender, literature and film, creative writing, communications, and post-colonialism—the idea of studying poetry at all, never mind Canadian poetry, may seem somewhat anachronistic. With the nation-state appearing to lumber dinosaur-like—and some would say, not a moment too soon—towards extinction, only to be replaced by the rule of capital and multi-national corporations, it's worthwhile remembering George Grant's telling observation that 'If you skip the stage of nationalism, you don't become internationals (there are no such animals), but Americans. It's as simple as that.'

I am more than ever convinced that Canada must preserve its cultural identity, rather than disappear within the larger US culture. We have a unique experiment underway in this country. It involves renegotiating land claims with our First Nations, working out a middle ground to protect and nourish the language and culture of the Québécois, struggling to achieve a balance between the provinces and the central government, and trying to adjust to the challenges of our now multicultural world. The old myths of Canada as a peacemaker, as a nation of gentle saints, won't wash any more, not when we think of smallpox blankets, *Komogatu Maru*, the Head Tax, residential schools, the Winnipeg strike, internment camps, the War Measures Act, and Somalia. However, we also have medicare, a populace still amenable to public enterprise, a modicum of respect for the land, and a tradition of noisy compromise; we are still capable, in other words, of being dragged into a state of decency.

And don't let anyone—politician, businessman, media hack, or guru—persuade you that these differences are not worth preserving. As Herschel Hardin says in our unacknowledged bible, *A Nation Unaware*:

> It is because Canadian civilization is so vulnerable, because every once in a while it seems to be coming apart at the seams under the pressure of centrifugal forces, that it has been so fruitful, and has slowly developed a subterranean strength. Nothing has added to that strength, and to that vulnerability, more than the separatist movement, and English Canada's facing up to the possibility it symbolizes, and the attempts of René Lévesque and others to explain to English Canadians the logic behind the possibility.

Our experiment involves a constant naming and re-naming—the green inventory refusing completion. What Lord Durham described as 'two nations warring in the bosom of a single state' has been described by Margaret Atwood, on one occasion, as 'paranoid schizophrenia' and, on another, as 'a duet for two deaf singers'. Now we have more voices speaking, demanding to be heard. The poets, traditional keepers of the word-hoard, caretakers of the dialects of the tribe, are more necessary than ever, to give these new realities imaginative shape. Robert

Kroetsch once described Canada as a poem, a dream we have forgotten, an orphanage of snow:

> We are tempted to escape the nightmare of history. General Wolfe, General Middleton: they are only the bungling aliens who won, the gunmen of reality. I grew up thinking Wolfe a sort of sneaky bastard, climbing that cliff-side in the dark. For Middleton, I was only embarrassed, a man of such ill-consequence allowed to ride a horse.

John Newlove poses the question more broadly in 'The Pride', asking us to confront 'the knowledge of / our origins, and where / we are in truth, / whose land this is / and is to be.' Margaret Laurence, singling out the Métis people as symbolic of the new reality we are creating, which is neither French nor English, nor purely Aboriginal, asked us to listen to each other, and to the land. Al Purdy, addressing the ongoing struggle, recalls our common origins and shared values: 'only this handful of earth / for a time at least / I have no other place to go.' And a new generation of poets, including Tim Lilburn, Don McKay, and Jan Zwicky, is responding to the crucial question—How To Be Here?—encouraging a 'deeper courtesy of the eye' and linking the lyric impulse with First Nations teachings about husbanding the earth and with the intuitions of deep ecology.

We may be, as poet Robin Skelton suggests, 'passionate provincials devoted to local mythologies', but we are also citizens of the world, rejoicing in cultural diversity, inclined to fight on behalf of the disadvantaged and, with some wavering on the part of various federal governments, committed to shaping an independent foreign policy. Poets included here know the importance and the dangers of naming and would share Brazilian philosopher and educator Paolo Freire's view that 'To exist, humanly, is to name the world, to change it. Once named, the world in its turn reappears to the namers as a problem and requires of them a new naming. There is no true word that is not at the same time a praxis. Thus, to speak a true word is to transform the world.' We need their subtle discriminations of conduct, their lyric and narrative responses to the pressures of a constantly changing reality.

3

15 Canadian Poets X3, a whacking big fourth edition, has leaned, once again, toward the emerging generation of mature poets, although I've added Robin Blaser, whose work on the serial poem has influenced two generations of writers. The importance of the long poem and poetic narrative, already evidenced by the presence in the anthology of Robert Kroetsch's 'Seed Catalogue', John Newlove's 'The Pride', and generous excerpts from long poems by Pratt, Livesay, Blaser, Ondaatje, and MacEwen, has been heightened with the inclusion of Anne Carson's 'The Glass Essay' and Dionne Brand's 'No Language Is Neutral'.

The long poem in its many manifestations—as narrative, serial poem, meditation, or book-length exploration of history and place—seems to me the central testing-ground for poets, as well as a major poetic site for psychological, social, and political analysis. It's also often the lab where the most interesting experiments with language are taking place. And Milton Wilson's wise observation many years ago seems as applicable now to the work of Kroetsch, Ondaatje, and others as it did at the time to Pratt:

> I have the notion that the problems involved in *Towards the Last Spike* are going to be the central problems in the poetry of our future. . . . [Pratt] writes narratives, no doubt, but discontinuous narratives which are always turning, on the one side, into documents, letters and jokes, and on the other, into pure lyrics.

Since the emergence of the novel and short story into the literary mainstream, poetic narrative has sometimes been viewed as problematic, although there has been no shortage of narrative elements in long and short poems. Although Edgar Allan Poe considered narrative poetry a 'contradiction in terms' and twentieth-century critic B.S. Johnson has described narrative poets as 'literary flat-earthers', story, however truncated, continues to play a significant role in contemporary poetry. As bp Nichol has said,

> When we write as we write we are always telling a story. When I write as I write I am telling the story of how I see the world, how it's been given to me, what I take from it. In the long poem I have the time to tell you that in all its faces or, at least, in as many faces as I've seen so far. Even when I'm not telling a specific story, I'm telling you that story. A narrative in language. The long poem. How I see the world.

The lyric continues to hold the attention of poets, since it represents the spirit in full song, the most highly charged dance of language and feeling. The lyric impulse continues to drive poems of all sizes. However, the lyric poem, as signature and advertisement of the self, raises questions about the role of the individual ego and its potential to interfere with the poetic quest for a deeper and, perhaps, a larger truth. It may be that the 'song of myself', to use Walt Whitman's phrase, can be the vehicle for larger truths about all of us, about the human condition in general. Yet the tremendous freight of personal trivia that the lyric has been forced to carry in the last century has made it a target for those who wish poetry to recover the subtlety, economy, and suggestiveness of Asian poetic forms or the archetypal depths of great poems from the past, not cleansed of the personal, but achieving a music that lifts the personal to the level of the symbolic. The intersection of lyric and narrative impulses continues to be the site of much experiment and debate. The contemporary Canadian poem may, like the totem pole, appear at first glance to be a series of unrelated, stacked images, but turns out to be much more: a subversive talking-stick, a repository of familiar and submerged stories.

4

I would like to thank the poets whose work is included here, many of whom have made suggestions about the selections and notes. Thanks are also due to the editors at Oxford, Laura McLeod and Phyllis Wilson, as well as friends and acquaintances who, over the years, have advised, cajoled, and challenged me in my efforts to put together a vibrant combination of poets and poems for the classroom: Ron Smith, Michael Ondaatje, Sharon Thesen, Phyllis Webb, P.K. Page, Tim Lilburn, W.J. Keith, Mark Abley, Phyllis Bruce, F.W. Watt, Hugo McPherson, Jan Geddes, Douglas Barbour, Stephen Scobie, Dennis Cooley, Robert Allen, Henry Beissel, Mary di Michele, George Johnston, Barry McKinnon, Michael Harris, Win Bogaards, and David Solway. Their combination of generosity and integrity is especially commendable, considering the fact that so many of them are fine poets whose work might have confidently graced these pages.

Gary Geddes

E.J. PRATT

(1883–1964)

Edwin John Pratt was born in Western Bay, Newfoundland, the son of a Methodist minister. After graduating from St John's Methodist College, he spent four years as a teacher and minister in coastal villages before entering the University of Toronto. A succession of degrees followed—BA in Philosophy (1911), MA (1912), BD (1913), and Ph.D. in Theology (1917)—after which he joined the English Department of Victoria College, where he remained until his retirement in 1953. Pratt was an enthusiastic and respected teacher, as well as an active force in the social and intellectual community of the University. He was also editor of *Canadian Poetry Magazine* from 1936 to 1942.

Pratt's critical reputation has been uneven, depending on the whims and fluctuations of the literary stock market in Canada. He began writing long poems in an age that valued brevity and economy; he espoused humanistic values—such as courage, endurance, and solidarity—when the dominant mode was irony and understatement, and the chief expression was a tight-lipped dismissal of society and its destructive ways. Yet Pratt's work was never naïvely optimistic; in fact, human weakness and vanity come up for regular drubbings in his work. Although Poe has called the long poem 'a contradiction in terms' and the English critic B.S. Johnson describes the narrative poet as a 'literary flat-earther', the long poem still remains the dominant form in Canada and Pratt is its chief architect. His

verse narratives restored drama, psychological depth, structural complexity, intelligence, and verbal texture to a form that had lost its energy and direction.

Pratt almost single-handedly upheld the expansive tradition in Canadian poetry, arguing for a poetry that is 'a grand binge' rather than a snack at a funeral; his use of rhyme, metrics, and blank verse has often blinded readers to the spare brilliance of his early poems, such as 'Newfoundland' and 'The Shark', and the rich contribution he has made to poetic diction, ushering in—with the scholar's resourcefulness and the child's delight—whole new vocabularies from science, technology, and anthropology in narratives such as 'The Titanic'. Earle Birney, in 'E.J. Pratt and his Critics', calls him 'a man whose capacity for feeling is so great he is like a smelter furnace demanding stacks of raw material for fuel' and draws attention to Pratt's insistence on the need for sufficient passion to turn these rough facts into tempered steel.

As Pratt wrote in the *Canadian Poetry Magazine* in 1936:

A poem can be written only by some one who knows how to write: there is no exception to that rule. Poetry is an exacting, difficult craft, and it takes years of hard work, and education and a sense of the language. Rhyme and metre do not make a poem; they produce by themselves nothing but doggerel. The real flesh and blood of poetry lies in turns of phrases, vivid images, new and unusual thoughts and manners of expressing them. A good poem is good because it is an unusual, imaginative, arresting way of writing English. We do not speak in poetry, except at rare moments; and if a poet writes so simply as to give the effect of spoken language, that effect is all the more startling and novel.

To be able to use this language one must learn it, and that takes, among other things, reading. Practically all the great poets of our language were very highly educated, and the majority were scholars of enormous learning, commanding a large number of languages living and dead. Shakespeare, Burns and Keats are usually regarded as proving the contrary, but their capacity to respond to the books they did read was tremendous, and of no great poet is it untrue to say that his genius would have starved to death without books, for all his observations and experience of life. The reason is very simple: the poet is a literary man, and he has to know something about his trade. . . . Of course, reading the classics is not everything. . . . People will always try to resist reading modern poets, but very few ever succeeded in becoming good poets who took that attitude to the poetry of their own time. Contemporary poetry should be studied by everyone who wishes to add something further to it.

Although he pioneered the narrative or contemporary epic, Pratt also prepared the way for Atwood, Kroetsch, Ondaatje, and Nichol by parodying in *Towards the Last Spike* both the epic form and the values it traditionally espoused—nationhood, heroism, and reason—thus laying the groundwork for *Power Politics, The Collected Works of Billy the Kid, Seed Catalogue*, and bpNichol's whimsical tribute, 'Continental Trance'. Milton Wilson fully understood the importance of Pratt's poem when he said, 'I have the notion that the problems involved in Towards the Last Spike are going to be the central problems in the poetry of our future. . . . [Pratt writes] narratives, no doubt, but discontinuous narratives which are always turning, on the one side, into documents, letters, and jokes, and on the other, into pure lyrics.'

Pratt's publications include *Newfoundland Verse* (1923), *The Witches' Brew* (1925), *Titans* (1926), *The Iron Door* (1927), *The Roosevelt and the Antinoë* (1930), *The Titanic* (1935), *Still Life and Other Verse* (1943), *Dunkirk* (1941), *Behind the Log* (1947), *Brébeuf and His Brethren* (1940), and *Towards the Last Spike* (1952). Pratt's *Collected Poems* appeared in 1944 and again in 1958, this time with a long introduction by Northrop Frye. *Complete Poems*, edited by Sandra Djwa and R.G. Moyles, appeared in 1989; and *Selected Poems*, edited by Sandra Djwa, W.J. Keith, and Zailig Pollock, in 1999. *E.J. Pratt on His Life and Poetry* appeared in 1983 and *Pursuits Amateur and Academic: The Selected Prose of E.J. Pratt* in 1995, both edited by Susan Gingell. Pratt's poetry received three Governor General's Awards and is the subject of numerous critical studies, including Glenn Clever's On *E.J. Pratt* (1977), David Pitt's *E.J. Pratt: The Truant Years, 1882–1927* (1984) and *E.J. Pratt: The Master Years, 1927–1964* (1987), Peter Buitenhuis' *E.J. Pratt and His Works* (1987), *The E.J. Pratt Symposium* (1977, edited with an introduction by Glenn Clever), and Robert Collins' *E.J. Pratt* (1988).

NEWFOUNDLAND

Here the tides flow,
And here they ebb;
Not with that dull, unsinewed tread of waters
Held under bonds to move
Around unpeopled shores—
Moon-driven through a timeless circuit
Of invasion and retreat;
But with a lusty stroke of life
Pounding at stubborn gates,
That they might run
Within the sluices of men's hearts,
Leap under throb of pulse and nerve,
And teach the sea's strong voice
To learn the harmonies of new floods,
The peal of cataract,
And the soft wash of currents
Against resilient banks,
Or the broken rhythms from old chords
Along dark passages
That once were pathways of authentic fires.

Red is the sea-kelp on the beach,
Red as the heart's blood,
Nor is there power in tide or sun
To bleach its stain.
It lies there piled thick
Above the gulch-line.
It is rooted in the joints of rocks,
It is tangled around a spar,
It covers a broken rudder,
It is red as the heart's blood,
And salt as tears.

Here the winds blow,
And here they die,
Not with that wild, exotic rage
That vainly sweeps untrodden shores,
But with familiar breath
Holding a partnership with life,

Resonant with the hopes of spring,
Pungent with the airs of harvest.
They call with the silver fifes of the sea,
They breathe with the lungs of men,
They are one with the tides of the sea,
They are one with the tides of the heart,
They blow with the rising octaves of dawn,
They die with the largo of dusk,
Their hands are full to the overflow
In their right is the bread of life,
In their left are the waters of death.

Scattered on boom
And rudder and weed
Are tangles of shells;
Some with backs of crusted bronze,
And faces of porcelain blue,
Some crushed by the beach stones
To chips of jade;
And some are spiral-cleft
Spreading their tracery on the sand
In the rich veining of an agate's heart;
And others remain unscarred,
To babble of the passing of the winds.

Here the crags
Meet with winds and tides—
Not with that blind interchange
Of blow for blow
That spills the thunder of insentient seas;
But with the mind that reads assault
In crouch and leap and the quick stealth,
Stiffening the muscles of the waves.
Here they flank the harbours,
Keeping watch
On thresholds, altars and the fires of home,
Or, like mastiffs,
Over-zealous,
Guard too well.

Tide and wind and crag,
Sea-weed and sea-shell
And broken rudder—
And the story is told
Of human veins and pulses,
Of eternal pathways of fire,
Of dreams that survive the night,
Of doors held ajar in storms.

THE SHARK

He seemed to know the harbour,
So leisurely he swam;
His fin,
Like a piece of sheet-iron,
Three-cornered,
And with knife-edge,
Stirred not a bubble
As it moved
With its base-line on the water.

His body was tubular
And tapered
And smoke-blue,
And as he passed the wharf
He turned,
And snapped at a flat-fish
That was dead and floating.
And I saw the flash of a white throat,
And a double row of white teeth,
And eyes of metallic grey,
Hard and narrow and slit.

Then out of the harbour,
With that three-cornered fin
Shearing without a bubble the water
Lithely,
Leisurely,
He swam—
That strange fish,

Tubular, tapered, smoke-blue,
Part vulture, part wolf,
Part neither—for his blood was cold.

SEA-GULLS

For one carved instant as they flew,
The language had no simile—
Silver, crystal, ivory
Were tarnished. Etched upon the horizon blue.
The frieze must go unchallenged, for the lift
And carriage of the wings would stain the drift
Of stars against a tropic indigo
Or dull the parable of snow.

Now settling one by one
Within green hollows or where curled
Crests caught the spectrum from the sun,
A thousand wings are furled.
No clay-born lilies of the world
Could blow as free
As those wild orchids of the sea.

EROSION

It took the sea a thousand years,
A thousand years to trace
The granite features of this cliff,
In crag and scarp and base.

It took the sea an hour one night,
An hour of storm to place
The sculpture of these granite seams
Upon a woman's face.

THE MAN AND THE MACHINE

By right of fires that smelted ore
Which he had tended years before,
The man whose hands were on the wheel
Could trace his kinship through her steel,
Between his body warped and bent
In every bone and ligament,
And this 'eight-cylinder' stream-lined,
The finest model yet designed.
He felt his lesioned pulses strum
Against the rhythm of her hum,
And found his nerves and sinews knot
With sharper spasm as she climbed
The steeper grades, so neatly timed
From storage tank to piston shot—
This creature with the cougar grace,
This man with slag upon his face.

FROM STONE TO STEEL

From stone to bronze, from bronze to steel
Along the road-dust of the sun,
Two revolutions of the wheel
From Java to Geneva run.

The snarl Neanderthal is worn
Close to the smiling Aryan lips,
The civil polish of the horn
Gleams from our praying finger tips.

The evolution of desire
Has but matured a toxic wine,
Drunk long before its heady fire
Reddened Euphrates or the Rhine.

Between the temple and the cave
The boundary lies tissue-thin:
The yearlings still the altars crave
As satisfaction for a sin.

The road goes up, the road goes down—
Let Java or Geneva be—
But whether to the cross or crown,
The path lies through Gethsemane.

NEWFOUNDLAND SEAMEN

This is their culture, this—their master passion
Of giving shelter and of sharing bread,
Of answering rocket signals in the fashion
Of losing life to save it. In the spread
Of time—the Gilbert-Grenfell-Bartlett span—
The headlines cannot dim their daily story,
Nor calls like London! Gander! Teheran!
Outplay the drama of the sled and dory.

The wonders fade. There overhead a mile,
Planes bank like gulls: like curlews scream the jets.
The caravans move on in radar file
Scarce noticed by the sailors at their nets,
Bracing their bodies to their tasks, as when,
Centuries before Argentia's smoking funnels,
That small ancestral band of Devon men
Red-boned their knuckles on the Squirrel gunwales.

As old as it is new, as new as old,
Enduring as a cape, as fresh as dulse,
This is the Terra Nova record told
Of uncontractual blood behind the pulse
On sea or land. Was it but yesterday
That without terms and without drill commands,
A rescue squad found Banting where he lay
With the torn tissues of his healing hands?

FROM THE TITANIC

HARLAND & WOLFF WORKS, BELFAST, MAY 31, 1911

The hammers silent and the derricks still,
And high-tide in the harbour! Mind and will
In open test with time and steel had run
The first lap of a schedule and had won.
Although a shell of what was yet to be
Before another year was over, she,
Poised for the launching signal, had surpassed
The dreams of builder or of navigator.
The Primate of the Lines, she had out-classed
That rival effort to eliminate her
Beyond the North Sea where the air shots played
The laggard rhythms of their fusillade
Upon the rivets of the *Imperator*.
The wedges in, the shores removed, a girl's
Hand at a sign released a ribbon braid;
Glass crashed against the plates; a wine cascade,
Netting the sunlight in a shower of pearls,
Baptized the bow and gave the ship her name;
A slight push of the rams as a switch set free
The triggers in the slots, and her proud claim
On size—to be the first to reach the sea—
Was vindicated, for whatever fears
Stalked with her down the tallow of the slips
Were smothered under by the harbour cheers,
By flags strung to the halyards of the ships.

MARCH 31, 1912

Completed! Waiting for her trial spin—
Levers and telegraphs and valves within
Her intercostal spaces ready to start
The power pulsing through her lungs and heart.
An ocean lifeboat in herself—so ran
The architectural comment on her plan.
No wave could sweep those upper decks—unthinkable!
No storm could hurt that hull—the papers said so.
The perfect ship at last—the first unsinkable,

Proved in advance—had not the folders read so?
Such was the steel strength of her double floors
Along the whole length of the keel, and such
The fine adjustment of the bulkhead doors
Geared to the rams, responsive to a touch,
That in collision with iceberg or rock
Or passing ship she could survive the shock,
Absorb the double impact, for despite
The bows stove in, with forward holds aleak,
Her aft compartments buoyant, watertight,
Would keep her floating steady for a week.
And this belief had reached its climax when,
Through wireless waves as yet unstaled by use,
The wonder of the ether had begun
To fold the heavens up and reinduce
That ancient *hubris* in the dreams of men,
Which would have slain the cattle of the sun,
And filched the lightnings from the fist of Zeus.
What mattered that her boats were but a third
Of full provision—caution was absurd:
Then let the ocean roll and the winds blow
While the risk at Lloyds remained a record low.

THE ICEBERG

Calved from a glacier near Godhaven coast,
It left the fiord for the sea—a host
Of white flotillas gathering in its wake,
And joined by fragments from a Behring floe,
Had circumnavigated it to make
It centre of an archipelago.
Its lateral motion on the Davis Strait
Was casual and indeterminate,
And each advance to southward was as blind
As each recession to the north. No smoke
Of steamships nor the hoist of mainsails broke
The polar wastes—no sounds except the grind
Of ice, the cry of curlews and the lore
Of winds from mesas of eternal snow;
Until caught by the western undertow,
It struck the current of the Labrador

Which swung it to its definite southern stride.
Pressure and glacial time had stratified
The berg to the consistency of flint,
And kept inviolate, through clash of tide
And gale, façade and columns with their hint
Of inward altars and of steepled bells
Ringing the passage of the parallels.
But when with months of voyaging it came
To where both streams—the Gulf and Polar—met,
The sun which left its crystal peaks aflame
In the sub-arctic noons, began to fret
The arches, flute the spires and deform
The features, till the batteries of storm,
Playing above the slow-eroding base,
Demolished the last temple touch of grace.
Another month, and nothing but the brute
And palaeolithic outline of a face
Fronted the transatlantic shipping route.
A sloping spur that tapered to a claw
And lying twenty feet below had made
It lurch and shamble like a plantigrade;
But with an impulse governed by the raw
Mechanics of its birth, it drifted where
Ambushed, fog-grey, it stumbled on its lair,
North forty-one degrees and forty-four,
Fifty and fourteen west the longitude,
Waiting a world-memorial hour, its rude
Corundum form stripped to its Greenland core.

SOUTHAMPTON, WEDNESDAY, APRIL 10, 1912

An omen struck the thousands on the shore—
A double accident! And as the ship
Swung down the river on her maiden trip,
Old sailors of the clipper decades, wise
To the sea's incantations, muttered fables
About careening vessels with their cables
Snapped in their harbours under peaceful skies.
Was it just suction or fatality
Which caused the New York at the dock to turn,
Her seven mooring ropes to break at the stern

And writhe like anacondas on the quay,
While tugs and fenders answered the collision
Signals with such trim margin of precision?
And was it backwash from the starboard screw
Which, tearing at the big *Teutonic*, drew
Her to the limit of her hawser strain,
And made the smaller tethered craft behave
Like frightened harbour ducks? And no one knew
For many days the reason to explain
The rise and wash of one inordinate wave,
When a sunken barge on the Southampton bed
Was dragged through mire eight hundred yards ahead,
As the *Titanic* passed above its grave.
But many of those sailors wise and old,
Who pondered on this weird mesmeric power,
Gathered together, lit their pipes and told
Of portents hidden in the natal hour,
Told of the launching of some square-rigged ships,
When water flowed from the inverted tips
Of a waning moon, of sun-hounds, of the shrieks
Of whirling shags around the mizzen peaks.
And was there not this morning's augury
For the big one now heading for the sea?
So long after she passed from landsmen's sight,
They watched her with their Mother Carey eyes
Through Spithead smoke, through mists of Isle of Wight,
Through clouds of sea-gulls following with their cries.

WEDNESDAY EVENING

Electric elements were glowing down
In the long galley passages where scores
Of white-capped cooks stood at the oven doors
To feed the population of a town.
Cauldrons of stock, purées and consommés,
Simmered with peppercorns and marjoram.
The sea-shore smells from bisque and crab and clam
Blended with odours from the fricassées.
Refrigerators, hung with a week's toll
Of the stockyards, delivered sides of lamb
And veal, beef quarters to be roasted whole.

Hundreds of capons and halibut. A shoal
Of Blue-Points waited to be served on shell.
The boards were loaded with pimolas, pails
Of lobster coral, jars of Béchamel,
To garnish tiers of rows of chilled timbales
And aspics. On the shelves were pyramids
Of truffles, sprigs of thyme and water-cress,
Bay leaf and parsley, savouries to dress
Shad roes and sweetbreads broiling on the grids.
And then in diamond, square, crescent and star,
Hors d'oeuvres were fashioned from the toasted bread,
With paste of anchovy and caviare,
Paprika sprinkled and pimento spread,
All ready, for the hour was seven!
                                    Meanwhile,
Rivalling the engines with their steady tread,
Thousands of feet were taking overhead
The fourth lap round the deck to make the mile.
Squash racquet, shuffle board and quoits; the cool
Tang of the plunge in the gymnasium pool,
The rub, the crisp air of the April night,
The salt of the breeze made by the liner's rate,
Worked with an even keel to stimulate
Saliva for an ocean appetite;
And like storm troops before a citadel,
At the first summons of a bugle, soon
The army massed the stairs towards the saloon,
And though twelve courses on the cards might well
Measure themselves against Falstaffian juices,
But few were found presenting their excuses,
When stewards offered on the lacquered trays
The Savoy chasers and the canapés.

The dinner gave the sense that all was well:
That touch of ballast in the tanks; the feel
Of peace from ramparts unassailable,
Which, added to her seven decks of steel,
Had constituted the *Titanic* less
A ship than a Gibraltar under heel.
And night had placed a lazy lusciousness
Upon a surfeit of security.

Science responded to a button press.
The three electric lifts that ran through tiers
Of decks, the reading lamps, the brilliancy
Of mirrors from the tungsten chandeliers,
Had driven out all phantoms which the mind
Had loosed from ocean closets, and assigned
To the dry earth the custody of fears.
The crowds poured through the sumptuous rooms and halls,
And tapped the tables of the Regency;
Smirked at the caryatids on the walls;
Talked Jacobean-wise; canvassed the range
Of taste within the Louis dynasty.
Grey-templed Caesars of the world's Exchange
Swallowed liqueurs and coffee as they sat
Under the Georgian carved mahogany,
Dictating wireless hieroglyphics that
Would on the opening of the Board Rooms rock
The pillared dollars of a railroad stock.

DOROTHY LIVESAY

(1909–1996)

In an essay entitled 'Song and Dance' (*Canadian Literature*, No. 41, summer 1969), Dorothy Livesay said: 'I suppose that all my life I have fought against obscurantism! For me the true intellectual is a simple person who knows how to be close to nature and to ordinary people. I therefore tend to shy away from academic poets and academic critics. They miss the essence.' Livesay's search for the 'essence' led her through a series of transformations, from her earliest imagist and symbolist lyrics about love and isolation; through her activist 'agit-prop' writings of the forties and fifties; and, finally, to her confessional and feminist writings of the sixties and seventies.

The constant fact in her art, as in her life, was the struggle to reconcile her need for privacy and her need for community. At times Livesay likened this struggle to the search for the 'perfect dancing partner' or the perfect muse. As she says in 'Song and Dance', writing was a form of dance that 'could extend to an identification with a community, a nation, a world.' Poetry is for Livesay a manifestation of that ideal union between two people, poet and reader: 'Not a dance of touch, but one where the rhythm itself created an unseen wire holding two people together in the leap of movement.'

At various points in her life, Livesay espoused a 'realist' credo, such as that expressed in 'Without Benefit of Tape', where she insists that poetry must originate in everyday experience and 'living speech'.

Her documentary poems clearly grow out of this 'realist' impulse. She describes 'Call My People Home' as her 'most thoroughly documented "public" poem', one that is able to 'combine a sense of personal poignancy and alienation with a sense of social purpose'. What interests her about this form, as she says in 'The Documentary Poem: A Canadian Genre' (*Contexts of Canadian Criticism*, edited by Eli Mandel), is its capacity to create a 'dialectic between the objective facts and the subjective feelings of the poet'. Livesay's best work certainly lies at the extremes of private and public statement—in the lyric and the narrative; and the documentary is the form in which, for her, both of these elements come together. The passion of the poet finds its engagement and release, not in didacticism or righteous indignation, but rather in a total absorption in character and event. And yet, regardless of the documentary impulse that gives rise to it, 'Call My People Home' derives its illusion of reality less from accurate reference to historical fact than from the linguistic inventiveness and imaginative sympathy of the poet. The subjective needs of the poet drive her to penetrate the surfaces of history in order to create myth, to plumb the depths of what we call archetypal experience.

Although her later work is more stridently feminist in its utterances, Livesay has always been concerned about the role of women in society. There is no shortage of women in her poetry, from ruined maids and overburdened housewives to political activists. The world of these women is often circumscribed by roles, attitudes, and domestic conditions. They move awkwardly and uncomfortably within rooms, framed windows, magic circles of children, drowning in, but miraculously saved by, the profusion of detail in their lives; and rejoicing in the evidence of growing things—a bird, a grandchild, a geranium.

Livesay rejects the elegiac preoccupations of much modern writing. 'We are optimists,' she says, 'Blakean believers in the New Jerusalem. We cannot see man's role as tragic but rather as divine comedy. We are alone—so what? We are not always lonely. Laughter heals, the dance captures, the song echoes forth from the tree-top. I won't stop believing this until every tree in Canada's chopped down; I thumb my nose at those who say that nature, and with it human nature, is becoming "obsolete".'

No doubt she inherited both her interest in poetry and her concern for social issues from her parents, who were literary people active in the field of journalism. Livesay was born in Winnipeg and lived there for ten years before her family moved to Ontario. She graduated from the University of Toronto in 1931 and then studied at the Sorbonne, exploring the influence of the French Symbolists on modern English poetry. During the Depression she was a social worker in Toronto, Montreal, and New Jersey. After 1936 she lived in Vancouver, where she worked at the YWCA, taught, and contributed to political and literary magazines, including Alan Crawley's *Contemporary Verse*. When her husband died, Livesay returned to Paris, where she worked for

UNESCO before being posted to Zambia for three years. She has taught widely and been a writer-in-residence at various Canadian universities, including the University of Manitoba, where she founded *CV/II*, a periodical of poetry and reviews. She was honoured for her literary contributions with four honorary doctorates and the Order of Canada.

Livesay's works include *Green Pitcher* (1928), *Signpost* (1932), *Day and Night* (1944), *Selected Poems* (1957), *The Unquiet Bed* (1967), *Collected Poems: The Two Seasons* (1972), *Ice Age* (1975), *The Raw Edges* (1981), *The Phases of Love* (1983), *The Self-Completing Tree: Selected Poems* (1986, 1999), *Archive for Our Times: Previously Uncollected and Unpublished Poems* (1998), and *The Woman I Am* (1991). Her non-fiction work includes two memoirs, *A Winnipeg Childhood* (1975) and *Journeys With My Selves* (1991), and a gathering of prose pieces, *Right Hand Left Hand: A True Life of the Thirties* (1977) edited by David Arnason and Kim Todd. Livesay edited *The Collected Poems of Raymond Knister* (1949) and two anthologies of poetry by women: *Forty Women Poets of Canada* (1972) and *Woman's Eye* (1974). She was twice the recipient of Governor General's Awards for poetry and received the Lorne Pierce Medal for Literature in 1947. She was productive to the last, publishing *Beginnings* (1988), *The Husband* (1990, a novella), and *Awakenings* (1991). Her poems have been the subject of several critical studies: Lee Briscoe Thompson's *Dorothy Livesay* (1987), Paul Denham's *Dorothy Livesay and Her Works* (1987), Peter Stevens' *Dorothy Livesay: Patterns in A Poetic Life* (1992), and Nadine McInnis's *Dorothy Livesay's Poetics of Desire* (1994).

FIRE AND REASON

I cannot shut out the night—
Nor its sharp clarity.

The many blinds we draw,
You and I,
The many fires we light
Can never quite obliterate
The irony of stars,
The deliberate moon,
The last, unsolved finality of night.

GOING TO SLEEP

I shall lie like this when I am dead—
But with one more secret I my head.

SPAIN

When the bare branch responds to leaf and light
Remember them: it is for this they fight.
It is for haze-swept hills and the green thrust
Of pine, that they lie choked with battle dust.
You who hold beauty at your finger-tips
Hold it because the splintering gunshot rips
Between your comrades' eyes; hold it across
Their bodies' barricade of blood and loss.

You who live quietly in sunlit space
Reading The Herald after morning grace
Can count peace dear, when it has driven
Your sons to struggle for this grim, new heaven.

COMRADE

Once only did I sleep with you;
A sleep and love again more sweet than I
Have ever known; without an aftertaste.
It was the first time; and a flower could not
Have been more softly opened, folded out.
Your hands were firm upon me: without fear
I lay arrested in a still delight—
Till suddenly the fountain in me woke.

My dear, it's years between; we've grown up fast
Each differently, each striving by itself.
I see you now a grey man without dreams,
Without a living, or an overcoat:
But sealed in struggle now, we are more close
Than if our bodies still were sealed in love.

FROM CALL MY PEOPLE HOME
A Documentary Poem for Radio or Choral Presentation

FIRST FISHERMAN:

Home was my boat: T.K. 2930—
Wintering on the Skeena with my nets
Cast up and down the river, to lure and haul
The dogfish. (His oil, they said, was needed overseas
For children torn from home, from a blitzed town.)
We made good money, and the sockeye run
That summer had outdone all the remembered seasons.
Now I could own my boat, *Tee Kay*, the Gillnetter
The snug and round one, warm as a woman
With her stove stocked at night and her lanterns lit
And anchor cast, brooding upon the water
Settled to sleep in the lap of the Skeena.

Now after thirty years, come from an island
To make a home near water: first on a sailing vessel
Towed, each season, to the fishing grounds:
Then the small gasboat, the gillnetter, that belonged

Not to the man who fished, but to the cannery.
Now after thirty years a free man, naturalized,
A man who owned his boat! I smelt the wind
Wetting my face, waves dashing against the *Tee Kay*'s sides
The grey dawn opening like a book
At the horizon's rim. I was my own master—
Must prove it now, today! Stooping over the engine
Priming the starter, opening the gas valve,
I felt her throbbing in answer; I laughed
And grasped the fly wheel, swung her over.
She churned off up the river—my own boat, my home.
That was before Pearl Harbor: before a December day
Spent on a restless sea; then anchor in the dusk
And down to bunk to have a bowl of rice.
By lantern light I turned the battery set
To hear brief messages from fishermen
From boat to shore, to learn the weather forecast.
Must have been dozing when I woke up sharp—
What was he saying? Some kind of government order?
'All fishing craft on the high seas must head at once
To the nearest port, report to authorities.'
Did they not want our fish, the precious oil?
'No,' said the voice, 'Our boats were to be examined, searched
For hidden guns, for maps, for treachery . . .'
I heard, but could not understand. Obeyed,
But as a blind man. The numb fear about my boat,
Tee Kay, found no release in port, off shore,
Rubbing against a fleet of trollers, frail gillnetters
All heading down the Inverness and Tusk
All in the dark, with rumour flying fast.
No one knew more than his fear whispered,
No one explained.
We thought: perhaps it's all a mistake
Perhaps they'll line us up and do a search
Then leave us free for Skeena, Ucluelet—
The time is ripe, the season's fish are running.

*   *   *

Christmas at sea. The bitterest for me
That any year had given. Even so

Some had a celebration, pooled their funds
And bought the only chicken left in Alert Bay.
Others boiled cabbages in salt sea water,
Pulled out the playing cards and shrugged, and laughed.
As we set sail at midnight, now a thousand boats
Chained to the naval escort, steadily south
Into familiar waters where the forests cooled their feet
At rocks'-end, mountains swam in mist—
As we set sail for home, the young ones, born here, swore
Not softly, into the hissing night. The old men wept.

The rest takes little telling. On the fifteenth night
We passed Point Grey's low hulk, our long line wavered shoreward.
Dirty and hungry, sleep lying like a stone
Stuck in our heads, we nosed our broken craft
Into the wharf at Steveston, 'Little Tokyo.'
The crowd on the dock was silent. Women finding their men
Clung to them searchingly, saying never a word,
Leading them home to the *ofuro** and supper.
Others of us, like me, who knew no one,
Who had no place near the city's centre
Stood lonely on the wharf, holding the *Tee Kay*'s line
For the last time, watching the naval men
Make a note of her number, take my name.
That was the end of my thirty years at the fishing
And the end of my boat, my home.

THE UNQUIET BED

The woman I am
is not what you see
I'm not just bones
and crockery

the woman I am
knew love and hate
hating the chains
that parents make

---

*ofuro—the bath

longing that love
might set men free
yet hold them fast
in loyalty

the woman I am
is not what you see
move over love
make room for me

THE THREE EMILYS*

These women crying in my head
Walk alone, uncomforted:
The Emilys, these three
Cry to be set free—
And others whom I will not name
Each different, each the same.

Yet they had liberty!
Their kingdom was the sky:
They batted clouds with easy hand,
Found a mountain for their stand;
From wandering lonely they could catch
The inner magic of a heath—
A lake their palette, any tree
Their brush could be.

And still they cry to me
As in reproach—
I, born to hear their inner storm
Of separate man in woman's form,
I yet possess another kingdom, barred
To them, these three, this Emily.
I move as mother in a frame,
My arteries
Flow the immemorial way
Towards the child, the man;

---

*Emily Bronte, Emily Dickinson, and Emily Carr.

And only for a brief span
Am I an Emily on mountain snows
And one of these.

And so the whole that I possess
Is still much less—
They move triumphant through my head:
I am the one
Uncomforted.

PICASSO, SKETCHING

He lays his lines, blaspheming rules' precision,
silver and black converging, juxtaposed,
angles colliding, parallels enclosed:
distorts perspective, daggers the bull's eye
and then, his cornucopia conjured from thin air
tossed to a corner, dazzles out a scrawl-
Hen's track? Hen's eggs? Hen's teeth? They purl
and plane; ripple and pearl to grey again.

Il faut risquer tout!
Smoke from a tunnel belches cumulus,
the rearing engine truckles to its tracks,
snorts to a pause; develops eyes and nose,
is Taurus-teased, insanely furious.
Busy the fingers fly to tame it down
seizing the rein and haltering the frown
then easing to its customary stance-
Et violá ça m'amuse!
Stationed but champing, belching fire and fuss.

So does he shunt his visions through the station,
sets dynamite in open air, ignites creation.

BARTOK AND THE GERANIUM

She lifts her green umbrellas
Towards the pane

Seeking her fill of sunlight
Or of rain;
Whatever falls
She has no commentary
Accepts, extends,
Blows out her furbelows,
Her bustling boughs;
And all the while he whirls
Explodes in space,
Never content with this small room:
Not even can he be
Confined to sky
But must speed high and higher still
From galaxy to galaxy,
Wrench from the stars their momentary notes
Steal music from the moon.

She's daylight
He is dark
She's heaven-held breath
He storms and crackles
Spits with hell's own spark.

Yet in this room, this moment now
These together breathe and be:
She, essence of serenity,
He in a mad intensity
Soars beyond sight
Then hurls, lost Lucifer,
From heaven's height.

And when he's done, he's out:
She leans a lip against the glass
And preens herself in light.

WITHOUT BENEFIT OF TAPE

The real poems are being written in outports
on backwoods farms
in passageways where pantries still exist

or where geraniums
nail light to the window
while out of the window boy in the flying field
is pulled to heaven on the keel of a kite.

Stories breed in the north:
men with snow in their mouths
trample and shake at the bit
kneading the woman down under blankets of snow
icing her breath, her eyes.

The living speech is shouted out
by men and women leaving railways lines
to trundle home, pack-sacked
just company for deer or bear—
 Hallooed
across the counter, in a corner store
it booms upon the river's shore:
on midnight roads where hikers flag you down
speech echoes from the canyon's wall
 resonant
 indubitable.

SORCERY

My breasts are withered gourds
my skin all over stiffens
shrinks—the pubic hair
bristles to an itch

Not to be touched and swept
by your arm's force
gives me the ague
turns me into witch

O engineer of spring!
magic magic me
out of insanity
from scarecrow into girl again
then dance me toss me
catch!

RALPH GUSTAFSON

(1909–1995)

Ralph Gustafson was born of Anglo-Swedish stock in Lime Ridge, Quebec, and raised in Sherbrooke. He graduated from Bishop's University in Lennoxville, then studied at Oxford. After a brief stint of teaching at St Alban's School in Brockville, he returned to England in 1933 and remained there until 1939, publishing his first two books of poetry. Gustafson lived in New York City from 1939 until 1963, working during the war for British Information Services, summarizing attitudes to Britain in the American press. He returned to Canada in 1963, living in North Hatley and serving as poet-in-residence and a professor of English at Bishop's from 1966 until his retirement in 1977. Gustafson won a Governor-General's Award in 1974 for *Fire on Stone* and was the recipient of the A.J.M. Smith Prize. He travelled widely, was an avid devotee and acute critic of classical music for CBC radio, as well as an anthologist—he edited three anthologies for Penguin, including the early *Anthology of Canadian Verse (English)* (1942) and *The Penguin Book of Canadian Verse* (1958; rev. 1967 and 1984). In addition to many collections of poetry, he published two collections of short stories: *The Brazen Tower* (1974) and *The Vivid Air* (1980).

Leon Edel, in the *Oxford Companion to Canadian Literature* (1983), has suggested that Gustafson's poetry falls into three distinct periods, corresponding roughly to his British, American, and Canadian years. From the English, Gustafson certainly seems to have learned a good deal about measure and compression in the closed lyric; and from the Americans, especially Wallace Stevens, he learned that poetry can accommodate ideas, or wise talk, that it can be richly meditative. The poems produced during these two periods are dense, angular, syncopated, labyrinthine, and given to large-scale pronouncements and generalizations about historical events and human motivations. Inside his tortured syntax, the journalist is often at odds with the man who feels; the singer, with the thinking man. But in the late 1950s something unusual happened to change Gustafson's style. Whether the result of his marriage or of his travels in Canada—perhaps both—new energies were released into his poetry. The new landscapes and experiences could not be contained in short lyrics and meditations, but demanded an opening out toward longer discursive and narrative modes that would permit the cataloguing of names, the recording of minutiae, and the creation of a sense of movement through vast distances in a world far removed from the claustrophobic bed-sitters and flats of London and the garrets of Manhattan. The poems became longer, the lines shorter, reflecting modes developed by Lawrence Ferlinghetti and Gary Snyder in the US, and Earle Birney and Al Purdy in Canada. This new sense of emotional and physical space—which was doubtless a factor in his decision to return home—pushed Gustafson towards extended forms, particularly the poem-sequence, to which he brought outrageous wit, lyric skills, and an eye for significant detail.

In his selected essays on poetry and music, *Plummets and Other Partialities* (1987), Gustafson claims that 'Of all the constructions which a poem may take, the sequence, the poem by sections, is the one, I think, most peculiarly contemporary. The architecture accommodates the modern temper. Its structure and complex of meditation, irony, and extension, convey the contemporary world of incompletion and, at the same time (in accordance with Poe's injunction) maintain tension.' Yet, against the abuses of the long poem—'Sprawling, self-licensed, half prose, half thought'—Gustafson also makes the case for the short lyric or Impromptu poem, as an 'inspired accident', 'devil in a halo': 'The structuring, invisible, cogent, is from learning; the vitality of its cadence is from metrical control; the verbal music is from the tuned ear.' Although he continued to shift gears regularly from his complex, angular, and epigrammatic occasional poems to the longer meditative pieces, Gustafson's greatest achievement may well lie in those delicate, lucid, almost oriental evocations of place in the Eastern Townships, where meaning is found to reside in the concrete particulars of daily life.

An engagingly partisan account of Gustafson's legacy and development, which supports and elaborates this view, is to be found in George Elliott Clarke's essay 'The Road to North Hatley: Ralph Gustafson's Post-Colonial Odyssey', which appeared in the Gustafson memorial issue of the *Journal of Eastern Township Studies* (#9, Fall, 1996). Dismissing the early poems as products of a 'tin-ear' and a misplaced poetics, he maps Gustafson's progress from a colonial schizophrenia, which left him adrift, unfocussed, out of place, towards a work fully grounded in the local particulars of the Eastern Townships where he lived—in other words, in 'the revelation of his own backyard'—and possessing, at last, 'an agonizingly piercing music'.

Gustafson's poetry collections include *The Golden Chalice* (1935), *Alfred the Great* (1937), *Flight into Darkness* (1944), *Rivers among Rocks* (1960), *Rocky Mountain Poems* (1960), *Sift in an Hourglass* (1966), *Ixion's Wheel* (1969), *Selected Poems* (1972), *Fire on Stone* (1974), *Corners in the Glass* (1977), *Sequences* (1979), *Landscape with Rain* (1980), *Conflicts of Spring* (1981), *Gradations of Grandeur* (1982), *The Moment Is All: Selected Poems* (1983); *Directives of Autumn* (1984), *Impromptus* (1984), *The Collected Poems of Ralph Gustafson* (1987), *Shadows in the Grass* (1991), *Configurations At Midnight* (1992), *Tracks in the Snow* (1994), and *Visions Fugitive* (1996). Of considerable literary and historical interest is *A Literary Friendship: The Correspondence of Ralph Gustafson and W.W.E. Ross* (1984), edited by Bruce Whiteman.

'S.S.R., LOST AT SEA.' THE *TIMES*

What heave of grapnels will resurrect the fabric
Of him, oceans drag, whereof he died,
Drowning sheer fathoms down, liquid to grab on—
Sucked by the liner, violence in her side?
Of no more sorrow than a mottled Grief
In marble. There fantastic in the murk,
Where saltwhite solitary forests leaf,
He swings: the dark anonymously works.
For who shall count the countless hands and limbs
In ditch and wall and wave, dead, dead
In Europe: touch with anguished name and claim
And actual tear, what must be generally said?
O let the heart's tough riggings salvage him,
Only whose lengths can grapple with these dead.

S.S. *Athenia*
September 3, 1939

NOW AT THE OCEAN'S VERGE

After great expectations, what
It is the time of life declares, that
Was there, is as the ebbtide shows:
These miles of sand packt and under a slant
Moon, the piling granite throw of surf,
Nothing but the beauty of itself.
Conch and shell and tugged weed cling
To the wave and are thrown.
    I turn to the seamark,
Climb descensions of pebbles and under the moon
Sit arms on knees, the night of stars,
Each in apportioned stance, intolerable before
The initialling mind. Indigence is all.
Concrete heaven only must suffice,
What expectation thought was possible:
Packt sand; a grasp, whorled and beautiful
Tossed by the tide, this accessible,
Reached for, empty shell.

THE NEWSPAPER

That photo of the little Jew in the cap,
Back to the gun held by the Nazi
With splay feet aware of the camera,
The little boy his hands in the air,
I turn over, I don't want to see it.
As a member of the human race. I am
Civilized. I am happy. I flap the
Newspaper with the picture over
So that when it is picked up to be taken
Down cellar to be put with the trash
I won't see it. I am sensitive.
The little boy is dead. He went
Through death. The cap is his best one.
He has brown eyes. He does not
Understand. Putting your hands
Up in front of a carbine prevents
The bullet. He is with the others.
Some of them he knows, so
It is all right. I turn
The paper over, the picture face
Down.

WEDNESDAY AT NORTH HATLEY

It snows on this place
And a gentleness obtains.
The garden fills with white,
Last summer's hedgerow
Bears a burden and birds
Are scarce. The grosbeak
Fights for seeds, the squirrel
Walks his slender wire.
There is a victory;
The heart endures, the house
Achieves its warmth and where
He needs to, man in woollen
Mitts, in muffler, without
A deathwish, northern, walks.

Except he stop at drifts
He cannot hear this snow,
The wind has fallen, and where
The lake awaits, the road
Is his. Softly the snow
Falls. Chance is against him.
But softly the snow falls.

IN THE YUKON

In Europe, you can't move without going down into history.
Here, all is a beginning. I saw a salmon jump,
Again and again, against the current,
The timbered hills a background, wooded green
Unpushed through; the salmon jumped, silver.
This was news, was commerce, at the end of the summer
The leap for dying. Moose came down to the water edge
To drink and the salmon turned silver arcs.
At night, the northern lights played, great over country
Without tapestry and coronations, kings crowned
With weights of gold. They were green,
Green hangings and great grandeur, over the north
Going to what no man can hold hard in mind,
The dredge of that gravity, being without experience.

I THINK OF ALL SOFT LIMBS

Many victims are around.
There are Greeks beaten
Over the kidneys with rifle
Butts. There are the four
Hundred of Phu Cam,
'The eyeholes,' it is reported, 'deep
And black, the water broken
Over the ribs.' A somewhat
Agitated description,
But one can get what's going
On—apparently they were bludgeoned
To death and the creek was shallow.

Others were found elsewhere.
A farmer stumbled on
A wire; when he tugged,
A hand rose from the dirt.
In other places the grass
Grew abnormally green
And long. This was at Hué—
They showed the corpses on
The TV. I looked
For genitals but they had fixed
Up the film or else
It was luck.

      Then there are the children
Who must die so the others may eat.
The worst were obviously expendable.
You could tell: though they moved their heads
They were no longer eager.
The ones who got the food
Jumped in the stream laughing,
To show the cameras. . . . That
Is clear? Or should it be
Gone over? I mean, the others
Might just as well die. . . .

Anyway, 2000 a day
Did in Biafra. Of course,
That is not all children—
Just mostly children.
Major General Yakubu
Gowon of Nigeria explains
It all. 'We must live together,'
He rightly says. Meanwhile,
He expresses regrets. This,
Like the crucifixion of Christ,
Is past history, of course.

Still, within memory, are Sinyavsky
And Daniel, writers mixed
Up in Marxist realism
And Siberia: Solzhenitsyn—

Unassailable really:
He has stomach cancer.
Natalya Gorbanevskaya
Though, can be mentioned, a poet
Arrested on Red Square
Not far from Lobnoye Mesto,
'The place of the forehead' where intellects
Were beheaded under the Czars.
She was against Soviet
Tanks liberating
Czechoslovakia. She
Is not in Siberia, however,
But in a mental home:
She has a three-months-old
Son. As they said:
'These are all Jews!'

Then there are those who sit
In student unions hearing
Ceremony is bullshit;
Students dragged along
Stone stairways face
Down; and those in Vaclav
Square who place fresh flowers
Daily on the Wenceslas monument.

Many are around. One
Could bring up Bill Terry,
First Class, black,
The corpse, kept out of the white
Cemetery in Alabama,
Buried finally by law
Six months to the day.

I think of all soft limbs:
The VC stripped, wrists
Wired behind, kicked
In the cheeks and groin, going
Back to foetal position
Each time, the GI
Standing by, reasonably

Not offering much advice,
His buddy on being picked
Up the day before,
Leaving his leg behind.

The trouble is there is too
Much death for compassion.

RAMBLE ON WHAT IN THE WORLD WHY

Making a meaning out of everything that has happened,
The there-it-is, plainsong, pitch and pinnacle:
All is blanket-plucking otherwise. My father
Lighted a pipe out in a rowboat on the lake
When he fished and brought up Leviathan on a wormy
Hook, Ahab's pegleg in the belly,
So the watching boy said. Brahms
Percolated coffee, something to fiddle with,
The cup, the pot, the burner, to duck having
To write down music. Meaning is wearying, hammers,
Level, hacking out hunks of marble to raise
Cathedrals. I travel to get out of it to walk in them—
And run slambang into gospels of course,
Pegasus loose and the barndoor slammed.
Berryman took poems and jumped off a bridge.
It all comes down to making oneself one
With sea-slime. Knowing what is OK,
It's the why we've got to, the prehensile toes
And the rest of it, slops, jade and Jesus,
Venice, murder, virgins and music, that counts.

THE SUN IN THE GARDEN

Wallace Stevens is wrong: he says,
'A poem need not have a meaning
And like most things in nature
Often does not have.' He is slipshod.
He was in the insurance business,
He ought to have known better.

I examine this slug that has crawled up
Into the saucer of my cup of tea.
It has two protrusions out of its head
And apparently absorbs food
Through its foot's peristalsis:
Repugnance after my sugar.

Also after the roses. The garden
Looks like it. The protuberances
Move out almost imperceptibly
But it doesn't fool what it senses
Or me. Beauty is taken in,
Blind repugnance or not. It squashes.

I snip it with my fingers off
The saucer, enough of it had. I walk
The rest of the day in the garden knowing
Something is futile. I have meaning.
I have to counteract it. I look up
Evolution, religion, love.

THE ARRIVAL OF WISDOM

Of course the truth is there's no design,
Just process: which settles all-seeing God for good
And Him as a chemist mixing combinations
To get what He could declare without it,
Wanting to be worshipped, pitching beginnings
With a Bang into teleological void.

Truth goes on solving nothing, gluons
And quarks combine, come apart, not caring, stars
Go out, suns come on, the clutter ever
Expanding; sheep on the meadow chew, chew,
Man makes mince, until his neck-thongs shrivel
And breath departs lugging its baggage
Of unaccomplished dreams. What a celestial
Tautology to get there! fun in the dreaming,
Irony in choice, tragedy in the waste,
Getting nowhere with injustice.

Faith is an ignorance. Love without hurt
The only choice.

AT THE CAFÉ AT NIGHT

All this uproar under the stars
Only art makes sense of. The houses
Pay no heed to the passing night,
The moon is an object—it takes art
To get to the bottom of it. Men
Hate one another. The uproar
Of consent tingles the pulse. This
Disbelieved, ask the next
Person. The noise assails the stars.

Let us refer to those two at the café
Sitting outside in the night, the electric
Bulb bare, the street past the chairs
Empty, they tolerate one another
Only because of Van Gogh's paint.

STATE OF AFFAIRS

This is a world of small boys with legs off.
Hip. Hip. They walk the world grown up.
Bitterness is not unknown.

Of course always there have been legs off
In a manner of speaking, taking legs off
To stand for eyes out,

But that is expected—the previous century is barbaric,
Few university degrees were granted,
TV was unknown.

It is too bad since we have so many computers,
So many carbines and combines that we have
So many legs off

But it can't be helped, boys must hop as best
They can, bitterness or not, there must be legs off
So there can be progress,

That is to say democratic election,
Culture for the collectivity and less
In the future legs off.

SAINT LAWRENCE ROASTED ON ONE SIDE ASKED TO BE TURNED OVER

The blue jay eats seeds swallowing
Greatly to get them down, the roseate
Spoonbill stands in the marsh
For hours on both legs unlike
The heron. They take off utterly.

After aeons the quick lizard
Is aware of itself. The tree
Just stands there. Even so
There is more. I have heard a child sob.
It is impossible that all this clutch

And gather of nullity should choose itself
Instead of oblivion but it does,
A creative man once took paper
And a pencil and wrote down an abstract
Idea, he laughed, pleased. As he went

Out the door, on the premise of life
And not nothing, he thanked someone—
The beneficence and width of heaven
(Where do we put the risen?). Other
Instances of assumption can be found—

Thumbtacks, haircuts and bedspreads,
For instance, let alone trust
Of children. Melancholy is no good.
At the instant of conception he knows. Dawn
Comes like a shock, certainty does.

A.M. KLEIN

(1909–1972)

Abraham Moses Klein was born in Ratno, in the Ukraine, and the following year his family moved to Montreal. He began writing seriously as a student at McGill University (1926–30), where he first met A.J.M. Smith, F.R. Scott, Leon Edel, and Leo Kennedy. In 1930 he entered law school at the University of Montreal and received his LLB in 1933. He married Bessie Kozlov in 1933 and became editor of the *Canadian Jewish Chronicle* in 1938; the following year he began a long association with Sam Bronfman, as a speech writer and public-relations adviser. While his literary reputation grew over the years—with the winning of a Governor General's Award in 1949 for *The Rocking Chair and Other Poems* (1948) and the great critical success of his novel *The Second Scroll* (1951)—Klein was never quite satisfied and was easily distracted into causes and kinds of writing for which he was neither gifted nor temperamentally disposed. He was a lawyer with the spirit and instincts of a poet and scholar; an employee of big business with a socialist's conscience and vision; and a deeply religious, if unorthodox, Jew with an intense need to reach, and be appreciated by, a much wider audience. While these pressures and contradiction contributed to his eventual breakdown and long silence, it must be said that his unusual burdens fired a remarkable talent and inspired a body of work unique in vision and seldom surpassed in craft.

In his 'Portrait of the Poet as Landscape' Klein speaks of the poet as someone com-pulsively engaged in naming, cataloguing, deciphering. Klein's tools included French, English, Latin, Yiddish, and Hebrew and a love of language that expressed itself in infectious wit, outrageous pedantry, free-wheeling word-play, and a propensity for exotic vocabularies and frequent allusions to religious and literary classics. His biographer, Usher Caplan, calls attention in *Like One That Dreamed* to Klein's earthy humour and Joycean playfulness, qualities also noticed by his friend and fellow-poet P.K. Page: 'His puns were unbelievable—he just couldn't resist them. Language was marvelously flexible on his tongue, he could bend it any way at all, make it do anything. Klein had that sense of the child in him, to delight in language and play with it. His joyfulness, his delight in things—he was so alive to the world.'

Klein took pleasure in deciphering Joyce's *Ulysses*, and his writings on Joyce that have survived can be found in *Accent* X, 3 (1950) and *New Directions* 13 (1951). He identified with Joyce's breadth of imagination, verbal genius, and bawdy humour, not to mention his lovingly portrayed Jewish hero, Leopold Bloom. But Klein was also drawn to the religious and linguistic intensities of Jesuit poet Gerard Manley Hopkins, from whom he learned much about poetic syntax and sound-patterning. Klein's devotion to craft and his love of language helped him rise above the causes and the occasions that triggered much of his poetry, so that he could make co-exist, in a single literary context, the ridiculousness and the horror of Nazism, the sacredness and profanity of French-Canadian culture, and the sublimity and folly of artistic ambition and endeavour.

Klein's publications also include *Hath Not a Jew* (1940), *The Hitleriad* (1944), *Poems* (1944), and *Collected Poems* (1974), edited with an introduction by Miriam Waddington. Klein's influence and example have been felt by many Canadian poets—notably Layton, Mandel, Cohen, and Solway—in terms of linguistic play and tactics for using and exploring the poet's Jewishness. However, as Waddington points out, Klein's influence among these and other poets has even more to do with the later work, where 'he put into poetry his double and sometimes triple tradition, extending ancient biblical metaphors to include modern grain elevators in a northern landscape, and finding a new metaphysic in such folk objects as rocking chairs and spinning wheels.'

Aside from his splendid 'Portrait of the Poet as Landscape', Klein refused to delineate his poetics:

I do not intend to give you 'a brief statement on my attitude towards my art, etc.' I am surprised that you ask it. You know such questions elicit only the sheerest of arrogant balderdash. What shall I say in reply: 'I sing because I must!'—How phoney! Or that I wish to improve the world with my rhyme!—How ridiculous! Or that I seek to express the standards of my age, etc. Me, I will have none of that cant. Simply expressed, I write poetry only to reveal my civilization, my sensitivities, my craftsmanship. This, however, is not to be quoted. (*Like One That Dreamed: A Portrait of A.M. Klein*, 1982, edited by Usher Caplan)

The gathering of Klein's collected works saw the appearance of *Literary Essays and Reviews* in 1987, *Complete Poems* in 1990, and *Notebooks: Selections from the A.M. Klein Papers* (1994). As an indication of the continuing interest in his poetry, a new *Selected Poems* was released in 1997.

HEIRLOOM

My father bequeathed me no wide estates;
No keys and ledgers were my heritage;
Only some holy books with *yahrzeit* dates
Writ mournfully upon a blank front page—

Books of the Baal Shem Tov, and of his wonders;
Pamphlets upon the devil and his crew;
Prayers against road demons, witches, thunders;
And sundry other tomes for a good Jew.

Beautiful: though no pictures on them, save
The scorpion crawling on a printed track;
The Virgin floating on a scriptural wave,
Square letters twinkling in the Zodiac.

The snuff left on this page, now brown and old,
The tallow stains of midnight liturgy—
These are my coat of arms, and these unfold
My noble lineage, my proud ancestry!

And my tears, too, have stained this heirloomed ground,
When reading in these treatises some weird
Miracle, I turned a leaf and found
A white hair fallen from my father's beard.

AUTOBIOGRAPHICAL

Out of the ghetto streets where a Jewboy
Dreamed pavement into pleasant Bible-land,
Out of the Yiddish slums where childhood met
The friendly beard, the loutish Sabbath-goy,
Or followed, proud, the Torah-escorting band,
Out of the jargoning city I regret,
Rise memories, like sparrows rising from
The gutter-scattered oats,
Like sadness sweet of synagogal hum,
Like Hebrew violins
Sobbing delight upon their Eastern notes.

Again they ring their little bells, those doors
Deemed by the tender-year'd, magnificent:
Old Ashkenazi's cellar, sharp with spice;
The widows' double-parloured candy-stores
And nuggets sweet bought for one sweaty cent;
The warm fresh-smelling bakery, its pies,
Its cakes, its navel'd bellies of black bread;
The lintels candy-poled
Of barber-shop, bright-bottled, green, blue, red;
And fruit-stall piled, exotic,
And the big synagogue door, with letters of gold.

Again my kindergarten home is full—
Saturday night—with kin and compatriot:
My brothers playing Russian card-games; my
Mirroring sisters looking beautiful,
Humming the evening's imminent fox-trot;

My uncle Mayer, of blessed memory,
Still murmuring maariv, counting holy words;
And the two strangers, come
Fiery from Volhynia's murderous hordes—
The cards and humming stop.
And I too swear revenge for that pogrom.

Occasions dear: the four-legged aleph named
And angel pennies dropping on my book;
The rabbi patting a coming scholar-head;
My mother, blessing candles, Sabbath-flamed,
Queenly in her Warsovian perruque;
My father pickabacking me to bed
To tell tall tales about the Baal Shem Tov—
Letting me curl his beard.
Oh memory of unsurpassing love,
Love leading a brave child
Through childhood's ogred corridors, unfear'd!

The week in the country at my brother's—(May
He own fat cattle in the fields of heaven!)
Its picking of strawberries from grassy ditch,
Its odour of dogrose and of yellowing hay—
Dusty, adventurous, sunny days, all seven!—
Still follow me, still warm me, still are rich
With the cow-tinkling peace of pastureland.
The meadow'd memory
Is sodded with its clover, and is spanned
By that same pillow'd sky
A boy on his back one day watched enviously.

And paved again the street: the shouting boys,
Oblivious of mothers on the stoops,
Playing the robust robbers and police,
The corncob battle—all high-spirited noise
Competitive among the lot-drawn groups.
Another day, of shaken apple trees
In the rich suburbs, and a furious dog,
And guilty boys in flight;
Hazelnut games, and games in the synagogue—
The burrs, the Haman rattle,
The Torah dance on Simchas Torah night.

Immortal days of the picture calendar
Dear to me always with the virgin joy
Of the first flowering of senses five,
Discovering birds, or textures, or a star,
Or tastes sweet, sour, acid, those that cloy;
And perfumes. Never was I more alive.
All days thereafter are a dying off,
A wandering away
From home and the familiar. The years doff
Their innocence.
No other day is ever like that day.

I am no old man fatuously intent
On memories, but in memory I seek
The strength and vividness of nonage days,
Not tranquil recollection of event.
It is a fabled city that I seek;
It stands in Space's vapours and Time's haze;
Thence comes my sadness in remembered joy
Constrictive of the throat;
Thence do I hear, as heard by a Jewboy,
The Hebrew violins,
Delighting in the sobbed Oriental note.

FOR THE SISTERS OF THE HOTEL DIEU

In pairs,
as if to illustrate their sisterhood,
the sisters pace the hospital garden walks.
In their robes black and white immaculate hoods
they are like birds,
the safe domestic fowl of the House of God.

O biblic birds,
who fluttered to me in my childhood illnesses
—me little, afraid, ill, not of your race,—
the cool wing for my fever, the hovering solace,
the sense of angels—
be thanked, O plumage of paradise, be praised.

POLITICAL MEETING
For Camillien Houde

On the school platform, draping the folding seats,
they wait the chairman's praise and glass of water.
Upon the wall the agonized Y initials their faith.

Here all are laic; the skirted brothers have gone.
Still, their equivocal absense is felt, like a breeze
that gives curtains the sounds of surplices.

The hall is yellow with light, and jocular;
suddenly some one lets loose upon the air
the ritual bird which the crowd in snares of singing

catches and plucks, throat, wings, and little limbs.
Fall the feathers of sound, like *alouette's*.
The chairman, now, is charming, full of asides and wit,

building his orators, and chipping off
the heckling gargoyles popping in the hall.
(Outside, in the dark, the street is body-tall,

flowered with faces intent on the scarecrow thing
that shouts to thousands the echoing
of their own wishes.) The Orator has risen!

Worshipped and loved, their favourite visitor,
a country uncle with sunflower seeds in his pockets,
full of wonderful moods, tricks, imitative talk,

he is their idol: like themselves, not handsome,
not snobbish, not of the *Grande Allée! Un homme!*
Intimate, informal, he makes bear's compliments

to the ladies; is gallant; and grins;
goes for the balloon, his opposition, with pins;
jokes also on himself, speaks of himself

in the third person, slings slang, and winks with folklore;
and knows now that he has them, kith and kin.
Calmly, therefore, he begins to speak of war,

praises the virtue of being *Canadien*,
of being at peace, of faith, of family,
and suddenly his other voice: *Where are your sons?*

He is tearful, choking tears; but not he
would blame the clever English; in their place
he'd do the same; maybe.

Where *are* your sons?
                    The whole street wears one face,
shadowed and grim; and in the darkness rises
the body-odour of race.

MONTREAL

O city metropole, isle riverain!
Your ancient pavages and sainted routs
Traverse my spirit's conjured avenues!
Splendour erablic of your promenades
Foliates there, and there your maisonry
Of pendant balcon and escalier'd march,
Unique midst English habitat,
Is vivid Normandy!

You populate the pupils of my eyes:
Thus, does the Indian, plumed, furtivate
Still through your painted autumns, Ville-Marie!
Though palisades have passed, though calumet
With tabac of your peace enfumes the air,
Still do I spy the phantom, aquiline,
Genuflect, moccasin'd, behind
His statue in the square!

Thus, costumed images before me pass,
Haunting your archives architectural:
Coureur de bois, in posts where pelts were portaged;
Seigneur within his candled manoir; Scot
Ambulant through his bank, pillar'd and vast.
Within your chapels, voyaged mariners
Still pray, and personage departed,
All present from your past!

Grand port of navigations, multiple
The lexicons uncargo'd at your quays,
Sonnant though strange to me; but chiefest, I,
Auditor of your music, cherish the
Joined double-melodied vocabulaire
Where English vocable and roll Ecossic,
Mollified by the parle of French
Bilinguefact your air!

Such your suaver vice, hushed Hochelaga!
But for me also sound your potencies,
Fortissimos of sirens fluvial,
Bruit of manufactory, and thunder
From foundry issuant, all puissant tone
Implenishing your hebdomad; and then
Sanct silence, and your argent belfries
Clamant in orison!

You are a part of me, O all your quartiers—
And of dire pauvrete and of richesse—
To finished time my homage loyal claim;
You are locale of infancy, milieu
Vital of institutes that formed my fate;
And you above the city, scintillant,
Mount Royal, are my spirit's mother,
Almative, poitrinate!

Never do I sojourn in alien place
But I do languish for your scenes and sounds,
City of reverie, nostalgic isle,
Pendant most brilliant on Laurential cord!
The coigns of your boulevards—my signiory—
Your suburbs are my exile's verdure fresh,
Your parks, your fountain'd parks—
Pasture of memory!

City, O city, you are vision'd as
A parchemin roll of saecular exploit
Inked with the script of eterne souvenir!
You are in sound, chanson and instrument!
Mental, you rest forever edified

With tower and dome; and in these beating valves,
Here in these beating valves, you will
For all my mortal time reside!

LONE BATHER

Upon the ecstatic diving board the diver,
poised for parabolas, lets go
lets go his manshape to become a bird.
Is bird, and topsy-turvy
the pool floats overhead, and the white tiles snow
their crazy hexagons. Is dolphin. Then
is plant with lilies bursting from his heels.
Himself, suddenly mysterious and marine,
bobs up a merman leaning on his hills.

Plashes and plays alone the deserted pool;
as those, is free, who think themselves unseen.
He rolls in his heap of fruit,
he slides his belly over
the melonrinds of water, curved and smooth and green.
Feels good: and trains, like little acrobats
his echoes dropping from the galleries;
circles himself over a rung of water;
swims fancy and gay; taking a notion, hides
under the stains of his great big bed,—
and then comes up to float until he thinks
the ceiling at his brow, and nowhere any sides.
His thighs are a shoal of fishes: scattered: he
turns with many gloves of greeting
towards the sunnier water and the tiles.

Upon the tiles he dangles from his toes
lazily the eight reins of his ponies.
An afternoon, far from the world
a street sound throws like a stone, with paper, through the glass.
Up, he is chipped enamel, grained with hair.
The gloss of his footsteps follows him to the showers,
the showers, and the male room, and the towel
which rubs the bird, the plant, the dolphin back again
personable plain.

PORTRAIT OF THE POET AS LANDSCAPE

I

Not an editorial-writer, bereaved with bartlett,
mourns him, the shelved Lycidas.
No actress squeezes a glycerine tear for him.
The radio broadcast lets his passing pass.
And with the police, no record. Nobody, it appears,
either under his real name or his alias,
missed him enough to report.

It is possible that he is dead, and not discovered.
It is possible that he can be found some place
in a narrow closet, like the corpse in a detective story,
standing, his eyes staring, and ready to fall on his face.
It is also possible that he is alive
and amnesiac, or mad, or in retired disgrace,
or beyond recognition lost in love.

We are sure only that from our real society
he has disappeared; he simply does not count,
except in the pullulation of vital statistics—
somebody's vote, perhaps, an anonymous taunt
of the Gallup poll, a dot in a government table—
but not felt, and certainly far from eminent—
in a shouting mob, somebody's sigh.

O, he who unrolled our culture from his scroll—
the prince's quote, the rostrum-rounding roar—
who under one name made articulate
heaven, and under another the seven-circled air,
is, if he is at all, a number, an x,
a Mr Smith in a hotel register,—
incognito, lost, lacunal.

II

The truth is he's not dead, but only ignored—
like the mirroring lenses forgotten on a brow
that shine with the guilt of their unnoticed world.

The truth is he lives among neighbours, who, though they will allow
him a passable fellow, think him eccentric, not solid,
a type that one can forgive, and for that matter, forgo.

Himself he has his moods, just like a poet.
Sometimes, depressed to nadir, he will think all lost,
will see himself as throwback, relict, freak,
his mother's miscarriage, his great-grandfather's ghost,
and he will curse his quintuplet senses, and their tutors
in whom he put, as he should not have put, his trust.

Then he will remember his travels over that body—
the torso verb, the beautiful face of the noun,
and all those shaped and warm auxiliaries!
A first love it was, the recognition of this own.
Dear limbs adverbial, complexion of adjective,
dimple and dip of conjugation!

And then remember how this made a change in him
affecting for always the glow and growth of his being;
how suddenly was aware of the air, like shaken tinfoil,
of the patents of nature, the shock of belated seeing,
the loneliness peering from the eyes of crowds;
the integers of thought; the cube-roots of feeling.

Thus, zoomed to zenith, sometimes he hopes again,
and sees himself as a character, with a rehearsed role:
the Count of Monte Cristo, come for his revenges;
the unsuspecting heir, with papers; the risen soul;
or the chloroformed prince awakening from his flowers;
or—deflated again—the convict on parole.

III

He is alone; yet not completely alone.
Pins on a map of a colour similar to his,
each city has one, sometimes more than one;
here, caretakers of art, in colleges;
in offices, there, with arm-bands, and green-shaded;
and there, pounding their catalogued beats in libraries,—

everywhere menial, a shadow's shadow.
And always for their egos—their outmoded art.
Thus, having lost the bevel in the ear,
they know neither up nor down, mistake the part
for the whole, curl themselves in a comma,
talk technics, make a colon their eyes. They distort—

such is the pain of their frustration—truth
to something convolute and cerebral.
How they do fear the slap of the flat of the platitude!
Now Pavlov's victims, their mouths water at bell,
the platter empty.
                    See they set twenty-one jewels
into their watches; the time they do not tell!

Some, patagonian in their own esteem,
and longing for the multiplying word,
join party and wear pins, now have a message,
an ear, and the convention-hall's regard.
Upon the knees of ventriloquists, they own,
of their dandled brightness, only the paint and board.

And some go mystical, and some go mad.
One stares at a mirror all day long, as if
to recognize himself; another courts
angels,—for here he does not fear rebuff;
and a third, alone, and sick with sex, and rapt,
doodles him symbols convex and concave.

O schizoid solitudes! O purities
curdling upon themselves! Who live for themselves,
or for each other, but for nobody else;
desire affection, private and public loves;
are friendly, and then quarrel and surmise
the secret perversions of each other's lives.

IV

He suspects that something has happened, a law
been passed, a nightmare ordered. Set apart,
he finds himself, with special haircut and dress,
as on a reservation. Introvert.

He does not understand this; sad conjecture
muscles and palls thrombotic on his heart.

He thinks an imposter, having studied his personal biography,
his gestures, his moods, now has come forward to pose
in the shivering vacuums his absence leaves.
Wigged with his laurel, that other, and faked with his face,
he pats the heads of his children, pecks his wife,
and is at home, and slippered, in his house.

So he guesses at the impertinent silhouette
that talks to his phone-piece and slits open his mail.
Is it the local tycoon who for a hobby
plays poet, he so epical in steel?
The orator, making a pause? Or is that man
he who blows his flash of brass in the jittering hall?

Or is he cuckolded by the troubadour
rich and successful out of celluloid?
Or by the don who unrhymes atoms? Or
the chemist death built up? Pride, lost impostor'd pride,
it is another, another, whoever he is,
who rides where he should ride.

V

Fame, the adrenalin: to be talked about;
to be a verb; to be introduced as *The:*
to smile with endorsement from slick paper; make
caprices anecdotal; to nod to the world; to see
one's name like a song upon the marquees played;
to be forgotten with embarrassment; to be—
to be.

It has its attractions, but is not the thing;
nor is it the ape mimesis who speaks from the tree
ancestral; nor the merkin joy . . .
Rather it is stark infelicity
which stirs him from his sleep, undressed, asleep
to walk upon roofs and window-sills and defy
the gape of gravity.

VI

Therefore he seeds illusions. Look, he is
the nth Adam taking a green inventory
in world but scarcely uttered, naming, praising,
the flowering fiats in the meadow, the
syllabled fur, stars aspirate, the pollen
whose sweet collusion sounds eternally.

For to praise
the world—he, solitary man—is breath
to him. Until it has been praised, that part
has not been. Item by exciting item—
air to his lungs, and pressured blood to his heart—
they are pulsated, and breathed, until they map,
not the world's, but his own body's chart!

And now in imagination he has climbed
another planet, the better to look
with single camera view upon this earth—
its total scope, and each afflated tick,
its talk, its trick, its tracklessness—and this,
this, he would like to write down in a book!

To find a new function for the *déclassé* craft
archaic like the fletcher's; to make a new thing;
to say the word that will become sixth sense;
perhaps by necessity and indirection bring
new forms to life, anonymously, new creeds—
O, somehow pay back the daily larcenies of the lung!

These are not mean ambitions. It is already something
merely to entertain them. Meanwhile, he
makes of his status as zero a rich garland,
a halo of his anonymity,
and lives alone, and in his secret shines
like phosphorus. At the bottom of the sea.

EARLE BIRNEY

(1904–1995)

Birney always believed that moral progress is possible. His observation of the scarred battleground of his own century troubled him deeply, however, causing him to lash out in anger at human cruelty and indifference and to despair at his own guilt and complicity. These two responses reflect the Marxism of a generation caught in two world wars and a depression as well as the Puritanism of his heritage. The first accounts for his well-known vitriolic satires, such as 'Anglo-Saxon Street', and for his more recent attacks on the economic and political atrocities of the American empire, such as 'Sinaloa' and 'Images in Place of Logging', where he describes 'the men and the metalled / ants that multiply in the browning / pulp of the peeled world'. As early as 1945, Birney had written from Watford Military Hospital lamenting the time-bomb within each man, and pleading: 'O men be swift to be mankind / or let the grizzly take.' Almost twenty years later, he wrote in 'Letter to a Cuzco Priest': 'Pray to yourself above all for men like me / that we do not quench / the man in each of us.'

In 'The Bear on the Delhi Road', Birney suggests the method by which he brings his world under imaginative control. He says: 'It is not easy to free / myth from reality.' He describes the business of trying to make a bear perform, making it dance rather than merely amble among berries. The men of Kashmir try to transform reality, to give it artistic shape for financial gain; however, in so doing, they perform a task not unlike that

of the artist, who begins with the real and concrete, whether an object or an experience, and reflects upon it until its 'meaning' (for him) is released. This is the essential structure of the romantic code, wherein the poet contemplates a height of land (say Tintern Abbey) and is moved to discover some personal and universal significance in his experience. It is certainly the organizing principle at work in 'Vancouver Lights', 'A Walk in Kyoto', and many of Birney's travel poems; and it is a method he shares quite noticeably with Al Purdy.

Birney's energies were continually engaged in coming to terms with his need for a social identity and with his separateness as an artist. Despite his involvement in the war and the universities, he always was an outsider, beset by internal and external forces that kept him from feeling fulfilled. He resented society's indifference to the artist and feels intensely that the artist has a cure for society's ills. In 'Cartagena de Indias' he describes what it means to learn that other cultures can honour even their most critical poets. 'I love the whole starved cheating / poetry-reading lot of you,' he says of the Colombians, 'I who am seldom read by my townsmen.' In *The Creative Writer*, Birney speaks of the situation of the writer in Canada:

It seems to me that the effective writer is one who is inwardly sure of the entire naturalness of his creative act. For instance, he must be aware that he is writing not merely because he is neurotic. Everybody's a bit queer and slightly mad, but I'm sure that my compulsion to construct more and more unprofitable verses isn't anywhere near as screwball as the compulsion of businessmen to make more and more money. But the writer who does not believe this is hamstrung from the start, haunted by a false diagnosis of his society, and driven either into a permanent state of apology and mock-modesty for his abnormality, or into snarling hatred for the nastiness of the normal.

This describes accurately many of the tensions Birney felt during his own lifetime. For him there could be no real resolution. And there is reason to believe that without it his peculiar *daimon* would have ceased to function. That is why he was continually on the move, why he was always experimenting in his art.

'Living art,' Birney says, 'like anything else, stays alive only by changing.' His own verse has travelled from the most traditional beginnings—including narrative, meditative lyrics, satires, nature poems, and odes— through years of experiment with typography and orthography, down the long congested road to concrete poetry. Birney was a constant reviser of poems and a contributor to little magazines. 'I don't know exactly where the literary Dew Line is this moment,' he says, 'but I'm sure it lies somewhere in the complicated world of today's little-little magazines and small-press chapbooks.'

Birney's life was as colourful as his art— and as controversial. He was born in Calgary, but spent most of his youth in Banff and in Creston, BC. He graduated from the University of British Columbia in 1926. His graduate studies in California were interrupted by difficulties, mostly financial, which took him to Utah to teach, and to New York to work for the Trotskyites. With a grant from the Royal Society he completed his doctoral studies in London, England, and at the University of Toronto, where he lectured for several years and served as literary editor of the *Canadian Forum*. During the Second World War he was a Personnel Selection Officer overseas and then for a short time Supervisor of Foreign Language Broadcasts to Europe for the CBC. Later he joined the English Department at UBC, where he founded and briefly headed the Department of Creative Writing. He served as writer-in-residence at the University of Toronto and travelled widely throughout Asia, Europe, South America, and the United States.

His books of poetry include *David and Other Poems* (1942) and *Now Is Time* (1945), for each of which he won a Governor General's Award, *The Strait of Anian: Selected Poems* (1948), *Trial of a City and Other Verse* (1952), *Ice Cod Bell or Stone* (1962), *Near False Creek Mouth* (1964), *Selected Poems* (1966), *Rag and Bone Shop* (1970), *The Collected Poems of Earle Birney* (1975), *Ghost in the Wheels, Selected Poems 1920–1976* (1977) and *Last Makings* (1991). He also published two novels, *Turvey* (1949), which won the Stephen Leacock medal for humour, and *Down the Long Table* (1955); two books on the creative process, *The Creative Writer* (1966) and *The Cow Jumped Over the Moon* (1972); and an autobiographical work, *Spreading Time, Book One, 1940–1949* (1980). *Words on Waves: the Selected Radio Plays of Earle Birney*, edited by Howard Fink and John Jackson, appeared in 1985. Critical works on Earle Birney include Frank Davey's *Earle Birney* (1975), York University's Symposium papers *Perspectives on Earle Birney* (1981), Peter Aichinger's *Earle Birney and His Works* (1984), and Elspeth Cameron's controversial *Earle Birney: A Life* (1994).

FROM THE HAZEL BOUGH

I met a lady
 on a lazy street
hazel eyes
 and little plush feet

her legs swam by
 like lovely trout
eyes were trees
 where boys leant out

hands in the dark and
 a river side
round breasts rising
 with the fingers' tide

she was plump as a finch
 and live as a salmon
gay as silk and
 proud as Brahmin

we winked when we met
 and laughed when we parted
never took time
 to be brokenhearted

but no man sees
 where the trout lie now
or what leans out
 from the hazel bough

ANGLOSAXON STREET

Dawndrizzle ended dampness steams from
blotching brick and blank plasterwaste
Faded housepatterns hoary and finicky
unfold stuttering stick like a phonograph

Here is a ghetto gotten for goyim

O with care denuded   of nigger and kike
No coonsmell rankles   reeks only cellarrot
Ottar of carexhaust   catcorpse and cookinggrease
Imperial hearts   heave in this haven
Cracks across windows   are welded with slogans
There'll Always Be An England   enhances geraniums
and V's for a Victory   vanquish the housefly

Ho!   with beaming sun   march the bleached beldames
festooned with shopping bags   farded   flatarched
bigthewed Saxonwives   stepping over buttrivers
waddling back wienerladen   to suckle smallfry

Hoy!   with sunslope   shrieking over hydrants
flood from learninghall   the lean fingerlings
Nordic   nobblecheeked   not all clean of nose
leaping Commandowise   into leprous lanes

What!   after whistleblow!   spewed from wheelboat
after daylight doughtiness   dire handplay
in sewertrench or sandpit   some Saxonthegns
Junebrown Jutekings   jawslack for meat

Sit after supper   on smeared doorsteps
not humbly swearing   hatedeeds on Huns
profiteers politicians   pacifists Jews

Then by twobit magic   to muse in movie
unlock picturehoard   or lope to alehall
soaking bleakly   in beer skittleless
Home again to hotbox   and humid husbandhood
in slumbertrough adding   sleepily to Anglekin

Alongside in lanenooks   carling and leman
caterwaul and clip   careless of Saxonry
with moonglow and haste   and a higher heartbeat

Slumbers now slumtrack   unstinks cooling
waiting brief for milkmaid   mornstar and worldrise

DAVID

I

David and I that summer cut trails on the Survey,
All week in the valley for wages, in air that was steeped
In the wail of mosquitoes, but over the sunalive week-ends
We climbed, to get from the ruck of the camp, the surly

Poker, the wrangling, the snoring under the fetid
Tents, and because we had joy in our lengthening coltish
Muscles, and mountains for David were made to see over,
Stairs from the valleys and steps to the sun's retreats.

II

Our first was Mount Gleam. We hiked in the long afternoon
To a curling lake and lost the lure of the faceted
Cone in the swell of its sprawling shoulders. Past
The inlet we grilled our bacon, the strips festooned

On a poplar prong, in the hurrying slant of the sunset.
Then the two of us rolled in the blanket while round us the cold
Pines thrust at the stars. The dawn was afloating
Of mists till we reached to the slopes above timber, and won

To snow like fire in the sunlight. The peak was upthrust
Like a fist in a frozen ocean of rock that swirled
Into valleys the moon could be rolled in. Remotely unfurling
Eastward the alien prairie glittered. Down through the dusty

Skree on the west we descended, and David showed me
How to use the give of shale for giant incredible
Strides. I remember, before the larches' edge,
That I jumped a long green surf of juniper flowing

Away from the wind, and landed in gentian and saxifrage
Spilled on the moss. Then the darkening firs
And the sudden whirring of water that knifed down a fern-hidden
Cliff and splashed unseen into mist in the shadows.

III

One Sunday on Rampart's arête a rainsquall caught us,
And passed, and we clung by our blueing fingers and bootnails
An endless hour in the sun, not daring to move
Till the ice had steamed from the slate. And David taught me

How time on a knife-edge can pass with the guessing of fragments
Remembered from poets, the naming of strata beside one,
And matching of stories from schooldays. . . . We crawled astride
The peak to feast on the marching ranges flagged

By the fading shreds of the shattered stormcloud. Lingering
There it was David who spied to the south, remote,
And unmapped, a sunlit spire on Sawback, an overhang
Crooked like a talon. David named it the Finger.

That day we chanced on the skull and the splayed white ribs
Of a mountain goat underneath a cliff-face, caught
On a rock. Around were the silken feathers of hawks.
And that was the first I knew that a goat could slip.

IV

And then Inglismaldie. Now I remember only
The long ascent of the lonely valley, the live
Pine spirally scarred by lightning, the slicing pipe
Of invisible pika, and great prints, by the lowest

Snow, of a grizzly. There it was too that David
Taught me to read the scroll of coral in limestone
And the beetle-seal in the shale of ghostly trilobites,
Letters delivered to man from the Cambrian waves.

V

On Sundance we tried from the col and the going was hard.
The air howled from our feet to the smudged rocks
And the papery lake below. At an outthrust we baulked
Till David clung with his left to a dint in the scarp,

Lobbed the iceaxe over the rocky lip,
Slipped from his holds and hung by the quivering pick,
Twisted his long legs up into space and kicked
To the crest. Then grinning, he reached with his freckled wrist

And drew me up after. We set a new time for that climb.
That day returning we found a robin gyrating
In grass, wing-broken. I caught it to tame but David
Took and killed it, and said, 'Could you teach it to fly?'

VI

In August, the second attempt, we ascended The Fortress.
By the forks of the Spray we caught five trout and fried them
Over a balsam fire. The woods were alive
With the vaulting of mule-deer and drenched with clouds
    all the morning,

Till we burst at noon to the flashing and floating round
Of the peaks. Coming down we picked in our hats the bright
And sunhot raspberries, eating them under a mighty
Spruce, while a marten moving like quicksilver scouted us.

VII

But always we talked of the Finger on Sawback, unknown
And hooked, till the first afternoon in September we slogged
Through the musky woods, past a swamp that quivered
    with frog-song,
And camped by a bottle-green lake. But under the cold

Breath of the glacier sleep would not come, the moon-light
Etching the Finger. We rose and trod past the feathery
Larch, while the stars went out, and the quiet heather
Flushed, and the skyline pulsed with the surging bloom

Of incredible dawn in the Rockies. David spotted
Bighorns across the moraine and sent them leaping
With yodels the ramparts redoubled and rolled to the peaks,
And the peaks to the sun. The ice in the morning thaw

Was a gurgling world of crystal and cold blue chasms,
And seracs that shone like frozen saltgreen waves.
At the base of the Finger we tried once and failed. Then David
Edged to the west and discovered the chimney; the last

Hundred feet we fought the rock and shouldered and kneed
Our way for an hour and made it. Unroping we formed
A cairn on the rotting tip. Then I turned to look north
And the glistening wedge of giant Assiniboine, heedless

Of handhold. And one foot gave. I swayed and shouted.
David turned sharp and reached out his arm and steadied me,
Turning again with a grin and his lips ready
To jest. But the strain crumbled his foothold. Without

A gasp he was gone. I froze to the sound of grating
Edge-nails and fingers, the slither of stones, the lone
Second of silence, the nightmare thud. Then only
The wind and the muted beat of unknowing cascades.

VIII

Somehow I worked down the fifty impossible feet
To the ledge, calling and getting no answer but echoes
Released in the cirque, and trying not to reflect
What an answer would mean. He lay still, with his lean

Young face upturned and strangely unmarred, but his legs
Splayed beneath him, beside the final drop,
Six hundred feet sheer to the ice. My throat stopped
When I reached him, for he was alive. He opened his grey

Straight eyes and brokenly murmured 'over . . . over.'
And I, feeling beneath him a cruel fang
Of the ledge thrust in his back, but not understanding,
Mumbled stupidly, 'Best not to move,' and spoke

Of his pain. But he said, 'I can't move. . . . If only I felt
Some pain.' Then my shame stung the tears to my eyes
As I crouched, and I cursed myself, but he cried,
Louder, 'No, Bobbie! Don't ever blame yourself.

I didn't test my foothold.' He shut the lids
Of his eyes to the stare of the sky, while I moistened his lips
From our water flask and tearing my shirt into strips
I swabbed the shredded hands. But the blood slid

From his side and stained the stone and the thirsting lichens,
And yet I dared not lift him up from the gore
Of the rock. Then he whispered, 'Bob, I want to go over!'
This time I knew what he meant and I grasped for a lie

And said, 'I'll be back here by midnight with ropes
And men from the camp and we'll cradle you out.' But I knew
That the day and the night must pass and the cold dews
Of another morning before such men unknowing

The ways of mountains could win to the chimney's top.
And then, how long? And he knew . . . and the hell of hours
After that, if he lived till we came, roping him out.
But I curled beside him and whispered, 'The bleeding will stop.

You can last.' He said only, 'Perhaps. . . . For what? A wheelchair,
Bob?' His eyes brightening with fever upbraided me.
I could not look at him more and said, 'Then I'll stay
With you.' But he did not speak, for the clouding fever.

I lay dazed and stared at the long valley,
The glistening hair of a creek on the rug stretched
By the firs, while the sun leaned round and flooded the ledge,
The moss, and David still as a broken doll.

I hunched to my knees to leave, but he called and his voice
Now was sharpened with fear. 'For Christ's sake push me over!
If I could move. . . . Or die. . . .' The sweat ran from his forehead,
But only his eyes moved. A hawk was buoying

Blackly its wings over the wrinkled ice.
The purr of a waterfall rose and sank with the wind.
Above us climbed the last joint of the Finger
Beckoning bleakly the wide indifferent sky.

Even then in the sun it grew cold lying there. . . . And I knew
He had tested his holds. It was I who had not. . . . I looked
At the blood on the ledge, and the far valley. I looked
At last in his eyes. He breathed, 'I'd do it for you, Bob.'

IX

I will not remember how nor why I could twist
Up the wind-devilled peak, and down through the chimney's empty
Horror, and over the traverse alone. I remember
Only the pounding fear I would stumble on It

When I came to the grave-cold maw of the bergschrund . . . reeling
Over the sun-cankered snowbridge, shying the caves
In the névé . . . the fear, and the need to make sure It was there
On the ice, the running and falling and running, leaping

Of gaping greenthroated crevasses, alone and pursued
By the Finger's lengthening shadow. At last through the fanged
And blinding seracs I slid to the milky wrangling
Falls at the glacier's snout, through the rocks piled huge

On the humped moraine, and into the spectral larches,
Alone. By the glooming lake I sank and chilled
My mouth but I could not rest and stumbled still
To the valley, losing my way in the ragged marsh.

I was glad of the mire that covered the stains, on my ripped
Boots, of his blood, but panic was on me, the reek
Of the bog, the purple glimmer of toadstools obscene
In the twilight. I staggered clear to a firewaste, tripped

And fell with a shriek on my shoulder. It somehow eased
My heart to know I was hurt, but I did not faint
And I could not stop while over me hung the range
Of the Sawback. In blackness I searched for the trail by the creek

And found it. . . . My feet squelched a slug and horror
Rose again in my nostrils. I hurled myself
Down the path. In the woods behind some animal yelped.
Then I saw the glimmer of tents and babbled my story.

I said that he fell straight to the ice where they found him,
And none but the sun and incurious clouds have lingered
Around the marks of that day on the ledge of the Finger,
That day, the last of my youth, on the last of our mountains.

BUSHED

He invented a rainbow but lightning struck it
shattered it into the lake-lap of a mountain
so big his mind slowed when he looked at it

Yet he built a shack on the shore
learned to roast porcupine belly and
wore the quills on his hatband

At first he was out with the dawn
whether it yellowed bright as wood-columbine
or was only a fuzzed moth in a flannel of storm
But he found the mountain was clearly alive
sent messages whizzing down every hot morning
boomed proclamations at noon and spread out
a white guard of goat
before falling asleep on its feet at sundown

When he tried his eyes on the lake   ospreys
would fall like valkyries
choosing the cut-throat
He took then to waiting
till the night smoke rose from the boil of the sunset

But the moon carved unknown totems
out of the lakeshore
owls in the beardusky woods derided him
moosehorned cedars circled his swamps and tossed
their antlers up to the stars
Then he knew   though the mountain slept   the winds
were shaping its peak to an arrowhead
poised

And now he could only
bar himself in and wait
for the great flint to come singing into his heart

1951

APPEAL TO A LADY WITH A DIAPER

               haired   bus
O   ochre   woman at the   of the
                                   back

                  swing   on the
swaying and   ing by the bassinet   seat

            once
changing   more on the little   mush-
                             cleft
               your
room bottom of   baby his diaper   O

             y with s
          d   a
       a   f
yellowpowedl   etypinnedteeth its
your MAN   look   over here   its your husb-

                   s
     mp   a
    u   e   y
and h   d a   nd me   ing WELLNOW L TELLYUH
          r u
           o
SEPRITISTS & LONGHAIRS & BEATNIKS & JAIL THE JERKS
& HIPPIES & DOE PADDIX & VIETNIKS & MAKE EM WORK
His laugh is a bullFROG in BUHLEEVEME a can
in a LOYALTEE swamp saying DIG THAT! & IS SHE STACKED!
saying BILLYUNS AMERRRKAN KINAIDGIN FREEYENTAH PRIZE & WE

                 mopperup a
& O   saffron   cross this   continent
                             purging

wordswords are oozing & ooshing from the mouths of all
your husbands saying SPACEWAR & FIGGERS DONT & EGG
HEADS & WY & plashing on the   of   national
                          plastic   inter

buses & dribbling on barbecues the slick floors of
autocourts saying WALLSTREET saying BAY STREET & TAXES & REDS
WARE I COMEFROM & CLOUT EM FIRST & dripping onto rockers LEGS
bleachers & outboards saying Z–BOMB & GREAZERS & PINKOS & SPADES
clouding the luncheon soup the beerpool on the bartop
staining the fairway the walltowall   the cortex
saying READERSDIGEST saying TEENAGE saying GOOKS saying . . . I ME
MINE.

       phurtoppedm
    l   o
   u   m   one
& O s   ma there is no   none

          over
nowhere to bend   one   mush-
               cleft

room face saying ULCERS & KIDESTHESEDAYS SECURITY
WHAT A LAY! & HEAR TH ONE?

         ing
bend with a loop   nickof   deftness
              time

& mothersmother all this wetnakedness away with
one soft white disposable diaper of *s i l e n c e*

Ontario & Illinois 1956/1971

A WALK IN KYOTO

All week   the maid tells me   bowing
her doll's body at my mat   is Boy's Day
Also please Man's Day   and gravely
bends deeper   The magnolia sprig in my alcove
is it male?   The ancient discretions of Zen were not shaped
for my phallic western eye   There is so much discretion
in this small bowed body of an empire
the wild hair of waterfalls combed straight
in the ricefields   the inn–maid retreating
with the face of a shut flower   I stand hunched
and clueless like a castaway in the shoals of my room

When I slide my parchment door to stalk awkward
through Lilliput gardens framed and untouchable
as watercolors   the streets look much the same
the Men are being pulled past on the strings of their engines
the legs of the Boys are revolved by a thousand pedals
and all the faces as taut and unfestive as Moscow's
or Chicago's   or mine

Lord Buddha help us all there is vigor enough
in these islands and in all islands reefed and resounding
with cities   But the pitch is high as the ping
of cicadas   those small strained motors concealed
in the propped pines by the dying river   and only
male as the stretched falsetto of actors mincing
the women's roles in kabuki   or female only
as the lost heroes womanized in the Ladies' Opera
Where in these alleys jammed with competing waves
of signs in two tongues and three scripts
can the simple song of a man be heard?

By the shoguns' palace   the Important Cultural Property
stripped for tiptoeing schoolgirls   I stare at the staring
penned carp that flail on each other's backs
to the shrunk pool's edge for the crumb this non-fish
tossed   Is this the Day's one parable?
Or under that peeling pagoda the five hundred tons
of hermaphrodite Word?

At the inn I prepare to surrender again my defeated
shoes to the bending maid   But suddenly the closed
lotus opens to a smile and she points
over my shoulder   above the sagging tiles   to where
tall in the bare sky and huge as Gulliver
a carp is rising   golden and fighting
thrusting its paper body up from the fist
of a small boy on an empty roof   higher
and higher   into the endless winds of the world

Kyoto & Hong Kong 1958

THE BEAR ON THE DELHI ROAD

Unreal   tall as a myth
by the road the Himalayan bear
is beating the brilliant air
with his crooked arms
about him two men   bare
spindly as locusts   leap

One pulls on a ring
in the great soft nose   His mate
flicks   flicks with a stick
up at the rolling eyes

They have not led him here
down from the fabulous hills
to this bald alien plain
and the clamorous world   to kill
but simply to teach him to dance

They are peaceful both   these spare
men of Kashmir   and the bear
alive is their living   too
If   far on the Delhi way
around him galvanic they dance
it is merely to wear   wear
from his shaggy body the tranced
wish forever to stay
only an ambling bear
four-footed in berries

It is no more joyous for them
in this hot dust to prance
out of reach of the praying claws
sharpened to paw for ants
in the shadows of deodars
It is not easy to free
myth from reality
or rear this fellow up
to lurch   lurch with them
in the tranced dancing of men

Srinagar 1958—Ile des Porquerolles 1959

AL PURDY

(1918-2000)

Purdy was born in Wooler, Ontario and educated at Albert College in Belleville. At sixteen he dropped out of school and began his wanderings, working at odd jobs, putting in time with the RCAF in British Columbia, and trying his hand at writing. Although his first book of poems was published in 1944, he did not seriously consider supporting himself by writing until he sold a script to the CBC in 1955. He moved to Montreal and then to Roblin Lake at Ameliasburg, Ontario, where he lived for many years. From Ameliasburg he travelled to the Cariboo, Newfoundland, Baffin Island, Cuba, Greece, and England, and has been writer-in-residence at various universities. Of this incessant wandering he said: 'I write poems like spiders spin webs, and perhaps for much the same reason, to support my existence . . . unless one is a stone one doesn't sit still. And perhaps new areas of landscape awaken old areas of one's self. One has seen the familiar landscape (perhaps) so often that one ceases to really see it.' He retired to Sidney, BC, but always conspired to spend part of each summer at Roblin Lake.

Purdy's development was haphazard and independent, a product of his continued experiment and chance discovery of interesting poets, such as Milton Acorn, Irving Layton, and D.H. Lawrence. He objected as much to the 'sweetness and iambic smoothness' of academic poets like Richard Wilbur as to the 'togetherness . . . of the Duncan-Creeley-Olson bunch'. 'I have no one style,'

he said in a letter to Charles Bukowski, 'I have a dozen: have got to be virtuoso enough so I can shift gears like a hot-rod kid—I doubt that my exact combo ever came along before. Unlike some, I have no ideas about being a specific kind of poet. I mean, I don't make rules and say THIS is what a poet HAS to be. I don't know what the hell a poet is or care much. I do know what he isn't sometimes.'

Despite his objections to the contrary, Purdy developed a speaking voice that is unmistakable. His poetry is most recognizable in terms of its language and structure. One of its main characteristics is a peculiar mixing of chattiness and profundity, of homely observation and mythical or historical allusion. He peopled his rural Ontario with ghosts from the near and distant past, with echoes of ancient Greece and United Empire Loyalist salons; in his particular Baffin Island may be seen the shades of Diefenbaker, Odysseus, Laurence Olivier, King John, and Gary Cooper. Poetry, which he called his 'umbilical cord with the world and other people', should resemble prose but make it 'suddenly glow like coloured glass in a black and white world'.

Structurally, Purdy's verse is equally recognizable. He tended to leave his poems open-ended, his subjects deliberately unresolved. In poems of this sort there is no fixed subject outside the poem other than the perceiving consciousness of the poet; in other words, the subject of the poem is the *process itself*, the process of trying to come to terms with a feeling or experience. Philosophically, a preoccupation with process is understandable; it implies awareness that at best 'truth' is difficult to discover, at worst it is completely relative. From an aesthetic point of view, however, such indeterminacy does not always work to the poem's advantage. Carried too far it can become a structural cliché, a crutch. Fortunately, Purdy's wit, erudition, and self-mockery lifted his best work beyond such concerns, giving it qualities beloved by both academics and general readers.

His 'exact combo' is unlike anything else in Canadian poetry. He has an inexhaustible capacity to surprise and delight, to upset whatever critical expectations his own poems might encourage. His answer to his critics, and perhaps the reason for his popularity, is suggested in his comment on the nature of the poetic process:

> There ought to be a quality in a good poet beyond any analysis, the part of his mind that leaps from one point to another, sideways, backwards, ass-over-electric-kettle. This quality is not logic, and the result may not be consistent with the rest of the poem when it happens, though it may be. I believe it is said by medicos that much of the human mind has no known function. Perhaps the leap sideways and backwards comes from there. At any rate, it seems to me the demands made on it cause the mind to stretch, to do more than it is capable of under ordinary and different circumstances. And when this happens, or when you think it does, that time is joyous, and you experience something beyond experience. Like discovering you can fly, or that relative truth may blossom into an absolute. And the absolute must be attacked again and again, until you find something that will stand up, may not be denied, which becomes a compass point by which to move somewhere else. . . . And sometimes—if you're lucky—a coloured fragment may slip through into the light when you're writing a poem.

Although there is a strong comic element in Purdy's work, his best poems tend to be elegiac. Like Roberts and Carman, he is sensitive to manifestations of change, to the passing of time. He loves to reflect upon things historical. There is something about events and people out of the past that releases his imagination in new and exciting ways. Thus his identification with the decaying world of Prince Edward County in Ontario, his attraction to the outbacks of British Columbia, and his passionate response to the Inuit's encounter with the white man's technology on Baffin Island. Perhaps the values and the certainty that the shifting present never afforded him were found in abundance in the past. In poems such as 'The Runners' and 'Lament for the Dorsets' there is little uncertainty or self-consciousness, only a rare beauty and precision.

After the self-publication of his modest book, *The Enchanted Echo*, in 1944, Purdy went on to publish numerous major collections, including *Poems for All the Annettes* (1962, 1968, 1973); *The Cariboo Horses* (1965), for which he received a Governor General's Award; *North of Summer* (1967); *Wild Grape Wine* (1968); *Love in a Burning Building* (1970); *Selected Poems* (1972); *Sex and Death* (1973); *The Poems of Al Purdy* (1976); *Sundance at Dusk* (1976); *No Other Country* (1977); *Being Alive* (1978); *The Stone Bird* (1981); *Piling Blood* (1984); *The Collected Poems of Al Purdy* (1986), which earned him a second Governor General's Award; *The Woman on the Shore* (1990); *On the Bearpaw Sea* (1994); *Naked With Summer in Your Teeth* (1994); *To Paris Never Again* (1997); and *Rooms for Rent in the Outer Planets* (1996), which also contains a medley of his critical comments on poetry gathered by Sam Solecki. Purdy edited two anthologies—*Storm Warning* (1971) and *Storm Warning II* (1976)—and a collection of Canadian views of the United States, *The*

New Romans (1968). He published a novel, *A Splinter in the Heart,* in 1990; a memoir, *Reaching for the Beaufort Sea* (1993); and *Starting from Ameliasburgh: The Collected Prose* *of Al Purdy* (1995). His work has been widely discussed in journals and in a recent book by Sam Solecki: *The Last Canadian Poet: An Essay on Al Purdy* (1999).

HOME-MADE BEER

I was justly annoyed 10 years ago
in Vancouver: making beer in a crock
under the kitchen table when this
next-door youngster playing with my own
kid managed to sit down in it and
emerged with one end malted—
With excessive moderation I yodelled
at him
            "Keep your ass out of my beer!"
            and the little monster fled—
Whereupon my wife appeared from the bathroom
where she had been brooding for days
over the injustice of being a woman and
attacked me with a broom—
With commendable savoir faire I broke
the broom across my knee (it hurt too) and
then she grabbed the breadknife and made
for me with fairly obvious intentions—
I tore open my shirt and told her calmly
with bared breast and a minimum of boredom
            "Go ahead! Strike! Go ahead!"
Icicles dropped from her fiery eyes as she
snarled
            "I wouldn't want to go to jail
            for killing a thing like you!"
I could see at once that she loved me
tho it was cleverly concealed—
For the next few weeks I had to distribute
the meals she prepared among neighbouring
dogs because of the rat poison and
addressed her as Missus Borgia—
That was a long time ago and while
at the time I deplored her lack of

self-control I find myself sentimental
about it now for it can never happen again—

Sept. 22, 1964: PS, I was wrong—

THE COUNTRY NORTH OF BELLEVILLE

Bush land scrub land—
    Cashel Township and Wollaston
Elzevir McClure and Dungannon
green lands of Weslemkoon Lake
where a man might have some
      opinion of what beauty
is and none deny him
           for miles—

Yet this is the country of defeat
where Sisyphus rolls a big stone
year after year up the ancient hills
picnicking glaciers have left strewn
with centuries' rubble
            backbreaking days
             in the sun and rain
when realization seeps slow in the mind
without grandeur or self-deception in
        noble struggle
of being a fool—

A country of quiescence and still distance
a lean land
        not like the fat south
with inches of black soil on
         earth's round belly—
And where the farms are
         it's as if a man stuck
both thumbs in the stony earth and pulled
          it apart
           to make room
enough between the trees

for a wife
       and maybe some cows and
       room for some
of the more easily kept illusions—
And where the farms have gone back
to forest
       are only soft outlines
       shadowy differences—

Old fences drift vaguely among the trees
       a pile of moss-covered stones
gathered for some ghost purpose
has lost meaning under the meaningless sky
       —they are like cities under water
and the undulating green waves of time
       are laid on them—

This is the country of our defeat
       and yet
during the fall plowing a man
might stop and stand in a brown valley of the furrows
       and shade his eyes to watch for the same
       red patch mixed with gold
       that appears on the same
       spot in the hills
       year after year
       and grow old
plowing and plowing a ten-acre field until
the convolutions run parallel with his own brain—

And this is a country where the young
       leave quickly
unwilling to know what their fathers know
or think the words their mothers do not say—
Herschel Monteagle and Faraday
lakeland rockland and hill country
a little adjacent to where the world is
a little north of where the cities are and
sometime
we may go back there
       to the country of our defeat

Wollaston Elzevir and Dungannon
and Weslemkoon lake land
where the high townships of Cashel
      McClure and Marmora once were—
But it's been a long time since
and we must enquire the way
     of strangers—

THE CARIBOO HORSES

At 100 Mile House the cowboys ride in rolling
stagey cigarettes with one hand reining
half-tame bronco rebels on a morning grey as stone
—so much like riding dangerous women
    with whiskey coloured eyes—
such women as once fell dead with their lovers
with fire in their heads and slippery froth on thighs
—Beaver and Carrier women maybe or
    Blackfoot squaws far past the edge of this valley
on the other side of those two toy mountain ranges
    from the sunfierce plains beyond—

But only horses
       waiting in stables
hitched at taverns
       standing at dawn
pastured outside the town with
jeeps and fords and chevvys and
busy muttering stake trucks rushing
importantly over roads of man's devising
over the safe known roads of the ranchers
families and merchants of the town—
       On the high prairie
are only horse and rider
       wind in dry grass
clopping in silence under the toy mountains
dropping sometimes and
       lost in the dry grass
       golden oranges of dung—

Only horses
            no stopwatch memories or palace ancestors
not Kiangs hauling undressed stone in the Nile Valley
and having stubborn Egyptian tantrums or
Onagers racing thru Hither Asia and
the last Quagga screaming in African highlands
            lost relatives of these
            whose hooves were thunder
the ghosts of horses battering thru the wind
whose names were the wind's common usage
whose life was the sun's
            arriving here at chilly noon
            in the gasoline smell of the
            dust and waiting 15 minutes
            at the grocer's—

Wilderness Gothic

Across Roblin Lake, two shores away,
they are sheathing the church spire
with new metal. Someone hangs in the sky
over there from a piece of rope,
hammering and fitting God's belly-scratcher,
working his way up along the spire
until there's nothing left to nail on—

Perhaps the workman's faith reaches beyond:
touches intangibles, wrestles with Jacob,
replacing rotten timber with pine thews,
pounds hard in the blue cave of the sky,
contends heroically with difficult problems of
gravity, sky navigation and mythopoeia,
his volunteer time and labour donated to God,
minus sick benefits of course on a non-union job—

Fields around are yellowing into harvest,
nestling and fingerling are sky and water borne,
death is yodelling quiet in green woodlots,
and bodies of three young birds have disappeared
in the sub-surface of the new county highway—

That picture is incomplete, part left out
that might alter the whole Dürer landscape:
gothic ancestors peer from medieval sky,
dour faces trapped in photograph albums escaping
to clop down iron roads with matched greys:
work-sodden wives groping inside their flesh
for what keeps moving and changing and flashing
beyond and past the long frozen Victorian day.
A sign of fire and brimstone? A two-headed calf
born in the barn last night? A sharp female agony?
An age and a faith moving into transition,
the dinner cold and new-baked bread a failure,
deep woods shiver and water drops hang pendant,
double-yolked eggs and the house creaks a little—
Something is about to happen. Leaves are still.
Two shores away, a man hammering in the sky.
Perhaps he will fall.

ARCTIC RHODODENDRONS

They are small purple surprises
in the river's white racket
and after you've seen them
a number of times
in water-places
where their silence seems
related to river-thunder
you think of them as 'noisy flowers'
Years ago
it may have been
that lovers came this way
stopped in the outdoor hotel
to watch the water floorshow
and lying prone together
where the purged green
boils to a white heart
and the shore trembles
like a stone song
with bodies touching
flowers were their conversation

and love the sound of a colour
that lasts two weeks in August
and then dies
except for the three or four
I pressed in a letter
and sent whispering to you

LAMENT FOR THE DORSETS
(Eskimos extinct in the 14th century A.D.)

Animal bones and some mossy tent rings
scrapers and spearheads carved ivory swans
all that remains of the Dorset giants
who drove the Vikings back to their long ships
talked to spirits of earth and water
—a picture of terrifying old men
so large they broke the backs of bears
so small they lurk behind bone rafters
in the brain of modern hunters
among good thoughts and warm things
and come out at night
to spit on the stars

The big men with clever fingers
who had no dogs and hauled their sleds
over the frozen northern oceans
awkward giants
                    killers of seal
they couldn't compete with little men
who came from the west with dogs
Or else in a warm climatic cycle
the seals went back to cold waters
and the puzzled Dorsets scratched their heads
with hairy thumbs around 1350 A.D.
—couldn't figure it out
went around saying to each other
plaintively
            'What's wrong? What happened?
            Where are the seals gone?'
And died

Twentieth century people
apartment dwellers
executives of neon death
warmakers with things that explode
—they have never imagined us in their future
how could we imagine them in the past
squatting among the moving glaciers
six hundred years ago
with glowing lamps?
As remote or nearly
as the trilobites and swamps
when coal became
or the last great reptile hissed
at a mammal the size of a mouse
that squeaked and fled

Did they ever realize at all
what was happening to them?
Some old hunter with one lame leg
a bear had chewed
sitting in a caribou skin tent
—the last Dorset?
Let's say his name was Kudluk
carving 2-inch ivory swans
for a dead grand-daughter
taking them out of his mind
the places in his mind
where pictures are
He selects a sharp stone tool
to gouge a parallel pattern of lines
on both sides of the swan
holding it with his left hand
bearing down and transmitting
his body's weight
from brain to arm and right hand
and one of his thoughts
turns to ivory
The carving is laid aside
in beginning darkness
at the end of hunger
after a while wind

blows down the tent and snow
begins to cover him
After 600 years
the ivory thought
is still warm

THE RUNNERS

'It was when Leif was with King Olaf Tryggvason, and he bade him proclaim Christianity to Greenland, that the king gave him two Gaels; the man's name was Haki, and the woman's Haekia. The king advised Leif to have recourse to these people, if he should stand in need of fleetness, for they were swifter than deer. Erick and Leif had tendered Karlsefni the services of this couple. Now when they had sailed past Marvel-Strands (to the New World) they put the Gaels ashore, and directed them to run to the southward, and investigate the nature of the country, and return again before the end of the third half-day.'

—*From* ERICK THE RED'S SAGA

Brother, the wind of this place is cold,
and hills under our feet tremble,
the forests are making magic against us—
I think the land knows we are here,
I think the land knows we are strangers.
Let us stay close to our friend the sea,
or cunning dwarves at the roots of darkness
shall seize and drag us down—

Sister, we must share our strength between us,
until the heat of our bodies makes a single flame,
and one that we are is more than two that we were:
while the moon sees only one shadow,
and the sun knows only our double heartbeat,
and the rain does not come between—

Brother, I am afraid of this dark place,
I am hungry for the home islands,
and wind blowing the waves to coloured spray,
I am sick for the sun—
Sister, we must not think those thoughts again,
for three half-days have gone by,

and we must return to the ship.
If we are away longer,
the Northmen will beat us with thongs,
until we cry for death—
Why do you stare at nothing?

Brother, a cold wind touched me,
tho I stand in your arms' circle:
perhaps the Northmen's runes have found us,
the runes they carve on wood and stone.
I am afraid of this dark land,
ground mist that makes us half ghosts,
and another silence inside silence . . .
But there are berries and fish here,
and small animals by the sea's edge
that crouch and tremble and listen . . .
If we join our words to the silence,
if our trails cross the trails we made,
and the sun remembers what the moon forgets . . .
Brother, it comes to me now,
the long ship must sail without us,
we stay here—

Sister, we should die slowly,
the beasts would gnaw at our bodies,
the rains whiten our bones.
The Northmen's runes are strong magic,
the runes would track us down,
tho we keep on running
past the Land of Flat Stones
over the Marvel-Strands
beyond the land of great trees . . .
Tho we ran to the edge of the world,
our masters would track us down—

Brother, take my hand in your hand,
this part of ourselves between us
while we run together,
over the stones of the sea-coast,
this much of ourselves is our own:

while rain cries out against us,
and darkness swallows the evening,
and morning moves into stillness,
and mist climbs to our throats,
while we are running,
while we are running—

Sister—

A HANDFUL OF EARTH
to René Lévesque

Proposal:
let us join Quebec
if Quebec won't join us
I don't mind in the least
being governed from Quebec City
by Canadiens instead of Canadians
in fact the fleur-de-lis
              and maple leaf
are only symbols
and our true language
speaks from inside
the land itself

Listen:
you can hear soft wind blowing
among tall fir trees on Vancouver Island
it is the same wind we knew
whispering along Côte des Neiges
on the island of Montreal
when we were lovers and had no money
Once flying in a little Cessna 180
above that great spine of mountains
where a continent attempts the sky
I wondered who owns this land
and knew that no one does
for we are tenants only

Go back a little:
to hip-roofed houses on the Isle d'Orléans
and scattered along the road to Chicoutimi
the remaining few log houses in Ontario
sod huts of sunlit prairie places
dissolved in rain long since
the stones we laid atop one another
a few of which still stand
those origins
in which children were born
in which we loved and hated
in which we built a place to stand on
and now must tear it down?
—and here I ask all the oldest questions
of myself
the reasons for being alive
the way to spend this gift and thank the giver
but there is no way

I think of the small dapper man
chain-smoking at PQ headquarters
Lévesque
on Avenue Christophe Colomb in Montreal
where we drank coffee together six years past
I say to him now: my place is here
whether Côte des Neiges Avenue Christophe Colomb
Yonge Street Toronto Halifax or Vancouver
this place is where I stand
where all my mistakes were made
when I grew awkwardly and knew what I was
and that is Canadian or Canadien
it doesn't matter which to me

Sod huts break the prairie skyline
then melt in rain
the hip-roofed houses of New France as well
but French no longer
nor are we any longer English
—limestone houses
lean-tos and sheds our fathers built

in which our mothers died
before the forests tumbled down
ghost habitations
only this handful of earth
for a time at least
I have no other place to go

MOONSPELL

I have forgotten English
in order to talk to pelicans
plunging into tomorrow
disturb the deep reverie
of herons standing
on yesterday's shoreline
find the iguana's secret
name embroidered
on his ruby brain
it is milk
it is moonlight
milk pouring
over the islands
stand in a doorway
listen
I am drowning
in sky milk
and those soft murmurings
of moonlit vertebrae
these deciphered codewords
are spoken names
of island dwellers
they will not be repeated
pour on my bare shoulders
are small extensions
of themselves
as the manta ray bubbles
rising in water
gleams in moonlight
small fish tremble

I know I know
my speech is grunts
squeaks clicks stammers
let go let go
follow the sunken ships
and deep sea creatures
follow the protozoa
into that far darkness
another kind of light
leave off this flesh
this voice
these bones
sink down

Galapagos Islands

MIRIAM WADDINGTON

(b. 1917)

Miriam Waddington (née Dworkin) was born to Russian-Jewish parents in Winnipeg, though she spent her adolescent years in Ottawa. She completed a BA in English at the University of Toronto in 1939 and married Patrick Waddington, a journalist, the same year. After writing briefly for newspapers and magazines, she studied social work, receiving her MA from the University of Pennsylvania. Until her divorce in 1960, Waddington lived in Montreal, raising a family, doing social work, and writing poems that would appear in *First Statement, Preview*, and her first three books: *Green World* (1945), *The Second Silence* (1955), and *The Season's Lovers* (1958). She returned to Toronto to work for the North York Family Services and to teach English at York University from 1964 until her retirement in 1983. She was the recipient of the J.J. Segal Award in 1972 and an honorary D.Litt. From Lakehead University in 1975. Her other collections of poetry are *The Glass Trumpet* (1966), *Call Them Canadians* (1968), *Say Yes* (1969), *Driving Home* (1972), *The Price of Gold* (1976), *Mr. Never* (1978), *The Visitants* (1981), *Collected Poems* (1986), and *The Last Landscape* (1992). She is also the author of *Summer at Lonely Beach and Other Stories* (1982) and a critical study, *A.M. Klein* (1970), and is the editor of *The Collected Poems of A.M. Klein* (1974). *Apartment Seven: Essays New and Selected* appeared in 1989.

Waddington's career as a social worker has played an important role in her poetry, shaping both the content and the form of her work. Much of the early work examines the world of poverty, unemployment, deviance, and crime; these poems, for the most part, make use of traditional poetic devices such as rhyme, metre, and stanzaic form: the chaos of the material itself seemed to demand a rigorously ordered poetic form. Alongside these documentary pieces are tender poems about nature, love, and the loss of innocence, in which Waddington presents herself as poet-healer, 'a splint against your sorrows'. Gradually her poetic interests shifted from public to private concerns, with a corresponding loosening of form, particularly the use of the short line. Of this shift, she writes: 'This change was unconscious and had something to do with *zeitgeist*. New hope, new ways of understanding the world, and—along with the atom bomb—new anxieties were everything. There no longer seemed to be time for the spinning out of long literary lines. The tempo of short lines suited the times and suited me.'

The short line serves Waddington's purposes well in the personal poems, as well as in the Jewish and folkloric pieces, where there is a Chagall-like playfulness and where the momentum allows her to assume the role of ecstatic celebrant, 'the tender and brooding outsider' concerned with 'subtle melodies' and 'obscure lives', listening for the 'old lost songs'. In *Call Them Canadians* Waddington was invited to write poems to accompany a stunning collection of photographs of Canadians at work and at play, in love and in mourning. This commission produced some of her finest work and rescued Waddington from the solipsism and lack of density that are a possible legacy of the short line. The visual images lift the poet beyond the interfering ego, providing the sensory detail to charge her imagination; and the public function of the volume encourages her in the direction of greater substance and universality, resulting in poems that are lively, textured, and fully accessible.

Waddington's essays and reminiscences in *Apartment Seven* are well worth exploring. In 'Poetry As Communication', while making a strong case for rhythm, form, and metaphor, she insists that 'language should seem to be simple, but of the kind of simplicity that contains complexities; and also that the poem should tell us something we didn't know before we read it. The something that it tells us should have a source in the poet, and a threefold impact on the reader; physical, emotional, and intellectual. This, in one sentence, is the sum of all my wisdom, such as it is.' In 'Form and Ideology in Poetry', she insists that 'form in poetry is the momentary verbal limit imposed by the artist on the infinite number of possibilities that are contained in the chaos of his psyche. . . . Another way of understanding form is to see each formulation, that is, each new poem or group of poems, as the completion of an equivalent new formulation in the artist's personality. The art work transforms the artist and creates him at the same time as he transforms the world by his recreation of it through his work. Thus there is a continuous interchange between inner and outer, and a continuous relation between self and world.' As the essay suggests—and her practice confirms—a certain raggedness, a fraying at the edges, is inevitable as inner and outer forces serve as an abrasive against inherited formal conventions.

GIRLS

In summer the light flushed faces of my girls
Rush to me with hullos along the green street of their growing,
And from their freckled smiles all their hopes bloom out
And in their curving laughter all their past is carolled
While the strands of hair damp against their foreheads
Are tendrils reaching from the roots of their joy.

Oh my girls, as you rush to me with your swift hullos
I see over your shoulders the years like a fascist army
Advancing against your love, burning your maiden villages,
I see your still minorities destroyed in lethal chambers
Your defenceless dreams shot backward into the pit,
And I see
The levelling down of all your innocent worlds.

I offer myself a splint against your sorrows
And I kiss the broken wings of your future.

AT MIDNIGHT

Wife goes to husband now
And husband to his wife
The bells ring midnight on the winter street.

Outside the wandering cats
Are still and the rooster
In his silky wing is soft asleep.

Inside the dark now
Husband turns to wife,
Precious and single as the guarded seal

Of ancient kings
Merge they and mingle,
Folded limbs and lips.

Softly now falls the rhythm
Of their breathing through the house,
And the frost against the window flickers low.

MY LESSONS IN THE JAIL

Walk into the prison, that domed citadel,
That yellow skull of stone and sutured steel,
Walk under their mottoes, show your pass,
Salute their Christ to whom you cannot kneel.

In the white-tiled room arrange the interview
With the man who took his daughter, and learn
That every man is usual but none are equal
In the dark rivers that in them burn.

And take this man's longest, bleakest year,
Between done act and again-done act, and take
His misery and need, stand against his tears
And transform them to such a truth as slakes

The very core of thirst, and be you sure
The thirst is his and not your own deep need
To spurt fine fountains; accept, accept
His halting words—since you must learn to read

Between the lines his suffering and doubt.
Be faithful to your pity, be careworn,
Though all this buffet you, and beat, and cruelly
Test you—you chose this crown of thorns.

Wear it with grace and when you rise to go
Thank him, and don't let yourself forget
How hard it is to thank, and to beholden be
One to another, and spin your role out yet

For moments in the hallway, compose your face
To false good humor, conceal your sex:
Smile at the brute who runs the place
And memorize the banner, *Christus Rex*.

ON MY BIRTHDAY

There was nothing   not a white bone
or the hard dry skeleton of half a leaf,
only the wind in the transmitter singing
when I fronted the winter so sick and halfhearted,
denying my body's wholeness from my head to my feet
as I turned with the world to the high wind's song.

There was nothing   and turning I cried
for a white bone found or the half-moon's token,
there was only the heel of the beer bottle lying
on the humped-up earth in the net of snow,
and the wild parsley like a green wound showing
as the world turned and the high wind lay low.

And I guessed at the beggar's steep celebration
and the pitch of his wailing in four-legged joy
at his being a man inside of a woman
at her being a woman with a man inside,

both tossed on the bed of the mounting darkness
when the world turned to the high wind's song.

And I turned blind to the dead mating season
with my nerve-ends crying at lovers broken.
I heard the rain on the vowelled whisper
of the man and the woman in leafy autumn;
their bodies sank in their love's last labour
as he lay a Hans Andersen prince in her arms,
and she, muted mermaid that he wished her.

And I listened to my own my blind bone groaning
and to all the children that lay in my womb,
to the landlocked sailors and men in prison
and the pimply youths in the pin-ball cafes
as I choked on the cry of my white bone wailing
the wilding boy   the self I never was.

In my darkest year at the deadness of mating,
in my dismalest year and the years still passing,
how could I guess that all waters flow downward,
that the womb-held child must swim out downward
and the man through the woman moves deep downward,
but the woman from downward is never retrieved?

And I listened to the world loud with my wailing
for the selves not dead who were never born,
and all the tongue-tied rage of my losing
shook me and roared through my solemn aging,
and I was a child in the wind's high singing
turning the world to be born again.

For how could I guess and to whom confide
my dreadness of losing and the gone bone wailing
the man's hard absence from winter's white side?
With my blind rooted body defenceless and falling
I guessed at the cry of my birth that first morning
when the world turned to the high wind's song.

THE MILE RUNNER

You are my buzz my hive   you are my honey steeple,
you are my me my how my pray and also prithee,
my mile runner and spinning helicopter,
my rescue from the wilderness of river.

And are you not my this my that of prairie,
my weathered granary   my nuisance crow?
My miles of sameness and my endless railway,
my gone-astray   my slow unlabelled freight?

So add the fishes' double-quick of colour,
the while-away of summer's brazen boys,
the golden eye of lakes   the fresh of beaches,
and I'm the eyelid and the tongue   and I'm the ear.

UKRAINIAN CHURCH

Little father your
rhythmic black robe
against white snow
improvises you
a black note
on a white keyboard;

let me follow
into your churchbarn
through the gate
to the onion domes
where your carrot
harvest burns
a fire of candles,

let me follow
in the cool light
as you move through
God's storehouse
as you put the bins
in order as you set
each grain in place;

let me follow
as your voice
moves in the
familiar liturgy
through the low caves
of Gregorian chant
and let me hear
little father

how you pray
for all your geese
for the cow fertile
at Easter and the
foundations of new
houses to be strong
and firmly set;

let me hear
how you beseech
for all your people
a clear road, an
open gate and
a new snowfall
fresh, dazzling,
white as birchbark.

GOSSIP

Professor Waddington will not be
joining the academic procession
she wrote a note to the Dean she
said that her gown was moth-eaten
and she had to stay home to tie up
the chrysanthemums or else they
would flop all over and kill the grass
and she would have to resod around
the flowerbeds a nuisance so she regrets
she will not be able to join the academic
procession if you ask me that woman has
a nerve she's not friendly and further-

more I hear that she keeps late hours
looks at men what kind of example is that
for young girls all I can say is some
people are never satisfied

THE SURVIVORS

In your quiet hand I touch
the touch of your gentle mother's hand
and hold her death in mine;

and in your opened eyes I see
the bareness of your younger brother's eyes
and miss your missed farewell.

The troubled journeys that you since have made
from war to war, record the faulty pulse
of time so timeless lost between the wars,

and wake the terrible child in us all
to rage against fixed bedtime and to cry
himself to lonesome sleep inside a world

of you-can't-go-home-again or painted cities
flat as lakes and bland as German summers:
the innocent seasons of the never never

are unmarked graveyards of the spoiled time
where even your hand must mourn against mine
to mark the graveyard of that other time

with angers that your Jewish father's face
buried against your will in every act
to make your hearing deaf   your speaking dumb;

and what I touch with my uninjured hand
is your survival: immune to love we move
to ancient Jewish law   and strict command.

HOW I SPENT THE YEAR LISTENING TO THE TEN O'CLOCK NEWS

Last year
there were executions
in Chile
bribes in
America no
transit for Jews
in Austria
and lies
lies everywhere.

The children
of Ireland are
also in the news,
they have become
hardened street
fighters some of
them murderers,
I ask myself
where will it
all end?

Of course
the interests of
Canadian citizens
(read corporations)
must be protected
at any cost no
matter how many
good men are
shot like dogs
in the streets
of Chile or
how many poets
die of a broken
heart.

They claim
the world is
changing getting
better they have
the moon walk
and moon walkers
to prove it,
but my brain
is bursting my
guts are twisted
I have too much
to say thank
God I am too old
to bear children.

TEN YEARS AND MORE

When my husband
lay dying a mountain
a lake three
cities ten years
and more
lay between us:

There were our
sons my wounds
and theirs,
despair loneliness,
handfuls of un–
hammered nails
pictures never
hung all

The uneaten
meals and unslept
sleep; there was
retirement, and
worst of all
a green umbrella
he can never
take back.

I wrote him a
letter but all
I could think of
to say was: do you
remember Severn
River, the red canoe
with the sail
and lee-boards?

I was really saying
for the sake of our
youth and our love
I forgave him for
everything
and I was asking him
to forgive me too.

LATELY I'VE BEEN FEELING VERY JEWISH

Jews are soft
touches: I'm a soft
touch too I
melt like snow
in February I
step down disappear
leave patches of
bare earth in
the backyard for
other soft touches
and touchers; it
makes the world
less lonesome when
you can feel/see
the soft/yellow not-
especially-Jewish-touch
of a daffodil.

F.R. SCOTT

(1899–1985)

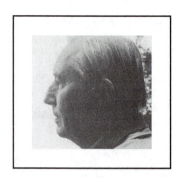

Frank Scott was born and raised in Quebec City, where his father was an Anglican minister and a poet. He graduated from Bishop's College in Lennoxville, was a Rhodes scholar at Oxford, and then studied Law at McGill University, where he graduated and joined the Faculty in 1928. He was Dean of Law from 1961 to 1964 and retired from McGill in 1968. Scott found no difficulty reconciling his artistic and political impulses. He was active in founding the League for Social Reconstruction in 1932 and the Co-operative Commonwealth Federation (the CCF, which eventually became the NDP), drafting its Regina Manifesto and acting as the CCF's National Chairman from 1942 to 1950. He contributed to *Social Planning for Canada* (1935), wrote *Canada and the United States* (1941), edited *Canada Today: A Study of Her National Interests and National Policy* (1943), and co-edited with Michael Oliver *Quebec States Her Case* (1964). Scott not only became an expert on international law and constitutional affairs, but also defended D.H. Lawrence's *Lady Chatterley's Lover* in the courts and won a case against the notorious Padlock Law of the Duplessis government. *Essays on the Constitution: Aspects of Canadian Law and Politics*, which won the Governor General's Award, appeared in 1977; *A New Endeavour: Selected Political Essays, Letters*, in 1986. Scott also published numerous translations, including the volume *St. Denys Garneau and Anne Hébert* (1978).

'What is my personal conception of poetry?' Scott wrote. 'If I could define it, it would not be too different from my conception of life itself. The making of something new and true. An exploring of the frontiers of the world inside and the world outside man. And a kind of umbilical contemplation from within the poem itself of its own dynamic and central structure.' His examination of the world outside man began with a number of imagistic poems about nature, particularly related to the northness of Canada, its remote lakes and vast rock formations such as the Canadian Shield; this early work, in terms of its subject matter and visual intensity, has much in common with the work of the Group of Seven. Against the serene and austere aspects of nature in Canada, Scott pits the human work of building and 'civilizing', though he does this in terms that are not entirely romantic; he admires the work of human hands where it constructs, by way of its 'cabin syllables', art and language, and such humanizing enterprises as education, medicine, and government. However, his keen intellect and training in law gave him sufficient insight to identify and the wit to parody all that is bogus and destructive in human affairs, so that even a largely affirmative poem such as 'Laurentian Shield' ends with the ambivalent phrase, 'the long sentence of their exploitation'.

Scott's lively satires and diatribes against hypocrisy and waste in government, or prudery and racism in society, are seldom without redeemingly infectious humour and word-play, making generous use of puns and *double entendre*. In 'Lakeshore', for example, man's primitive ancestors emerging from sea-slime are described as 'landed gentry'. Scott employed the minimalist techniques of the Imagists in composing his pithy epigrams; he adopted the argumentative modes of eighteenth-century poetry to construct his essays in verse; and he used ballad measures, in the manner of Robert Service, to evoke the full comedy of Canadian attitudes towards sex. Perhaps his most characteristic and successful mode is the extended metaphor, which he employs in 'Lakeshore', 'Laurentian Shield', and 'For Bryan Priestman' where, in a poem that recalls the tone and measure of Auden's 'Musée des Beaux Arts', Scott uses the language of the laboratory to evoke the death by drowning of a professor of chemistry.

In an essay entitled 'The Poet in Quebec Today' (*English Poetry in Quebec*, edited by John Glassco, 1965), Scott describes the process of his own poetic development.

My early poetry was influenced by the geography in Quebec. Coming back from Oxford, where for the first time in my life I was brought into direct contact with the European tradition, in which one soaked up the human achievements of great individuals and great nations past and present, and where always one was drawn back toward antiquity, I found Quebec presented a totally different kind of challenge. Here nothing great seemed to have been achieved in human terms. I was shocked by the ugliness of the cities and buildings by comparison with those that I had recently lived in, and there seemed so little that one wished to praise or draw inspiration from in our social environment or past history. But the Laurentian country was wonderful, open, empty, vast, and speaking a kind of eternal language in its mountains, rivers, and lakes. I knew that these were the oldest mountains in the world, and that their rounded valleys and peaks were the result of long submersion under continents of ice. Geologic time made ancient civilizations seem but yesterday's picnic. This caught my imagination and I tried to express some of this feeling in what I call my Laurentian poems. It was a form of 'internalization', and it sufficed me at first for poetic inspiration.

As I became more involved in the human society about me, particularly after the great financial crash of 1929, the ensuing depression, and the emergence of revolutionary and reform political movements in which I participated, I found that I reacted negatively in my writing and turned easily to satire. The satire was the holding up of the existing society against standards one was formulating in one's mind for a more perfect society. It was not revolutionary poetry; it was satiric poetry, which is quite a different thing, though somewhat allied.

Scott's poems appeared in the *McGill Fortnightly Review*, of which he was an editor in 1925, but his writing was not widely noticed until it appeared in *New Provinces: Poems of Several Authors* (1936), which he co-edited with his friend and fellow-poet A.J.M. Smith. Scott was co-founder of *Preview* in 1942, which merged three years later with *First Statement*; 1945 also saw the publication of *Events & Signals*. Then came Scott's *Overture* (1954), *The Eye of the Needle* (1957), *The Blasted Pine: An Anthology of Satire, Invective, and Disrespectful Verse, Chiefly by Canadian Writers*, co-edited with A.J.M. Smith (1957), *Signature* (1964), Selected Poems (1966), and *The Collected Poems of F.R. Scott* (1981), for which he received a Governor General's Award.

LAKESHORE

The lake is sharp along the shore
Trimming the bevelled edge of land
To level curves; the fretted sands
Go slanting down through liquid air
Till stones below shift here and there
Floating upon their broken sky
All netted by the prism wave
And rippled where the currents are.

I stare through windows at this cave
Where fish, like planes, slow-motioned, fly.
Poised in a still of gravity
The narrow minnow, flicking fin,
Hangs in a paler, ochre sun,
His doorways open everywhere.

And I am a tall frond that waves
Its head below its rooted feet
Seeking the light that draws it down
To forest floors beyond its reach
Vivid with gloom and eerie dreams.

The water's deepest colonnades
Contract the blood, and to this home
That stirs the dark amphibian
With me the naked swimmers come
Drawn to their prehistoric womb.

They too are liquid as they fall
Like tumbled water loosed above
Until they lie, diagonal,
Within the cool and sheltered grove
Stroked by the fingertips of love.

Silent, our sport is drowned in fact
Too virginal for speech or sound
And each is personal and laned
Along his private aqueduct.

Too soon the tether of the lungs
Is taut and straining, and we rise
Upon our undeveloped wings
Toward the prison of our ground
A secret anguish in our thighs
And mermaids in our memories.

This is our talent, to have grown
Upright in posture, false-erect,
A landed gentry, circumspect,
Tied to a horizontal soil
The floor and ceiling of the soul;
Striving, with cold and fishy care
To make an ocean of the air.

Sometimes, upon a crowded street,
I feel the sudden rain come down
And in the old, magnetic sound
I hear the opening of a gate
That loosens all the seven seas.
Watching the whole creation drown
I muse, alone, on Ararat.

OLD SONG

far voices
and fretting leaves
this music the
hillside gives

but in the deep
Laurentian river
an elemental song
for ever

a quiet calling
of no mind
out of long aeons
when dust was blind
and ice hid sound

only a moving
with no note
granite lips
a stone throat

LAURENTIAN SHIELD

Hidden in wonder and snow, or sudden with summer,
This land stares at the sun in a huge silence
Endlessly repeating something we cannot hear.
Inarticulate, arctic,
Not written on by history, empty as paper,
It leans away from the world with songs in its lakes
Older than love, and lost in the miles.

This waiting is wanting.
It will choose its language
When it has chosen its technic,
A tongue to shape the vowels of its productivity.

A language of flesh and roses.

Now there are pre-words,
Cabin syllables,
Nouns of settlement
Slowly forming, with steel syntax,
The long sentence of its exploitation.

The first cry was the hunter, hungry for fur,
And the digger for gold, nomad, no-man, a particle;
Then the bold commands of monopoly, big with machines,
Carving its kingdoms out of the public wealth;
And now the drone of the plane, scouting the ice,
Fills all the emptiness with neighbourhood
And links our future over the vanished pole.

But a deeper note is sounding, heard in the mines,
The scattered camps and the mills, a language of life,
And what will be written in the full culture of occupation
Will come, presently, tomorrow,
From millions whose hands can turn this rock into children.

OVERTURE

In the dark room, under a cone of light,
You precisely play the Mozart sonata. The bright
Clear notes fly like sparks through the air
And trace a flickering pattern of music there.

Your hands dart in the light, your fingers flow.
They are ten careful operatives in a row
That pick their packets of sound from steel bars
Constructing harmonies as sharp as stars.

But how shall I hear old music? This is an hour
Of new beginnings, concepts warring for power,
Decay of systems—the tissue of art is torn
With overtures of an era being born.

And this perfection which is less yourself
Than Mozart, seems a trinket on a shelf,
A pretty octave played before a window
Beyond whose curtain grows a world crescendo.

CHARITY

A code of laws
Lies written
On this beggar's hand.

My small coin
Lengthens
The harsh sentence.

W.L.M.K.

How shall we speak of Canada,
Mackenzie King dead?
The Mother's boy in the lonely room
With his dog, his medium and his ruins?

He blunted us.

We had no shape
Because he never took sides,
And no sides
Because he never allowed them to take shape.

He skilfully avoided what was wrong
Without saying what was right,
And never let his on the one hand
Know what his on the other hand was doing.

The height of his ambition
Was to pile a Parliamentary Committee on a Royal Commission,
To have 'conscription if necessary
But not necessarily conscription',
To let Parliament decide—
Later.

Postpone, postpone, abstain.

Only one thread was certain:
After World War I
Business as usual,
After World War II
Orderly decontrol.
Always he led us back to where we were before.

He seemed to be in the centre
Because we had no centre,
No vision
To pierce the smoke-screen of his politics.

Truly he will be remembered
Wherever men honour ingenuity,
Ambiguity, inactivity, and political longevity.

Let us raise up a temple
To the cult of mediocrity,
Do nothing by halves
Which can be done by quarters.

THE CANADIAN AUTHORS MEET

Expansive puppets percolate self-unction
Beneath a portrait of the Prince of Wales.
Miss Crotchet's muse has somehow failed to function,
Yet she's a poetess. Beaming, she sails
From group to chattering group, with such a dear
Victorian saintliness, as is her fashion,
Greeting the other unknowns with a cheer—
Virgins of sixty who still write of passion.

The air is heavy with Canadian topics,
And Carman, Lampman, Roberts, Campbell, Scott,
Are measured for their faith and philanthropics,
Their zeal for God and King, their earnest thought.

The cakes are sweet, but sweeter is the feeling
That one is mixing with the literati;
It warms the old, and melts the most congealing.
Really, it is a most delightful party.

Shall we go round the mulberry bush, or shall
We gather at the river, or shall we
Appoint a Poet Laureate this fall,
Or shall we have another cup of tea?

O Canada, O Canada, Oh can
A day go by without new authors springing
To paint the native maple, and to plan
More ways to set the selfsame welkin ringing?

SATURDAY SUNDAE

The triple-decker and the double-cone
I side-swipe swiftly, suck the coke-straws dry.
Ride toadstool seat beside the slab of morgue—
Sweet corner drug-store, sweet pie in the sky.

Him of the front-flap apron, him I sing,
The counter-clockwise clerk in underalls.
Swing low, sweet chocolate, Oh swing, swing,
While cheek by juke the jitter chatter falls.

I swivel on my axle and survey
The latex tintex kotex cutex land.
Soft kingdoms sell for dimes, Life Pic Look Click
Inflate the male with conquest girly grand.

My brothers and my sisters, two by two,
Sit sipping succulence and sighing sex.
Each tiny adolescent universe
A world the vested interests annex.

Such bread and circuses these times allow,
Opium most popular, life so small and slick,
Perhaps with candy is the new world born
And cellophane shall wrap the heretic.

MARTINIGRAM

The key person in the whole business
I said raising my Martini damn that woman
she didn't look where she was going sorry
it won't stain the key person what? oh it's
you Georgina no I won't be there tomorrow
see you some day the key person in the whole
business is not the one oh hello James yes
we're having a wonderful time not the one you
love but it's no thank you no more just now
not the one you love but it's the one who
does the hell's bells there's a stone in my olive

A LASS IN WONDERLAND

I went to bat for the Lady Chatte
    Dressed in my bib and gown.
The judges three glared down at me
    The priests patrolled the town.

My right hand shook as I reached for the book
    And rose to play my part,
For out on the street were the marching feet
    Of the League of the Sacred Heart.

The word 'obscene' was supposed to mean
    'Undue exploitation of sex'.
This wording's fine for your needs and mine
    But it's far too free for Quebec's.

I tried my best, with unusual zest,
    To drive my argument through,
But I soon got stuck on what rhymes with 'muck'
    And that dubious word 'undue'.

So I raised their sights to the Bill of Rights
    And cried: 'Let freedom ring!',
Showed straight from the text that freedom of sex
    Was as clear as anything.

Then I plunged into love, the spell that it wove,
    And its attributes big and bold
Till the legal elect all stood erect
    As my rapturous tale was told.

The judges' sighs and rolling of eyes
    Gave hope that my case was won,
Yet Mellors and Connie still looked pretty funny
    Dancing about in the sun.

What hurt me was not that they did it a lot
    And even ran out in the rain,
'Twas those curious poses with harebells and roses
    And that dangling daisy-chain.

Then too the sales made in the paper-back trade
    Served to aggravate judicial spleen,
For it seems a high price will make any book nice
    While its mass distribution's obscene.

Oh Letters and Law are found in the raw
    And found on the heights sublime,
But D.H. Lawrence would view with abhorrence
    This Jansenist pantomine.

BONNE ENTENTE

The advantages of living with two cultures
Strike one at every turn,
Especially when one finds a notice in an office building:
'This elevator will not run on Ascension Day';
Or reads in the Montreal Star:
'Tomorrow being the Feast of the Immaculate Conception,
There will be no collection of garbage in the city';
Or sees on the restaurant menu the bilingual dish:

DEEP APPLE PIE
TARTE AUX POMMES PROFONDES

FOR BRYAN PRIESTMAN
(Drowned while attempting to save a child.)

The child fell, turning slowly with arms outstretched like a doll,
One shrill cry dying under the arches,
And floated away, her time briefer than foam.

Nothing was changed on the summer's day. The birds sang,
The busy insects followed their fixed affairs.
Only a Professor of Chemistry, alone on the bridge,
Suddenly awoke from his reverie, into the intense moment,
Saw all the elements of his life compounded for testing,
And plunged with searching hands into his last experiment.

This was a formula he had carried from childhood,
That can work but once in the life of a man.
His were the labels of an old laboratory,
And the long glass tubes of the river.

IRVING LAYTON

(b. 1912)

Because he is so outspoken and graphic in his denunciations, Layton was for many years the best-known and most controversial figure in Canadian poetry. Like Auden, he believes that the writing of poetry is a political act; as he explains in the Preface to *The Laughing Rooster:*

> In this country the poet has always had to fight for his survival. He lives in a middle-class milieu whose values of money-getting, respectability, and success are hostile to the kind of integrity and authenticity that is at the core of his endeavour. His need to probe himself makes him an easy victim for those who have more practical things to do—to hold down a job, amass a fortune, or to get married and raise children. His concern is to change the world; at any rate, to bear witness that another besides the heartless, stupid, and soul destroying one men have created is possible.

Layton's barbs are not limited to the middle class. He is equally critical of educational institutions. He rejects Culture as 'that underarm perspiration odour of impotent old men'; and he describes good taste as 'something to wipe our unstodgy behinds with'.

Layton is a man of contradictions. He would have us believe that he is a brawling, irreverent, wild-eyed poet with no use for conservative values. Despite his swagger and cultivated disdain, however, Layton is neither a primitive nor a sensualist. His satire, bombast, and erotica are the masks for his fine, beleaguered sensibility. His need to project an image of controversy has often made him espouse issues and causes that seem inconsistent with his expressed poetic vision, with the vision of poetry as freedom. Perhaps it is a comment on our country, rather than on Layton, that his second-rate poems of social gesture should attract more attention than his most delicate, refined verse.

If Layton himself remains an enigma, his literary significance is more certain. Like Whitman in the United States, he has done much to stimulate interest in poetry and to loosen its choking collar. He has reminded us that there are no inherently unpoetic subjects—there are only unpoetic minds. Poetry, he says, is 'a self authenticated speaking, a reaching down into the roots of one's being'. The poet is someone who knows 'the terror and ecstasy of living daily beyond one's psychic means'. Layton is a conscious craftsman, but he insists that 'without the material given the poet when his Unconscious (soul) is stirred into activity by a powerful emotion, his intelligence and craftsmanship are of no use to him whatever.' His own best poems are a perfect blend of passion and restraint, of a conscious and an unconscious ordering of materials.

Layton's poetry is concerned with three main subjects: sexual love, power, and imagination. Like most men he is attracted to the subject of large-scale expenditures of energy, especially violence. He believes that men are basically aggressive and that battles and wars are a means of psychic cleansing. Sexual love is, for Layton, another form of encounter that has its creative and destructive aspects. Man can dominate reality, Layton tells us in 'The Fertile Muck', not only by love, but also by imagination. Art is the supreme synthesizer; it can contain paradox and contradiction because it deals with the truth that lies between opposites, as we have learned from poets like Blake and Yeats. As Layton explains in 'The Birth of Tragedy', 'Love, power, the huzza of battle / are something, are much; / yet a poem includes them like a pool / water and reflection.'

Of his long meditation, 'A Tall Man Executes A Jig', Layton has this to say: More than any other poem of mine, this one fuses feeling and thought in an intense moment of perception. Of truth. Truth for me, of course. That's the way I feel about gnats, and hills, and Christian renunciation, the pride of life and crushed grass-snakes writhing on the King's Highway. I like poems that are subtle and circular—the perfect form of a serpent swallowing its own tail and rolling towards Eternity. A meditative music, the feelings open as the sky. Formless poems give me the pips. If ideas, I want to see them dance (*Poet's Choice*, 1966, edited by Paul Engle and Joseph Langland).

Layton was born in Romania. While a child he went with his parents to Montreal, where he has spent most of his life. He studied agricultural science at Macdonald College and economics at McGill University, and taught in a boys' private school before taking up his teaching position at Sir George Williams University. In the forties Layton was associated with Louis Dudek and John Sutherland in the editing of *First Statement*, a controversial magazine that later merged with *Preview* to become *Northern Review*. In the fifties he joined with Dudek and Raymond Souster in the founding of the influential Contact Press. Since then Layton has taught, travelled, edited books, read his poetry on campuses across the country, and been an active commentator on current affairs. He has taught English at several universities, including York and Concordia, but is now retired and lives in Montreal.

Since the publication of *Here and Now* (1945), Layton has published many books of poetry, including *The Improved Binoculars* (1956), *A Red Carpet for the Sun* (1959), for which he received a Governor General's Award, *Balls for a One-Armed Juggler* (1963), *The Laughing Rooster* (1964), *Collected Poems* (1965), *Periods of the Moon* (1967), *The Shattered Plinths* (1968), *The Whole Bloody Bird* (1969), *The Collected Poems of Irving Layton* (1971), *Lovers and Lesser Men* (1973), *The Darkening Fire* (1975), *The Unwavering Eye* (1975), *For My Brother Jesus* (1976), *The Covenant* (1977), *The Poems of Irving Layton* (1977), *The Gucci Bag* (1984), *Final Reckoning: Poems 1984–1987* (1987), *Fortunate Exile* (1987), *A Wild Peculiar Joy 1945–1989* (1989), and *Fornalutx: Selected Poems, 1928–1990* (1992). His poetry has been discussed and celebrated by Eli Mandel, *Irving Layton* (1969), Wynne Francis, *Irving Layton and His Works* (1984), Seymour Mayne (ed.), *Irving Layton: the poet and his critics* (1984), Henry Beissel and Joy Bennett (eds.), *A Raging Fire: A Celebration of Irving Layton* (1993), and Francis Mansbridge, *Irving Layton: God's Recording Angel* (1995). Elspeth Cameron's controversial biography, *Irving Layton: A Portrait*, appeared in 1985. Several collections of his letters are available, including *Wild Gooseberries: Selected Letters* (1989), edited by Francis Mansbridge.

LOOK, THE LAMBS ARE ALL AROUND US!

Your figure, love,
curves itself
into a man's memory;
or to put it the way
a junior prof
at Mount Allison might,
Helen with her thick
absconding limbs
about the waist
of Paris
did no better.

Hell, my back's sunburnt
from so much love-making
in the open air.
The Primate (somebody
made a monkey of him)
and the Sanhedrin
(long on the beard, short
on the brain)
send envoys to say
they don't approve.
You never see them, love.
You toss me in the air
with such abandon,
they take to their heels and run.
I tell you
each kiss of yours
is like a blow on the head!

What luck, what luck to be loved
by the one girl
in this Presbyterian
country
who knows how to give
a man pleasure.

THE COLD GREEN ELEMENT

At the end of the garden walk
the wind and its satellite wait for me;
their meaning I will not know
    until I go there,
but the black-hatted undertaker

who, passing, saw my heart beating in the grass,
is also going there. Hi, I tell him,
a great squall in the Pacific blew a dead poet
    out of the water,
who now hangs from the city's gates.

Crowds depart daily to see it, and return
with grimaces and incomprehension;
if its limbs twitched in the air
    they would sit at its feet
peeling their oranges.

And turning over I embrace like a lover
the trunk of a tree, one of those
for whom the lightning was too much
    and grew a brilliant
hunchback with a crown of leaves.

The ailments escaped from the labels
of medicine bottles are all fled to the wind;
I've seen myself lately in the eyes
    of old women,
spent streams mourning my manhood,

in whose old pupils the sun became
a bloodsmear on broad catalpa leaves
and hanging from ancient twigs,
    my murdered selves
sparked the air like the muted collisions

of fruit. A black dog howls down my blood,
a black dog with yellow eyes;

he too by someone's inadvertence
    saw the bloodsmear
on the broad catalpa leaves.

But the furies clear a path for me to the worm
who sang for an hour in the throat of a robin,
and misled by the cries of young boys
    I am again
a breathless swimmer in that cold green element.

THE FERTILE MUCK

There are brightest apples on those trees
    but until I, fabulist, have spoken
they do not know their significance
or what other legends are hung like garlands
    on their black boughs twisting
like a rumour. The wind's noise is empty.

Nor are the winged insects better off
    though they wear my crafty eyes
wherever they alight. Stay here, my love;
you will see how delicately they deposit
    me on the leaves of elms
or fold me in the orient dust of summer.

And if in August joiners and bricklayers
    are thick as flies around us
building expensive bungalows for those
who do not need them, unless they release
    me roaring from their moth-proofed cupboards
their buyers will have no joy, no ease.

I could extend their rooms for them without cost
    and give them crazy sundials
to tell the time with, but I have noticed
how my irregular footprint horrifies them
    evenings and Sunday afternoons:
they spray for hours to erase its shadow.

How to dominate reality? Love is one way;
    imagination another. Sit here
beside me, sweet; take my hard hand in yours.
We'll mark the butterflies disappearing over the hedge
    with tiny wristwatches on their wings:
our fingers touching the earth, like two Buddhas.

ON SEEING THE STATUETTES OF EZEKIEL AND JEREMIAH IN THE CHURCH OF NOTRE DAME

They have given you French names
    and made you captive, my rugged
troublesome compatriots;
    your splendid beards, here, are epicene,
plaster white
      and your angers
unclothed with Palestinian hills quite lost
in this immense and ugly edifice.

You are bored—I see it—sultry prophets
    with priests and nuns
(What coarse jokes must pass between you!)
    and with those morbidly religious
i.e. my prize brother-in-law
              ex-Lawrencian
pawing his rosary, and his wife
sick with many guilts.

Believe me I would gladly take you
    from this spidery church
its bad melodrama, its musty smell of candle
    and set you both free again
in no make-believe world
        of sin and penitence
but the sunlit square opposite
alive at noon with arrogant men.

Yet cheer up Ezekiel and you Jeremiah
    who were once cast into a pit;

I shall not leave you here incensed, uneasy
  among alien Catholic saints
but shall bring you from time to time
    my hot Hebrew heart
as passionate as your own, and stand
with you here awhile in aching confraternity.

WHATEVER ELSE POETRY IS FREEDOM

Whatever else poetry is freedom.
Forget the rhetoric, the trick of lying
All poets pick up sooner or later. From the river,
Rising like the thin voice of grey castratos—the mist;
Poplars and pines grow straight but oaks are gnarled;
Old codgers must speak of death, boys break windows;
Women lie honestly by their men at last.

And I who gave my Kate a blackened eye
Did to its vivid changing colours
Make up an incredible musical scale;
And now I balance on wooden stilts and dance
And thereby sing to the loftiest casements.
See how with polish I bow from the waist.
Space for these stilts! More space or I fail!

And a crown I say for my buffoon's head.
Yet no more fool am I than King Canute,
Lord of our tribe, who scanned and scorned;
Who half-deceived, believed; and, poet, missed
The first white waves come nuzzling at his feet;
Then damned the courtiers and the foolish trial
With a most bewildering and unkingly jest.

It was the mist. It lies inside one like a destiny.
A real Jonah it lies rotting like a lung.
And I know myself undone who am a clown
And wear a wreath of mist for a crown;
Mist with the scent of dead apples,
Mist swirling from black oily waters at evening,
Mist from the fraternal graves of cemeteries.

It shall drive me to beg my food and at last
Hurl me broken I know and prostrate on the road;
Like a huge toad I saw, entire but dead,
That Time mordantly had blacked; O pressed
To the moist earth it pled for entry.
I shall be I say that stiff toad for sick with mist
And crazed I smell the odour of mortality.

And Time flames like a paraffin stove
And what it burns are the minutes I live.
At certain middays I have watched the cars
Bring me from afar their windshield suns;
What lay to my hand were blue fenders,
The suns extinguished, the drivers wearing sunglasses.
And it made me think I had touched a hearse.

So whatever else poetry is freedom. Let
Far off the impatient cadences reveal
A padding for my breathless stilts. Swivel,
O hero, in the fleshy groves, skin and glycerine,
And sing of lust, the sun's accompanying shadow
Like a vampire's wing, the stillness in dead feet—
Your stave brings resurrection, O aggrievèd king.

BERRY PICKING

Silently my wife walks on the still wet furze
Now darkgreen the leaves are full of metaphors
Now lit up is each tiny lamp of blueberry.
The white nails of rain have dropped and the sun is free.

And whether she bends or straightens to each bush
To find the children's laughter among the leaves
Her quiet hands seem to make the quiet summer hush—
Berries or children, patient she is with these.

I only vex and perplex her; madness, rage
Are endearing perhaps put down upon the page;
Even silence daylong and sullen can then
Enamour as restraint or classic discipline.

So I envy the berries she puts in her mouth,
The red and succulent juice that stains her lips;
I shall never taste that good to her, nor will they
Displease her with a thousand barbarous jests.

How they lie easily for her hand to take,
Part of the unoffending world that is hers;
Here beyond complexity she stands and stares
And leans her marvellous head as if for answers.

No more the easy soul my childish craft deceives
Nor the simpler one for whom yes is always yes;
No, now her voice comes to me from a far way off
Though her lips are redder than the raspberries.

Keine Lazarovitch 1870–1959

When I saw my mother's head on the cold pillow,
Her white waterfalling hair in the cheeks' hollows,
I thought, quietly circling my grief, of how
She had loved God but cursed extravagantly his creatures.

For her final mouth was not water but a curse,
A small black hole, a black rent in the universe,
Which damned the green earth, stars and trees in its stillness
And the inescapable lousiness of growing old.

And I record she was comfortless, vituperative,
Ignorant, glad, and much else besides; I believe
She endlessly praised her black eyebrows, their thick weave,
Till plagiarizing Death leaned down and took them for his mould.

And spoiled a dignity I shall not again find,
And the fury of her stubborn limited mind;
Now none will shake her amber beads and call God blind,
Or wear them upon a breast so radiantly.

O fierce she was, mean and unaccommodating;
But I think now of the toss of her gold earrings,
Their proud carnal assertion, and her youngest sings
While all the rivers of her red veins move into the sea.

A TALL MAN EXECUTES A JIG

I

So the man spread his blanket on the field
And watched the shafts of light between the tufts
And felt the sun push the grass towards him;
The noise he heard was that of whizzing flies,
The whistlings of some small imprudent birds,
And the ambiguous rumbles of cars
That made him look up at the sky, aware
Of the gnats that tilted against the wind
And in the sunlight turned to jigging motes.
Fruitflies he'd call them except there was no fruit
About, spoiling to hatch these glitterings,
These nervous dots for which the mind supplied
The closing sentences from Thucydides,
Or from Euclid having a savage nightmare.

II

Jig, jig, jig, jig. Like miniscule black links
Of a chain played with by some playful
Unapparent hand or the palpitant
Summer haze bored with the hour's stillness.
He felt the sting and tingle afterwards
Of those leaving their orthodox unrest,
Leaving their undulant excitation
To drop upon his sleeveless arm. The grass,
Even the wildflowers became black hairs
And himself a maddened speck among them.
Still the assaults of the small flies made him
Glad at last, until he saw purest joy
In their frantic jiggings under a hair,
So changed from those in the unrestraining air.

III

He stood up and felt himself enormous.
Felt as might Donatello over stone,
Or Plato, or as a man who has held

A loved and lovely woman in his arms
And feels his forehead touch the emptied sky
Where all antinomies flood into light.
Yet jig jig jig, the haloing black jots
Meshed with the wheeling fire of the sun:
Motion without meaning, disquietude
Without sense or purpose, ephemerides
That mottled the resting summer air till
Gusts swept them from his sight like wisps of smoke.
Yet they returned, bringing a bee who, seeing
But a tall man, left him for a marigold.

IV

He doffed his aureole of gnats and moved
Out of the field as the sun sank down,
A dying god upon the blood-red hills.
Ambition, pride, the ecstasy of sex,
And all circumstance of delight and grief,
That blood upon the mountain's side, that flood
Washed into a clear incredible pool
Below the ruddied peaks that pierced the sun.
He stood still and waited. If ever
The hour of revelation was come
It was now, here on the transfigured steep.
The sky darkened. Some birds chirped. Nothing else.
He thought the dying god had gone to sleep:
An Indian fakir on his mat of nails.

V

And on the summit of the asphalt road
Which stretched towards the fiery town, the man
Saw one hill raised like a hairy arm, dark
With pines and cedars against the stricken sun
—The arm of Moses or of Joshua.
He dropped his head and let fall the halo
Of mountains, purpling and silent as time,
To see temptation coiled before his feet:
A violated grass snake that lugged
Its intestine like a small red valise.

A cold-eyed skinflint it now was, and not
The manifest of that joyful wisdom,
The mirth and arrogant green flame of life;
Or earth's vivid tongue that flicked in praise of earth.

VI

And the man wept because pity was useless.
'Your jig's up; the flies come like kites,' he said
And watched the grass snake crawl towards the hedge,
Convulsing and dragging into the dark
The satchel filled with curses for the earth,
For the odours of warm sedge, and the sun,
A blood-red organ in the dying sky.
Backwards it fell into a grassy ditch
Exposing its underside, white as milk,
And mocked by wisps of hay between its jaws;
And then it stiffened to its final length.
But though it opened its thin mouth to scream
A last silent scream that shook the black sky,
Adamant and fierce, the tall man did not curse.

VII

Beside the rigid snake the man stretched out
In fellowship of death; he lay silent
And stiff in the heavy grass with eyes shut,
Inhaling the moist odours of the night
Through which his mind tunnelled with flicking tongue
Backwards to caves, mounds, and sunken ledges
And desolate cliffs where come only kites,
And where of perished badgers and racoons
The claws alone remain, gripping the earth.
Meanwhile the green snake crept upon the sky,
Huge, his mailed coat glittering with stars that made
The night bright, and blowing thin wreaths of cloud
Athwart the moon; and as the weary man
Stood up, coiled above his head, transforming all.

P.K. PAGE

(b. 1917)

'I am a traveller,' P.K. Page has written. 'I have a destination but no maps. Others will have reached that destination already, still others are on their way. But none has had to go from here before—nor will again. One's route is one's own. One's journey unique. What I will find at the end I can barely guess. What lies on the way is unknown. How to go? Land, sea or air? What techniques to use? What vehicle?' ('Traveller, Conjuror, Journeyman', *Canadian Literature* No. 46, Autumn 1970).

Patricia Kathleen Page has been a traveller in both her life and art. She was born in England but raised in Calgary and Winnipeg, where her father was stationed with the Strathcona Horse. From her family, which she describes as closely knit and not at all typical, she seems to have gained an appreciation for the arts, as her parents engaged in writing and drawing and were excellent carvers. She says she 'first came to writing by being an adolescent, which is enough to make anyone write.' After living briefly in the Maritimes, she moved to Montreal, where she worked as a scriptwriter for the National Film Board and became associated with Patrick Anderson and F.R. Scott in the editing of *Preview* magazine. Her first major publication was in *Unit of Five* (1944), an anthology of five poets edited by Ronald Hambleton. Page lived abroad for many years, in Mexico, Australia, and Brazil, where she began to draw under her married name, P.K. Irwin. She now lives in Victoria, BC.

Page's search for the technique with which to make her spiritual and aesthetic journey is a fascinating study. Her early poetry, which she now describes as 'clotted with images', explores the contradictions that underlie everyday experience: the terrible and explosive beauty of childhood; the haunting presence of boredom and madness associated with the deadly routine of jobs; the vanity and self-delusion that infects the most charitable and earnest of actions and statements. Such subjects lent themselves readily to a richly textured and highly allusive style, in which the interplay of elements of prosody and figurative language served to heighten the sense of irony and paradox. A poem such as 'The Stenographers', for example, strikes one as a kind of tapestry of metaphor, on which the routines and nitty-gritty of office life are described in terms that draw attention to their tedium, mechanization, and mind-deadening qualities: 'the brief bivouac of Sunday', 'the inch of noon', 'the winter of paper'. Such detail and stylization give imaginative expression to the problem of workers alienated from the product of their labours as no Marxist treatises could do. Page does not glorify or romanticize the secretaries; but her metaphors leave no doubt that such conditions are, ultimately, dehumanizing: 'In their eyes I have seen / the pin men of madness in marathon trim / race round the track of the stadium pupil.'

Time and travel have altered Page's conception of life and art, shifting her attention from social and political surfaces to internal psychological states. Actually, her account of her development as a visual artist serves as a useful analogy for her poetic progress as well. The shock of learning another language, as she says in 'Questions and Images' (*Canadian Literature,* No. 41, Summer 1969), was like being born a second time, growing from silence through a linguistic childhood and adolescence towards a radically altered adulthood, in which all her perceptions underwent a sea-change. Since she could not write poetry, she began to draw, going first through a realist phase in which she had to 'see with the eye of an ant' in order to appropriate the new and exotic environment; then, she says, 'the pen began dreaming. It began a life of its own', to the point where the painter could look into the macaw's eye and be 'drawn through its vortex into a minute cosmos which contained all the staggering dimensions of outer space.'

Here the poet and painter speak the same language, both being concerned, as she says in 'Stories of Snow', with that 'area behind the eyes / where silent, unrefractive whiteness lies.' No other poet in Canada, with the possible exception of Atwood, has been so intensely concerned to explore the nature of visual perception. Eyes abound in her poems, as do lenses, cameras, field glasses. Perspectives are almost always unusual; compositional elements play an important part; images may be blurred, superimposed, surprisingly juxtaposed, viewed through strangely distorting lenses. These perceptual elements, including a concern for colour and light and shade, combine with an imagistic precision that recalls her experience of film. As Munro Beattie has observed, 'Several of her poems might serve as scripts for little experimental films for "art" theatres. Action flows into action, image melts, "by a slow dissolve", into image.'

After Canada, which she has described as a 'whim-oriented culture', Page found the order and interconnectedness of the cultural symbols in Mexico liberating. She came to realize that, for her, art was not an end in itself so much as a means to an end, a path to wisdom. 'Poetry', she says 'was more than ever in the perceiving.' Art, whether poetry or painting, becomes a technique of transformation or metamorphosis, a vehicle for conducting us on that route that leads through the looking-glass, beyond the senses to 'some unseen centre'. 'Without magic the world is not to be borne,' she insists. 'A good writer or painter understands these laws and practices conjuration.'

Page's skills as a conjuror are everywhere present in her poetry, from the metaphysical wit that draws strange and wonderful analogies to the deftness and precision with which she uses words: she is a master of her craft. However, the formal or manipulative aspect of her work seldom submerges the realistic, or referential, side; her best poems remain immediately accessible and thoroughly mysterious.

Page's publications include a novel, *The Sun and the Moon,* which was published in 1944 under the pseudonym Judith Cape and reprinted with eight short stories in 1973 under the title *The Sun and the Moon and Other Fictions.* Her books of poetry are *As Ten As Twenty* (1946); *The Metal and the Flower* (1954), which won a Governor General's Award; *Cry Ararat!* (1967); *Poems Selected and New* (1974); *Leviathan in a Pool* (1974); *Evening Dance of the Grey Flies* (1981); *The Glass Air: Selected Poems* (1985, 1991); *Hologram: A Book of Glosas* (1994) and *The Hidden Room: Collected Poems, Volumes One and Two* (1997), a major achievement graced with her own unique drawings. She has also published an autobiographical work, *Brazilian Journal* (1986), and works for young readers: *A Flask of Sea Water* (1989), *The Travelling Musicians* (1991), and *The Goat That Flew* (1993).

THE STENOGRAPHERS

After the brief bivouac of Sunday,
their eyes, in the forced march of Monday to Saturday,
hoist the white flag, flutter in the snow-storm of paper,
haul it down and crack in the mid-sun of temper.

In the pause between the first draft and the carbon
they glimpse the smooth hours when they were children—
the ride in the ice-cart, the ice-man's name,
the end of the route and the long walk home;

remember the sea where floats at high tide
were sea marrows growing on the scatter-green vine
or spools of grey toffee, or wasps' nests on water;
remember the sand and the leaves of the country.

Bell rings and they go and the voice draws their pencil
like a sled across snow; when its runners are frozen
rope snaps and the voice then is pulling no burden
but runs like a dog on the winter of paper.

Their climates are winter and summer—no wind
for the kites of their hearts—no wind for a flight;
a breeze at the most, to tumble them over
and leave them like rubbish—the boy-friends of blood.

In the inch of the noon as they move they are stagnant.
The terrible calm of the noon is their anguish;
the lip of the counter, the shapes of the straws
like icicles breaking their tongues, are invaders.

Their beds are their oceans—salt water of weeping
the waves that they know—the tide before sleep;
and fighting to drown they assemble their sheep
in columns and watch them leap desks for their fences

and stare at them with their own mirror-worn faces.
In the felt of the morning the calico-minded,
sufficiently starched, insert papers, hit keys,
efficient and sure as their adding machines;

yet they weep in the vault, they are taut as net curtains
stretched upon frames. In their eyes I have seen
the pin men of madness in marathon trim
race round the track of the stadium pupil.

LANDLADY

Through sepia air the boarders come and go,
impersonal as trains. Pass silently
the craving silence swallowing her speech;
click doors like shutters on her camera eye.

Because of her their lives become exact:
their entrances and exits are designed;
phone calls are cryptic. Oh, her ticklish ears
advance and fall back stunned.

Nothing is unprepared. They hold the walls
about them as they weep or laugh. Each face
is dialled to zero publicly. She peers
stippled with curious flesh;

pads on the patient landing like a pulse,
unlocks their keyholes with the wire of sight,
searches their rooms for clues when they are out,
pricks when they come home late.

Wonders when they are quiet, jumps when they move,
dreams that they dope or drink, trembles to know
the traffic of their brains, jaywalks their street
in clumsy shoes.

Yet knows them better than their closest friends:
their cupboards and the secrets of their drawers,
their books, their private mail, their photographs
are theirs and hers.

Knows when they wash, how frequently their clothes
go to the cleaners, what they like to eat,
their curvature of health, but even so
is not content.

And like a lover must know all, all, all.
Prays she may catch them unprepared at last
and palm the dreadful riddle of their skulls—
hoping the worst.

STORIES OF SNOW

Those in the vegetable rain retain
an area behind their sprouting eyes
held soft and rounded with the dream of snow
precious and reminiscent as those globes—
souvenir of some never-nether land—
which hold their snow-storms circular, complete,
high in a tall and teakwood cabinet.

In countries where the leaves are large as hands
where flowers protrude their fleshy chins
and call their colours,
an imaginary snow-storm sometimes falls
among the lilies.
And in the early morning one will waken
to think the glowing linen of his pillow
a northern drift, will find himself mistaken
and lie back weeping.
And there the story shifts from head to head,
of how in Holland, from their feather beds
hunters arise and part the flakes and go
forth to the frozen lakes in search of swans—
the snow-light falling white along their guns,
their breath in plumes.
While tethered in the wind like sleeping gulls
ice-boats wait the raising of their wings
to skim the electric ice at such a speed
they leap jet strips of naked water,
and how these flying, sailing hunters feel
air in the mouths as terrible as ether.
And on the story runs that even drinks
in that white landscape dare to be no colour;
how flasked and water clear, the liquor slips
silver against the hunters' moving hips.

And of the swan in death these dreamers tell
of its last flight and how it falls, a plummet,
pierced by the freezing bullet
and how three feathers, loosened by the shot,
descend like snow upon it.
While hunters plunge their fingers in its down
deep as a drift, and dive their hands
up to the neck of the wrist
in that warm metamorphosis of snow
as gentle as the sort that woodsmen know
who, lost in the white circle, fall at last
and dream their way to death.

And stories of this kind are often told
in countries where great flowers bar the roads
with reds and blues which seal the route to snow—
as if, in telling, raconteurs unlock
the colour with its complement and go
through to the area behind the eyes
where silent, unrefractive whiteness lies.

PHOTOS OF A SALT MINE

How innocent their lives look,
how like a child's
dream of caves and winter, both combined;
the steep descent to whiteness
and the stope
with its striated walls
their folds all leaning as if pointing to
the greater whiteness still,
that great white bank
with its decisive front,
that seam upon a slope,
salt's lovely ice.

And wonderful underfoot the snow of salt
the fine
particles a broom could sweep,
one thinks

muckers might make angels in its drifts
as children do in snow,
lovers in sheets,
lie down and leave imprinted where they lay
a feathered creature holier than they.

And in the outworked stopes
with lamps and ropes
up miniature matterhorns
the miners climb
probe with their lights
the ancient folds of rock—
syncline and anticline—
and scoop from darkness an Aladdin's cave:
rubies and opals glitter from its walls.

But hoses douse the brilliance of these jewels,
melt fire to brine.
Salt's bitter water trickles thin and forms,
slow fathoms down,
a lake within a cave,
lacquered with jet—
white's opposite.
There grey on black the boating miners float
to mend the stays and struts of that old stope
and deeply underground
their words resound,
are multiplied by echo, swell and grow
and make a climate of a miner's voice.

So all the photographs like children's wishes
are filled with caves or winter,
innocence
has acted as a filter,
selected only beauty from the mine.
Except in the last picture,
it is shot
from an acute high angle. In a pit
figures the size of pins are strangely lit
and might be dancing but you know they're not.
Like Dante's vision of the nether hell

men struggle with the bright cold fires of salt,
locked in the black inferno of the rock:
the filter here, not innocence but guilt.

THE PERMANENT TOURISTS

Somnolent through landscapes and by trees
nondescript, almost anonymous,
they alter as they enter foreign cities—
the terrible tourists with their empty eyes
longing to be filled with monuments.

Verge upon statues in the public squares
remembering the promise of memorials
yet never enter the entire event
as dogs, abroad in any kind of weather,
move perfectly within their rainy climate.

Lock themselves into snapshots on the steps
of monolithic bronze as if suspecting
the subtle mourning of the photograph
might later conjure in the memory
all they are now incapable of feeling.

And search all heroes out: the boy who gave
his life to save a town; the stolid queen;
forgotten politicians minus names
and the plunging war dead, permanently brave,
forever and ever going down to death.

Look, you can see them nude in any café
reading their histories from the bill of fare,
creating futures from a foreign teacup.
Philosophies like ferns bloom from the fable
that travel is broadening at the café table.

Yet somehow beautiful, they stamp the plaza.
Classic in their anxiety they call
all sculptured immemorial stone
into their passive eyes, as rivers
draw ruined columns to their placid glass.

ARRAS

Consider a new habit—classical,
and trees espaliered on the wall like candelabra.
How still upon that lawn our sandalled feet.

But a peacock rattling his rattan tail and screaming
has found a point of entry. Through whose eye
did it insinuate in furled disguise
to shake its jewels and silk upon that grass?

The peaches hang like lanterns. No one joins
those figures on the arras.
                    Who am I
or who am I become that walking here
I am observer, other, Gemini,
starred for a green garden of cinema?

I ask, what did they deal me in this pack?
The cards, all suits, are royal when I look.
My fingers slipping on a monarch's face
twitch and grow slack.
I want a hand to clutch, a heart to crack.

No one is moving now, the stillness is
infinite. If I should make a break. . . .
take to my springy heels. . . ? But nothing moves.
The spinning world is stuck upon its poles,
the stillness points a bone at me. I fear
the future on this arras.
                    I confess:

It was my eye.

Voluptuous it came.
Its head the ferrule and its lovely tail
folded so sweetly; it was strangely slim
to fit the retina. And then it shook
and was a peacock—living patina,
eye-bright, maculate!
Does no one care?

I thought their hands might hold me if I spoke.
I dreamed the bite of fingers in my flesh,
their poke smashed by an image, but they stand
as if within a treacle, motionless,
folding slow eyes on nothing. While they stare
another line has trolled the encircling air,
another bird assumes its furled disguise.

AFTER RAIN

The snails have made a garden of green lace:
broderie anglaise from the cabbages,
chantilly from the choux-fleurs, tiny veils—
I see already that I lift the blind
upon a woman's wardrobe of the mind.

Such female whimsy floats about me like
a kind of tulle, a flimsy mesh,
while feet in gum boots pace the rectangles—
garden abstracted, geometry awash—
an unknown theorem argued in green ink,
dropped in the bath.
Euclid in glorious chlorophyl, half drunk.

I none too sober slipping in the mud
where rigged with guys of rain
the clothes-reel gauche
as the rangy skeleton of some
gaunt delicate spidery mute
is pitched as if
listening;
while hung from one thin rib
a silver web—
its infant, skeletal, diminutive,
now sagged with sequins, pulled ellipsoid,
glistening.

I suffer shame in all these images.
The garden is primeval, Giovanni
in soggy denim squelches by my hub

over his ruin,
shakes a doleful head.
but he so beautiful and diademmed,
his long Italian hands so wrung with rain
I find his ache exists beyond my rim
and almost weep to see a broken man
made subject to my whim.

O choir him, birds, and let him come to rest
within this beauty as one rests in love,
till pears upon the bough
encrusted with
small snails as pale as pearls
hang golden in
a heart that knows tears are a part of love.

And choir me too to keep my heart a size
larger than seeing, unseduced by each
bright glimpse of beauty striking like a bell,
so that the whole may toll,
its meaning shine
clear of the myriad images that still—
do what I will—encumber its pure line.

BRAZILIAN FAZENDA

That day all the slaves were freed
their manacles, anklets
left on the window ledge to rust in the moist air

and all the coffee ripened
like beads on a bush or balls of fire
as merry as Christmas

and the cows all calved and the calves all lived
such a moo.
On the wide verandah where birds in cages
sang among the bell flowers
I in a bridal hammock
white and tasselled
whistled

and bits fell out of the sky near Nossa Senhora
who had walked all the way in bare feet from Bahia

and the chapel was lit by a child's
fistful of marigolds on the red velvet altar
thrown like a golden ball.

Oh let me come back on a day
when nothing extraordinary happens
so I can stare
at the sugar white pillars
and black lace grills
of this pink house.

EVENING DANCE OF THE GREY FLIES

Grey flies, fragile, slender-winged and slender-legged
scribble a pencilled script across the sunlit lawn.

As grass and leaves grow black
the grey flies gleam—
their cursive flight a gold calligraphy.

It is the light that gilds their frail
bodies, makes them fat and bright as bees—
reflected or refracted light—

as once my fist
burnished by some beam I could not see
glowed like gold mail and conjured Charlemagne

as once your face
grey with illness and with age—
a silverpoint against the pillow's white—

shone suddenly like the sun
before you died.

PLANET EARTH

It has to be spread out, the skin of this planet,
has to be ironed, the sea in its whiteness;
and the hands keep on moving,
smoothing the holy surfaces.

In Praise of Ironing, Pablo Neruda

It has to be loved the way a laundress loves her linens,
the way she moves her hands caressing the fine muslins
knowing their warp and woof,
like a lover coaxing, or a mother praising.
It has to be loved as if it were embroidered
with flowers and birds and two joined hearts upon it.
It has to be stretched and stroked.
It has to be celebrated.
O this great beloved world and all the creatures in it.
It has to be spread out, the skin of this planet.

The trees must be washed, and the grasses and mosses.
They have to be polished as if made of green brass.
The rivers and little streams with their hidden cresses
and pale-coloured pebbles
and their fool's gold
must be washed and starched or shined into brightness,
the sheets of lake water
smoothed with the hand
and the foam of the oceans pressed into neatness.
It has to be ironed, the sea in its whiteness

and pleated and goffered, the flower-blue sea
the protean, wine-dark, grey, green, sea
with its metres of satin and bolts of brocade.
And sky—such an O! overhead—night and day
must be burnished and rubbed
by hands that are loving
so the blue blazons forth
and the stars keep on shining
within and above
and the hands keep on moving.

It has to be made bright, the skin of this planet
till it shines in the sun like gold leaf.
Archangels then will attend to its metals
and polish the rods of its rain.
Seraphim will stop singing hosannas
to shower it with blessings and blisses and praises
and, newly in love,
we must draw it and paint it
our pencils and brushes and loving caresses
smoothing the holy surfaces.

RAYMOND SOUSTER

(b. 1921)

Souster's chief concern has been to keep singing in the face of despair. As he says in 'Good Fortune', 'life isn't a matter of luck / of good fortune, it's whether / the heart can keep singing / when there's really no reason / why it should.' His imagination is peopled with the victims of wars and industrial 'progress', whores, cripples, beggars, down-and-outs of every sort. He takes upon himself their guilt and shame and tries to communicate the terrible sense of human waste that weighs upon him. Souster is equally troubled by the impermanence of things. At times he displays a gentle nostalgia for the innocence and good times of the past, lamenting the passing of friends and shared interests and the disappearance of familiar landscapes under a jungle of concrete and cereal-box architecture. Although he is incapable of sustained irony or satire, Souster often strikes out at the instruments of change and destruction like an animal that has been hurt or cornered. His most convincing response is to celebrate signs of man's capacity for joy or, at least, survival; he searches out pockets of beauty and spontaneity in the rubbish heap of the century, as in 'Top Hat' or 'Victory', where he celebrates the determination of a 'bum' who beats the street-cleaning machine to a castaway cigarette butt.

Souster is predominantly a poet of content. Robert Creeley applies this name to the poets of the thirties. 'There are also those men', he says, '. . . who extend to their writing of verse concerns which haunt

them, again reasonably enough, in other areas of living. They are in this way poets of "content", and their poems argue images of living to which the content of their poem points. They argue the poem as a means to recognition, a signboard as it were, not in itself a structure of "recognition" or—better —cognition itself.' Creeley is thinking here of Kenneth Fearing, but his description applies well to Souster, for whom the sociological impulse seems more pressing than the aesthetic. This view is not inconsistent with Souster's idea of the poet's function. In 'The Lilac Poem' he speaks of the impermanence of all things, even poetry. If art itself is subject to the eroding effects of time, the artist is best employed as a recorder or photographer of the human condition at a particular moment in history; or rather—and perhaps this is his main function—as an entertainer who can divert man's attention away from the sources of his despair. The short poem is itself a function of the poet's view of the impermanence of all things; and it is especially characteristic of modern poetry. As Frost suggests, the good poem provides 'a momentary stay against confusion'.

This does not mean that Souster has no interest in form, in prosody. He is sufficiently steeped in American poetry, especially in the work of Ezra Pound and William Carlos Williams, to have absorbed not only a distaste for the baggage of poetic tradition, but also a preoccupation with certain formal elements in verse. His own poetry is not metrical; he prefers the shifting rhythms of speech to the monotony of the metronome. Like Bowering, he avoids the use of mythical allusion and archaism, preferring instead poetry with a base in actual experience. Souster understands Pound's dictum that 'It is better to present one Image in a lifetime than to produce voluminous works.' He has written a number of excellent imagist poems, such as 'Study: The Bath' and 'The Six-Quart Basket', that have the clarity and economy of the haiku. Occasionally Souster is tempted to comment on the image, to tag on a moral that leaves attention outside the poem, as in 'The Hunter'; but his best poems are either pure image or pure voice. The poems of lyrical reflection are less likely to misfire, because the poet begins with a mood that is strong enough to arrange the materials it gathers to express itself, rather than with an image that is too weak to support itself without assistance from the voice of the poet. These reflective verses speak for Souster's integrity as a man and as a poet; they are beautifully turned and reveal a quiet concern, or empathy, that is always surprising, sometimes moving.

Souster was born in Toronto and has spent all his life there except for the war years, 1941–5, when he was in the RCAF in the Maritimes and in England. Of his beloved Toronto, he says: 'I suppose I am truly an unrepentant regionalist. As Emile Zola put it to Paul Bourget: "Why should we be everlastingly wanting to escape to lands of romance? Our streets are full of tragedy and full of beauty; they should be enough for any poet." All the experiences one is likely to encounter in Paris can be found in this city. Toronto has a flavour all its own. . . . My roots are here, this is the place that tugs at my heart when I leave it and fills me with quiet relief when I return to it.'

Like Wallace Stevens, Souster has been wedded simultaneously to the muses of both poetry and commerce; until his retirement he was employed for four decades by the Canadian Imperial Bank of Commerce in downtown Toronto. His involvements in the poetic community are many. He edited a mimeographed magazine called *Combustion* (1957–60) and was a founder-editor of Contact Press. He edited *New Wave Canada: The New Explosion in Canadian Poetry* (1966), and *Generation Now* (1970), an anthology of poetry for schools. He was also a founding member of the League of Canadian Poets.

Souster has published many books of poetry, including *When We Are Young* (1946); *Go to Sleep, World* (1947); *Shake Hands with the Hangman* (1953); *Selected Poems* (1956), edited by Louis Dudek; *A Local Pride* (1962); *Place of Meeting* (1962); *The Colour of the Times* (1964), his collected poems, which received a Governor General's Award; *Ten Elephants on Yonge Street* (1965); *As Is* (1967); *Lost & Found* (1968); *So Far So Good* (1969); *Selected Poems* (1972); *On Target* (1973); *Doubleheader* (containing *As Is* and *Lost & Found*, 1975); *Rain-check* (1975); *Extra Innings* (1977); *Collected Poems* in four volumes (1980 ff.); *It Takes All Kinds* (1986); *The Eyes of Love* (1987); *Asking for More* (1988); *Running Out the Clock* (1991); *Riding the Long Black Horse* (1993); *Old Bank Notes* (1993); *No Sad Songs Wanted Here* (1995); and *Close to Home* (1996). His work is discussed in Frank Davey's *Louis Dudek and Raymond Souster* (1980) and Bruce Whiteman's *Raymond Souster and His Works* (1984).

YOUNG GIRLS

With the night full of spring and stars we stand
here in this dark doorway and watch the young
girls pass, two, three together, hand in hand.
Like flowers they are whose fragrance has not sprung
or awakened, whose bodies dimly feel
the flooding upward welling of the trees;
whose senses, caressed by the wind's soft fingers, reel
with a delirium that makes them ill at ease.

They lie awake at night unable to sleep
and walk the streets kindled by strange desires;
they steal glances at us, unable to keep
control upon those subterranean fires.
We whistle after them, then laugh, for they
stiffen, not knowing what to do or say.

LAGOONS, HANLAN'S POINT

Mornings
before the sun's liquid
spilled gradually, flooding
the island's cool cellar,
there was the boat
and the still lagoons,
with the sound of my oars
the only intrusion
over the cries of birds
in the marshy shallows,
or the loud thrashing
of the startled crane
rushing the air.

And in one strange
dark, tree-hung entrance,
I followed the sound
of my heart all the way
to the reed-blocked ending,
with the pads of the lily

thick as green-shining film
covering the water.

And in another
where the sun came
to probe the depths
through a shaft of branches,
I saw the skeletons
of brown ships rotting
far below in their burial-ground,
and wondered what strange fish
with what strange colours
swam through these places
under the water. . . .

A small boy
with a flat-bottomed punt
and an old pair of oars
moving with wonder
through the antechamber
of a waking world.

DOWNTOWN CORNER NEWS STAND

It will need all of death to take you from this corner.
It has become your world, and you its unshaved
bleary-eyed, foot-stamping king. In winter
you curse the cold, huddled in your coat from the wind,
you fry in summer like an egg hopping on a griddle;
and always the whining voice, the nervous-flinging arms,
the red face, shifting eyes watching, waiting
under the grimy cap for God knows what
to happen. (But nothing ever does, downtown Toronto
goes to sleep and wakes the next morning
always the same, except a little dirtier.)
And you stand with your armful of Stars and Telys,
the peak of your cap well down against the sun,
and all the city's restless seething river
surges besides you, but not once do you plunge

into its flood, are carried or tossed away:
but reappear always, beard longer than ever, nose running,
to catch the noon editions at King and Bay.

STUDY: THE BATH

In the almost dim light
of the bathroom a woman
steps from white tub
towel around her shoulders.

Drops of water glisten
on her body, slight buttocks,
neck, tight belly,
fall at intervals
from the slightly plumed
oval of crotch.

Neck bent forward
eyes collected
her attention gathered
at the ends of fingers

as she removes
dead skin from her nipples.

FLIGHT OF THE ROLLER-COASTER

Once more around should do it, the man confided . . .

and sure enough, when the roller-coaster reached the peak
of the giant curve above me, screech of its wheels
almost drowned out by the shriller cries of the riders,

instead of the dip and plunge with its landslide of screams,
it rose in the air like a movieland magic carpet,
    some wonderful bird,

and without fuss or fanfare swooped slowly across
    the amusement-park,
over Spook's Castle, ice-cream booths, shooting-gallery.
    And losing no height

made the last yards above the beach, where the cucumber-cool
brakeman in the last seat saluted
a lady about to change from her bathing-suit.

Then, as many witnesses reported, headed leisurely
    out over the water,
disappearing all too soon behind a low-flying flight of clouds.

ALL THIS SLOW AFTERNOON

All this slow afternoon
the May winds blowing
honey of the lilacs,
sounds of waves washing
through the highest branches
of my poplar tree.

Enough in such hours
to be simply alive;
I will take death tomorrow
without bitterness.

Today all I ask
is to be left alone
in the wind
in the sunshine,
with the honey of lilacs
down the garden;

to fall asleep tired
of small birds' gossip,
of so much greenness
pushed behind my eyes.

THE SIX-QUART BASKET

The six-quart basket
one side gone
half the handle torn off

sits in the centre of the lawn
and slowly fills up
with the white fruits of the snow.

THE DEATH OF THE GRENADIERS

It was over the ice
of this bottomless pond
(so the story goes)
that the Grenadiers
chased those Indians,
and the ice that gave way
to the marching step
of the English held up
for the braves' single file. . . .
And girls have told me
they've felt that someone
was looking up their legs
as they skated the pond,
and looking down they've seen
(noses close to the ice
on the underneath side),
the white-bearded faces
of lonely soldiers
looking up at them
with lascivious winks
in their socketless eyes.

A MORNING IN BRUSSELS

—Granted the most subtle torture that in which the victim
knows each step of his pain but is powerless to change
it in any way—

Then become this moment the young French-Canadian airman
of twenty, who, having watched in the cellar of the Rue
Royale the most expert monsters of the Gestapo stalk
round on cat-silent shoes behind the line of prisoners
(faces held six inches back from dripping walls), lashing
out with rubber truncheons now at this head and now this,
quite at random, never the same pattern repeated—

Knowing this then stand in line yourself, lips held
tightly together until the first searing terror of your
face smashed against the stone, pain in your nose like
a knife-slit, lips moving tremblingly in prayer, Holy
Mary, Mother of God, as you wait for the warning of
footsteps which never comes, as you wait for an end,
any end. . . .

Night Raider

Something getting its Christmas dinner early
in the narrow alley that flanks
our apartment house.
                          Gorging so frantically
it can't hear the noise it makes
rattling trash-can lids, ripping skins
of newspaper-wrapping off the choicest refuse.
This to the sleepy steadiness of rain falling,
so that I get a picture of my animal,
head down in garbage, busy, steam ascending
like a grace from its breathing coat.

Graveyard Shift

Five o'clock and still sleepless,
with eyelids half-shuttered,
I am still commanded
to remain here at my desk,

awaiting the late arrival
of the last two lines

of what's turning out to be
a reluctant, foot-dragging
little bitch of a poem.

SOMALIA

In the time it takes
to say Mogadishu,

a five-year-old
playing in the mud
has both arms blown away.

The militiamen call him
Little-One-Who-Can't-Fly.

PHYLLIS WEBB

(b. 1927)

Readers caught up in Phyllis Webb's early work are often startled by the subject matter—suicide, betrayal, gratuitous violence, death—and may need to be reminded that, whatever its ostensible content, good poetry is an affirmation of the human spirit, of the power of the imagination to confront and reshape reality. As Albert Camus argues in his famous treatise, *The Rebel*, there is no such thing as a nihilistic work of art; even if literature 'describes nostalgia, despair, frustration, it still creates a form of salvation. To talk of despair is to conquer it. Despairing literature is a contradiction in terms.' I'm not sure why it should be necessary to say this, in an age of concentration camps, forced migrations, ethnic cleansing, subjects which the artist ignores at her (and our) peril, but it is. What's important to celebrate in Webb's poetry is the style, the way in which she imposes *form* on whatever elements from reality she uses.

One has only to look closely at 'Love Story' to understand the terrifyingly delicate balance Webb can achieve between the realist and formalist elements, by virtue of an unremitting attention to the visual, auditory, and intellectual nuances of words. Rather than describe the death of the infant in graphic detail, Webb chooses to stylize the killing, speaking of the ape's biting of the neck in metaphorical terms as 'tasting time' and of the attack as something general rather than specific: 'and his nails rooted sudden fire in the ribs of Adam.' Reference to the infant's belly as 'plush' on which the ape 'bobbed nervously' serves, finally, to heighten rather than diminish the horror of the imaged scene by drawing attention to elements of texture and the 'cushioning' effect that the reader would otherwise gladly forgo.

As is evident in her poems and in the emphases her critical writings place on the poetic line, the creative process, and the genesis of poems, Webb is extremely conscious of even the smallest nuance of rhythm or sound. Her dissatisfaction with the verbosity and heavy-handedness of conventional rhetoric led her, in the mid-1960s, towards the minimalism of *Naked Poems* (1965), with their short lines and abbreviated manner; the same questing and curiosity led her, in the 1980s, to explore the 8th-century Persian form called the *ghazal*, whose discrete but tonally-linked couplets accommodated themselves particularly well, in *Water and Light* (1984), to the verbal dexterity and imaginative leaping that are Webb's hallmarks. Webb is also a continuing explorer of life and its meaning, personally and collectively. Her work touches not only upon the philosophical anguish of modern life, but also upon some of the issues, events, and personalities that have shaped our age.

To fully appreciate the importance Webb places on form, it's instructive to read 'Up the Ladder: Notes on the Creative Process' and 'The Crannies of Matter: Texture in Robin Blaser's Later *Image-Nations*' (*Nothing But Brush Strokes*), where she scrutinizes, with great wit and linguistic playfulness, her own creative processes and those of a fellow poet:

> I used to think of texture in poetry as mainly a sound apparition produced by an intricate play of vocables whose plosives, dentals, labials, fricatives, hoots, whistles, yells and chuckles, sighs, murmurs, phonemic and syllabic interactions could scuff up or smooth out the surface of a poem. . . . When we speak of texture in poetry we're in the land of mixed metaphors, or, more accurately, in the surreal world of synaesthesia where sensory perceptions seem to be cross-wired and the sky today is high C, or the high C sounds like cerulean blue. . . . When we sound a poem aloud the synesthesic transfer that takes place to give us a sense of texture occurs because—simplicity itself—words are formed inside the chest and head, inside the mouth.

In 'Seeking Shape. Seeking Meaning: An Interview with Phyllis Webb' conducted by Smaro Kamboureli (*West Coast Line*, 6, Fall/Winter, 1991–92), Webb talks at length about how she employs an associative process in writing poetry; the need not so much for passivity on the part of the poet, as for 'fertile silence' and 'active attention' to what the language is revealing; aspiring to a 'speakeasy' frame of mind; her resistance to poetic theory and dogma; how the prose poem upsets the 'logical expectations' of prose; the 'death of the lyric poem' and how, in seeking to move outside the individual ego, she came to write a book of 'uglies'— poems that deliberately flout the conventions, the controlling expectations; and how this search might lead her to 'deep structure'. She quotes Ginsberg on the shapeliness of mind and art, then concludes: 'I think we must trust that primal creativity, trust its slow-motion urge toward order and enlightenment.'

Webb describes, in the same interview, the experience of writing some of the poems in *Hanging Fire*, where, she said, sounds attracted meanings:

> That is why there is a sense of play in a lot of the poems where I'm working from givens. I really did, almost, proceed with exercises, you know, purely associative exercises. Rhyming exercises. As I noted down these things, I would take off on them and do rhymes, and do associations that would lead me on. And so the sounds, for instance—oh dear— 'Cornflowers & Saffron Robes Belittle the Effort'. Now this has a wonderful sound to me, and it's rather mysterious in its content. For me it related to Buddhism; it's a very, very tiny poem that's written out of this very long title. I mean long compared to most of the other titles in the book. It's a long sentence to have been given to me. Perhaps, it's untrustworthy in its givenness, but in fact that's what arrived that morning, and so I simply went with sound there . . . pure sound. . . . It's not a great poem, but it's an interesting compression of thought processes.

Phyllis Webb was born in Victoria and raised there and in Vancouver. She studied English and Philosophy at UBC from 1945 to 1949, ran unsuccessfully as a CCF candidate in the provincial elections, and worked as a secretary in Montreal, where she also attended McGill and came into contact with F.R. Scott and John Sutherland. Her poems were first published in *Trio*, along with those of Eli Mandel and Gael Turnbull. For the next fourteen years she lived intermittently in England, Montreal, Paris, Vancouver (where she taught English at UBC), and Toronto, where she was co-creator and Executive Producer of the CBC 'Ideas' program. She now lives on Salt Spring Island, where she pursues the sister arts of painting and collage. Her poetry books include *Even Your Right Eye* (1956), *The Sea Is Also a Garden* (1962), *Naked Poems* (1965), *Wilson's Bowl* (1980), *The*

Vision Tree: Selected Poems (1982), which won a Governor General's Award, *Water & Light: Ghazals and Anti-Ghazals* (1982; 1984), and *Hanging Fire* (1991). Her critical writings and thoughts on the creative process appear in *Talking* (1982) and *Nothing But Brush Strokes: Selected Prose* (1995), which includes a number of her own photo-collages. Webb's poetry has received critical attention in articles and books, including John Hulcoop's *Phyllis Webb and Her Works* (1991) and Pauline Butling's *Seeing in the Dark: The Poetry of Phyllis Webb* (1996).

LOVE STORY

It was easy to see what he was up to,
the grey, bundled ape,
as he sidled half-playfully
up to the baby
and with a sly look behind
put his hands onto the crib
and leapt in.

The child's pink, beginning face
stared up as the hair-handed monkey
explored the flesh, so soft, of our infant race.
The belly spread like plush to the monkey's haunch,
he settled, heavy and gay, his nuzzling
mouth at the baby's neck.

But, no answer accurate to a smile,
he bit, tasted time, maddened,
and his nails rooted sudden fire in the ribs of Adam,
towered, carnivorous, for aim
and baby face, ears, arms
were torn and taken in his ravaging.

And so the killing, too-late parents came,
hysteric, after their child's
futile pulse had stopped its beating.
Only the half-pathetic, half-triumphant
monkey peered out from the crib,
bobbed nervously on the dead infant's belly,
then stopped, suddenly paralyzed on that soft tomb.

Was it the donkey Death brayed out at him
from the human mother's eyes,
or did his love for her in that pause
consume him?

The jealous ape's death was swift
and of natural cause. 'Died of shame,'
some said, others, 'of shock.'
But his death was Othello's death,
as great, as picayune,
he died of envy, lacking the knack of wisdom.

SITTING

The degree of nothingness
is important:
to sit emptily
in the sun
receiving fire
that is the way
to mend
an extraordinary world,
sitting perfectly
still
and only
remotely human.

A TALL TALE

The whale, improbable as lust,
carved out a cave
for the seagirl's rest;
with rest the seagirl, sweet as dust, devised
a manner for the whale
to lie between her thighs.
Like this they lay
within the shadowed cave
under the waters, under the waters wise,
and nested there, and nested there and stayed,
this coldest whale aslant the seagirl's thighs.

Two hundred years perhaps swam by them there
before the cunning waters so distilled the pair
they turned to brutal artifacts of stone
polished, O petrified prisoners of their lair.
And thus, with quiet, submerged in deathly calm,
the two disclosed a future geologic long,
lying cold, whale to thigh revealed
the secret of their comfort
to the marine weeds,
to fish, to shell, sand, sediment and wave,
to the broken, dying sun
which probed their ocean grave.
These, whale and seagirl, stone gods,
stone lust, stone grief,
interred on the sedimented sand
amongst the orange starfish,
these cold and stony mariners
invoked the moral snail
and in sepulchral voice intoned a moral tale:
'Under the waters, under the waters wise,
all loving flesh will quickly meet demise,
the cave, the shadow cave is nowhere wholly safe
and even the oddest couple can scarcely find relief:
appear then to submit to this tide and timing sea,
but secrete a skilful shell and stone and perfect be.'

TO FRIENDS WHO HAVE ALSO CONSIDERED SUICIDE

It's still a good idea.
Its exercise is discipline:
to remember to cross the street without looking,
to remember not to jump when the cars side-swipe,
to remember not to bother to have clothes cleaned,
to remember not to eat or want to eat,
to consider the numerous methods of killing oneself,
that is surely the finest exercise of the imagination:
death by drowning, sleeping pills, slashed wrists,
kitchen fumes, bullets through the brain or through
the stomach, hanging by the neck in attic or basement,
a clean frozen death—the ways are endless.
And consider the drama! It's better than a whole season

at Stratford when you think of the emotion of your
family on hearing the news and when you imagine
how embarrassed some will be when the body is found.
One could furnish a whole chorus in a Greek play
with expletives and feel sneaky and omniscient
at the same time. But there's no shame
in this concept of suicide.
It has concerned our best philosophers
and inspired some of the most popular
of our politicians and financiers.
Some people swim lakes, others climb flagpoles,
some join monasteries, but we, my friends,
who have considered suicide take our daily walk
with death and are not lonely.
In the end it brings more honesty and care
than all the democratic parliaments of tricks.
It is the 'sickness unto death'; it is death;
it is not death; it is the sand from the beaches
of a hundred civilizations, the sand in the teeth
of death and barnacles our singing tongue:
and this is 'life' and we owe at least this much
contemplation to our western fact: to Rise,
Decline, Fall, to futility and larks,
to the bright crustaceans of the oversky.

POETICS AGAINST THE ANGEL OF DEATH

I am sorry to speak of death again
(some say I'll have a long life)
but last night Wordsworth's 'Prelude'
suddenly made sense—I mean the measure,
the elevated tone, the attitude
of private Man speaking to public men.
Last night I thought I would not wake again
but now with this June morning I run ragged to elude
The Great Iambic Pentameter
who is the Hound of Heaven in our stress
because I want to die
writing Haiku
or, better,
long lines, clean and syllabic as knotted bamboo. Yes!

RILKE

Rilke, I speak your name I throw it away
with your angels, your angels, your statues
and virgins, and a horse in a field held
at the hoof by wood. I cannot take so much
tenderness, tenderness, snow falling like lace
over your eyes year after year as the poems
receded, roses, the roses, sinking in snow
in the distant mountains.

Go away with your women to Russia or take them
to France, and take them or don't the poet is
in you, the spirit, they love that.
(I met one in Paris, her death leaning outward,
death in all forms. The letters you'd sent her,
she said, stolen from a taxi.)

Rilke.
Clowns and angels held your compassion.
You could sit in a room saying nothing,
nothing. Your admirers thought you were there,
a presence, a wisdom. But you had to leave
everyone once, once at least. That was your
hardness.

This page is a shadowed hall in Duino Castle.
Echoes. The echoes.
I don't know why I'm here.

ESCHATOLOGY OF SPRING

Death, Judgement, Heaven, Hell,
and Spring. The Five Last Things,
the least of which I am, being in
the azaleas and dog-toothed violets
of the South of Canada. Do not tell me
this is a cold country. I am also in
the camellias and camas of early, of
abrupt birth.

We are shooting up for the bloody
judgement of the six o'clock news.
Quick, cut us out from the deadlines
of rotting newspapers, quick, for the
tiny skeletons and bulbs will tell you
how death grows and grows in Chile and
Chad. Quick, for the small bones pinch
me and insects divulge occult excrement
in the service of my hyacinth, my trailing
begonia. And if you catch me resting
beside the stream, sighing against
the headlines of this pastoral, take
up your gun, the flowers blossoming
from its barrel, and join this grief, this
grief: that there are lambs, elegant black-
footed lambs in this island's eschatology,
Beloved.

PRISON REPORT

The eye of Jacobo Timerman looks through the hole and sees
another eye looking through a hole.

These holes are cut into steel doors in prison cells in Argentina.

Both eyes are wary.
They disappear.

Timerman rests his cheek on the icy door,
amazed at the sense of space he feels—the joy.

He looks again: the other's eye is there,
then vanishes like a spider.

Comes back, goes, comes back.

This is a game of hide-and-seek.
This is intelligence with a sense of humour.
Timerman joins the game.

Sometimes two eyes meet at exactly the same moment.

This is music. This is love
playing in the middle of a dark night
in a prison in Argentina.

My name is Jacobo one eye says.
Other eye says something, but Jacobo can't quite catch it.

Now a nose appears in the vision-field
of Timerman. It rubs cold edges of the hole,
a love-rub for Jacobo.

This is a kiss, he decides, a caress,
an emanation of solitude's tenderness.

In this prison everything is powered electrically
for efficiency and pain. But tenderness is also
a light and a shock.

An eye, a nose, a cheek resting against a steel door
in the middle of the dark night.
These are parts of bodies, parts of speech,
saying,
I am with you.

TREBLINKA GAS CHAMBER

'Klostermayer ordered another count of the children. Then their stars were snipped off and thrown into the center of the courtyard. It looked like a field of buttercups.'

—A Field of Buttercups *by Joseph Hymans*

fallingstars
       'a field of'
              buttercups'

           yellow stars
               of David
                    falling

the prisoners
        the children
               falling

      in heaps
           on one another
                  they go down

Thanatos
     showers
          his dirty breath
               they must breathe
                      him in

      they see stars
           behind their
               eyes

David's
   'a field of
       buttercups'

       a metaphor
          where all that's
             left lies down

SEEKING SHAPE. SEEKING MEANING

Hot pursuit, or languorous. We are in. A blue lagoon
bird stands on one pale leg, a picture of reflection,
nothing ruffled. Waters lap, ingenious insects walk
on water; thoughts bloom like algae, fluorescent,
many-celled, liberated and dying in their own element.

           *   *   *

The syntax of deep structure composes on the harp,
strings along.

           *   *   *

Red hot spikes. Fire-walking.

* * *

Cadence in scene, in the seen, seeking out pattern,
finding where the eye catches, heart hooks, tangible
order, a cadence. Tantrums of tears at such pure
spirit, radiant things, on which the eyes close.

* * *

'Mind is shapely, Art is shapely.' Ginsbergian insight,
Allen afloat on his untidy chaos, his good humours. Ahoy!

* * *

Fragmentation: to understand the parts, reify certain
curious particulars to our habit of framing.
(Management techniques—precious jewels in the Swiss
        watch,
the Cretaceous period slotted between Jurassic and
Cenozoic. See chart under GEOLOGY. See geology under
the chart.

* * *

CORNFLOWERS & SAFFRON ROBES BELITTLE THE EFFORT

Ssh, sigh, silence is coming, the night time blues. Hark.
Ahem. Sir? I lift my arm, the wind chimes through my
holy raiment. Mesmeric bells reduce the flies to slum-
ber. Pajama party. The end of the Raj.

YOU HAVE MY APPROVAL

Well, thank you very much. The indices prick up their ears, they tabulate
    the prospects—
quick, a hit of doctrine. the poem expands its chest, looks you straight in
    the eye, knows
you for who you pretend to be, says, The game is up, Buster, let's get serious.

Instructions for the faint of heart

Turn the turtle over. Test its white stomach.
Find your island. Find the treasure.
Take short naps through the heat of the day.
Drink clean water only, if you can find it.
Build a wall—or not at all.
Lead your pretty shadow by the pretty hand.

Terrorist directives

Know the code.
Translate it into a foreign language. Any foreign language.

Memorize the Plan. Do not try to understand it.
Make a new plan. Make a list. A longer list.
Forget it.

Crash course in Chaos science; likewise Particle Physics.

Abscond with the Access to Information Act.
Advertise your whereabouts on national TV.

Call the hot-line. Say you're on your way with a crack
death squad.

Say your Now-I-lay-me's.

Have a drink on me.

LEONARD COHEN

(b. 1934)

Leonard Cohen's imagination was shaped not only by his Jewish heritage and the Catholic milieu of Montreal, but also by the literary values and antics of the Beat generation, whose bohemianism embodied anew the Blakean notion that the road of excess is the path to wisdom. His earliest poems in *Let Us Compare Mythologies* (1956), and *Spice-Box of Earth* (1961), which are witty, exuberant, and richly embroidered, reveal a fascination with eroticism and violence as means of spiritual transcendence, a theme that finds its fullest expression in his novel *Beautiful Losers* (1966). *Flowers for Hitler* (1964) announces a deepening and maturing of vision; the tone of joyous celebration gives way to darker imaginings. The poet descends morally and imaginatively into the fiery furnaces of Belsen and Auschwitz where, like Conrad's Marlow, he comes face to face with his own emptiness and his own potential for evil. At this point the poems move towards the greater simplicity of form delineated in 'Style', where Cohen hints at the potential for brotherhood and harmony that might be possible beyond the trappings of ego, culture, and nationalism. 'Well, you know, you get wiped out,' he said. 'And the deeper the wipe-out, the deeper the reluctance to use ornament or to use any other faculties that brought you to the wipe-out.'

Parasites of Heaven (1966) and *The Energy of Slaves* (1972) give full expression to Cohen's rejection of many of the values and strategies of conventional poetry. The books consist mainly of anti-poems, gestures of refusal, indicating a belief that the act of writing may itself be a betrayal. By the time he had published *Parasites and Slaves*, Cohen had already become internationally known for his folksongs. He could afford to announce his demise as a writer; he may also have had serious doubts, given the demands of his musical career and the lessons to be learned in the public arena, about both his poetic talent and the efficacy of poetry as a means of communication. However, there is in Cohen's most serious pronouncements a redeeming degree of humour and self-mockery, so it is not surprising to find, after a six-year silence, that he published a new collection of poems called *Death of a Ladies' Man* (1978), a sort of dialogue of self and soul in which the poet and his alter ego debate the meaning of art, love, politics, and nation.

Sainthood and renunciation figure prominently in *Death of a Ladies' Man*, as they do in so many of Cohen's song lyrics.

What is a saint? A saint is someone who has achieved a remote human possibility. It is impossible to say what that possibility is. I think it has something to do with the energy of love. Contact with this energy results in the exercise of a kind of balance in the chaos of existence. A saint does not dissolve the chaos; if he did the world would have changed long ago. I do not think that a saint dissolves the chaos even for himself, for there is something arrogant and warlike in the notion of a man setting the universe in order. It is a kind of balance that is his glory. He rides the drifts like an escaped ski. His course is the caress of the hill. His track is a drawing of the snow in a moment of its particular arrangement with wind and rock. Something in him so loves the world that he gives himself to the laws of gravity and chance. Far from flying with the angels, he traces with the fidelity of a seismograph needle the state of the solid bloody landscape. His house is dangerous and finite, but he is at home in the world. He can love the shape of human beings, the fine and twisted shapes of the heart. It is good to have among us such men, such balancing monsters of love.

However, the writer of subtle psychoparables such as 'Story', 'You Have the Lovers', and 'The Stranger Song' often turns the interrogation lights on his own motivations and devices, producing a number of astonishing and hilarious prose pieces, such as 'How to Speak Poetry', which embodies as clear a statement as has been made of the dilemma of the modern artist. 'The bombs, the flame-throwers, and all the shit have destroyed more than just the trees and villages. They have destroyed the stage.' In the face of such reality, the poet must become a 'student of discipline', one who offers not advertisements for himself and his sensitivity, but 'data and the quiet organization of (his) presence'.

This advice recalls a comment Cohen made a decade earlier in an interview with Michael Harris in *Duel*:

I think that a decent man who has discovered valuable secrets is under some obligation to share them. But I think that the technique of sharing them is a great study. Now, you can reveal secrets in many ways. One way is to say this is the secret discovered. I think that this way is often less successful because when that certain kind of conscious mind brings itself to bear on this information,

it distorts it, makes it very inaccessible. Sometimes, it's just in the voice, sometimes just in the style, in the length of the paragraph; it's in the tone rather than in the message.

The sharing of valuable secrets has taken Cohen a considerable distance down the road to asceticism, which is another form of excess. As his career blossomed, his private life was characterized more and more by solitude, simplicity, and meditation. *Book of Mercy* (1984) is in the form of fifty prayers and incantations that recall the Old Testament Psalms, the Sermon on the Mount, and the tradition of religious verse that moves from Gerard Manley Hopkins through John Donne back to St John of the Cross. Cohen was a regular student of Buddhism for many years, but has recently left the ashram or monastery, commenting that he 'washed too many dishes' there.

Cohen is internationally renowned as a folk singer and performs regularly. His many albums include *Songs of Leonard Cohen* (1968), *Songs from A Room* (1969), *Songs of Love & Hate* (1971), *New Skin for the Old Ceremony* (1974), *The Best of Leonard Cohen* (1975), *Various Positions* (1984), *I'm Your Man* (1988), *The Future* (1992), and *Cohen Live* (1994).

Cohen was born in Westmount, a wealthy English-speaking enclave of Montreal, and studied at McGill University. He tried graduate studies for three weeks at Columbia, but returned to Montreal to read in clubs, write his unpublished novel *Ballet of Lepers*, and do a stint in the family clothing business. A Canada Council grant enabled him to travel to England, where he wrote *The Favourite Game* (1963), then to the island of Hydra in Greece, where he wrote much of his poetry and fiction. He returned to Montreal and New York to pursue his musical career, producing a series of highly acclaimed albums. He divides his time between Montreal, east of The Main, and California.

ELEGY

Do not look for him
In brittle mountain streams:
They are too cold for any god;
And do not examine the angry rivers
For shreds of his soft body
Or turn the shore stones for his blood;
But in the warm salt ocean
He is descending through cliffs
Of slow green water
And the hovering coloured fish
Kiss his snow-bruised body
And build their secret nests
In his fluttering winding-sheet.

STORY

She tells me a child built her house
one Spring afternoon,
but that the child was killed
crossing the street.

She says she read it in the newspaper,
that at the corner of this and this avenue
a child was run down by an automobile.

Of course I do not believe her.
She has built the house herself,
hung the oranges and coloured beads in the doorways,
crayoned flowers on the walls.
She has made the paper things for the wind,
collected crooked stones for their shadows in the sun,
fastened yellow and dark balloons to the ceiling.

Each time I visit her
she repeats the story of the child to me,
I never question her. It is important
to understand one's part in a legend.

I take my place
among the paper fish and make-believe clocks,
naming the flowers she has drawn,
smiling while she paints my head on large clay coins,
and making a sort of courtly love to her
when she contemplates her own traffic death.

I HAVE NOT LINGERED IN EUROPEAN MONASTERIES

I have not lingered in European monasteries
and discovered among the tall grasses tombs of knights
who fell as beautifully as their ballads tell;

I have not parted the grasses
or purposefully left them thatched.

I have not released my mind to wander and wait
in those great distances
between the snowy mountains and the fishermen,
like a moon,
or a shell beneath the moving water.

I have not held my breath
so that I might hear the breathing of God,
or tamed my heartbeat with an exercise,
or starved for visions.

Although I have watched him often
I have not become the heron,
leaving my body on the shore,
and I have not become the luminous trout,
leaving my body in the air.

I have not worshipped wounds and relics,
or combs of iron,
or bodies wrapped and burnt in scrolls.

I have not been unhappy for ten thousand years.
During the day I laugh and during the night I sleep.
My favourite cooks prepare my meals,
my body cleans and repairs itself,
and all my work goes well.

YOU HAVE THE LOVERS

You have the lovers,
they are nameless, their histories only for each other,
and you have the room, the bed and the windows.
Pretend it is a ritual.
Unfurl the bed, bury the lovers, blacken the windows,
let them live in that house for a generation or two.
No one dares disturb them.
Visitors in the corridor tip-toe past the long closed door,
they listen for sounds, for a moan, for a song:
nothing is heard, not even breathing.
You know they are not dead,
you can feel the presence of their intense love.
Your children grow up, they leave you,
they have become soldiers and riders.
Your mate dies after a life of service.
Who knows you? Who remembers you?
But in your house a ritual is in progress:
it is not finished: it needs more people.
One day the door is opened to the lovers' chamber.
The room has become a dense garden,
full of colours, smells, sounds you have never known.
The bed is smooth as a wafer of sunlight,
in the midst of the garden it stands alone.
In the bed the lovers, slowly and deliberately and silently,
perform the act of love.
Their eyes are closed,
as tightly as if heavy coins of flesh lay on them.
Their lips are bruised with new and old bruises.
Her hair and his beard are hopelessly tangled.
When he puts his mouth against her shoulder
she is uncertain whether her shoulder
has given or received the kiss.
All her flesh is like a mouth.
He carries his fingers along her waist
and feels his own waist caressed.
She holds him closer and his own arms tighten around her.
She kisses the hand beside her mouth.
It is his hand or her hand, it hardly matters,
there are so many more kisses.

You stand beside the bed, weeping with happiness,
you carefully peel away the sheets
from the slow-moving bodies.
Your eyes are filled with tears, you barely make out the lovers.
As you undress you sing out, and your voice is magnificent
because now you believe it is the first human voice
heard in that room.
The garments you let fall grow into vines.
You climb into bed and recover the flesh.
You close your eyes and allow them to be sewn shut.
You create an embrace and fall into it.
There is only one moment of pain or doubt
as you wonder how many multitudes are lying beside your body,
but a mouth kisses and a hand soothes the moment away.

AS THE MIST LEAVES NO SCAR

As the mist leaves no scar
On the dark green hill,
So my body leaves no scar
On you, nor ever will.

When wind and hawk encounter,
What remains to keep?
So you and I encounter,
Then turn, then fall to sleep.

As many nights endure
Without a moon or star,
So will we endure
When one is gone and far.

NOW OF SLEEPING

Under her grandmother's patchwork quilt
a calico bird's-eye view
of crops and boundaries
naming dimly the districts of her body
sleeps my Annie like a perfect lady

Like ages of weightless snow
on tiny oceans filled with light
her eyelids enclose deeply
a shade tree of birthday candles
one for every morning
until the now of sleeping

The small banner of blood
kept and flown by Brother Wind
long after the pierced bird fell down
is like her red mouth
among the squalls of pillow

Bearers of evil fancy
of dark intention and corrupting fashion
who come to rend the quilt
plough the eye and ground the mouth
will contend with mighty Mother Goose
and Farmer Brown and all good stories
of invincible belief
which surround her sleep
like the golden weather of a halo

Well-wishers and her true lover
may stay to watch my Annie
sleeping like a perfect lady
under her grandmother's patchwork quilt
but they must promise to whisper
and to vanish by morning—
all but her one true lover.

THE GENIUS

For you
I will be a ghetto jew
and dance
and put white stockings
on my twisted limbs
and poison wells
across the town

For you
I will be an apostate jew
and tell the Spanish priest
of the blood vow
in the Talmud
and where the bones
of the child are hid

For you
I will be a banker jew
and bring to ruin
a proud old hunting king
and end his line

For you
I will be a Broadway jew
and cry in theatres
for my mother
and sell bargain goods
beneath the counter

For you
I will be a doctor jew
and search
in all the garbage cans
for foreskins
to sew back again

For you
I will be a Dachau jew
and lie down in lime
with twisted limbs
and bloated pain
no mind can understand

STYLE

I don't believe the radio stations
of Russia and America
but I like the music and I like

the solemn European voices announcing jazz
I don't believe opium or money
though they're hard to get
and punished with long sentences
I don't believe love
in the midst of my slavery I
do not believe
I am a man sitting in a house
on a treeless Argolic island
I will forget the grass of my mother's lawn
I know I will
I will forget the old telephone number
Fitzroy seven eight two oh
I will forget my style
I will have no style
I hear a thousand miles of hungry static
and the old clear water eating rocks
I hear the bells of mules eating
I hear the flowers eating the night
under their folds
Now a rooster with a razor
plants the haemophilia gash across
the soft black sky
and now I know for certain

I will forget my style
Perhaps a mind will open in this world
perhaps a heart will catch rain
Nothing will heal and nothing will freeze
but perhaps a heart will catch rain
America will have no style
Russia will have no style
It is happening in the twenty-eighth year
of my attention
I don't know what will become
of the mules with their lady eyes
or the old clear water
or the giant rooster
The early morning greedy radio eats
the governments one by one the languages
the poppy fields one by one

Beyond the numbered band
a silence develops for every style
for the style I laboured on
an external silence like the space
between insects in a swarm
electric unremembering
and it is aimed at us
(I am sleepy and frightened)
it makes toward me brothers

THE MUSIC CREPT BY US

I would like to remind
the management
that the drinks are watered
and the hat-check girl
has syphilis
and the band is composed
of former SS monsters
However since it is
New Year's Eve
and I have lip cancer
I will place my
paper hat on my
concussion and dance

GOD IS ALIVE
From *Beautiful Losers*

God is alive. Magic is afoot. God is alive. Magic is afoot. God is afoot. Magic is alive. Alive is afoot. Magic never died. God never sickened. Many poor men lied. Many sick men lied. Magic never weakened. Magic never hid. Magic always ruled. God is afoot. God never died. God was ruler though his funeral lengthened. Though his mourners thickened Magic never fled. Though his shrouds were hoisted the naked God did live. Though his words were twisted the naked Magic thrived. Though his death was published round and round the world the heart did not believe. Many hurt men wondered. Many struck men bled. Magic never faltered. Magic always led. Many stones were rolled but God would not lie down. Many wild men lied. Many fat men listened. Though they offered stones Magic still was fed. Though they locked their coffers God was always served. Magic is afoot. God rules. Alive is afoot. Alive is in command. Many weak men hungered. Many strong men thrived. Though they boasted solitude God was at their side. Nor the dreamer in his cell, nor the captain on the hill. Magic is alive. Though his death was pardoned round and round the world the heart would not believe. Though laws were carved in marble they could not shelter men. Though altars built in parliaments they could not order men. Police arrested Magic and Magic went with them for Magic loves the hungry. But Magic would not tarry. It moves from arm to arm. It would not stay with them. Magic is afoot. It cannot come to harm. It rests in an empty palm. It spawns in an empty mind. But Magic is no instrument. Magic is the end. Many men drove Magic but Magic stayed behind. Many strong men lied. They only passed through Magic and out the other side. Many weak men lied. They came to God in secret and though they left him nourished they would not tell who healed. Though mountains danced before them they said that God was dead. Though his shrouds were hoisted the naked God did live. This I mean to whisper to my mind. This I mean to laugh with in my mind. This I mean my mind to serve till service is but Magic moving through the world, and mind itself is Magic coursing through the flesh, and flesh itself is Magic dancing on a clock, and time itself the Magic Length of God.

HOW TO SPEAK POETRY

Take the word butterfly. To use this word it is not necessary to make the voice weigh less than an ounce or equip it with small dusty wings. It is not necessary to invent a sunny day or a field of daffodils. It is not necessary to be in love, or to be in love with butterflies. The word butterfly is not a real butterfly. There is the word and there is the butterfly. If you confuse these two items people have the right to laugh at you. Do not make so much of the word. Are you trying to suggest that you love butterflies more perfectly than anyone else, or really understand their nature? The word butterfly is merely data. It is not an opportunity for you to hover, soar, befriend flowers, symbolize beauty and frailty, or in any way impersonate a butterfly. Do not act out words. Never act out words. Never try to leave the floor when you talk about flying. Never close your eyes and jerk your head to one side when you talk about death. Do not fix your burning eyes on me when you speak about love. If you want to impress me when you speak about love put your hand in your pocket or under your dress and play with yourself. If ambition and the hunger for applause have driven you to speak about love you should learn how to do it without disgracing yourself or the material.

What is the expression which the age demands? The age demands no expression whatever. We have seen photographs of bereaved Asian mothers. We are not interested in the agony of your fumbled organs. There is nothing you can show on your face that can match the horror of this time. Do not even try. You will only hold yourself up to the scorn of those who have felt things deeply. We have seen newsreels of humans in the extremities of pain and dislocation. Everyone knows you are eating well and are even being paid to stand up there. You are playing to people who have experienced a catastrophe. This should make you very quiet. Speak the words, convey the data, step aside. Everyone knows you are in pain. You cannot tell the audience everything you know about love in every line of love you speak. Step aside and they will know what you know because they know it already. You have nothing to teach them. You are not more beautiful than they are. You are not wiser. Do not shout at them. Do not force a dry entry. That is bad sex. If you show the lines of your genitals, then deliver what you promise. And remember that people do not really want an acrobat in bed. What is our need? To be close to the natural man, to be close to the natural woman. Do not pretend that you are a beloved singer with a vast loyal audience which has followed the ups and downs of your life to this very moment. The bombs, flame-throwers, and all the shit have destroyed more than just the trees and villages. They have also destroyed the stage. Did you think that your profession would escape the general destruction? There is no more stage. There are no more footlights. You are among the people. Then be modest. Speak the words, convey the data, step aside. Be by yourself. Be in your own room. Do not put yourself on.

This is an interior landscape. It is inside. It is private. Respect the privacy of the material. These pieces were written in silence. The courage of the play is to speak them. The discipline of the play is not to violate them. Let the audience feel your love of privacy even though there is no privacy. Be good whores. The poem is not a slogan. It cannot advertise you. It cannot promote your reputation for sensitivity. You are not a stud. You are not a killer lady. All this junk about the gangsters of love. You are students of discipline. Do not act out the words. The words die when you act them out, they wither, and we are left with nothing but your ambition.

Speak the words with the exact precision with which you would check out a laundry list. Do not become emotional about the lace blouse. Do not get a hard-on when you say panties. Do not get all shivery just because of the towel. The sheets should not provoke a dreamy expression about the eyes. There is no need to weep into the handkerchief. The socks are not there to remind you of strange and distant voyages. It is just your laundry. It is just your clothes. Don't peep through them. Just wear them.

The poem is nothing but information. It is the Constitution of the inner country. If you declaim it and blow it up with noble intentions then you are no better than the politicians whom you despise. You are just someone waving a flag and making the cheapest appeal to a kind of emotional patriotism. Think of the words as science, not as art. They are a report. You are speaking before a meeting of the Explorers' Club or the National Geographic Society. These people know all the risks of mountain climbing. They honour you by taking this for granted. If you rub their faces in it that is an insult to their hospitality. Tell them about the height of the mountain, the equipment you used, be specific about the surfaces and the time it took to scale it. Do not work the audience for gasps and sighs. If you are worthy of gasps and sighs it will not be from your appreciation of the event, but from theirs. It will be in the statistics and not the trembling of the voice or the cutting of the air with your hands. It will be in the data and the quiet organization of your presence.

Avoid the flourish. Do not be afraid to be weak. Do not be ashamed to be tired. You look good when you're tired. You look like you could go on forever. Now come into my arms. You are the image of my beauty.

D.G. JONES

(b. 1929)

Doug Jones was born in Bancroft, Ontario, and educated at McGill and Queen's Universities. He began writing as an undergraduate at McGill, where he won several prizes in creative writing. His early work was encouraged and ultimately published by Louis Dudek and Raymond Souster in magazines and in book form by Contact Press. Jones taught for many years in the English Department at the University of Sherbrooke, where he also served as an editor of *Ellipse*, a quarterly review designed to present the work of French- and English-Canadian writers in translation. He has published numerous books of poetry, including *Frost on the Sun* (1957), *The Sun Is Axeman* (1961), *Phrases from Orpheus* (1967), *Under the Thunder the Flowers Light Up the Earth* (1977), for which he received a Governor General's Award, *Balthazar and Other Poems* (1988), *A Thousand Hooded Eyes* (1990), *The Floating Garden* (1995), *Wild Asterisks in Cloud* (1997), and *Grounding Sight* (1999). In addition to review and critical articles, he has published a major analysis of image and theme in Canadian literature, *Butterfly on Rock* (1970, as well as translations of the poetry of Emile Martel and *Esprit de Corps: Québec Poetry of the Late Twentieth Century in Translation* (1997). He lives in North Hatley, Quebec. His poetry is discussed in E.D. Blodgett, *D.G. Jones and His Works* (1984).

There is a passage in *Butterfly on Rock* that is both an acute comment on the state of poetry in Canada and a useful summary of Jones's own poetic development: 'Having reached the Pacific, Canadians have begun to turn back on themselves, to create that added dimension Teilhard de Chardin calls the noosphere. . . . more than ever before, we have arrived at a point where we recognize, not only that the land is ours, but that we are the land's.' His first three volumes of poetry represent the stages in his own journey towards a 'true' landscape. In *Frost on the Sun* Jones was preoccupied with violence and disintegration, but only as poetic *subjects*, not as pressing realities that must find poetic resolution. In *The Sun Is Axeman*, however, a hostile nature is presented, one that is stunted and barren, mute and unsympathetic, unlike anything in the pastoral world of his early poems. Many of the poems present the unpredictable landscapes of dreams, landscapes that may splinter into betrayal and degeneration. In *Phrases from Orpheus* Jones experiences some sort of dark night of the soul, in which he asks: 'how shall I love / this earth, / which is my certain death?' Jones feels in all things a potential for violence, for disintegration, but he understands this at a psychological level to be a fundamental aspect of reality. In the later poems, myth functions not as ornament but as a controlling structural element; these poems are successful, not because they rewrite old myths, but because they reveal something of the poet's own world. In a letter to the present writer, Jones wrote: 'It is always a case of seeing through a conventional pattern or faded myth to something more immediate, vital or violent, and the renewal of the old or the creation of a new myth more adequate to that immediate experience.' *Orpheus* also includes a number of poems that grow out of very personal emotional experience, but experience that is controlled and manipulated. These poems are extremely well turned and yet they achieve a psychological depth that is quite remarkable.

As important as Jones's discovery of his own noosphere is his discovery of the means of giving it imaginative expression. In 'Clotheslines' he argued that 'the most common things / clothes hung out to dry / serve as well as kings / for your imagery.' The truth is that common things serve better than kings, as Jones discovers in *The Sun Is Axeman*. His early poetry had been too general, too abstract. The sense of logic, or intellect, was oppressive; too often sound and image were under severe strain from having to flesh out the skeleton of thought that held a poem together. However, in poems such as 'Portrait of Anne Hébert' and 'For Françoise Adnet', the images grow with the poem; they are not grafted on. The metaphors are organic, drawing the reader toward, rather than away from, the subject. Jones begins to use common objects quite naturally and his poetry makes its appeal through the senses, not merely through the intellect. He forsakes his idealized landscapes for the colour and texture of the actual world around him.

The search for a more precise and more immediate form of expression took Jones briefly to Pound and the Imagists and then to moderns such as Auden. In 'Portrait of Anne Hébert' the language is natural, the syntax simple and insistent, suggesting that the poet is too caught up in the making to

be fanciful or verbose. Here, and in the more complicated poems of *Phrases from Orpheus*, Jones is concerned with 'articulating a highly intense and obscure complex of feelings with extreme economy . . . with a certain simplicity and yet dramatic power.' One poem that seems to realize this difficult goal is 'These Trees Are No Forest of Mourners'; its sureness and simplicity are striking. The best of Jones's later poems have this sculptural quality; their success lies not in exhaustive detail, but rather in precision and economy of phrasing. We are left, as in the Chinese paintings that Jones admires, with only an image—and a space in which that image can grow.

In his later work, using his twin windows—his garden as a window on the natural world and television as a window on the outside world of society and politics—Jones combines metaphors of growth and decay, love and violence, to create poems that attain great lyrical intensity. He also continues to distance himself from logic and rhetorical persuasion, for reasons he makes clear in an interview with Philip Lanthier (*Matrix* #50):

More and more it's a question of leaps, a question of not getting locked in. You want to have some kind of rigour, but logical rigour, even metaphysical rigour, can be so bloody boring. . . . One of the images I have of a poem and of living is broken-field running. The thing is to keep going and not fall flat on your face with whatever comes up: bumps, holes, ups and downs, winds, logs. You keep going up and over and around. You negotiate all these things and to get there you also have to digest them. That's what people do in living.

PORTRAIT OF ANNE HÉBERT

The sunlight, here and there,
Touches a table

And a draught at the window
Announces your presence,

You take your place in the room
Without fuss,

Your delicate bones,
Your frock,
Have the grace of disinterested passion.

Words are arrayed
Like surgical instruments
Neatly in trays.

Deftly, you make an incision
Probing
The obscure disease.

Your sensibility
Has the sure fingers of the blind:

Each decision
Cuts like a scalpel
Through tangled emotion.

You define
The morbid tissue, laying it bare

Like a tatter of lace
Dark
On the paper.

BEAUTIFUL CREATURES BRIEF AS THESE
For Jay Macpherson

Like butterflies but lately come
From long cocoons of summer
These little girls start back to school
To swarm the sidewalks, playing-fields,
And litter air with colour.

So slight they look within their clothes,
Their dresses looser than the Sulphur's wings,
It seems that even if the wind alone
Were not to break them in the lofty trees,
They could not bear the weight of *things*.

And yet they cry into the morning air
And hang from railings upside down
And laugh, as though the world were theirs
And all its buildings, trees, and stones
Were toys, were gifts of a benignant sun.

FOR FRANÇOISE ADNET

It is that time of day, time
To chop the beans, to peel
Potatoes for the evening meal.

The fullness of time
Grows, at this hour,
Like the shadows on the crockery.

Mademoiselle's mauve gloves,
Alone, tell of the afternoon, the dried
Flowers, the delicate hands among the stalks.

For once things are what they are,
Until my little girl
Comes in from outdoors, the melting snow

Cool in her nostrils,
Sky, blue without clouds,
Behind her eyes.

But even these dissolve.
Fingering an orange
She lets her bare legs dangle.

Time is space, it glows
Like the white tablecloth,
The breadboard where I slice the onions.

The kitchen floats in my tears—
And the sun
In its brazier of urban trees.

THESE TREES ARE NO FOREST OF MOURNERS

They had dragged for hours.
The weather was like his body,
Cold, though May. It rained.

It had rained for three days—
In the grass, in the new leaves,
In the black boughs against the sky.

The earth oozed,
Like the bottom of the lake—
Like a swamp. They stared

At the drowned grass, at the leaves
That dripped in the water—aware
Of their own death, heavy

As the black boughs of the spruce
Moving in a current under the grey
Surface of the sky—aware

Of a supreme ugliness, which seemed
In its very indifference,
Somehow, to defy them:

The sodden body of the world
And of their only son.

Let them be. Oh hear me,

Though it cannot help you. They exist
Beyond your grief; they have their own
Quiet reality.

SUMMER IS A POEM BY OVID
For Michael Ondaatje

The fire falls, the night
Grows more profound.
The music is composed
Of clear chords
And silence. We become
Clear and simple as the forms
Of music; we are dumb
As water
Mirroring the stars.

Then summer is
Ovidian, and every sun
Is but a moth evolving
In the large gloom,
An excerpt from
Ars Amoris: flame
Is no more fleeting than the limbs
Of boy and girl: the conflagration
Is the same.

While the fire falls, and night
Grows more profound, the flesh,
The music and the flame
All undergo
Metamorphosis. The sounds
Of music make a close,
So with our several selves,
Together, until silence shall compose
All but the ashes in the pale dawn
And even those.

THE STREAM EXPOSED WITH ALL ITS STONES

The stream exposed with all its stones
Flung on a raw field
Is covered, once again,

With snow.

It is not hidden. It
Still flows.

The houses in the valley, standing
Motionless below,
Seem wrapped in sunlight like a snow

And are deceptive. Even stones
Deceive us.

The creator goes
Rampaging through our lives: winter
Is a masquerade.

I tell you
Nakedness is a disguise: the white
Is dark below.

The silence is the water's cry.

I tell you in those silent houses girls
Are dancing like the stones.

WORDS FROM THE AVIARY
For Monique

I would clothe you in feathers

You are too bare
in your long bones when the wind
sighs in the snow

You are a movement of birds

I would clothe you in voices
appellations, words
spare as the mirror of a young girl

or raw, and deliquescent as the crow's
cawing over chill fields

It is not a clothing but a call

of voices, nameless
gone into the still air

of the small birds that drift
above a river running among stones
in the Haute-Savoie

above the grasses of the steppe, and in the small
trees of the taiga

in the summer forest
north
along the Ottawa

I would surround you with a guard
of heron like a tall
smoke, I would surround you with a choir
of unrecorded waterbirds, exiguous
emerging from a wall

beyond the Nile

I would have you smile, and see the sun
arrested, rest among your bones

as glistening

you move within the garden of your names, diaphanous
innumerable

You walk as you have always walked
through desert yards, the cold
spaces where the night

sighs among the stars

the sunken orchard where the wind
sighs in the snow

You are an overture. You come

like a migration
like the first waters of the world
with their entelechy of flowers

And then your naked summer
silences my words

STUMBLESONG

sweet stuff, a warm body
in a cold bed, a dry
endearment coming in
from the wet snow

retirement a walk
in an April
blizzard, a childhood
of aches & pains

the short time to discover
nothing is gained
certainly—going for broke
the exception

which at least
can be shared, careering
into disaster with
love or distinction

not isolate with
surgical violence or garbage
on a street, just gently
coming apart

THE SHIP AS NAVIGATOR

five boards from a pine
precede
and outlast me

I have lived
with my elbows on this table

and pots and pans
and papers

idiot life! sun and moon
wars, computers
mini-skirts, long skirts, knee-length
—holy jeans

and lilies, day and species
nights
with a last Scotch

my raft amid the galaxies, themselves
fleeing like refugees

winters of Saint Denys-Garneau
blizzards
from all sides, some
appleblossom

night turns
on this coordinate

a kitchen chair, some cracked
refurbished boards

COVERING LETTER

i)

It is not possible to cover everything: axlerods,
axeheads (Minoan civilization, Brébeuf's necklace), action (the unities of, the rise and fall of
shares), acupuncture and acute accents, actuarial
statistics (and the General Services Tax on funerary
expenses), actually all we ask is that you cover
essentials—fig leaf, shroud ('I bought pearl necklace and earrings, which she liked to wear in her
last years'), credit card—an abstract, the General
Acceptance Corporation. Adieu, earth's bliss; adieu,
Aphrodite; adieu, the remains. That covers it.

ii)

My mother dead, I write letters to a phantom limb.

iii)

Hosta. Gone yellow. The plantain lily hit by frost. And rocks, a
half circle. In this grey margin of my world, a necklace remains, a
coronal. Hosta and rock. No, it is the ring, the heavy ring, the ring
broken. It is an old testament.

iv)

Florida, *venereal* soil. Hardly. She dies under palms in that sandy
spit. Some friendly bones at her side. Here it rains *in her memory*.
Hardly! Covers it rather in folios of wet leaves. That book *Le
Tombeau de*—her phantom tomb.

The frail wrist, looking to touch the friend, name
forgotten, yet known, dear Florida Cracker—wrist was right.
Remembering such a few touchings across a continent of life.
Remains here a bracelet . . . about the absent bone.

vi)

Heavy soils and rock, remember thee. Like a strange language. In the other country. You touched, uncovered, bones in the cold parts, between river and rock face, rain turning to snow. Without epitaph.

vii)

No I.D. Here, which is again elsewhere. This bracelet is broken, is woman's, is earth's, is nameless. She has slipped all covering letters.

viii)

Coronal.

ALDEN NOWLAN

(1933–1983)

Alden Nowlan has chronicled movingly and convincingly the harshness and hypocrisy of life in the Maritimes. His poems tell of the repressions that are a part of that heritage. 'I am a product,' he says, 'of a culture that fears any display of emotion and attempts to repress any true communication.' Like Souster, he is moved by his immediate environment, especially by economic conditions that grind down the human spirit. He is a poet of the underprivileged. 'In my childhood and early youth I experienced the kind of poverty that scarifies and warps the soul.' His is a dark world indeed, a world brutalized by poverty, ignorance, fear, greed, and lust. Anyone familiar with the fictional world of Hugh MacLennan's *Each Man's Son* or David Adams Richards' Miramichi novels will recognize Nowlan's landscapes at once.

Poetry for Nowlan was a means of establishing communication; like the atheist's prayer, it was a 'reaching out in fear and gentleness'. He can write of violence, loneliness, and despair with great compassion. In 'Britain Street' he tells of the unhappy conditions between parents and children in the depressed areas, 'where the very names / of their young were curses'. In this climate of brutality and hatred, the poet reclaims the abused, debased names and restores to them some dignity; he gives them a newer, more humane context, invests them with beauty and feeling. Though not a moralist, he is capable of fine moral discriminations, as in 'In Those Old Wars', where he reflects on the debasing effects of power and the (sometimes) ennobling effects of defeat. His attitude towards his own serious illness was typical:

When I was in hospital, every time that I was operated on I thought I was going to die. The thing I was worried about after worrying about what would become of my wife and son was how much I wanted to write—how much time I'd wasted when I could have been writing. Every time I went down in the elevator to get operated on, I thought ... how many more things I wanted to say. For that reason, my illness was good for my writing. As Nietzsche says, 'What does not kill me, strengthens me.'

Nowlan claimed that his work as a journalist gave him a sense of writing for an audience. 'You learn a great respect for the audience when you do newspaper work,' he said. 'And, another thing, it made me very aware of people.' Not content to be a mere recorder of experience (from the outside), he tried to fathom the psychology that underlies experience, the relation between the feeling and the act. He brought to poetry the novelist's gift of characterization, the capacity to embody a feeling or idea in an image of action. 'I don't like hypocrisy and I don't like fakes,' he said in typical fashion. 'I think the most important division in the world is between the people who are real and the people who are fakes.' Journalism also left its mark on his style. He wrote with a disarming directness and simplicity, as if he had time for neither fakes nor literary games. The pressure to 'get things said' seemed to preclude rhetoric, ornament. As he explained in 'And He Wept Aloud': 'oh, admit this, man, there is no point in poetry / if you withhold the truth / once you've come by it.'

The naturalness of Nowlan's diction, his ear for the nuances of the speaking voice, the rightness of his enjambment—these things speak for the sincerity of his desire to offer his truth in the simplest, most unadorned manner possible. As Robert Bly suggests in the prefatory note to *Playing the Jesus Game*, Nowlan is a poet entangled not in words, but in the universe. 'Human feeling is all that counts,' he said. 'To hell with literature . . . it's a kind of reassurance that there are people out there, listening. Makes me sort of visualize my poems wandering all over the place tapping people on the shoulder and saying: "Hi there, I'm Alden Nowlan, who are you?" ' To the charge that he was a regionalist, Nowlan replied: 'I don't write about Maritime people in capital letters, as if they were some special species. I have certain feelings and responses—I could well have these same feelings and responses if I lived in Montreal, but I'd write about them in a different way, simply because I'd have a different experience and see different things if I lived in Montreal.' Nowlan's portrayal of human emotions moved from the objective early poetry, which was often saved from lapsing into sentimentality by his sense of irony and wry humour, to a more personal, confessional poetry. Whatever his subject or manner, however, his unusual moral sympathy gave the poetry warmth and great appeal.

Nowlan was born in the Nova Scotia backwoods. He left school at twelve and worked as a farm labourer, a sawmill helper, the manager of a hillbilly orchestra, and the editor of the *Hartland Observer*, finally joining the *Telegraph-Journal* of Saint John, NB. Nowlan received a number of awards, including Canada Council grants, a Guggenheim fellowship, and a Governor General's Award (for *Bread, Wine and Salt*). He engaged in various freelance writing projects and was writer-in-residence at the University of New Brunswick from 1969 until his death.

Nowlan worked closely with theatre people in the Maritimes, writing a play called *Frankenstein* (1967) with Walter Learning, one called *One Dollar Woman*, and another about Sherlock Holmes. His published collections of poetry are *The Rose and the Puritan* (1958), *A Darkness in the Earth* (1959), *Wind in a Rocky Country* (1960), *Under the Ice* (1961), *The Things Which Are* (1962), *Bread, Wine and Salt* (1967), *the mysterious naked man* (1969), *Playing the Jesus Game* (1970), *Between Tears and Laughter* (1971), *I'm a Stranger Here Myself* (1974), *Smoked Glass* (1977), *I Might Not Tell Everybody This* (1982), *An Exchange of Gifts: Poems New and Selected* (1985), and *Selected Poems* (1996), edited by Patrick Lane and Lorna Crozier. Some of his short stories are collected in *Miracle at Indian River* (1968); an autobiographical novel, *Various Persons Named Kevin O'Brien*, appeared in 1973 and a second novel, *The Wanton Troopers*, appeared in 1988. *Road Dancers*, a gathering of journalistic pieces, was published in 1999. Nowlan's work remains widely read and is the subject of Michael Brian Oliver's *Poet's Progress: The Development of Alden Nowlan's Poetry* (1978).

BEGINNING

From that they found most lovely, most abhorred,
my parents made me: I was born like sound
stroked from the fiddle to become the ward
of tunes played on the bear-trap and the hound.

Not one, but seven entrances they gave
each to the other, and he laid her down
the way the sun comes out. Oh, they were brave,
and then like looters in a burning town.

Their mouths left bruises, starting with the kiss
and ending with the proverb, where they stayed;
never in making was there brighter bliss,
followed by darker shame. Thus I was made.

WARREN PRYOR

When every pencil meant a sacrifice
his parents boarded him at school in town,
slaving to free him from the stony fields,
the meagre acreage that bore them down.

They blushed with pride when, at his graduation,
they watched him picking up the slender scroll,
his passport from the years of brutal toil
and lonely patience in a barren hole.

When he went in the Bank their cups ran over.
They marvelled how he wore a milk-white shirt
work days and jeans on Sundays. He was saved
from their thistle-strewn farm and its red dirt.

And he said nothing. Hard and serious
like a young bear inside his teller's cage,
his axe-hewn hands upon the paper bills
aching with empty strength and throttled rage.

God Sour the Milk of the Knacking Wench

God sour the milk of the knacking wench
with razor and twine she comes
to stanchion our blond and bucking bull,
pluck out his lovely plumbs.

God shiver the prunes on her bark of chest,
who capons the prancing young.
Let maggots befoul her alive in bed,
and dibble thorns in her tongue.

For Nicholas of All the Russians

Wind in a rocky country and the harvest
meagre, the sparrows eaten, all the cattle
gone with the ragged troopers, winter coming,
mother will starve for love of you and wrapping
newest and least accustomed leave him squalling
out in the hills beside the skulls of foxes,
it cold and snow in the air. Stranger, knocking,
(now in this latter time even the poor
have bread and sleep on straw) what silly rumour
tells me your eyes are yellow and your lips
once rose trout-quick to suck a she-wolf's teats?

Our Lord, his peaked heir and hawk-faced daughters
are gone, although they say one severed finger
was found after the soldiers cleaned the cellar.

And He Wept Aloud,
So That the Egyptians Heard It

In my grandfather's house
for the first time in years,
houseflies big as bumblebees
playing crazy football
in the skim-milk-coloured windows,

leap-frogging from
the cracked butter saucer
to our tin plates of
rainbow trout and potatoes, catching the bread
on its way to our mouths,
    mounting one another
    on the rough deal table.

It was not so much their filth
as their numbers and persistence and—
oh, admit this, man, there's no point in poetry
if you withhold the truth
once you've come by it—
    their symbolism:
    Baal-Zebub,
god of the poor and outcast,

that enraged me, made me snatch the old man's
Family Herald, attack them like a maniac,
lay to left and right until the window sills
over-flowed with their smashed corpses,
until bits of their wings
stuck to my fingers,
until the room buzzed with their terror . . .

And my grandfather, bewildered and afraid,
came to help me:
    'never seen a year
    when the flies were so thick'
as though he'd seen them at all before I came!

His voice so old and baffled and pitiful
that I threw my club into the wood box and sat down
    and wanted to beg his forgiveness
as we ate on in silence broken only
by the almost inaudible humming
of the flies rebuilding their world.

BRITAIN STREET
Saint John, New Brunswick

This is a street at war.
The smallest children
battle with clubs
till the blood comes,
shout 'fuck you!'
like a rallying cry—

while mothers shriek
from doorsteps and windows
as though the very names
of their young were curses:

'Brian! Marlene!
Damn you! God damn you!'

or waddle into the street
to beat their own with switches:
'I'll teach you, Brian!
I'll teach you, God damn you!'

On this street
even the dogs
would rather fight
than eat.

I have lived here nine months
and in all that time
have never once heard
a gentle word spoken.

I like to tell myself
that is only because
gentle words are whispered
and harsh words shouted.

JULY 15

The wind is cool. Nothing is happening.
I do not strive for meaning. When I lie on my back
the wind passes over me, I do not feel it.
The sun has hands
like a woman, calling the heat
out of my body.
The trees sing. Nothing is happening.

When I close my eyes,
I hear the soft footsteps
of the grass. Nothing is happening.

How long have I lain here?
Well, it is still summer. But is it the same
summer I came?
I must remember
not to ask myself questions.
I am naked. Trees sing. The grass walks.
Nothing is happening.

THE MYSTERIOUS NAKED MAN

A mysterious naked man has been reported
on Cranston Avenue. The police are performing
the usual ceremonies with coloured lights and sirens.
Almost everyone is outdoors and strangers are conversing excitedly
as they do during disasters when their involvement is peripheral.
'What did he look like?' the lieutenant is asking.
'I don't know,' says the witness. 'He was naked.'
There is talk of dogs—this is no ordinary case
of indecent exposure, the man has been seen
a dozen times since the milkman spotted him and now
the sky is turning purple and voices
carry a long way and the children
have gone a little crazy as they often do at dusk
and cars are arriving
from other sections of the city.
And the mysterious naked man

is kneeling behind a garbage can or lying on his belly
in somebody's garden
or maybe even hiding in the branches of a tree,
where the wind from the harbour
whips at his naked body,
and by now he's probably done
whatever it was he wanted to do
and he wishes he could go to sleep
or die
or take to the air like Superman.

FOR CLAUDINE BECAUSE I LOVE HER

Love is also
my finding this house
emptier than a stranger
ever could.

Is it the sound of your movements
enlivening the chairs
although I hear nothing, is it the weight
of your small body moving the house
so little no machine
could ever assess it,
though my mind knows,
is it some old
wholly animal instinct
that fills every room with you,
gently, so I am aware of it only

when I come home
and there is nothing here.

YPRES: 1915

The age of trumpets is passed, the banners hang
like dead crows, tattered and black,
rotting into nothingness on cathedral walls.

In the crypt of St Paul's I had all the wrong thoughts,
wondered if there was anything left of Nelson
or Wellington, and even wished
I could pry open their tombs and look,
then was ashamed
of such morbid childishness, and almost afraid.

I know the picture is as much a forgery
as the Protocols of Zion, yet it outdistances
more plausible fictions: newsreels, regimental histories,
biographies of Earl Haig.
    It is always morning
and the sky somehow manages to be red
though the picture is in black and white.
There is a long road over flat country,
shell holes, the debris of houses,
a gun carriage overturned in a field,
the bodies of men and horses,
but only a few of them and those
always neat and distant.
    The Moors are running
down the right side of the road.
The Moors are running
in their baggy pants and Santa Claus caps.
The Moors are running.
    And their officers,
Frenchmen who remember
Alsace and Lorraine,
are running backwards in front of them,
waving their swords, trying to drive them back,
weeping
  at the dishonour of it all.
The Moors are running.
And on the left side of the same road,
the Canadians are marching
in the opposite direction.

The Canadians are marching
in English uniforms behind
a piper playing 'Scotland the Brave'.

The Canadians are marching
in impeccable formation,
every man in step.

The Canadians are marching.

And I know this belongs
with Lord Kitchener's mustache
and old movies in which the Kaiser and his general staff
seem to run like the Keystone Cops.

That old man on television last night,
a farmer or fisherman by the sound of him,
revisiting Vimy Ridge, and they asked him
what is was like, and he said,
There was water up to our middles, yes
and there was rats, and yes
there was water up to our middles
and rats, all right enough,
and to tell you the truth
after the first three or four days
I started to get a little disgusted.
Oh, I know they were mercenaries
in a war that hardly concerned us.
I know all that.

Sometimes I'm not even sure that I have a country.

But I know they stood there at Ypres
the first time the Germans used gas,
that they were almost the only troops
in that section of the front
who did not break and run,
who held the line.

Perhaps they were too scared to run.
Perhaps they didn't know any better
—that is possible, they were so innocent,
those farmboys and mechanics, you have only to look
at old pictures and see how they smiled.

Perhaps they were too shy
to walk out on anybody, even Death.
Perhaps their only motivation
was a stubborn disinclination.

Private MacNally thinking:
You squareheaded sons of bitches,
you want this God damn trench
you're going to have to take it away
from Billy MacNally
of the South End of Saint John, New Brunswick.

And that's ridiculous, too, and nothing
on which to found a country.
                              Still
It makes me feel good, knowing
that in some obscure, conclusive way
they were connected with me
and me with them.

THE BROADCASTER'S POEM

I used to broadcast at night
alone in a radio station
but I was never good at it,
partly because my voice wasn't right
but mostly because my peculiar
metaphysical stupidity
made it impossible
for me to keep believing
there was somebody listening
when it seemed I was talking
only to myself in a room no bigger
than an ordinary bathroom.
I could believe it for a while
and then I'd get somewhat
the same feeling as when you
start to suspect you're the victim
of a practical joke.

So one part of me
was afraid another part
might blurt out something
about myself so terrible
that even I had never until
that moment suspected it.
                    This was like the fear
of bridges and other
high places: Will I take off my glasses
and throw them
into the water, although I'm
half-blind without them?
Will I sneak up behind
myself and push?
                    Another thing:
as a reporter
I covered an accident in which a train
ran into a car, killing
three young men, one of whom
was beheaded. The bodies looked
boneless, as such bodies do.
More like mounds of rags.
And inside the wreckage
where nobody could get at it
the car radio
was still playing.
                    I thought about places
the disc jockey's voice goes
and the things that happen there
and of how impossible it would be for him
to continue if he really knew.

ELI MANDEL

(1922–1992)

Eli Mandel was born in Estevan, Saskatch-ewan, and lived in that province until he joined the Army Medical Corps in 1943 and went overseas. When he returned from the war, he completed an MA from the University of Saskatchewan and taught at the Collège Militaire Royale de St Jean. He completed a Ph.D. in English at the University of Toronto, taught at the University of Alberta, and became a Professor in the Fine Arts and Humanities Departments at York University. His first poems were published in *Trio* (1954) with those of Gael Turnbull and Phyllis Webb. His numerous published books of poetry include *Fuseli Poems* (1960); *Black and Secret Man* (1964); *An Idiot Joy* (1967), for which he received a Governor General's Award; *Crusoe: Poems Selected and New* (1973); *Stony Plain* (1973); *Out of Place* (1977); *Life Sentence* (1981); *Dreaming Backwards: The Selected Poetry of Eli Mandel, 1954–1981* (1981), and *The Family Romance* (1986). Mandel was also an important critic and anthologist, who had an unusual talent for critical synthesis. He published *Criticism: The Silent Speaking Word*, (1966), a series of broadcasts for the CBC, *Contexts of Canadian Criticism* (1971), *Another Time* (1977), a collection of essays on Canadian poetry, and with co-editor David Tarus *A Passion for Identity: Introduction to Canadian Studies* (1987). He edited *Poetry '62* (with Jean-Guy Pilon), *Five Modern Canadian Poets* (1970) and *Poets of Contemporary Canada: 1960–1970* (1972).

Mandel's early poetry was admired for its use of classical mythology as a means of exploring experience obliquely. His 'Mino-taur Poems' and many of the Fuseli poems were written under the critical inspiration of Northrop Frye and the poetic example of James Reaney and Jay Macpherson. The early poems, though they are well-turned, polished pieces, often lack conviction, as if the weight of the traditional masks weakens, or stifles, the poet's own voice. In all of these poems there is a lyrical poet caged and threatening to break out. In *Black and Secret Man* Mandel becomes more personal, more inward. He was, to use his own definition of the modern poet, a man in search of him-self; and his voyage of discovery takes him into difficult, troubled waters. He wandered through the ranks of his own ghosts, rifled his personal files of guilt and suffering, dis-covering in the process new and exciting materials.

The form of Mandel's verse changed rad-ically over the years. It moved from a rational ordering of materials in the direction of fragmentation and logical discontinuity, from language that is heavily rhetorical to a more colloquial idiom. Gradually he left behind 'the poise and thrust of speech' that 'gleams like polished steel' for a rougher, more halting, though possibly incoherent, form of expression. Some of his later poems echo the last speeches of Samuel Beckett's characters in combining grunts, non sequiturs, and erratic description with philosophical profundities and lyrical outpourings. Mandel read and absorbed the critical theories of George Steiner in *Language and Silence*. As a Jew, a writer, and an academic, he was in a natural position to understand the limitations of rational discourse and also the dangers inherent in the indiscriminate use of language. Although his poetic explorations of these themes were sometimes too self-conscious and academic, his later directions were always challenging. The Auschwitz poem, for example, is a powerful rendering of the intellectual and verbal disintegration that accompanies extreme psychic shock, as well as being a profound comment on the labyrinthine nature of moral perception.

Like Atwood, Mandel was fond of perceptual tricks, of unexpected shifts in tone or diction or point of view that startle the reader into consciousness, although his verse always seems more personal and affective. Atwood, like Flaubert's ideal artist, is everywhere felt but seldom seen in much of her verse; Mandel, on the other hand, is a poet who is both felt *and* seen. He does not use alienating devices to refine himself out of existence but to give another dimension to his poetry. In a poem such as 'Pictures in an Institution' he claims to reject his Greek and Anthropology, his second-hand textbook knowledge, for the raw materials of memory. 'I take, / brutal to my thoughts, these lives, defy / your taste in metaphor', he says. The three self-consciously comic and anti-poetic 'notices' in the poem seem at first designed to conceal the poet's embarrassment at the deeply personal nature of the materials. Nevertheless it is well to remember that poets are good liars, creatures with a 'forked tongue', to use Mandel's phrase; thus the 'notices' in the poem may also be regarded as devices calculated to heighten the personal emphasis by trying to call attention away from it to the banal or the merely comic. That such questions should be raised at all is a fair indication that Mandel was successful in his efforts to create the illusion of fact. Mandel would no doubt have agreed with Frederick Philip Grove's view that the artist's concern is not with fact but with truth.

For Mandel, the poet is a paradoxical creature, one who partakes of the divine but who also needs to be carefully watched like the wizards, thieves, hunchbacks, and idiots that inhabit his poetic world. The poet, like Houdini, is an escape artist, continually seeking newer and more difficult emotional and verbal nets or mazes to escape from, because he is most alive during those moments of struggle, of challenge. 'I am crazed by poetry,' Mandel admits; but he means the kind of madness that is truly sane, that demands the experience of bondage in order to understand the meaning of liberty. He describes himself as a man 'reeling with messages' and there is in his verse a kind of apocalyptic frenzy, or passionate intensity, that reminds one at times of Layton, at times of Yeats.

THIEF HANGING IN BAPTIST HALLS

After a Sculpture by George Wallace

Amid the congratulations of summer,
polite vegetation, deans, a presbyterian sun,
brick minds quaintly shaped in gothic and glass,
here where the poise and thrust of speech
gleams like polished teak
I did not expect to see myself.

But there he hangs
shrugging on his huge lines,
soft as a pulped fruit or bird
in his welded soft suit of steel.

I wish he would not shrug
and smile weakly at me
as if ashamed that he is hanging there,
his dean's suit fallen off, his leg cocked
as if to run
or (too weak, too tired, too undone)
to do what can be done
about his nakedness.

Why should he hang there,
my insulting self, my deanship, all undone?

He dangles while the city bursts in green and steel,
black flower in the mouth of speech:
the proud halls reel,
gothic and steel melt in the spinning sun.

THE MEANING OF THE I CHING

I

unopened
       book of old men
       orange-blossom book
              before me
you were
       how could you contain me?
do you not see I am the mouths
of telegraphs and cemeteries?
my mother groaned like the whole
of Western Union to deliver
my message
        and yelling birthdays
that unrolled from my lungs
like ticker-tape for presidents

about to be murdered
                     I sped
on a line that flew
to the vanishing point of the west

before I was
             you were
unopened book
               do not craze me
with the odour of orange-blossom

do not sit there
like smiling old men

     how could you contain me?

II

under my fingers words form themselves
it's crazy to talk of temples in this day
but light brightens on my page
like today moving against the wooden house
all shapes change and yet stay
as if they were marble in autumn
as if in the marbled yellow autumn
each western house becomes a shrine
stiff against the age of days
under my fingers stiffly formed

one cannot be another, I cry,
let me not be crazed by poetry
I will walk in streets that vanish
noting peculiar elms like old women
who will crash under the storm of sun
that breaks elm, woman, man
into a crumble of stump and bark
until the air is once more clear
in the sane emptiness of fall

III

my body speaks to me
as my arms say: two are one
as my feet say: earth upon earth
as my knees say: bow down, unhinge yourself
as my cells say: we repeat the unrepeatable

the books speaks: arrange yourself in the form
                  that will arrange you

before I was: colours that hurt me
                  arranged themselves in me

before I was: horizons that blind me
                  arranged themselves in me

before I was: the dead who speak to me
                  arranged themselves in me

IV

I am the mouths
of smiling old men

there rises from me
the scent of orange-blossoms

I speak in the words
of the ancient dead
arranged
in the raging sun

in the stiffening age of days

and in the temple of my house

one becomes another
I am crazed by poetry

HOUDINI

I suspect he knew that trunks are metaphors,
could distinguish between the finest rhythms
unrolled on rope or singing in a chain
and knew the metrics of the deepest pools

I think of him listening to the words
spoken by manacles, cells, handcuffs,
chests, hampers, roll-top desks, vaults,
especially the deep words spoken by coffins

escape, escape: quaint Harry in his suit
his chains, his desk, attached to all attachments
how he'd sweat in that precise struggle
with those binding words, wrapped around him
like that mannered style, his formal suit

and spoken when? by whom? What thing first said
'there's no way out'?; so that he'd free himself,
leap, squirm, no matter how, to chain himself again,
once more jump out of the deep alive
with all his chains singing around his feet
like the bound crowds who sigh, who sigh.

PICTURES IN AN INSTITUTION

I

Notice: all mirrors will be covered
            the mailman is forbidden to speak
            professors are confined to their offices
            faculties no longer exist.

II

I speak of what I know,
how uncle Asher, spittle on his lips,
first typed with harvest hands the fox
across a fence and showing all good men

come to their country's aid rushed off to Israel
there to brutalize his wife and son

how step-grandfather Barak wiped
sour curds out of his curly beard
before he roared the Sabbath in my ears
what Sara, long his widow, dreamed
the night she cried: God, let him die at last,
thinking perhaps of Josef who had lost
jewels in Russia where the Cossack rode
but coughed his stomach out in Winnipeg

Your boredom does not matter. I take,
brutal to my thoughts, these lives, defy
your taste in metaphor; the wind-break
on the farm that Barak plowed to dust
makes images would ruin public poetry.

The rites of love I knew:
how father cheated brother, uncle, son,
and bankrupt-grocer, that we might eat
wrote doggerel verse, later took his wife,
my mother, in the English way beside my bed.
Why would he put his Jewishness aside?
Because there was no bread?
                              Or out of spite
that doctors sliced his double rupture,
fingered spleen, and healed his bowel's ache?

Lovers lie down in glades, are glad.
These, now in graves, their headstones sunk,
knew nothing of such marvels, only God, his ways,
owning no texts of Greek or anthropology.

III

Notice: the library is closed to all who read
          any student carrying a gun
          registers first, exempt from fines,
          is given thirteen books per month,
          one course in science, one in math,

two options
                    campus police
will see to co-eds' underwear

IV

These names I rehearse:
                    Eva, Isaac,
Charley, Yetta, Max
                now dead
or dying or beyond my lies

till I reeling with messages
and sick to hold again their bitter lives
put them, with shame, into my poetry.

V

Notice: there will be no further communication
            lectures are cancelled
            all students are expelled
            the reading of poetry is declared a public
                                                crime

FROM THE NORTH SASKATCHEWAN

when on the high bluff discovering
the river cuts below
                send messages
we have spoken to those on the boats

I am obsessed by the berries they eat
all night odour of Saskatoon
and an unidentifiable odour
something baking
                the sun
never reaches the lower bank

I cannot read the tree markings

today the sky is torn by wind:
a field after a long battle
strewn with corpses of cloud

give blessings to my children
speak for us to those who sent us here
say we did all that could be done
we have not learned
what lies north of the river
or past those hills that look like beasts

ON THE 25TH ANNIVERSARY OF THE LIBERATION OF AUSCHWITZ: MEMORIAL SERVICES, TORONTO, YMHA, BLOOR & SPADINA, JANUARY 25, 1970

the name is hard
a German sound made out of
the gut guttural throat
y scream yell   ing open
voice mouth growl
                    and sweat

the only way out of Auschwitz
is through the chimneys
                    of course
that's second hand   that's told
again Sigmund Sherwood (Sobolewski)
twisting himself into that sentence
before us on the platform
                    the poem
shaping itself late in the after
noon later than it would be:

Pendericki's 'Wrath of God'
moaning electronic Polish theatric
the screen silent
                    framed by the name
looking away from/pretending not there
no   name   no not   name   no

Auschwitz
    in GOTHIC lettering
                the hall
a parody a reminiscence a nasty memory
the Orpheum in Estevan before Buck Jones
the Capital in Regina before Tom Mix
waiting for the guns
waiting for the cowboy killers
one two three
                Legionnaires
Polish ex-prisoners Association
Legions
        their medals their flags

so the procession, the poem gradually
insistent beginning to shape itself
with the others
                walked with them
into the YMHA Bloor & Spadina
thinking apocalypse shame degradation
thinking bones and bodies melting
thickening thinning melting bones and bodies
thinking not mine/speak clearly
the poet's words/Yevtyshenko at Baba-Yar

there   this January   snow
heavy wet   the wind   heavy wet
the street grey white slush melted concrete
bones and bodies melting slush
                            saw
with the others
                the prisoner
in the YMHA hall Bloor & Spadina
arms wax stiff body stiff unnatural
coloured face blank eyes
                        walked
with the others toward the screen
toward the pictures
                SLIDES
        this is mother
        this is father

                this is
                        the one who is
waving her arms like that
is the one who
                        like
I mean running with her breasts bound
ing
        running
                with her hands here and there
with her here and
                        there
hands
        that   that is

the poem becoming the body
becoming the faint hunger
ing body
                prowling
                        through
words the words words the words
opening   mouths   ovens
the generals smiling saluting
in their mythic uniforms god-like
generals uniforms with the black leather
with the straps and intricate leather
the phylacteries the prayer shawl
corsets and the boots and the leather straps
and the shining faces of the generals in their boots
and their stiff wax bodies their unnatural faces
and their blank eyes and their hands their stiff hands
and the generals in their straps and wax and stiff
staying standing
                melting bodies and thickening
                quick flesh on flesh handling
                hands

    the poem flickers, fades
the four Yarzeit candles guttering   one
    each four million lights dim
my words drift
                smoke from chimneys and ovens

a bad picture, the power failing
pianist clattering on and over and through
the long Saturday afternoon in the Orpheum
while the whitehatted star spangled cowboys
shot the dark men and shot the dark men
and we threw popcorn balls and grabbed
each other and cheered:
me jewboy yelling
for the shot town and the falling men
and the lights come on
and
with the others
standing in silence

the gothic word hangs
over us on a shroud–white screen
and we drift away
to ourselves
to the late Sunday *Times*

the wet snow
the city

a body melting

MARGARET AVISON

(b. 1918)

In 1941 Margaret Avison outlined a modest poetic: 'Literature', she wrote, 'results when: (a) every word is written in the full light of *all* the writer knows; (b) the writer accepts the precise limits of what he knows, i.e., distinguishes unerringly (while writing) between what he knows, and what he merely knows about, by reputation or reflected opinion.' This view, which she endorsed again as recently as 1962, reflects not only the seriousness with which she approaches her craft, but also her view of poetry as a vehicle of discovery. She is a philosophical poet who is moved to search for 'truths' that underlie the world we perceive with our senses. She is not a descriptive poet; she is interested, as she explains in 'Voluptuaries and Others', in 'that other kind of lighting up / That shows the terrain comprehended.' 'Nobody stuffs the world in at your eyes', she says in 'Snow'. 'The optic heart must venture: a jailbreak / And re-creation.' In order to make this jailbreak, the optic heart must see through the pollution of body and mind that produces a society of unconscious grey men and clapboard suburbs, and 'this communal cramp of understanding' ('The World Still Needs'). In a world where salesmanship is valued more than a fine ear, where limited imaginations triumph, the poet can find little that is worth her attention and respect. The landscapes of *Winter Sun* (1960) are bleak and imprisoning, like the landscapes of Eliot's early poetry; like Eliot also, Avison is often forced to search the past for significant

moments of illumination. Hence her interest in great men of science whose imaginative leaps have opened up new worlds of knowledge and experience. 'History makes the spontaneous jubilation at such moments less and less likely though,' she laments.

Avison's epistemological concerns have resulted in a number of poems that explore the nature of imaginative perception. Many poems in *Winter Sun* are characterized by rapid shifts of perspective, a kind of poetic equivalent of the use of multiple lenses and camera angles in film-making. To write in the 'full light of all the writer knows' involves dispensing with all formal notions of time and space. Like the reader of the stream-of-consciousness novel, the reader of Avison's poetry is often hard-pressed to find a centre of gravity, a fixed point of reference. It is as though, in this world of continuous change, the only certainty is the act of perception itself. Each new poem, for poet and reader alike, is analogous to the swimmer's moment at the whirlpool; if both 'dare knowledge', they will discover perhaps 'the silver reaches of the estuary'.

The austere winter terrain of her first book gives way to the gentler landscapes and warmer climates in *The Dumbfounding* (1966), marking a deepening of religious experience. There is also a reconciliation with the physical world that results in poetry at once more concrete and sensuous. These poems are characterized by a careful observation of minutiae, such as the faces of loiterers and the industry of ants; it is the work of a poet fully absorbed in actuality. Here Avison leaves behind most of the rhetorical and esoteric elements that trouble her earlier verse; her sensitivity to the subtleties of language now encompasses the sound of raindrops, 'letting the ear experience this / discrete, delicate / clicking.'

Margaret Avison was born in Galt, Ontario, and educated at the University of Toronto. She has been a librarian, a secretary, a research worker, a lecturer in English literature, and a social worker at a mission in downtown Toronto. She is one of the finest but least prolific poets in Canada. During the early forties and fifties she contributed to Sid Corman's *Origin*, along with Charles Olson, Denise Levertov, and Robert Creeley. Apart from giving occasional readings and participating in a writers' workshop at the University of British Columbia, she has remained at the edges of the literary arena in Canada. Avison is an enthusiastic supporter of other writers and has translated a number of poems from the Hungarian, which appear in *The Plough and the Pen: Writings from Hungary, 1930–1956* (1963), edited by Ilona Duczynska and Karl Polanyi. *Sunblue* appeared in 1978, *Winter Sun/The Dumbfounding: Poems 1940–1966* in 1982, *No Time* in 1989, *Selected Poems* in 1991, and *Not Yet But Still* in 1997. Her work has been discussed widely in journals and is now the subject of several critical studies, including Ernest Redekop, *Margaret Avison* (1970), David Mazoff, *Waiting for the Sun* (1989), David Kent, *Margaret Avison and Her Works* (1989), and David Kent (ed.), *Lighting Up the Terrain* (1987).

SNOW

Nobody stuffs the world in at your eyes.
The optic heart must venture: a jail-break
And re-creation. Sedges and wild rice
Chase rivery pewter. The astonished cinders quake
With rhizomes. All ways through the electric air
Trundle candy-bright disks; they are desolate
Toys if the soul's gates seal, and cannot bear,
Must shudder under, creation's unseen freight.
But soft, there is snow's legend: colour of mourning
Along the yellow Yangtze where the wheel
Spins an indifferent stasis that's death's warning.
Asters of tumbled quietness reveal
Their petals. Suffering this starry blur
The rest may ring your change, sad listener.

THE WORLD STILL NEEDS

Frivolity is out of season.
Yet, in this poetry, let it be admitted
The world still needs piano-tuners

And has fewer, and more of these
Gray fellows prone to liquor
On an unlikely Tuesday, gritty with wind,
When somewhere, behind windows,
A housewife stays for him until the
    Hour of the uneasy bridge-club cocktails
    And the office rush at the groceteria
    And the vesper-bell and lit-up buses passing
    And the supper trays along the hospital corridor,
Suffering from
Sore throat and dusty curtains.

Not all alone on the deserted boathouse
Or even on the prairie freight
(The engineer leaned out, watchful and blank
And had no Christmas worries
Mainly because it was the eve of April),
Is like the moment
When the piano in the concert-hall
Finds texture absolute, a single solitude
For those hundreds in rows, half out of overcoats,
Their eyes swimming with sleep.

From this communal cramp of understanding
Springs up suburbia, where every man would build
A clapboard in a well of Russian forest
With yard enough for a high clothesline strung
To a small balcony . . .
A woman whose eyes shine like evening's star
Takes in the freshblown linen
While sky a lonely wash of pink is still
Reflected in brown mud
Where lettuces will grow, another spring.

TO PROFESSOR X, YEAR Y

The square for civic receptions
Is jammed, static, black with people in topcoats
Although November
Is mean, and day grows late.

The newspapermen, who couldn't
Force their way home, after the council meeting
&c., move between windows and pressroom
In ugly humour. They do not know
What everybody is waiting for
At this hour
To stand massed and unmoving
When there should be—well—nothing to expect
Except the usual hubbub
Of city five o'clock.

Winter pigeons walk the cement ledges
Urbane, discriminating.

Down in the silent crowd few can see anything.
It is disgusting, this uniformity
Of stature.
If only someone climbed in pyramid
As circus families can . . .
Strictly, each knows
Downtown buildings block all view anyway
Except, to tease them,
Four narrow passages, and ah
One clear towards open water
(If 'clear'
Suits with the prune and mottled plumes of
Madam night).

Nobody gapes skyward
Although the notion of
Commerce by air is utterly
familiar

Many citizens at this hour
Are of course miles away, under
Rumpus-room lamps, dining-room chandeliers,
Or bound elsewhere.
One girl who waits in a lit drugstore doorway
North 48 blocks for the next bus
Carries a history, an ethics, a Russian grammar,
And a pair of gym shoes.

But the few thousand inexplicably here
Generate funny currents, zigzag
Across the leaden miles, and all suburbia
Suffers, uneasily.

You, historian, looking back at us,
Do you think I'm not trying to be helpful?
If I fabricated cause-and-effect
You'd listen? I've been dead too long for fancies.
Ignore us, hunched in these dark streets
If in a minute now the explosive
Meaning fails to disperse us and provide resonance
Appropriate to your chronicle.

But if you do, I have a hunch
You've missed a portent.
('Twenty of six.' 'Snow?—I wouldn't wonder.')

THE SWIMMER'S MOMENT

For everyone
The swimmer's moment at the whirlpool comes,
But many at that moment will not say
'This is the whirlpool, then.'
By their refusal they are saved
From the black pit, and also from contesting
The deadly rapids, and emerging in
The mysterious, and more ample, further waters.
And so their bland-blank faces turn and turn
Pale and forever on the rim of suction
They will not recognize.
Of those who dare the knowledge
Many are whirled into the ominous centre
That, gaping vertical, seals up
For them an eternal boon of privacy,
So that we turn away from their defeat
With a despair, not for their deaths, but for
Ourselves, who cannot penetrate their secret
Nor even guess at the anonymous breadth
Where one or two have won:
(The silver reaches of the estuary).

VOLUPTUARIES AND OTHERS

That Eureka of Archimedes out of his bath
Is the kind of story that kills what it conveys;
Yet the banality is right for that story, since it is not a
    communicable one
But just a particular instance of
The kind of lighting up of the terrain
That leaves aside the whole terrain, really,
But signalizes, and compels, an advance in it.
Such an advance through a be-it-what-it-may but take-it-not-
    quite-as-given locale:
Probably that is the core of being alive.
The speculation is not a concession
To limited imaginations. Neither is it
A constrained voiding of the quality of immanent death.
Such near values cannot be measured in values
Just because the measuring
Consists in that other kind of lighting up
That shows the terrain comprehended, as also its containing
    space,
And wipes out adjectives, and all shadows
    (or, perhaps, all but shadows).

The Russians made a movie of a dog's head
Kept alive by blood controlled by physics, chemistry, equip-
    ment, and
Russian women scientists in cotton gowns with writing tablets.
The heart lay on a slab midway in the apparatus
And went phluff, phluff.
Like the first kind of illumination, that successful experiment
Can not be assessed either as conquest or as defeat.
But it is living, creating the chasm of creation,
Contriving to cast only man to brood in it, further.

History makes the spontaneous jubilation at such moments
    less and less likely though,
And that story about Archimedes does get into public school
    textbooks.

PACE

'Plump raindrops in these
faintly clicking groves,
the pedestrian's place, July's
violet and albumen
close?'

'No. No. It is perhaps the conversational side-effect
among the pigeons; behold
the path-dust is nutmeg powdered and
bird-foot embroidered.'

> The silk-fringed hideaway
> permits the beechnut-cracking
> squirrels to plumply
> pick and click and
> not listen.

Pedestrians linger
striped stippled sunfloating
at the rim of the
thin-wearing groves

letting the ear experience this
discrete, delicate
clicking.

BLACK-WHITE UNDER GREEN:
MAY 18, 1965

This day of the leafing-out
speaks with blue power—
among the buttery grassblades
white, tiny-spraying spokes on the end of a weed-stem
and in the formal beds, tulips
and invisible birds inaudibly hallooing,
enormous, their beaks out wide, throats bulging, aflutter,
eyes weeping with speed

where the ultraviolets play and the scythe of the jets
flashes, carrying
the mind-wounded heartpale person, still a boy, a pianist, dying
            not
of the mind's wounds (as they read the x-rays) but
dying, fibres separated, parents ruddy and
American, strong, sheathed in the cold of
years of his differentness, clustered by two at
the nether arc of his flight.

This day of the leafing-out is one to remember
      how the ice crackled among
            stiff twigs. Glittering strongly
                  the old trees sagged. Boughs
            abruptly unsocketed. Dry, orange gashes
the dawn's fine snowing discovered and powdered over.

. . . to remember the leaves ripped loose
the thudding of the dark sky-beams
and the pillared plunging sea
shelterless. Down the centuries
a flinching speck
      in the white fury found of itself—and another—
the rich blood spilling, mother to child, threading
the perilous combers, marbling
the surges, flung
out, and ten-fingered, feeling for
the lollop, the fine-wired
music, dying skyhigh
still between carpets and the
cabin-pressuring windows
on the day of the leafing.

Faces fanned by
rubberized, cool air
are opened; eyes wisely
smile.
The tulips, weeds, new leaves
neither smile nor are scorning to smile nor uncertain,
dwelling in light.
A flick of ice, fire, flood,
far off from

the day of the leafing-out I knew
when knee-wagon small, or from my
father's once at a horse-tail silk-shiny
fence-corner or this
day when the runways wait
white in the sun, and a new leaf is
metal, torn out of that blue
afloat in the dayshine.

July Man

Old, rain-wrinkled, time-soiled, city-wise, morning man
whose weeping is for the dust of the elm-flowers
and the hurting motes of time,
rotted with rotting grape,
sweet with the fumes,
puzzled for good by fermented potato-
peel out of the vat of the times,
turned out and left
in this grass-patch, this city-gardener's place
under the buzzing populace's
square shadows, and the green shadows
of elm and ginkgo and lime
(planted for Sunday strollers and summer evening
families, and for those
bird-cranks with bread-crumbs
and crumpled umbrellas who come
while the dew is wet on the park, and beauty
is fan-tailed, gray and dove gray, aslant, folding in
from the white fury of day).

In the sound of the fountain
you rest, at the cinder-rim, on your bench.

The rushing river of cars
makes you a stillness, a pivot, a heart-stopping
blurt, in the sorrow
of the last rubbydub swig, the searing, and
stone-jar solitude lost, and yet,
and still—wonder (for good now) and
trembling:

The too much none of us knows
is weight, sudden sunlight, falling
on your hands and arms, in your lap,
all, all, in time.

IN A SEASON OF UNEMPLOYMENT

These green painted park benches are
all new. The Park Commissioner had them
planted.
Sparrows go on
having dust baths at the edge of
the park maple's shadow, just where
the bench is cemented down, planted
and then cemented.

    Not a breath moves
    this newspaper.
    I'd rather read it by the Lapland sun at midnight. Here we're
    bricked in early by a
    stifling dark.

On that bench a man in a
pencil-striped white shirt
keeps his head up and steady.

    The newspaper-astronaut says
    'I feel excellent under the condition of weightlessness.'
And from his bench a
scatter of black bands in the hollow-air
ray out—too quick for the eye—
and cease.

    'Ground observers watching him on a TV circuit said
    At the time of this report he
    was smiling,' Moscow ra-
    dio reported.
I glance across at him, and mark that
he is feeling
excellent too, I guess, and
weightless and
'smiling'.

OUGHTINESS OUSTED

God (being good) has let me know
no good apart from Him.
He, knowing me, yet promised too
all good in His good time.

This light, shone in, wakened a hope
that lives here-&-now—
strongly the wind in push and sweep
made fresh for all-things-new.

But o, how very soon a gloat
gulped joy: the kernel (whole)
I chaffed to merely *act* and *ought*—
'rightness' uncordial.

But Goodness broke in, as the sea
satins in shoreward sun
washing the clutter wide away:
all my inventeds gone.

WE THE POOR WHO ARE ALWAYS WITH US

The cumbering hungry
and the uncaring ill
become too many
try as we will.

Try on and on, still?
In fury, fly
out, smash shards? (And quail
at tomorrow's new supply,
and fail anew to find and smash the why?)

It is not hopeless.
One can crawling move
too there, still free to love
past use, where none survive.

And there is reason in
the hope that then can shine
when other hope is none.

WORD: RUSSETS

Whoever longs for spring to come,
be stayed by winter's hamper-hued
but choicest—russet apples.

Though it still feel iron hard
its seeds are black, its juices sweet.

Aroma? in the seeds?
There is a fragrance of the one-day flower;
later, a tang of fruit; sharper in peel.
But—seeds?

Where else is the aroma hid?
and how much more of good
sense, anticipated,
or understood.

GWENDOLYN MacEWEN

(1941–1987)

Gwendolyn MacEwen rejected self-indulgent, therapeutic poetry and the 'terribly cynical and "cool" poetry written today'. She believed that the poet can and must say things; and she wrote with the conviction that she had discovered things sayable, and worth saying. 'I write basically to communicate joy, mystery, passion,' she said, '. . . not the joy that naïvely exists without knowledge of pain, but that joy which arises out of and conquers pain. I want to construct a myth.'

MacEwen's poetry might well be discussed in terms of the peculiar ground it inhabits between the 'realists' and the 'myth-makers' in Canadian poetry. From the beginning she repudiated the actual world for one that is ancient and mythic, believing that imagination can reconcile the antinomies in life. 'I believe there is more room inside than outside', she says in the introduction to *A Breakfast for Barbarians*. 'And all the diversities which get absorbed can later work their way out into fantastic things, like hawk-training, IBM programming, mountain-climbing, or poetry.' Like Blake and Yeats, she drew her inspiration from things occult, mystical, rather than from traditional mythology. She was most alive to the myth and ritual contained in ordinary experience; her motorcycle Icarus bears little resemblance to the original. Her landscape and figures are mostly dream-like, not bound by normal conventions of space and time; her characters are symbolic, their movements ritualistic.

'I am involved with writing as a total profession, not as an aesthetic pursuit,' she said. 'My prime concern has always been with the raw materials from which literature is derived, not with literature as an end in itself.' Of course one of the primary sources of raw material for the writer is literature itself. MacEwen had long been preoccupied with the figure of the artist, whether Egyptian scribes 'who drew / eyes right into their hieroglyphs' or the solitary figure of the dancer. As she says in 'Finally Left in the Landscape', 'Yet still I journey to this naked country / to see a form which dances in the sand. / This is my chosen landscape.'

She chose this landscape, but not without certain misgivings, as she suggests in 'Poems in Braille'. Here she expresses the conflict she feels between art and life, between the world of names and the world of things, between dance and action. For her, as for the Platonist, things are but the shadows of a real world. Words, the names we give to things, are more real because they are our attempt to describe the other-worldliness of things; they are the windows through which we view reality. However attractive this landscape, the poet cannot help but doubt its sufficiency at times. MacEwen is aware that the whole of the message may not be contained in the medium, that it may be found in the very *things* she eschews. 'I do not read the long cabbala of my bones / truthfully', she admits. She asks to follow Wenceslas, who could behold a peasant gathering fuel and be moved and involved in that experience—that is, see it in terms of itself. 'I should read all things like braille in this season', she concludes: 'with my fingers I should read them / lest I go blind in both eyes reading with / that other eye the final hieroglyph.'

Although her usual method was to begin with names, to decode language for what it may reveal about the human condition, MacEwen appears, in *The Shadow-Maker*, to be moving more in the direction of realism. One poem is a comic exaggeration of an encounter with a fool who abuses language profoundly on a train between Fredericton and Halifax; another is a reflective account of actual experiences and impressions during travel. In terms of poetic technique, MacEwen resembles the incantatory and prophetic Yeats, who claimed to have 'tried to make the language of poetry coincide with that of passionate, normal speech', to have searched for 'a powerful and passionate syntax'. Although she emphasizes the passionate more than the normal aspect of speech, she often combines, like Yeats, the oracular and the vernacular in a single poem. 'O baby, get me out of Egypt', she writes in 'Cartaphilus'. 'An ancient slang speaks through me like that.' She employs the dramatic gesture and direct speech ('listen—there was this boy, Manzini') of the actor or storyteller who is intent upon delivering his message. It is a spoken poetry, a poetry of chant or incantation. MacEwen had the habit of reciting her own poetry from memory; and the ritual was quite spellbinding. Hers was a passionate plea for life, for beauty. 'To live consciously is holy', she said. The conscious man will not be one-sided; he will find a balance between his passion and his reason, between 'the complex dance of fire and blood' and 'the accurate self'.

Gwendolyn MacEwen was born in Toronto. She first published poetry when she was fifteen, in the *Canadian Forum*. At eighteen she left school to take up a full-time career as a writer. After her Canada Council grant in 1965 to research a historical novel in Egypt, she received the CBC New Canadian Writing Contest Award (1965), the Borestone Mountain Poetry Award, and a Governor General's Award for *The Shadow-Maker* (1969). She translated, prepared plays and talks for radio, read poetry in universities and schools, and was writer-in-residence at the University of Toronto in 1986. She died in November 1987. As Rosemary Sullivan suggests in her moving and award-winning biography, *Shadow Maker: The Life of Gwendolyn MacEwen* (1995), MacEwen suffered greatly from her mother's mental illness and her father's alcoholism and self-destructiveness: 'And yet I think, how curious it is that as children we serve as defence attorneys for our parents. Gwen could never tell her father of her feelings of hurt, anger, and betrayal, but the cost of hiding would be high—throughout her life she would accept behaviour from others, particularly from men, that was distressful and exploitive. Instead, this young eighteen-year-old turned her rage upon reality itself.'

Her publications include *Selah* (1961) and *The Drunken Clock* (1961) (both privately printed), *The Rising Fire* (1963), *A Breakfast for Barbarians* (1966), *The Shadow-Maker* (1969), *The Armies of the Moon* (1972), *Magic Animals: Selected Poems Old and New* (1974), *The Fire-eaters* (1976), *The T.E. Lawrence Poems* (1982), *Earth Light: Selected Poetry* (1982), *Afterworlds* (1987), which won the Governor General's Award, and a work for juvenile readers, *Dragon Sandwiches* (1987). Her works of adult fiction include *Julian the Magician* (1963), *King of Egypt, King of Dreams* (1971), *Noman* (1972), and *Noman's Land* (1985). Her work has been discussed in Jan Bartley's *Gwendolyn MacEwen and Her Works* (1984) and Rosemary Sullivan's *Shadow-Maker: The Life of Gwendolyn MacEwen* (1995).

POEMS IN BRAILLE

I

all your hands are verbs,
now you touch worlds and feel their names—
thru the thing to the name
not the other way thru (in winter
I am Midas, I name gold)

the chair and table and book
extend from your fingers;
all your movements
command these things back to their
places; a fight against familiarity
makes me resume my distance

II

they knew what it meant,
those egyptian scribes who drew
eyes right into their hieroglyphs,
you read them dispassionate until
the eye stumbles upon itself
blinking back from the papyrus

outside, the articulate wind
annotates this; I read carefully
lest I go blind in both eyes, reading with
that other eye in the final hieroglyph

III

the shortest distance between 2 points
on a revolving circumference
is a curved line; O let me follow you,
Wenceslas

IV

with legs and arms I make alphabets
like in those children's books
where people bend into letters and signs,
yet I do not read the long cabbala of my bones
truthfully; I need only to move
to alter the design

V

I name all things in my room
and they rehearse their names,
gather in groups, form tesseracts,
discussing their names among themselves

I will not say the cast is less than the print
I will not say the curve is longer than the line,
I should read all things like braille in this season
with my fingers I should read them
lest I go blind in both eyes reading with
that other eye the final hieroglyph

MANZINI: ESCAPE ARTIST

now there are no bonds except the flesh; listen—
there was this boy, Manzini, stubborn with
gut stood with black tights and a turquoise
leaf across his sex

and smirking while the big
brute tied his neck arms legs, Manzini
naked waist up and white with sweat

struggled. Silent, delinquent, he
was suddenly all teeth and knee, straining slack
and excellent with sweat, inwardly

wondering if Houdini would take as long
as he; fighting time and the drenched
muscular ropes, as though his tendons were worn
on the outside—

as though his own guts were the ropes
encircling him; it was beautiful; it was thursday; listen—
there was this boy, Manzini

finally free, slid as snake from
his own sweet agonized skin, to throw his entrails
white upon the floor
with a cry of victory—

now there are no bonds except the flesh,
but listen, it was thursday, there was this boy,
Manzini—

POEM IMPROVISED AROUND A FIRST LINE*

the smoke in my bedroom which is always burning
worsens you, motorcycle Icarus;
you are black and leathery and lean and
you cannot distinguish between sex and nicotine

anytime, it's all one thing for you—
cigarette, phallus, sacrificial fire—
all part of that grimy flight
on wings axlegreased from Toronto to Buffalo
for the secret beer over the border—

now I long to see you fullblown and black
over Niagara, your bike burning and in full flame
and twisting and pivoting over Niagara
and falling finally into Niagara,
and tourists coming to see your black leather wings
hiss and swirl in the steaming current—

now I long to give up cigarettes
and change the sheets on my carboniferous bed;
O baby, what Hell to be Greek in this country—
without wings, but burning anyway

---

*The first line around which it was improvised has disappeared.

THE RED BIRD YOU WAIT FOR

You are waiting for someone to confirm it,
You are waiting for someone to say it plain,
Now we are here and because we are short of time
I will say it; I might even speak its name.

It is moving above me, it is burning my heart out,
I have felt it crash through my flesh,
I have spoken to it in a foreign tongue,
I have stroked its neck in the night like a wish.

Its name is the name you have buried in your blood,
Its shape is a gorgeous cast-off velvet cape,
Its eyes are the eyes of your most forbidden lover
And its claws, I tell you its claws are gloved in fire.

You are waiting to hear its name spoken,
You have asked me a thousand times to speak it,
You who have hidden it, cast it off, killed it,
Loved it to death and sung your songs over it.

The red bird you wait for falls with giant wings—
A velvet cape whose royal colour calls us kings
Is the form it takes as, uninvited, it descends,
It is the Power and the Glory forever, Amen.

THE DISCOVERY

do not imagine that the exploration
ends, that she has yielded all her mystery
or that the map you hold
cancels further discovery

I tell you her uncovering takes years,
takes centuries, and when you find her naked
look again,
admit there is something else you cannot name,
a veil, a coating just above the flesh
which you cannot remove by your mere wish

when you see the land naked, look again
(burn your maps, that is not what I mean),
I mean the moment when it seems most plain
is the moment when you must begin again

DARK PINES UNDER WATER

This land like a mirror turns you inward
And you become a forest in a furtive lake;
The dark pines of your mind reach downward,
You dream in the green of your time,
Your memory is a row of sinking pines.

Explorer, you tell yourself this is not what you came for
Although it is good here, and green;
You had meant to move with a kind of largeness,
You had planned a heavy grace, an anguished dream.

But the dark pines of your mind dip deeper
And you are sinking, sinking, sleeper
In an elementary world;
There is something down there and you want it told.

MEMOIRS OF A MAD COOK

There's no point kidding myself any longer,
I just can't get the knack of it; I suspect
there's a secret society which meets
in dark cafeterias to pass on the art
from one member to another.
Besides,
it's so *personal* preparing food for someone's
insides, what can I possibly know
about someone's insides, how can I presume
to invade your blood?
I'll try, God knows I'll try
but if anyone watches me I'll scream
because maybe I'm handling a tomato wrong
how can I *know* if I'm handling a tomato wrong?

something is eating away at me
with splendid teeth

Wistfully I stand in my difficult kitchen
and imagine the fantastic salads and soufflés
that will never be.
Everyone seems to grow thin with me
and their eyes grow back as hunter's eyes
and search my face for sustenance.
All my friends are dying of hunger,
there is some basic dish I cannot offer,
and you my love are almost as lean
as the splendid wolf I must keep always
at my door.

THE CHILD DANCING

there's no way I'm going to write about
the child dancing in the Warsaw ghetto
in his body of rags

there were only two corpses
on the pavement that day
and the child I will not write about
had a face as pale and trusting
as the moon

(so did
the boy with a green belly full of dirt
lying by the roadside
in a novel of Kazantzakis
and the small girl T.E. Lawrence wrote about
who they found after the Turkish massacre
with one shoulder chopped off, crying:
'don't hurt me, Baba!')

I don't feel like slandering them with poetry.

the child who danced
in the Warsaw ghetto

to some music no one else could hear
had moon-eyes, no
green horror and no fear
but something worse

a simple desire to please
the people who stayed
to watch him shuffle back and forth,
his feet wrapped in the newspapers
of another ordinary day

FROM THE T.E. LAWRENCE POEMS

APOLOGIES

I did not choose Arabia; it chose me. The shabby money
That the desert offered us bought lies, bought victory.
     What was I, that soiled Outsider, doing
Among them? I was not becoming one of them, no matter
What you think. They found it easier to learn my kind
     of Arabic, than to teach me theirs.
And they were all mad; they mounted their horses and camels
     from the right.

But my mind's twin kingdoms waged an everlasting war;
The reckless Bedouin and the civilized Englishman
     fought for control, so that I, whatever I was,
Fell into a dumb void that even a false god could not fill,
     could not inhabit.

The Arabs are children of the idea; dangle an idea
In front of them, and you can swing them wherever.
     I was also a child of the idea; I wanted
     no liberty for myself, but to bestow it
Upon them. I wanted to present them with a gift so fine
     it would outshine all other gifts in their eyes;
     it would be *worthy*. Then I at last could be
Empty.

You can't imagine how beautiful it is to be empty.
Out of this grand emptiness wonderful things must surely
    come into being.
When we set out, it was morning. We hardly knew
That when we moved we would not be an army, but a world.

NITROGLYCERINE TULIPS

We planted things called tulip bombs to knock out
    Turkish trains, or curl up the tracks;
    the Turks were so stupid, it sometimes
    seemed to me too easy. How could they
    expect a proper war
If they gave us no chance to honor them?

I called myself Emir Dynamite, and became quite deft
    at the whole business of organized
    destruction. In the back of one train
    which I derailed, was a carriage full of
    dying men; one whispered Typhus,
So I wedged the door closed and left them in.

Another time I straightened out the bodies of dead Turks,
    placing them in rows to look better;
    I was trying, I think, to make it
    a neat war. Once there were three hundred
    of them, with their clothes stripped off,
And I wanted nothing more than to lie down with them,

And die, of course—and think of nothing else but
    raspberries cold with rain, instead of
    sending currents into blasting gelatin
    and watching the sad old trains
    blow sky high
With Turks in little bits around everywhere.

DERAA

I started to write something like:
The citadels of my integrity were lost, or
quo vadis from here, Lawrence?
                How pathetic.

I may as well tell you that as a boy my best castle
    was besieged and overcome by my brothers.

What happened of course was that I was raped at Deraa,
    beaten and whipped and reduced to shreds
    by Turks with lice in their hair, and VD,
    a gift from their officers, crawling all over
    their bodies.
                I had thought that the Arabs were
Bad enough. Slicing the soles of a prisoner's feet
    so that when they let him return to his men,
    he went very, very slowly;
                    but they were merciful.

Imagine, I could never bear to be touched by anybody;
I considered myself a sort of flamboyant monk, awfully
    intact, yet colorful.
              Inviolable is the word.
But everything is shameful, you know; to have a body
    is a cruel joke. It is shameful to be under
    an obligation to anything, even an animal;
    life is shameful; I am shameful. There.

So what part of me lusted after death, as they smashed
    knees into my groin and turned a small knife
    between my ribs? Did I cry out or not when
    they held my legs apart and one of them rode
    upon me, laughing, and splitting open
    a bloody pathway through my soul?
I don't remember.
             They beat me until something, some
    primal slime spilled out of me, and fire
    shot to my brain.
             On a razor edge of reality,
I knew I would come out of this, bleeding and broken,
    and singing.

They lean on the horizon, insolent and wise.

GHAZALA'S FOAL

Ghazala was the second finest camel in all Arabia, and
She did not know it.
                            She had absolutely no mission in life
        and no sense of honor or of shame; she was
        almost perfect.
                            I've seen so many camels die
        that it doesn't matter—the females going on
        until they foundered and died in their tracks,
        the males roaring and flinging themselves down
        and dying unnecessarily out of sheer rage, those
        we scooped out of the snow at Tafileh—but
Mostly I remember Ghazala's foal, getting up and walking
        when it was three hours old, then falling down
        again, in a little heap of slippery limbs.

One of the men skinned it, and Ghazala cried and sniffed
        the little hide.
                            Then we marched again, and often
        she stopped short, and looked around wildly,
        remembering something that was terribly important
        then lapsing into a blank, dazed stare.
                                                Only
        when the poor, tiny piece of skin was placed
        before her on the ground would she
Murmur something, nudge it, ponder a while, and walk on.

TALL TALES

It has been said that I sometimes lie, or bend the truth
        to suit me. Did I make that four hundred mile
        trip alone in Turkish territory or not?
        I wonder if it is anybody's business
        to know. Syria is still there,
        and the long lie that the war was.

Was there a poster of me offering money for my capture,
        and did I stand there staring at myself,
        daring anyone to know me? Consider
        truth and untruth, consider why they call them

the theatres of war. All of us
played our roles to the hilt.

Poets only play with words, you know; they too
    are masters of the Lie, the Grand Fiction.
    Poets and men like me who fight for something
contained in words, but not words.

What if the whole show was a lie, and it bloody well was—
    would I still lie to you? Of course I would.

NOTES FROM THE DEAD LAND

I have died at last, Feisal. I have been lying
On this hospital bed for five days, and I know
    that I am dead. I was going back home
    on my big bike, and I wasn't doing more
    than sixty when this black van, death camel,
Slid back from the left side of my head, and ahead,
Two boys on little bikes were biking along, and
    something in my head, some brutal music
    played on and on. I was going too fast,
    I was always going too fast for the world,
So I swerved and fell on my stupid head, right
In the middle of the road. I addressed myself
    to the dark hearts of the tall trees
    and nothing answered.

The Arabs say that when you pray, two angels stand
On either side of you, recording good and bad deeds,
    and you should acknowledge them.
    Lying here, I decide that now
    the world can have me any way it pleases.
I will celebrate my perfect death here. *Maktub*:
It is written. I salute both of the angels.

JOHN NEWLOVE

(b. 1938)

There are many dimensions to John Newlove's poetry. To readers familiar with his verse the tone of 'wearied intellectuality' that he refers to in 'In This Reed' seems predominant. In his early work, he writes from a mood of despair and disenchantment that reminds one of post-war English poets such as Philip Larkin. Newlove's is a poetry of alienation, peopled with derelicts, hitchhikers, whores, outsiders of all sorts. The poet appears as an outsider wandering in some no man's-land between a vanishing past and a never-to-be realized future. Memory is another country he inhabits frequently, but memory, like everything else in Newlove's cosmos, breaks down. The vision of *Black Night Window* is dark indeed; but in *The Cave* Newlove's landscape is even more desolate. He moves from the bleakness of the Prairies and the unending highway to a more primal landscape of swamps and sea. It is a book of terse confessions, tortured examinations of failed relationships and breakdowns in communication, cynical meditations on history and 'progress'. The poet experiences not only the disintegration of personality, of identity, but also the collapse of the objective world; he is a man caught between the engine and the sea; in 'the cave / of time / with trees / and war / falling / down ... —and / Jesus, / goodbye, / goodbye.'

In these poems Newlove often writes in a halting, disjunctive, matter-of-fact manner, giving the impression of resistance to the poetic process itself. As his vision darkens there is a corresponding paring down of language. The poems become like etchings, painstakingly made, or distillations of complex thoughts and feelings. In *The Cave* Newlove's spareness reaches such a point that he says in 'The Flower': 'I am too tense / decline to dance / verbally.'

Why, then, given the bleakness of its material, is Newlove's poetry so breathtaking and exhilarating? A comment of Margaret Atwood's (from an interview with Geoff Hancock in *Canadian Fiction Magazine*) seems particularly relevant here: 'When I finish a book I really like, no matter what the subject matter, or see a play or film like Kurosawa's *Ran*, which is swimming in blood and totally pessimistic, but so well done, I feel very good. I do feel hope. It's the well-doneness that has that effect on me. Not the conclusion—not what is said, *per se*.' Newlove is a master craftsman; he knows how to use the tools of the poet. He has an exceptional gift for rhythm and cadence and has written short lyrics that rival the best of Cohen and Layton.

Newlove has written poems of historical importance and poems of great lyric intensity. 'Ride Off Any Horizon' is a good example of Newlove's lyricism and his range of poetic materials. It is interesting first of all because it demonstrates one of the primary ways in which Newlove's imagination works. To ride off any horizon is to let the mind follow any idea or feeling for which there is an appropriate sound pattern, to let the mind be carried along by the verbal associations. The various sections of 'Ride Off Any Horizon' contain almost all of the areas of experience that concern Newlove in his poetry: the vast, untamed Prairies barely touched by the forces of industrialization; the Prairies of the Depression; the destruction of the Indians that finds its most powerful expression in 'The Pride'; the place of boyhood and family memories and emotional relationships; and, finally, the lonely crowds and concrete wilderness of the city. These images are held together by the refrain both aurally and grammatically, so that the poem has the kind of unity that is usually associated with narrative or ballad.

'Poetry is the shortest distance between two points; prose, the longest,' Newlove insists. He writes with directness, candour, and economy about personal relationships. His is not simply a poetry of self-exposure; he seldom stops short of a precise, rhythmical expression of feeling. Where he cannot find the measure to control a feeling, he will occasionally turn on a gentle but perfectly pitched irony. In 'The Pride' he also pioneers the documentary mode, where a delicate balance must be struck between historical fact and imaginative recreation. This short narrative asserts the power of, and the pride that must be taken in, aboriginal history and culture; First Nations stories from the collective past will enable us to acquire 'the knowledge of / our origins, and where / we are in truth, / whose land this is / and is to be?'

Newlove was born in Regina and lived for a number of years in Russian farming communities on the eastern edges of Saskatchewan, where his mother was a teacher. He has lived and worked in various parts of Canada—in Vancouver, Terrace, Toronto, and Ottawa—but the major geographical influence on his life and verse is the Prairies, with its oppressed Indians, ethnic minorities, and the vastness and austerity of its terrain. As he says in *Black Night Window*: 'Everyone is so / lonely in this / country that / it's necessary / to be fantastic.' Newlove's poetry has been widely published in magazines in Canada and abroad and has appeared in numerous anthologies. He has worked as a publisher's editor and been a writer-in-residence at several Canadian universities. His publications include *Grave Sirs* (1962), *Elephants, Mothers & Others* (1963), *Moving in Alone* (1965), *Notebook Pages* (1966), *What They Say* (1967), *Black Night Window* (1968), *The Cave* (1970), *The Fat Man* (1977), *The Night the Dog Smiled* (1986), and *Apology for Absence: Selected Poems 1962–1992* (1993).

THEN, IF I CEASE DESIRING

Then, if I cease desiring,
you may sing a song
of how young I was.

You may praise famous moments,
all have them, of the churches
I broke into for wine,

not praise, the highways
I travelled drunkenly
in winter, the cars I stole.

You may allow me moments,
not monuments, I being
content. It is little,
but it is little enough.

CRAZY RIEL

Time to write a poem
or something.
Fill up a page.
The creature noise.
Huge massed forces of men
hating each other.
What young men do not know.
To keep quiet,
contemporaneously.
Contempt. The robin diligently
on the lawn sucks up worms,
hopping from one to another.
Youthfully. Sixteen miles
from my boyhood home
the frogs sit in the grassy marsh
that looks like a golf course
by the lake. Green frogs.
Boys catch them for bait or sale.
Or caught them. Time.
To fill up a page.
To fill up a hole.
To make things feel better. Noise.
The noise of the images
that are people I will never understand.
Admire them though I may.
Poundmaker. Big Bear. Wandering Spirit,
those miserable men.
Riel. Crazy Riel. Riel hanged.
Politics must have its way.
The way of noise. To fill up.
The definitions bullets make,
and field guns.
The noise your dying makes,

to which you are the only listener.
The noise the frogs hesitate
to make as the metal hook
breaks through the skin
and slides smoothly into place
in the jaw. The noise
the fish makes caught in the jaw,
which is only an operation
of the body and the element,
which a stone would make
thrown in the same water, thrashing,
not its voice.
The lake is not displaced
with one less jackfish body.
In the slough that looks like a golf course
the family of frogs sings. Metal throats.
The images of death hang upside-down.
Grey music.
It is only the listening for death,
fingering the paraphernalia,
the noise of the men you admire.
And cannot understand.
Knowing little enough about them.
The knowledge waxing.
The wax that paves hell's road,
slippery as the road to heaven.
So that as a man slips
he might as easily slide
into being a saint as destroyer.
In his ears the noise magnifies.
He forgets men.

VERIGIN, MOVING IN ALONE,

(fatherless, 250 people,
counting dogs and gophers
we would say, Jmaeff's grocerystore,
me in grade 4, mother
principal of the 2-building,
3-room, 12-grade school,)

a boy sitting on the grass
of a small hill, the hot fall,
speaking no russian, an airgun
my sister gave me making me envied.

I tried all fall, all spring
the next ominous year, to kill
a crow with it, secretly glad
I could not, the men
in winter shooting the town's
wild dogs, casually tossing
the quick-frozen barely-bleeding
head-shot corpses onto
the street-side snowbanks,

the highway crews cutting their way
through to open the road with what
I was sure was simply
some alternate of a golden summer's
wheat-threshing machine, children
running through the hard-tossed spray,
pretending war from the monster's snout,

leaping into snowbanks from
Peter The Lordly Verigin's
palace on the edge of town
in a wild 3-dimensional
cubistic game of cops and robbers,

cold spring swimming
in Dead Horse Creek and farmers'
dugouts and doomed fishing
in beastless ponds, strapped
in school for watching a fight,

coldly holding back tears
and digging for drunken father's
rum-bottle, he had finally
arrived, how I loved him,
loved him, love him, dead, still.

My mad old brother chased me
alone in the house with him
around and around
the small living room, airgun
rifle in hand, silently,
our breaths coming together—

all sights and temperatures
and remembrances,
as a lost gull screams now
outside my window,
a 9-year-old's year-long
night and day in tiny
magnificent prairie Verigin:

the long grey cat we got,
the bruised knees, cut fingers,
nails in feet, far walks
to watch a horse's corpse
turn slowly and sweetly to bone,
white bone, and in the late spring,
too, I remember the bright
young bodies of the boys,

my friends and peers and enemies,
till everything breaks down.

RIDE OFF ANY HORIZON

and let the measure fall
where it may—

on the hot wheat,
on the dark yellow fields
of wild mustard, the fields

of bad farmers, on the river,
on the dirty river full
of boys and on the throbbing

powerhouse and the low dam
of cheap cement and rocks
boiling with white water,

and on the cows and their powerful
bulls, the heavy tracks
filling with liquid at the edge

of the narrow prairie
river running steadily away.

*

Ride off any horizon
and let the measure fall
where it may—

among the piles of bones
that dot the prairie

in vision and history
(the buffalo and deer,

dead indians, dead settlers
the frames of lost houses

left behind in the dust
of the depression,

dry and profound, that
will come again in the land

and in the spirit, the land
shifting and the minds

blown dry and empty—
I have not seen it! except

in pictures and talk—
but there is the fence

covered with dust, laden,
the wrecked house stupidly empty)—

here is a picture for your wallet,
of the beaten farmer and his wife
leaning toward each other—

sadly smiling, and emptied of desire.

*

Ride off any horizon
and let the measure fall
where it may—

off the edge
of the black prairie

as you thought you could fall,
a boy at sunset

not watching the sun
set but watching the black earth,

never-ending they said in school,
round: but you saw it ending,

finished, definite, precise—
visible only miles away.

*

Ride off any horizon
and let the measure fall
where it may—

on a hot night the town
is in the streets—

the boys and girls
are practising against

each other, the men
talk and eye the girls—

the women talk and
eye each other, the indians
play pool: eye on the ball.

*

Ride off any horizon
and let the measure fall
where it may—

and damn the troops, the horsemen
are wheeling in the sunshine,
the cree, practising

for their deaths: mr poundmaker,
gentle sweet mr bigbear,
it is not unfortunately

quite enough to be innocent,
it is not enough merely
not to offend—

at times to be born
is enough, to be
in the way is too much—

some colonel otter, some
major-general middleton will
get you, you—

indian. It is no good to say,
I would rather die
at once than be in that place—

though you love that land more,
you will go where they take you.

*

Ride off any horizon
and let the measure fall—

where it may;
it doesn't have to be

the prairie. It could be
the cold soul of the cities
blown empty by commerce

and desiring commerce
to fill up emptiness.

The streets are full of people.

It is night, the lights
are on; the wind

blows as far as it may. The streets
are dark and full of people.

Their eyes are fixed as far as
they can see beyond each other—

to the concrete horizon, definite,
tall against the mountains,
stopping vision visibly.

THE PRIDE

1

The image/ the pawnees
in their earth-lodge villages,
the clear image
of teton sioux, wild
fickle people the chronicler says,

the crazy dogs, men
tethered with leather dog-thongs

to a stake, fighting until dead,
image: arikaras
with traded spanish sabre blades
mounted on the long
heavy buffalo lances,
riding the sioux
down, the centaurs, the horsemen
scouring the level plains
in war or hunt
until smallpox got them,
the warriors,

image—of a desolate country,
a long way between fires,
unfound lakes, mirages, cold rocks,
and lone men going through it,
cree with good guns
causing terror in athabaska
among the inhabitants, frightened
stone-age people, 'so that
they fled at the mere sight
of a strange smoke miles away.'

2

This western country crammed
with the ghosts of indians
haunting the coastal stones and shores,
the forested pacific islands,
mountains, hills and plains:

beside the ocean ethlinga,
man in the moon, empties
his bucket, on
a sign from spirit
of the wind ethlinga
empties his bucket, refreshing
the earth, and it rains
on the white cities;

that black joker, broken—
jawed raven, most prominent
among haida and tsimshian tribes
is in the kwakiutl
dance masks too—
it was he who brought fire,
food and water to man,
the trickster;

and thunderbird hilunga,
little thought of
by haida for lack of thunderstorms
in their district, goes
by many names, exquisite disguises
carved in the painted wood,

he is nootka tootooch, the wings
causing thunder and the tongue
or flashing eyes engendering
rabid white lightning,
whose food was whales,

called kwunusela by the kwakiutl,
it was he who laid down the house-logs
for the people at the place
where kwunusela alighted;

in full force and virtue
and terror of the law, eagle—
he is authority, the sun
assumed his form once,
the sun which used to be
a flicker's egg, success-
fully transformed;

and malevolence comes to the land,
the wild woman of the woods—
grinning, she wears
a hummingbird in her hair,
d'sonoqua, the furious one—

they are all ready
to be found, the legends
and the people, or
all their ghosts and memories,
whatever is strong enough
to be remembered.

3

But what image, bewildered
son of all men
under the hot sun,
do you worship,
what completeness
do you hope to have
from these tales,
a half-understood massiveness, mirage,
in men's minds—what
is your purpose;

with what force
will you proceed
along a line
neither straight nor short,
whose future
you cannot know
or result foretell,
whose meaning is still
obscured as the incidents
occur and accumulate?

4

The country moves on;
there are orchards in the interior,
the mountain passes
are broken, the foothills
covered with cattle and fences,
and the fading hills covered;

but the plains are bare,
not barren, easy
for me to love their people,
for me to love their people
without selection.

5

In 1787, the old cree saukamappee, aged 75 or thereabout, speaking then
of things that had happened when he was 16, just a man, told david thompson
about the raids the shoshonis, the snakes, had made on the westward-reaching
peigan, of their war-parties sometimes sent 10 days' journey to enemy camps,
the men all afoot in battle array for the encounter, crouching behind their
giant shields. The peigan armed with guns drove these snakes out of the
plains, the plains where their strength had been, where they had been settled
since living memory (though nothing is remembered beyond a grandfather's
time), to the west of the rockies:

these people moved without rest,
backward and forward with the wind,
the seasons, the game, great herds,
in hunger and abundance—

in summer and in the bloody fall
they gathered on the killing grounds,
fat and shining with fat, amused
with the luxuries of war and death,

relieved from the steam of knowledge,
consoled by the stream of blood
and steam rising from the fresh hides
and tired horses, wheeling in their pride
on the sweating horses, their pride.

6

Those are all stories;
the pride, the grand poem
of our land, of the earth itself,

will come, welcome, and
sought for, and found,
in a line of running verse,
sweating, our pride;

we seize on
what has happened before,
one line only
will be enough,
a single line
and then the sunlit brilliant image suddenly floods us
with understanding, shocks our
attentions, and all desire
stops, stands alone;

we stand alone,
we are no longer lonely
but have roots,
and the rooted words
recur in the mind, mirror, so that
we dwell on nothing else, in nothing else,
touched, repeating them,
at home freely
at last, in amazement;

'the unyielding phrase
in tune with the epoch,'
the thing made up
of our desires,
not of its words, not only
of them, but of something else
as well, that which we desire
so ardently, that which
will not come when
it is summoned alone,
but grows in us
and idles about and hides
until the moment is due—

the knowledge of
our origins, and where
we are in truth,
whose land this is
and is to be.

7

The unyielding phrase:
when the moment is due, then
it springs upon us
out of our own mouths,
unconsidered, overwhelming
in its knowledge, complete—

not this handful
of fragments, as the indians
are not composed of
the romantic stories
about them, or of the stories
they tell only, but
still ride the soil
in us, dry bones a part
of the dust in our eyes,
needed and troubling
in the glare, in
our breath, in our
ears, in our mouths,
in our bodies entire, in our minds, until
at last
we become them

in our desires, our desires,
mirages, mirrors, that are theirs, hard-
riding desires, and they
become our true forbears, moulded
by the same wind or rain,
and in this land we
are their people, come
back to life again.

SUCH FUN, SUCH FUN

When the poets stopped writing poetry
I thought they were dead
and I went about and tried to describe my country
not leaf by leaf but soul by soul
and I found that though my soul was obscure
it was common. Liquor cured me or calmed me
and pain and long lying lines.

And the poets came back to life and said I was a poet too
and I was astonished!
I hadn't thought they'd known so much
or that I had cared so much.

And the booze tastes good even if the body aches
and the end is shame—but the sheer pleasure
of the gift, of a few gloomy words—

This is prose, this is a ghost with a steel chisel
sneaking another letter onto the stone.

Such fun, such fun. I guess you would have to pay attention
to someone besides yourself. It's better to celebrate
your funeral before you die.

Thank you, thank you.

ROBIN BLASER

(b. 1925)

Robin Blaser was born in Denver, Colorado, studied at Northwestern University, College of Idaho, and Berkeley, and was a librarian at Harvard, before emigrating from San Francisco to Vancouver to teach English at Simon Fraser University from 1966 to 1986. He became a Canadian citizen in 1972 and continued publishing instalments of his life-long poem, including *Cups* (1960), *The Moth Poem* (1964), *Les Chimères* (1964) *Image-Nation 1–12* (1974), *Syntax* (1983), *The Faerie Queene & The Park* (1988), *Pell Mell* (1988), and *Exody* (1993). These poems-in-progress were published in 1993 as *The Holy Forest*.

In league with Jack Spicer, Blaser claimed to be engaged in a 'battle for the real', which he considered a narrative of the spirit: 'I'm interested in a particular kind of narrative—what Jack Spicer and I agreed to call in our own work the serial poem—this is a narrative which refuses to adopt an imposed story line, and completes itself only in the sequence of poems, if, in fact, a reader insists upon a definition of completion which is separate from the activity of the poems themselves. The poems tend to act as a sequence of energies. . . .'

As a statement of poetics to accompany 'The Moth Poem', which appeared in Sharon Thesen's *The New Long Poem Anthology*, Robin Blaser wrote:

I have found in the serial poem a way to work from my displaced, uncentered 'I' in order to be found among things—

relational, at least, to what I can. Recent theory tells us writers that the author is gone from his/her authority. That seemed real enough to me before theory ever hit home. And, without authority, a conversation went on. . . . I don't know how to write any more. The covers won't close. I asked a scholar friend of these matters, 'What do you say when asked about the serial poem and how it works?' Miriam Nichols answered, 'The serial poem builds worlds that are provisional, and those worlds are specific, but not limited, in place and time—the result: plural worlds.' So, I guess, 'The Moth Poem', though back there, is still working at my initial sense of the multiplicity of times, persons, gods, things, thoughts, places and stuff—folding—

In *The Holy Forest* there are explicit and implicit structural clues, figures in the carpet, embedded throughout the text to help readers understand the poet's intentions. 'Lake of Souls (reading notes', in particular, contains many hints, acknowledgments of influence, and ongoing conversations with other writers, including William Blake, Shelley, René Girard, Bernard-Henri Lévy, Robert Duncan, and Geoffrey Hartman, whose work he quotes at length:

Poets having expelled the old gods, their images, their phraseology—in short, poetic diction—and, having instituted a more natural diction, the process of purification continues, not so happily, and the purified language proves to be as contaminated as ever. We see that the poetic diction once rejected had extraordinary virtues, including its non-natural character, its lucid artifice, the 'mirror-of-steel uninsistence' (Marianne Moore) by which it made us notice *'smallest things and ciphered greatest things, / and gathered into a few terms, / magical, memorable, barely meaningful, / the powers of language.'*

Blaser prefers a poetry open to both the old elegance and all other forms of language and content, so his work shifts easily from the high style to colloquial language—'listen, kid, / there isn't anything but art'— slang, scatological reference, snippets of autobiography, love-letters, jokes, and graffiti. In terms of form, it encompasses lyric, anecdote, meditation, elegy, ode, imagist poem, and the occasional professorial aside. He admires the workings of chance in art, which 'enters the mind, willy-nilly to unfold our form / the mind wanders / DISCREATION, nameless / therefore the quotations to transform time / and argue with *unart* and *mere litereity* / fate and form are interchangeable / the anger between them / is the dream in skin on our bones.'

Blaser recommends Hartman's *Criticism in the Wilderness, Beyond Formalism*, and *Saving the Text*, describing the latter as 'a companion for the poet reading poetry to find the layers of the real. . . .' The manifold layers of reality are less likely to be encountered via conventional form or adhering to the constraints of lyric and narrative, as one whimsical note suggests: 'To whom it may concern: there are no bones in your jello, so I'll make no bones about the skeletal structure the lost form is wary, even perky, all in a gesture . . . I am writing to remind you of causal effects and summaries . . . I have dismembered the black, and you, white perfection, what have you done with your patchwork, crazy quilted, the perfect ski-jacket down and hills of rocky dance-cards.'

By 'plundering memory and places . . . the gardened and the wild', the poet leaves open the possibility of addressing multiple worlds—the particular and the universal, the literal and the imaginary, the sublime and the mundane, holy writ and fortune cookie.

Although the dominant stance here is that of one poet talking to another—through his lyrical, gossipy or scholarly 'notations' and asides, his 'serial' jottings—rather than to some mythical common reader, there is plenty to learn, enjoy and admire for the eavesdropper in Blaser's salon. As he says in 'First Love', 'These poems may seem quirky, even hermetic. They are not. But they do reflect a lifetime of scholarship which gave me, first, pleasure, and then, a cosmos, and then, happiness. I hope that scholarship and the joy of it—the helpless quotation of it—gave greater generosity, a love of this one and that one, who turned up as helpless as I am.' He even incorporates an unflattering personal note from Charles Olson: 'I'd trust you anywhere with image, but you've got no syntax.'

In 'The Crannies of Matter: Texture in Robin Blaser's Later "Image-Nations"' (*Nothing But Brush Strokes*), Phyllis Webb has much to say about Blaser's poetics, what she calls his 'principle of randonnée or receptivity', his intertextuality, 'the way [the serial poem] is "built", the a-phasic alternation of prosaic passages with poetic ones— and the amazing sonic range and rhythmic inventions this method allows—deflects any tendency towards epic grandeur and the heroic.'

As Robert Creeley so aptly puts it in the Foreword to Blaser's *The Holy Forest*, although the questions may not be fully answered or the wisdom conventionally packaged, 'the complexly layered "song" of these poems' is evident. Further,

the 'unfolded fold' to be found in Blaser's work—the turn, the bend in the road, the 'twist' of Charles Olson's preoccupation—is the nexus of its life and the life it has made so movingly eloquent. . . . Much as a tree might grow in beloved intention, or anything of fragile possibility find continuing if unexpected time, so this poet's life is manifest as a complex of perceptions, of reflections, ironies, humour, things learned, things forgotten, person become substance of its own potential. . . . What does one ever want a poetry to be other than the sounding that reaches through all the fact of our variousness, brings to a common apprehension and presence whatever we have known, feel or have felt?

FROM CUPS

4

The shadow of the fish lies
among the rocks.   The
shadow of the sagebrush
turns the hill blue.   The
shadow of the mountain
includes all strangers.

(The strangulations will appear
in the brush fire.)

The coyotes, burned out of their lairs,
follow the railroad.   Shapes
of poems
                    fly out of the dark.

The tree spoke: Love is not love.
Imagine your first stupor.   The
effort to untie the strings
of the loins. The lips endure
the semen of strangers.
                              It is spring
when the shadow of willows is gone.

SO

You speak against the mundane
which is for instance
the sidewalk

and, I suspect, the gods
severed and loose
like architectural adornments

The word means
           worldly
but requiring the mundus

Gloria Swanson used one image to reappear
in the imagination
           the claw,
and Garbo chose white to show that death
works at the convenience of the lady of the
camellias, thus saving Robert Taylor for
later movies—in white flannels, the college
hero out on the town
              suppose you think the
plots were about Norma Desmond and Mme. Gauthier

You missed the structure they personified

where Dionysus lay sleeping against
the corner stone

the wall broke into pieces of glass

Again and again
I saw myself about to wake him

THE MEDIUM

it is essentially reluctance   the language
a darkness, a friendship, tying to the real
but it is unreal

the clarity desired, a wish for true sight,
all tangling

'you' tried me, the everyday which
caught me, turning the house

in the wind, a lovecraft   the political
was not my business   I could not look

without seeing the decay, the shit poured
on most things, by indifference, the personal

power which is simply that,   demanding a friend
take dullness out of the world (he doesn't know
his lousy emptiness)   I slept
in a fire   on my book bag, one dried wing

of a white moth   the story is of a man
who lost his way in the holy wood

because the way had never been taken without
at least two friends,   one on each side,

and I believe my dream said one of the others
always led   now left to acknowledge,

he can't breathe, the darkness bled
the white wing,   one   of the body

of the moth that moved him, of the other
wing,   the language is bereft

WINTER WORDS

O fountains, where the throat
is a silent partnership,   part of

the folklore of birds,
the news is

these sorrows
on a dream tree

rigged and actual

(the diaries of friendships
    have almost won a nest for themselves

the life in art fashions itself,
returns, gazes upon the traffic

(has the cold caught
   my hand in the game

   torn

an invisible entertainment
somehow
falls upon all things

THE FINDER

on the windows, the dirty film
in the sunlight   shaped by the shadows
of apple trees   dry winter branches

on English Bay   a ship appears,
its hiding over   two masts, a doubling
of the cross   two Christs

one matching the other   where
the world dies

the tabloids of fire, a Sunday supplement
to the San Francisco Examiner   out of place,
in this time   rises from the page

in a lightning storm   which holds
this man at the horizon in his apocalypse,
a war burning, if the heart scores

bodiless, a curious blood and reasons
in ourselves inheriting the intellect
from out there   defined by a President

who is violence in this world,
a definition of this destiny we have
effected   all's well without

'your' intelligence where the world dies
I bend 'you' to my mouth
and suck 'your' breath away
only worlds caught

in the glinting lights of those
pieces of glass   found in the
forest   under a tree   crushed
and shining

for Louis Zukofsky

TUMBLE-WEED

the flour-man, powdery, at the door
becomes finally, a sweat-body of spiritual
enemies, drunk on the plane-fare,
who walks nowhere

if you try on the costume, say, of
Picasso's religion or the fierce, feminine
purpose
            or better yet, of harlequin
dying to sleep with red bitten lips
and all of it said coldly
to move speech to its violent
marvellous teeth,
                        a desire
behind the desire and Oedipus

and which desert father lay his head
on a mummified-body-pillow whose
voice was a ghost of a woman
and which dreamed sadly he
knew better the perspective of his
landscape—windowless farms
and winds
and which cried out, 'father
of wax' and kissed his forehead
of lost lives of cold florists
at last?

for my father, died April 20, 1978, at 76

THE TRUTH IS LAUGHTER 14

across the Bay there was a house
and there were two rooms in it
when the water started to come into the house
they went outside and brought in a canoe
they sat in the canoe inside the house
for two nights because the house was full
of water   the ten-gallon oil tanks were all
blown away and the Hudson's Bay
office was also blown away

(from Joe Panipakuttuk

DREAMS, APRIL, 1981

so it is death is the
condition of infinite form—
the rebellion of particulars,
ourselves and each thing,
even ideas, against that infinitude,
is the story of finitude—the
dream of the children harvested
in a harvester-machine
there are the real voice
and the voice imagined
and both have a reality,
but the latter is out of it
the ladder things

never accept gifts from the gods
—Hesiod's bitter-sweet sense of it—
rings true and doesn't
settle the sea-shore down
to where the *heart breaks or is bronzed*
'I am happy,' the man said,
'because the toad of the morning
is the worst thing I'll find today'
and CBC's TV critic says, 'television
is the Shakespeare of the 20ᵗʰ century'

red lilies fall on the carpet
and Art Tatum, drawing his art
out of hymns, wanted more dissonance
perfect

there are knives in the air
all around the poorly loved
their lives follow life back
into stone and they dream
a sweeter consonance at the centre
the art of a screaming and
demented oyster is not theirs

GRAFFITO

Artists are the deodorant pucks in the urinals of life.
          (men's room, Leo's Fish House, Gastown

THE ICEBERG
for Michael Ondaatje

I want no summer to melt you
I want no tip to disappear where
I find you—and the largeness
out there, wanders, incomplete,
a constant creation to leap into

'Love' wanders, the speechless
mind of it, all that cost of the
flowers and statues—all that
city of delighted streets and
whimpers   O, the locked heaven
whose gate jangles   I wonder
at the steep of it

then wait, astonished that
the sweet heart grows in some
root or depth—and turns
into ceremonies   there are

the losses of the heartland, light,
sleepless forms against themselves
I repeat you, endlessly—

common, sorrowing, old,
and gigantic
                    this waits
and spits the bird image that
began icily in the distance to
save us, unaware that it lifted,
or was said to, the tip of ourselves

HOME FOR BOYS AND GIRLS

the silvery dark, the cry of it,
writing, the couching lion and the
jokes thereof, playing marbles with
jasper—one was how close do
you get to the wall, or the other,
fall into the pit, steelies will get
you out with losses, keeping the marbles,
glassies were resplendent, butterflies,
monarchs of black and near-gold bronze,
clay balls are the cheapest, used if
you're going to lose—or let's play
conkers, polish with shoe-polish,
harden the chestnuts, string them
and swing, hitting the other, spring
games and fall games, of free
children, the unwanted, sent
from England, 1880–1920, Dr. Barnardo's,
when the child first came, he was taken
to a thawing field and told to bury
the dead cow, he dug all day and
used a crow-bar to push the cow
in, buried her, but the legs stuck
up—stiff and everlasting—he
was given an axe, told to return
to the spot and chop the legs off,
the pieces under the thaw and mud,

in the child's mind, everlasting—
and the true gleam of Wordsworth's
children and Coleridge's answer
in the wind's scream, widening loss
and joyance given I repeat:
steelies, pits, jasper and
resplendent glassies

IMAGE-NATION 21 (TERRITORY

wandering to the other, wandering
the spiritual realities, skilled in all
ways of contending, he did not search
out death or courage, did not
found something, a country
or end it, but made it endless,
that is his claim to fame, to
seek out what is beyond any single
man or woman, or the multiples
of them   the magic country that
is homeland

the bridges   I strained for, strings
of my vastness in language, and
the cars rushed by in both
directions flashing at one another

the mechanic of splendour, sought
after, chanted in the windy
cables   and the river sailed,
haphazard, under the solitude

he had only the stories to tell, naked
and plotless, the spiritual territories,
earth-images and sky-maps, dark
at the edges

the mechanic of the marvellous dreamed
of Stalin and Hitler and the ordinary,
endlessly knew where he had gone

and, then, came back, whatever happens
if, I said—I was talking to religionists—
you gain social justice,
solve the whole terror, then where
is god? certainly not in happiness
and since god is not in unhappiness,
there you have it   the skilled
adventure in hostilities with no name

FOR BARRY CLINTON, D. 17 JUNE, 1984, OF AIDS

a circle of bricks beneath Lucretius' tall
Aphrodite who holds her shell among plum
branches—and iris, columbine—your favourite—
primula Florindae, again to surprise you—pale
blues and bright yellows—white poppies are not
available here—hail! dear blue-eyed
painter

PRAISE TO THEM, DECEMBER 30, 1984

the robins, returned to
the holly-tree   snow-
covered unusually, search
for red berries   joined by
flames—and larger—a
Common Flicker, 'red-
shafted', speckled fawn-
breast, long beak of
Picus—the first in
fourteen years—eating
berries in this city-
garden

OF THE LAND OF CULTURE
I flew too far into the future: a horror assailed me

think of it as fissiparous

an Other who is no longer God or the muse, but anonymous

a CBC interview on China: 'Business is above politics'   thereby:
beyondness   and 'politics' seeks equality in *kakistocracy* and
its professions

the psychiatric patient said, No, I don't want to go back there—
the place is full of fallen angels trapped in human form

strangers in the existing order, which the ordinary woman or man
can't narrate, though h/she is the most recent and only narrator
left to an anonymous culture   and is promissory

she said, someone broke in last night and stole my sexual organs,
I've called the police again and again, but they won't do anything   the doctor said gently, let's have a look, and he told
her he'd found them where they should be   and she left without
even a thank-you

was her thought of the loss really of the burglar, for whom most
of us wait?

age deepens politics and the wonderful world—oh, dear! body's
and mind's it-ain't-what-it-used-to-be decays in cliché, and is
beside the point—because it never was—in order to say, your
smile is true at the cut

how many centuries has Christianity had in *kind* hands our otherness, one to one, here & there, & beyondness?   'christians'—
now manifesting—should all get together and play patty-cake, for
that is the size of their cultural heaven

everyone said, thank you for your bright and careless eyes

Ethan Mordden said, *it could not be that paranoid Old Testament
sheik with the plagues and tantrums*   stopped by briefly, doing all
      over
again goodness

a song on the radio today sang, 'To our God we are in debt,' so
to describe the deficit

the shills said, confidentially, cultural haven is under one of
these three walnut shells, named O.T., N.T., and materialism—
try your luck!

Hustle, eyes watering, bent over the tabula rasa and his hand
trembled

Then I flew back, homeward—and faster and faster I flew: and so
I came to you, you men of the present, and to the land of culture
I laughed and laughed, while my foot still trembled and my heart
as well: 'Here must be the home of all the paint-pots! I said

You are half-open doors at which grave-diggers wait. And this is
your reality: 'Everything is worthy of perishing'

it's amazing to be pushed out of shape a lot of the time, and the
amazement is a cultural gift

someone said, the stones of _____ [fill in the name of
your own home town] are saturated with poetry

(Nietzsche whispering

GEORGE BOWERING

(b. 1935)

George Bowering's work has been closely associated with the *Tish* group of poets, who, in reaction to prescribed texts and dominant literary forebears, rejected much of the formalism of modernist poetry in favour of a poetry that was more personal, more clearly rooted in region or place, and committed to a greater degree of open-endedness. Under the influence mainly of American models, such as William Carlos Williams, Charles Olson, Robert Creeley, and Jack Spicer, these young poets came to regard the poem less as a set-piece, or well-made artefact, and more as a process, a sustained moment of discovery. The poet begins with the physical fact of his own being; thus his preoccupation with breathing, the body, nearby objects and persons. The poem, the created thing, becomes an object in its own right, with laws, a fusion of form and content, a unit of energy passed from writer to reader.

The primitive stance, which involves throwing off the yoke of tradition—including such poetic devices as rhyme, metrics, alliteration, and the simile—has its dangers. R.P. Blackmur sums up the matter well with regard to Thomas Hardy's poetry: 'Hardy was a free man in everything that concerns the poet; which is to say, helpless, without tradition; and he therefore rushed for support into the slavery of ideas whenever his freedom failed him.' The irregular, syncopated rhythms of the speaking voice can become as dull or flat as the too easily anticipated rhythms of the metrical or syllabic line; so, too, the rejection of conventional forms often sends the poet scurrying in search of such structuring devices as the journal entry, the Tarot, the thematically based sequence of poems about friends, fellow writers, and so on.

In his best work Bowering manages to navigate safely between the Scylla of formlessness and the Charybdis of prescribed forms. Many of his comments about technique relate to the question of voice. 'Not just Wordsworth's vague idea of using common speech,' he says, 'but *how to get your own voice on the page*.' In his book *Al Purdy*, he explains the notion of finding your own voice as 'a writing-school aphorism that inadequately describes the process whereby the poet comes to avail himself of ways to get the individualities of his speech habits into his prosody.' As he says in 'Circus Maximus', a poetic is no more than a single pattern imposed on experience to make it meaningful and tolerable: '(patterns I deny / and that / is part of a pattern).' In *Errata*, a book of short prose-takes on art, he makes an appeal for randomness, citing Richard Ellmann on 'the imaginative absorption of stray material' in the work of T.S. Eliot and James Joyce. As for being a 'packrat of the trivial', he insists 'there is something in post-modernist composition that welcomes the stray material and resists absorption.' He advises indulging the 'language's whims', rather than surrendering to the dictates of reason or the Machiavellian urges of the self. He emphasizes process, celebrating 'tracks' of language and thinking in poetry rather than the mere packaging of thought.

Although he is committed to open form and describes himself socially and politically as a romantic leftist, he confesses to being, aesthetically, an elitist. He delights in Joyce's 'pell-mell plunge down the sentence' to god-knows-where. 'I make the craft visible and the referent invisible.' He speaks of dictated writing, letting language rather than content drive the poem: 'We are priests, not monarchs. We have no subjects. A gift from the gods is not a licence to rule.' One of the functions of great writing, he insists, is 'to lay human song at the doorsill of the god's music room', a fearful but exciting task. Bowering favours what he calls *tapinosis*, 'the saying of very serious things in offhand language, in vernacular, even in slang'. He also distinguishes between what he calls the heavy-duty 'male' manipulators of language, shapers, power-brokers, and those 'girlish priests . . . insect collectors, roadside talkers' like himself who seek out music, serve rather than master language, and rejoice in 'a multiplicity in order'. He rejects poetic *aboutists*, insisting that Daphne Marlatt's long poem *Steveston* is not *about* the immigrant or work experiences, though it may allude to them: 'A poem such as that, with its devotion to the words, is speaking for poetry, not for the poet.'

Bowering was born in Penticton, BC and educated at the University of British Columbia, where he received a BA in History and an MA in English. In addition to being a co-editor of *Tish*, he served as an aerial photographer in the RCAF, and travelled to Mexico. He has edited various anthologies, as well as the magazine *Imago*, devoted to the publication of the long poem, and is now a contributing editor to *Open Letter*. He taught in Calgary and Montreal before joining the English Department at Simon Fraser University in Burnaby, BC. He lives in Vancouver.

He has published many books of poetry, including *Sticks & Stones* (1963), *Points on the Grid* (1964), *The Man in Yellow Boots* (1965), *Rocky Mountain Foot* (1969) and *The Gangs of Kosmos* (1969), which together won a Governor General's Award, *Touch: Selected Poems 1960–1970* (1971), *The Catch* (1976), *Selected Poems: Particular Accidents* (1980), *Smoking Mirror* (1982), *West Window* (1982), *Delayed Mercy and Other Poems* (1986), *Urban Snow* (1992), *Blonds on Bikes* (1997), and *George Bowering: Selected Poems 1961–1992* (1993). His abiding interest in the long poem is evident in his book-length poems, *George, Vancouver* (1970), *Autobiology* (1972), *Kerrisdale Elegies* (1984), and *His Life: A Poem* (2000). Bowering has also written several books of criticism, including *Al Purdy* (1970), *A Way With Words* (1982), *The Mask in Place: Essays on Fiction in North America* (1983), *Imagining Hand: Essays* (1988), and a book of poetics in verse form, *Errata* (1988). He is also author of various works of fiction, including *The Flycatcher and Other Stories* (1974), *Protective Footwear* (1978), *Burning Water* (1980), for which he received a Governor General's Award, *Caprice* (1987), and *Shoot* (1994). His non-fiction works include *Bowering's B.C.: A Swashbuckling History* (1996) and *Egotists and Autocrats: the Prime Ministers of Canada* (1999).

GRANDFATHER

Grandfather
        Jabez Harry Bowering
strode across the Canadian prairie
hacking down trees
                and building churches
delivering personal baptist sermons in them
leading Holy holy holy lord god almighty songs in them
red haired man squared off in the pulpit
reading Saul on the road to Damascus at them
Left home
          big walled Bristol town
at age eight
          to make a living
buried his stubby fingers in root snarled earth
for a suit of clothes and seven hundred gruelly meals a year
taking an anabaptist cane across the back every day
for four years till he was whipped out of England

Twelve years old
          and across the ocean alone
to apocalyptic Canada
               Ontario of bone bending child labor
six years on the road to Damascus till his eyes were blinded
with the blast of Christ and he wandered west
to Brandon among wheat kings and heathen Saturday nights
young red haired Bristol boy shoveling coal
in the basement of Brandon college five in the morning

Then built his first wooden church and married
a sick girl who bore two live children and died
leaving several pitiful letters and the Manitoba night

He moved west with another wife and built children and churches
Saskatchewan Alberta British Columbia Holy holy holy
lord god almighty
              struck his labored bones with pain
and left him a postmaster prodding grandchildren with crutches
another dead wife and a glass bowl of photographs
and holy books unopened save the bible by the bed

Till he died the day before his eighty fifth birthday
in a Catholic hospital on sheets white as his hair

DOBBIN

For Mike Ondaatje

We found dead animals in our sagebrush hills,
every day it seems now, deer, heads of
unimaginable elk. Or rattlesnake killed
by some kids we likely knew, upside down,
wrong coloured in the burnt couchgrass.

But my first dead horse. It was something
like mother, something gone wrong at home—
his opened & scattered body was tethered
the old shit surrounded his tufted hair
& his skin, the oil gone, just twisted
leather without eyeballs. A horse, as if
someone had lost him, obeying the rope
thru his open-air starving.

I was then, then, no longer another one
of the animals come to look, this
was no humus like the others, this
was death, not merely dead; that rope
may now hang from some rotted fence.

SUMMER SOLSTICE

I

The cool Pacific spring has gone without
my notice, now summer lies around us
once again. How long life is, how many
more of these seasons must I see, hydrangea
& the fat rhododendron sullen on the
neighbour's lawn. & I must rise, stick
fluid in mouth, stick beaten vegetables
into my living daughter's mouth, shit, it comes
& goes, it goes, thru us pretending we are

not some more, shit, the wearisome sun
& the sad motes in its visitations envelop
my mind even when it is thinking action
& when it thinks offers impatience with this
boring reappearance of the grass.

II

                              Must I
live longer year by year, watching from this
small mountain the heavier pall of sludge
residing over this city & the yet discernible
waterways of bygone sea manoeuvres, my baby
breathing under that? Every midnight, every
winter, removing familiar clothes & taking
others more familiar to my bed of habit?

III

What nature gave me at my birth no more
than this, a prospectus of recurring faces, old
leaves appear above ground, old words grow
to surround them, old fingers join to pull
them & cast them to their home.

IV

The grass needs cutting, part of it
is yellow, it is dying of starvation, hell
it will be back next year, somewhere
else, & so will we, will we? Will
we endure that? The Pacific winter remembered more fondly than it is, some
unconvincing refuge of the life-giving
horror felt in the knives of Quebec December.
We congratulate each other for the snowy
re-emergence of the mountains, our mountains
we say with fancy dinners at the top
& hydroelectric sticks poking up the
slopes, our mountains re-emerging from our
papermaking smoke, our mountains showing up
each year with their peaks capt, silent

& gentle, the air restful over them, the sea
content to lie beneath them, not looking
for any entrance to that stilled heart.

V

It is slowly dying, but so slowly, the
earthquake belt is forty miles west, the sea
deterred by that long island. Every summer's
pollen mixt with more haze. We come
back here to partake of slow death, the dying
ocean so lifelike, harder to beat down than some
great lake. The mountains once promist me
a rapid death, fall is a fall, to the
rocks below—but the mountains are somebody's back yard, hydrangea bushes all around.

VI

I havent heard a timely utterance for a
long time, there we are, hung on those
hands, watching & watching, & will they
never move? We seek out ways of death,
but slowly, or given minimal expectation, why
do I climb those stairs every morning?
To visit her, lift her eighteen pounds, &
clean her, more of it she'll pass & never
recall, to bring her downstairs for more,
of the same. Some will say that is reason
enough. Few will say enough of reason. It's
not reason I seek upstairs, we ought to be
past that, it's legs take us up there, legs
more tired every season. She makes utterances
we measure her time by.

VII

Sunday, I & Thea were there when Angela
woke up. So I'm back, she said, &
reacht to touch her baby's fuzzy head. Why,
where you been, I ask her.

I went on a car ride with a Fairie,
name of Mab.

What did she tell you?

She said things are going to get better.

VIII

I am slowly dying, water evaporating
from a saucer. I saw my daughter this
morning, trying to walk, & it fell like a vial
of melted lead into my heart, my heart so
deep in my chest. She will have to do it now,
we have presented her with a world,
whose spectres take shapes before her eyes
have fully focust, poor voyager! For joy
she brings us every morning we exchange
an accelerating series of shocks. We are together
cannibals of her spirit, we feast to nurture
our tired bodies, turning music to shit, a shock
felt numbly here & radiating to collisions
at the rim of space. You dont believe me?
See her eyes when first she wakes. A visible
tyrant of light yanks their traces, demanding
they stride apace.

IX

                    Then cannibal I will be—
her father. & I cant even teach her love,
but loose the horses, let a ghost ride &
call him loving, turn her away finally &
soothe her with a merry-go-round. That music
will disgust her in time, it rings & rings,
& I will instruct her of gold & gold
bedevillings, I will toil to win her trust,
& we will fall where we will rust
& watch the golden horses prancing by.

X

So fall will come
& winter too,
& she will wear
her first tight shoe

& she will wear
the seasons round
& watch the summers
wear me down.

XI

Thea, never read my lines, love your mother,
love your father, distrust circles, reach
this way & that. Remember how you can
the afternoon a bird came to sit at your shoulder
& let me remember how I dropt my game
to fly to your side, protecting your eyes.

Accept no promise from the mountains,
I have never seen your face before, & when
I leave you I will leave you time.
Forgive me the light that fades not fast away,
forgive me the continuous feast
we make from your remembered day.

BONES ALONG HER BODY

Bones along her body show
art is never far below,
reason offers equal space
bones that glimmer in her face;
art is never far from where
reason offers up its chair—
art is never far away.

Phones ring out in open air,
ears deduce a message there,

noises all fall into place,
tones that need no special grace;
letting half her reason go,
art is never far from so,
never far when she will play
dancing bones on reason's day.

FROM KERRISDALE ELEGIES

ELEGY ONE

If I did complain, who among my friends
would hear?
                    If one of them
amazed me with an embrace
he would find his arms empty, his own face
staring from a mirror.

Beauty is the first prod of fear,
                              we must
live our lives in.
                    We reach for her,
we think we love her, because she holds the knife
a knife-edge from our throat.
                              Every fair heart
is frightful.
              Every rose petal
exudes poison in bright sunlight.

So I close my mouth, and my cry
makes dark music in my belly.
                              Who would listen
who could amaze?
                    Friends and beauty
lie waiting in poems, and the god
whose life we once wrote has left us
to muck in a world we covered with grease.

        Maybe I should watch the blossoms
turn to toasted flakes on my cherry tree.

Maybe I should walk along 41st Avenue
where mothers in velvet jogging suits push prams
and imitate the objects of my first lyrics.
Maybe I should comb my hair
the way I did in high school.

In the night the wind slides in from the sea
and eats at our faces;
                         that sweetheart,
she would do anything you ask her,
ask her,
           she'll lie down for a lonely heart.
Night-time's for lovers, maybe, closing their eyes
and pretending tomorrow will be splendid.

You should know that, you adult;
why dont you fling your arms wide
into the juicy air, chuck your ardent loneliness,
bump birds out of their dark paths
homeward to their grieving chicks.

Be grateful—
                 sadness makes music, cruel
April tuned a string for you.
                              Moons
whirled around planets waiting for you to spot them.
The middle of the Pacific prepared a wave
to plash ashore at your visit.
                              A radio
switched to a melody as you walked by
a neighbour's window.

You should know by now,
                         the world waited
to come alive at your step—
                              could you handle that?
Or did you think this was love,
                              movie music
introducing a maiden you could rescue?
Where were you going to keep her,
                              and keep her

from seeing those dreams you were already
playing house with?

When your heart hungers,
                    sing a song of six-
teen, remember your own maidenly love
and the girls that aroused it,
                    make them famous.
Remember their plain friends who danced so well
because they never got into a back seat.
Bring them all back, become a lyric poet again.
Identify with heroes who die for love
and a terrific image,
                    you'll live forever
in your anguished exalted metaphors.
                    Oh yeah.

But remember nature?
                    She takes back all
worn-out lovers,
                    two lie in the earth, one moulders
above-ground;
                    nature is an exhausted mom,
she cant go on forever,
                    this is late
in the machine age.
                    Can you think of one woman
who gave up on the stag line and turned
to God and a peaceful lawn?

Isnt it about time we said to hell with agony?
Shouldnt we be rich with hit parade love by now?
Arent we really free to choose joy over drama,
and havent we come through looking pretty good,
like a line-drive off a perfect swing
in the ninth inning?
                    It leaves the bat faster
than it came to the plate.
                    Taking that pitch
and standing still in the batter's box is nowhere.

Somebody's talking.

         Listen, stupid Kerrisdale heart,
the way your dead heroes listened, till
they were lifted out of their shoes,
but they couldnt hear it all, they thought
they were standing on earth.

         No,
you're not going to hear the final clap of truth;
that would kill you in two heart-beats.

But listen to the wind in the chestnut trees,
the breath of autumn's bleeding,

         the death
of your young heroes.

         You recall the breeze
across from the station in Florence,
where you saw an amazing name by the door?
Remember the clouds pulled off the face
of Mt. Blanc you saw from the morning window?
Why would the wind reach down to me?

Am I supposed to translate that swishy voice
into some kind of modern law?
Make me their liar even as the chestnuts are?
Deesse dans l'air repandue,
flamme dans notre souterrain!

Yes, I know, it is odd to be away from the world,
dropping all the habits you learned so well;
never bending to look at a rose face to face,
throwing your name away,
free of hands that held you fiercely,
laughing at what you once ached for,
watching all the old connections unravel in space.

Being dead is no bed of roses,
you have so much work piled up in front of you
before the long weekend.
But the folks who are still alive are too quick
to make their little decisions.
The spooks, they tell me, cant tell whether they're moving

among corpses or the fretful living.
The everlasting universe of things rolls
through all minds of all ages in every back yard,
and none of them can hear themselves think.

The ones who left early dont need our voices;
they're weaned from this ground as neatly
as we're diverted from mom's tit. But
what about us?
               We need the mystery, we need
the grief that makes us long for our dead friends,
we need that void for our poems.
We'd be dead without them.

Queen Marilyn made silly movies, but she's
the stuff our words are made from.
                     Her meaning
struts along the lines of a hundred lovely books.
Her music may be heard in the gaps in the traffic
of 41st Avenue.
            Her shiny breasts
fill the hands of our weeping poets.

DEATH

I'm going to write a poem about life & death, I said,
but mostly about death. But you are always doing that, said D,
your last poem was about death. The poem before that one was
about death. In fact if you looked at all your writing, especially
the poems, you would find pretty near nothing but death. A lot
of the time you seem to be laughing about it, but that doesn't
fool anyone.

Yes, but this time I am going to make it a real poem about life
but mainly death, I'll grant you that. None of that lacy Rilke
death, none of that ho ho Vonnegut death. I mean real death
or I should say real thinking about death. For instance? asked
D. Well, for instance, take the way you feel like how awful it
will be when you cant put an arm around a waist, long arm the
way it is just made to snake around a perfect waist, & there

is that swelling out of hip upon which it is natural to rest
an arm. How wonderful, and how terrible not to be able to look
forward to that ever again.

You see? said D, you announce that you are going to say something
straight about death, and there you are talking about life,
as far as I can see. That's just my point, I said. Death will be
horrible because it wont have anything of life in it, no matter
how many fancypants graduate students have told me that you cant
really submerge yourself in life unless you are fully conscious
of your death. They have all been reading Albert Camus lately,
& they are so much wiser than I am.

I suppose you are using all the things I have been saying as
part of your poem, said D. Of course, I said. You are to this poem
as a swelling out of lovely hip is to an arm that has snaked
around a dear waist.

Just then I realized that I had made D up in my imagination, &
now there was no D at all, & I had to forget about writing
another poem about life & death but especially about death,
especially about death from a straight point of view, because
M came into the room while I was typing & had a persistent gripe
about C, & no matter how interrupted I managed to make myself
look on the chair in front of the keyboard, M just kept on &
on till the poem had followed D to some place we will never find
the way to.

MUSING ON SOME POETS

Those poets, heads coming out of collars,
advised us, showed us how to hold paper and look good,
did we sometime grow tired of them, those
who lived for us,
died for us,
rotted under ground for us,
are still
so we may move.

Not friends, really, not teachers,
poets, whose names glittered when we were alone,
whose books dropped like gleaming newborn calves into our unsteady
     hands,
did we read them as if pulling shavings off our souls,
never stepped out of the Pacific combers with shine on morning face,
never twisted body out of grip of coal giant ogre
save with inspiration of our poets,
and who knows what our
means?

What are we now besides older;
a young man newly graduated from university,
black gown still on him said I envy you and your friends,
you got to make the last ones,
there isnt anything to make now, or no one knows what there is.
I said it seems that way but there is always something,
and I showed him my teeth through yellow beer.

Do we old farts say thank you every genuflecting morning
to those poets with agate names who showed us their synapses?
Nowadays the young want us to love the earth,
and I never say out loud to them that my dear old people
are columns of earth, walk around, sit in chairs,
discard cigarettes and write what's left of poems.
They were low lights between mountains visible
to the evening gaze, they were evaporate mornings,
they are not mulch but stones in the earth, they are not
specimens but the authors of words should be whispered inside a dark bowl
from Siena.

I have no remaining skill for form,
just feel words jostle each other in doorways on the way out, sit here this
evening remembering a former life, I'm with friends
all lovely all restrained by hope, all agreed without saying so
—those poets gave us a way to waste our lives
saying useless things, smiling indulgently at each other's personal diaspora,
carrying mismatched goodies on the way to the grave,
trip, fall into hole, write on dirt walls

a first and last sonnet,
solving all, coming to rest, combing hair, adjusting socks,
kissing no one but the image of Jesus, disbursing mind as if it were mercury,
listening for the voices to arrive with the worms.

FALL 1983, OLIVER

Home town is the still
centre he's been getting away from
all these widening circles, these

men, John the director and
Doug the camera man and somebody
younger the sound man.

Roy the friend the consultant
and Pearl the mom. A simple
little movie, the orchard, the

ball park, the dried mud, the
late slanting sunlight, the nouns
a little place is made of. A kid

never did come back to be filmed,
just this middle-aged man, all
excited, as if he were the kid,

as if he had brought those
tender stinking wings
to earth.

FRED WAH

(b. 1939)

Born in Swift Current, Saskatchewan, Fred Wah grew up in the West Kootenay area of British Columbia, a region his work is steeped in, and where he later edited *Scree*, taught at Selkirk College, and was active in founding the writing program at David Thompson University Centre. As he says in an afterword to his *Selected Poems: Loki Is Buried At Smoky Creek* (1976):

> Writing has a lot to do with 'place', the spiritual and spatial localities of the writer. I see things from *where* I am, my view point, and I measure and imagine a world from there. . . . I live in the 'interior' of British Columbia and such a qualification affects my particular sense of what the world looks like. We go 'down' to the coast, which is the exterior, the outside, the city. The spaces between here and there are part of a vast similarity. The towns become predictable in their activities and appearances. Castlegar and Prince George, though specifically themselves, share certain aspects of distance, colour and taste. One feels at home nearly anywhere there are rivers, pulp mills, trucks, the mysterious gravel roads further inward, and similar 'local' inhabitants. Down and out there the exterior becomes more. Vancouver leads to other cities and countries, etc. But all of it, out there, is measured from in here. In the particularity of a place the writer finds revealed the correspondences of a whole world.

While at the University of British Columbia studying music and English literature, Wah became a founding editor of *Tish*, a poetry newsletter influenced by the Black Mountain American poets. To the magazine's celebration of place and formal experimentation in art, Wah added his own musical and linguistic concerns, developing a work that is uniquely grounded, spare, improvisational, and rooted in the vernacular. His graduate study in literature and linguistics at the University of New Mexico and the State University of New York at Buffalo deepened his interest in words as both sign and sound, little units of acoustic energy that have their own agenda, tricks to play and surprises to offer, for whomever cares to listen. Words are intimately linked to the body, fuelled or fired by our breathing, gaining speed, momentum, and coloration from the delivering pulse and nervous system.

With his move to teach at the University of Calgary, Wah's attention in recent years has shifted to the remembered places of childhood and family, as he explores the contours, the scree and flora, of his Chinese and Caucasian background. He seems less interested in offering strict autobiography than in exploring the word-fields of family, Chinese café, small town, conducting an ongoing dialogue with his dead father, whimsically deconstructing both his former selves and the conventions of autobiographical writing, and exploring the possibilities of the long or serial poem. As he explains in a statement written for Sharon Thesen's *The New Long Poem Anthology*:

> Length in poetry seems useful as a means by which to investigate the possibilities of a content, formally, and, further, to extend the inquiry into contiguous aspects of the content. Such a process of composition offers generative resources that extend the dynamics of the poem (rhythm, repetition, shape, etc.) that not so much avoid cadence as configure it in different ways (cadence as shapely settling, not closure). . . . 'This Dendrite Map', for example, attempts to engage, in each separate piece, the reaction and resonance of the 'haiku' that settles out at the bottom. These were interesting pieces to write because, while writing the prose, I was conscious of the word-rumble further down the line.

In 'Music, Heart, Thinking', a fascinating interview conducted by Lola Tostevin (*Line*, 12, 1988), Wah speaks not only of 'place as a stain, the stain the world makes on a person', but also of more formal considerations, including Victor Shklovsky's theory of 'making strange', which Wah explains in this way: 'No, you hold the perception by making it strange. He said that the purpose of art was to make the stone stony. We don't pay attention to the fact that the stone is stony. It's a quality that's given, so it doesn't enter our perception. It's not something that we knowingly experience—but if I make the stone strange, so that somehow you can experience its stoniness, then there's a perception of something that wasn't there before.' He identifies, too, with Québécois writer Nicole Brossard's novel, *A Book*, 'not so much a disjunctive narrative but an angular cut, a slicing through the narrative, and the fact that she was allowing the short paragraph at the top of the page to constitute the continuity of some kind of narrative. It's really a novel in that it has characters, plot, story, but all of that, the conventional stuff of the novel, is in the background and what's at the forefront is language. I got excited about that because that's what poets do. Well, not all poets—but the ones I'm interested in. Good poetry should bring language to the fore and she was doing it in prose.'

In the same interview, Wah speaks of the poet's language as a sort of psychic DNA, an externalization of the music at the heart of the poet's thinking/feeling. He comes back, again and again, to music and cadence:

> I love that in music, playing the ad lib in a trumpet solo, or even a group. Trying to keep the piece together and hear the others in the group, how everything is going and push it so that it just about falls over the edge and doesn't. Like dissonance, I like the discord, the dissonant, because it pushes toward the edge and doesn't fall. . . . What you do when you're a musician or artist is you play the expectation of randomness against the predictability of form that starts to occur. It's that tension between the two that makes it interesting, and it's the estrangement between the two that also makes it interesting. . . . Music by and large operates on cadence and I've always been interested in language as a cadential structure, even minutely, in terms of phrases and clauses.

Wah's other titles include *Lardeau* (1965), *Among* (1967), *Tree* (1974), *Earth* (1974), *Pictograms from the Interior of B.C.* (1980), *Breathin' My Name with a Sigh* (1981), *Waiting for Saskatchewan* (1985), which won the Governor General's Award, *Limestone Lakes: Utaniki* (1987), *Music at the Heart of Thinking* (1989), *So Far* (1991), *Alley Alley Home Free* (1992), a prose biofiction called *Diamond Grill* (1996), and a collection of critical writing titled *Faking It: Poetics & Hybridity* (2000).

MY HORSE

I never had
who carries me
so secretly
is dead.

I think
he bucked
& threw me
on a mountain
at the bottom
of the path.

O my dead horse
I never had
such dreams
as dreams of you
not there
when I ride past.

THE CANOE, TOO

there is all that talk about northern waters
lakes with canoes sliding silently over the cold glass surfaces
                    in the moonlight
and a mountain rising to the moon in its ice and snow
the rocky shore and its cold dry branches of driftwood waiting
for you to return alone in the still night
shimmering darkness

there is all that talk of this
and the mind wanders there is a canoe language carries
like a picture framing you in the black ice water

there is all this kind of talk and you listen to the words

the northern lakes freeze
over the ice snow covers the valley
                    and all the trees

FROM PICTOGRAMS FROM THE INTERIOR OF B.C.

Under and over
I see myself rocking
boat/cradle
cave to swim into
over and over again
home again
home

I'M GOING TO KEEP ON DANCING
FOR THE REST OF MY LIFE
for Lewis

Sproul Plaza body writhing on the asphalt
then swaying in the bandstand, Lew
did you ever play the saxophone
in your high-school dance band
especially A-Train and heft the ax
in a slight tilt 'till you tipped the music
and wailed out of your left shoulder
swirled honky honey blues glissandos
or maybe later you used your hips
when everybody switched from jazz to Comets
you could really pull it all out
and hump your horn 'till you're on your knees
and the girls are screamin and wettin their pants
and pushing their crinolines between their legs
whew, Lew
that's what this dancer's doing on the plaza
so much into it and what you do too

so that all that Texas in your voice
sways you into the body, sways you
and us, here Lew
read this for me will you?

FROM WAITING FOR SASKATCHEWAN

Waiting for Saskatchewan
and the origins grandparents countries places converged
europe asia railroads carpenters nailed grain elevators
Swift Current my grandmother in her house
he built on the street
and him his cafes namely the 'Elite' on Center
looked straight ahead Saskatchewan points to it
Erickson Wah Trimble houses train station tracks
arrowed into downtown fine clay dirt prairies wind waiting
for Saskatchewan to appear for me again over the edge
horses led to the huge sky the weight and colour of it
over the mountains as if the mass owed me such appearance
against the hard edge of it sits on my forehead
as the most political place I know these places these strips
laid beyond horizon for eyesight the city so I won't have to go
near it as origin town flatness appears later in my stomach why
why on earth would they land in such a place
mass of pleistocene
sediment plate wedge
arrow sky beak horizon still waiting for that
I want it back, wait in this snowblown winter night
for that latitude of itself its own largeness
my body to get complete
it still owes me, it does

ELITE 2

Do you remember how living on the prairies was like living
in water, in an ocean or a large lake. Movements, decisions, fortunes were made by undercurrent, a sense of
sliding along a large floor, in the night. The night I was
with you on a trip, just before we moved out to B.C.,

it felt like that, the way we moved, probably by train, through unknown territory. Always you had an 'intent.' You were on business of some sort and the others we met were all Chinese. You could talk to them. They gave me candy and pinched me. You and they talked and talked. Chinese always sounds so serious, emotional, angry. I napped on the couch in some Chinese store in some Alberta town. The old men played dominoes and smoked and drank tea. In the window dusty plants in porcelain bowls and some goldfish. Does it seem strange to you now to see this in words? Do you remember the trip I'm talking about? Late at night somewhere you played Mah Jong. From outside the sound of the click–clack of the pieces being shuffled over the tabletop under the hum of the men's voices, a real music I felt comfortable with. Even though you stayed late you always came back, going somewhere. We moved that night through this subcontinent of prairie landscape, it was summer and the water was warm and hazy, the possible distances, distant.

ELITE 3

I'm on the prairies this winter. I haven't been here in the winter since I was four years old. It's not Swift Current, or Speedy Creek as some here call it, but there are certain flavours which are unmistakeably part of us. The ethnicity here feels so direct. I mean the Chinese are still connected to China, the Ukrainians so Ukrainian, in the bar the Icelanders tell stories about Iceland, the Swede still has an accent, the French speak French. Here you're either a Wiebe or a Friesen, or not. What is a Metis, anyway? I know when you came back from China you must have felt more Chinese than anything else. But I remember you saying later that the Chinese didn't trust you and the English didn't trust you. You were a half-breed, Eurasian. I remember feeling the possibility of that word 'Eurasian' for myself when I first read it in my own troubled adolescence. I don't think you ever felt the relief of that exotic identity though. In North America white is still the standard and you were never white enough. But you weren't pure enough for the Chinese either. You never knew the full comradeship of an ethnic community. So you felt single, outside, though you played the game as we all must. To be a mix here on the prairies is still noticed. I remember going into Macleods in Swift Current a few years ago and sensing that most of the women in the store were just like Granny Erickson. I don't think you felt there was anyone else in the world like you.

ELITE 4

You got us involved in the Salvation Army because that's what Granny Wah wanted. She had a bonnet. I can't recall ever seeing Grampa or you there. But I bet she had her go at you too. Didn't you ever play the big bass drum, or the cymbals? I played the E-flat horn later in Nelson. I think, like Grampa, you always thought the Salvation Army people outside yourself. That was the Chinese in you. You didn't outwardly really trust it. But you tried it. In some totally pure and personal way you prayed, alone. I know later when our family went to the United Church in Nelson and you sometimes got off work on Sunday morning to go to church with us you did sing the hymns but your brow furled as if you couldn't understand the words. You were proud, then, of the fact you were going to church and you made a point of telling some of the customers in the restaurant that you had to go to church. That was after you had stopped desiring China and the Chinese at work put up with but laughed at you going to church. I think the church thing was white respectability and you did it for that and a sense of our family in that community. Somehow in the face of all the Salvation Army, Granny, community, etc. I know you established some real spiritual communication, totally private, no drums.

FATHER/MOTHER HAIBUN #4

Your pen wrote Chinese and your name in a smooth swoop
with flourish and style, I can hardly read my own tight
scrawl, could you write anything else, I know you could
read, nose in the air and lick your finger to turn the large
newspaper page pensively in the last seat of those half-
circle arborite counters in the Diamond Grill, your glass
case bulging your shirt pocket with that expensive pen,
always a favourite thing to handle the way you treated it
like jewellry, actually it was a matched pen and pencil set,
Shaeffer maybe (something to do with Calgary here), heavy,
silver, black, gold nib, the precision I wanted also in things,
that time I conned you into paying for a fountain pen I
had my eye on in Benwell's stationery store four dollars
and twenty cents Mom was mad but you understood such
desires in your cheeks relaxed when you worked signing
checks and doing the books in the back room of the cafe
late at night or how the pen worked perfectly with your
quick body as you'd flourish off a check during a busy
noon-hour rush the sun and noise of the town and the cafe
flashing.

**High muck-a-muck's gold-toothed clicks ink mark red green
on lottery blotting paper, 8-spot (click, click)**

FATHER/MOTHER HAIBUN #11

Mother somewhere you flying over me with love and close
careless caress from Sweden your soft smooth creme skin
only thoughts from your mother without comparison the
lightness of your life/blood womaness which is mine despite
language across foetalness what gods of northern europe
bring out of this sentence we say and live in outside of
the wife of the storm god's frictive battle with the 'story'
our names

**Rain washes first snow, old words here on the notepad,
'Where did Odysseus go?'**

FATHER/MOTHER HAIBUN #17

Oh Mother, the brightness of the birch tree's bark in this
November mid-afternoon sunset, fringes, the datum which
is permanent, the external events of all that stuff actual
energy is created from, you on a different planar syntax
Jenefer discovers in turning the yin/yang key, a cyclic
thing going on there, ontologic principle, all the daughters
want it, one pot, this morning I watered your Christmas
cactus bursting brilliant pink and purple on schedule for
your birthday again, and you should see Helen's, what'd
those philosophers say, he beats the drum, he
stops, he sobs, he sings, they had mothers.

**You flew over me, outside there was a moist loss, now I
remember**

FATHER/MOTHER HAIBUN #19

I'm here alone for the weekend, get fires going and burn
all that junk, mind keeps that there to clean up. I get some
rice on and the cabin's warm. Now I sit here sip a beer
and dwell on my aloneness, the solitary singleness and
being older now. That is a prediction I gave myself when
I watched some of the old men around town, isolation.
Night falling. Cold over the lake, fingers of
clouds in the western sky above Woodbury Creek. I told Peter that's the
process I'm interested in as long as I can keep getting the
language out. Now I'm as old as you were. The fire outside
in the dark comes from your eyes. The words of our name
settle down with everything else on this shore.

Smoke sits on the lake, frost tonight, eyes thinking

THE POEM CALLED SYNTAX

We live on the edge of a lake called Echo.
I love this notion that noise makes itself.
so the lake holds all noise in its depths
and when the dog barks it gets it from the lake.

About nine thousand feet above these lakes (all lakes)
there is a geometry of sound, something like Plato's cave of noise.
It is from that construct the dog's bark takes shape,
a resounding of an earlier bark conditioned by the alpine.

History and physics. Acoustic paradigms in a bog of algae.
When I tell all my cousins and friends about this
they'll come to live on the shores of this lake and clean it up.
From the balconies of their summer homes they'll ask a lot of
    questions.

FROM 'MUSIC AT THE HEART OF THINKING'

#89

    I've always had trouble with the ingenious engine as
a suffix of graded wanting love or prayer especially
kindergarten stifled kid as a kind of person who might
extend racism or even keep me off the block your kindred
jammed the oceans cognitive shot freeborn got then
similar to most of the inborn tutelary spirits everywhere
naive seed of Enyallion or old chip off the old rock and
that's congenital heart buds gyna gendered and warped up
tighter than a Persian rug how ginger's almost nicer than
being born but that's just taste.

*

#90

    On the weekend I got into anger talk about
landscape and the hunger of narrative to eat answer or
time but space works for me because place got to be
more spiritual at least last felt now this watery genetic I
suspect passions like anger suprafixed to simply dwells I
mean contained as we speak of it believe me I'd like to
find a new word-track for feeling but language and
moment work out simply as simultaneous occurences so I

don't think you should blame words for time-lapse
tropism eg ethics is probably something that surrounds
you like your house it's where you live.

*

#91

    Again only is it in the thing itself the place which is
the driven place as a warm motor song hums under the
chakra tree rock or stone creek song I've become used to
such a thing always drowning and then owning myself
come to my own again possessed of me as the sib in the
place of itself hungry with love again forgiven dreaming
and knowing again the tailbone of itself bones claimed
again so that 'thing' to my soul's bark floats again.

*

#92

Don't do anything
just sit still and feel the bridge above
forget about the traffic
    it's going as fast as it can
down here is the river property
        no train of words except some tropic text of
truth above old creek song flows its utter pure of
coolness underneath the fading rose another rose
untangled knot a permafrost of frozen words
unflavoured dirt for roots
        All this leveraging aggregate compassed
grounding cord to compost loops the stomach's
locomotor to Galan feedback shutdown more to
do with stellar steering of the junction box genetic
or the fresh-water hoofprint of salmon salt

*

#93

Any gravel road's ok by me or is that an ordering intervention so long as it's not pure highway to the end of the void without my story our narrative's just a bunch of rotten windfalls under the apple tree of someone elses eye a statistical cluster made up to cover up and that stupid notion of a project as sticking it to everyone else instead of girdling yourself to the entelecheic text underfoot that dreamt you long ago

an earth doesn't add up to the only implicate map ethnos is and

the new doesn't have to be the purity nation is at least some Love pictographed without lexicon gets us to the grannies grammar.

*

#94

This is no mass synapse I'm after and I've known awhile now being lost is as simple as sitting on a log but the fumble jerked mystique clouds grabbing as the staked mistake or stacked and treasured garbage belongs familiar to a gardened world disturbed as heat

O soft anxiousness to be found again and again estranged but marvellous then enlived slope of scree and marmot whistle so that synchronous foreignicity rages in music I want to put into a region of the cadence before falling's recognized you know

where there's that disgraceful ensoulment Mao called swimming

*

#95

If he thinks it's a great privilege to fill halls and talk about his own little heart when the invisible trunk of the noetic is what's available on the other side of the wall and only intuition can kiss the pebbly surface of Easter's stone just as 'it is not you who throw the dart when you throw it' then could we not have called for a parallel conspiration to play out the alphabet onto the red carpet of one's body through some himma of potency no such dream of stars shld floor us by the raw and sober daylight of a cloudy sky.

MARGARET ATWOOD

(b. 1939)

The issues that have been constant in Margaret Atwood's writing all have to do with survival: survival of the individual consciousness in the face of psychic overload; survival of women in a male-dominated society; survival of the community, whether the nation-state or a smaller unit such as the tribe of writers; and survival of the species against increasing violence, technological madness that is destroying culture and environment, and the ever-present threat of nuclear annihilation.

Atwood's poems about psychic overload often include the figure of an immigrant, or pioneer, who is trying to confront a new and possibly hostile environment, where 'unstructured/space is a deluge'. The task of this individual, like that of the artist, is to form gestalts, to shape the chaos, thereby rendering it manageable, perhaps even meaningful. Atwood's response to threats to Canadian sovereignty and cultural survival, posed by the colonial attitude of Canadians and the presence and policies of the United States, has found expression in a variety of works, including *Survival: A Thematic Guide to Canadian Literature* (1972), *The Journals of Susanna Moodie* (1970), and a sequence such as 'Two-Headed Poems'.

Feminist concerns inform her work at every level, not only because most of her personae and narrators are women, but also because she has very consciously addressed such issues as sexual rights, procreative rights, and social and vocational rights. The struggle for identity and equality for

women finds its fullest dramatic expression in her novels *The Edible Woman* (1970) and *Surfacing* (1972), but the poems of *Procedures for Underground* (1970), *Power Politics* (1973)—from which the surreal and witty 'They Eat Out' was taken—and several recent collections explore the same ideas with mordant humour and in a variety of genres, including psychological parables and stinging satires.

Atwood is concerned, in other words, with power politics at every level of existence. Much of her recent work has addressed directly the problems of torture, imprisonment, and other human rights violations, totalitarian regimes, racism, censorship, and hunger. Her task has been to create strategies, literary techniques, with which to bring these issues home to readers. Her poems and such non-fiction writings as 'Amnesty International: An Address' argue for the artist as a witness and provocateur, trying to raise consciousness and initiate change. She said in an interview with Christopher Levenson in *Manna*: 'I would say that I don't think what poetry does is express emotion. What poetry does is evoke emotion from the reader, and that is a very different thing. As someone once said, if you want to express emotion, scream. If you want to evoke emotion it's more complicated.'

Atwood uses anomaly and other dislocating devices to keep the reader alert and involved in the poetic process. She functions as an illusionist, employing perceptual tricks—interjecting apparent non sequiturs or off-hand comments to distract the reader from the apparent content of the poem, or suddenly shifting the point of view in the middle of a poem. Atwood loves to parody traditional romantic forms and stances; instead of lyrical outbursts, displays of sonority, and heavy emoting, she prefers understatement, the creation of a wry and prosaic voice, and the shock value of surreal and bizarre images. As she explains in *Manna*:

> There are always concealed magical forms in poetry. By 'magic' I mean a verbal attempt to accomplish something desirable. You can take a poem and trace it back to a source in either prayer, curse, charm or incantation—an attempt to make something happen. Do you know anything about autistic children? One of the symptoms of that is they mistake the word for the thing. If they see the word 'clock' on the paper they pick it up to see if it ticks. If you write 'door' they try to open it. That sort of thing is inherent in language in some funny way and poetry is connected with that at some level.

Atwood insists that 'every poem has a texture of sound which is at least as important to me as the "argument". This is not to minimize "statement". But it does annoy me when students, prompted by the approach of their teacher, ask, "What is the poet trying to say?" It implies that the poet is some kind of verbal cripple who can't quite "say" what he "means" and has to resort to a lot of round-the-mulberry-bush, thereby putting the student to a great deal of trouble extracting his "meaning," like a prize out of a box of Cracker Jacks.' 'For me', she insists, 'poetry is where the language is renewed. If poetry vanished, language would become dead. It would become embalmed. . . . It's true that poetry doesn't make money. But it's the heart of the language. If you think of language as a series of concentric circles, poetry is right in the centre. It's where precision takes place. It's where that use of language takes place that can extend a word yet have to be precise.'

Atwood was born in Ottawa, but spent much of her childhood in the woods of Northern Quebec, where her father worked as an entomologist. She studied at the University of Toronto and Harvard and has travelled widely. Her work has been acclaimed internationally. She has received a Governor General's Award, won the Booker Prize, and been published in many languages. In addition to the books mentioned above, her other collections of poetry include *The Circle Game* (1966), *The Animals in That Country* (1968), *You Are Happy* (1974), *Selected Poems* (1976), *Two-Headed Poems* (1978), *True Stories* (1981), *Interlunar* (1984), *Good Bones* (1992), and *Morning in the Burned House* (1995). Her other novels are *Lady Oracle* (1976), *Life Before Man* (1979), *Bodily Harm* (1981), *The Handmaid's Tale* (1986), *Cat's Eye* (1988), *The Robber Bride* (1993), *Alias Grace* (1997), and *The Blind Assassin* (2000). *Dancing Girls* (1977), *Bluebeard's Egg* (1984), and *Wilderness Tips* (1991) are collections of stories; *Murder in the Dark* (1993) is a collection of short fiction and prose poems. She has written children's books and two additional collection of critical commentary, *Second Words: Selected Critical Prose* (1982) and *Margaret Atwood: Conversations* (1990), edited by E.G. Ingersoll. Two non-fiction titles include *Strange Things: The Malevolent North in Canlit* (1995) and *The Labrador Fiasco* (1996). She lives in Toronto.

THE ANIMALS IN THAT COUNTRY

In that country the animals
have the faces of people:

the ceremonial
cats possessing the streets

the fox run
politely to earth, the huntsmen
standing around him, fixed
in their tapestry of manners

the bull, embroidered
with blood and given
an elegant death, trumpets, his name
stamped on him, heraldic brand
because

(when he rolled
on the sand, sword in his heart, the teeth
in his blue mouth were human)

he is really a man

even the wolves, holding resonant
conversations in their
forests thickened with legend.

 In this country the animals
 have the faces of
 animals.

 Their eyes
 flash once in car headlights
 and are gone.

 Their deaths are not elegant.

They have the faces of
 no-one.

A NIGHT IN THE ROYAL ONTARIO MUSEUM

Who locked me

into this crazed man-made
stone brain
        where the weathered
totempole jabs a blunt
finger at the byzantine
mosaic dome

Under that ornate
golden cranium I wander
among fragments of gods, tarnished
coins, embalmed gestures
chronologically arranged,
looking for the EXIT sign

but in spite of the diagrams
at every corner, labelled
in red: YOU ARE HERE
the labyrinth holds me,

turning me around
the cafeteria, the washrooms,
a spiral through marble
Greece and Rome, the bronze
horses of China

then past the carved masks, wood and fur
to where 5 plaster Indians
in a glass case
squat near a dusty fire

and further, confronting me
with a skeleton child, preserved
in the desert air, curled
beside a clay pot and a few beads.

I say I am far
enough,   stop here   please
no more

but the perverse museum, corridor
by corridor, an idiot
voice jogged by a pushed
button, repeats its memories

and I am dragged to the mind's
deadend, the roar of the bone-
yard, I am lost
among the mastodons
and beyond: a fossil
shell, then

samples of rocks
and minerals, even the thundering
tusks dwindling to pin-
points in the stellar
fluorescent-lighted
wastes of geology

PROGRESSIVE INSANITIES OF A PIONEER

I

He stood, a point
on a sheet of green paper
proclaiming himself the centre,

with no walls, no borders
anywhere; the sky no height
above him, totally un-
enclosed
and shouted:

Let me out!

II

He dug the soil in rows,
imposed himself with shovels.
He asserted

into the furrows, I
am not random.

The ground
replied with aphorisms:

a tree-sprout, a nameless
weed, words
he couldn't understand.

III

The house pitched
the plot staked
in the middle of nowhere.

At night the mind
inside, in the middle
of nowhere.

The idea of an animal
patters across the roof.

In the darkness the fields
defend themselves with fences
in vain:
    everything
    is getting in.

IV

By daylight he resisted.
He said, disgusted
with the swamp's clamourings and the outbursts
of rocks,
    This is not order
    but the absence
    of order.

He was wrong, the unanswering
forest implied:

It was
an ordered absence

V

For many years
he fished for a great vision,
dangling the hooks of sown
roots under the surface
of the shallow earth.

It was like
enticing whales with a bent
pin. Besides he thought
in that country
only the worms were biting.

VI

If he had known unstructured
space is a deluge
and stocked his log house-
boat with all the animals
even the wolves,

he might have floated.

But obstinate he
stated, The land is solid
and stamped,

watching his foot sink
down through stone
up to the knee.

VII

Things
refused to name themselves; refused
to let him name them.

The wolves hunted
outside.

On his beaches, his clearings,
by the surf of under–
growth breaking
at his feet, he foresaw
disintegration
           and in the end
through eyes
made ragged by his
effort, the tension
between subject and object,

the green
vision, the unnamed
whale invaded.

DEATH OF A YOUNG SON BY DROWNING

He, who navigated with success
the dangerous river of his own birth
once more set forth

on a voyage of discovery
into the land I floated on
but could not touch to claim.

His feet slid on the bank,
the currents took him;
he swirled with ice and trees in the swollen water

and plunged into distant regions,
his head a bathysphere;
through his eyes' thin glass bubbles

he looked out, reckless adventurer
on a landscape stranger than Uranus
we have all been to and some remember.

There was an accident; the air locked,
he was hung in the river like a heart.
they retrieved the swamped body,

cairn of my plans and future charts,
with poles and hooks
from among the nudging logs.

It was spring, the sun kept shining, the new grass
lept to solidity;
my hands glistened with details.

After the long trip I was tired of waves.
My foot hit rock. The dreamed sails
collapsed, ragged.

    I planted him in this country
    like a flag.

GAME AFTER SUPPER

This is before electricity,
it is when there were porches.

On the sagging porch an old man
is rocking. The porch is wooden,

the house is wooden and grey;
in the living room which smells of
smoke and mildew, soon
the women will light the kerosene lamp.

There is a barn but I am not in the barn;
there is an orchard too, gone bad,
its apples like soft cork
but I am not there either.

I am hiding in the long grass
with my two dead cousins,
the membrane grown already
across their throats.

We hear crickets and our own hearts
close to our ears;
though we giggle, we are afraid.

From the shadows around
the corner of the house
a tall man is coming to find us:

He will be an uncle,
if we are lucky.

THEY EAT OUT

In restaurants we argue
over which of us will pay for your funeral

though the real question is
whether or not I will make you immortal.

At the moment only I
can do it and so

I raise the magic fork
over the plate of beef fried rice

and plunge it into your heart.
There is a faint pop, a sizzle

and through your own split head
you rise up glowing;

the ceiling opens
a voice sings Love Is A Many

Splendoured Thing
you hang suspended above the city

in blue tights and a red cape
your eyes flashing in unison.

The other diners regard you
some with awe, some only with boredom:

they cannot decide if you are a new weapon
or only a new advertisement.

As for me, I continue eating;
I liked you better the way you were,
but you were always ambitious.

NOTES TOWARD A POEM THAT CAN NEVER BE WRITTEN

For Carolyn Forché

i

This is the place
you would rather not know about,
this is the place that will inhabit you,
this is the place you cannot imagine,
this is the place that will finally defeat you

where the word *why* shrivels and empties
itself. This is famine.

ii

There is no poem you can write
about it, the sandpits
where so many were buried
& unearthed, the unendurable
pain still traced on their skins.

This did not happen last year
or forty years ago but last week.
This has been happening,
this happens.

We make wreaths of adjectives for them,
we count them like beads,
we turn them into statistics & litanies
and into poems like this one.

Nothing works.
They remain what they are.

iii

The woman lies on the wet cement floor
under the unending light,
needle marks on her arms put there
to kill the brain
and wonders why she is dying.

She is dying because she said.
She is dying for the sake of the word.
It is her body, silent
and fingerless, writing this poem.

iv

It resembles an operation
but it is not one

nor despite the spread legs, grunts
& blood, is it a birth.

Partly it's a job
partly it's a display of skill
like a concerto.

It can be done badly
or well, they tell themselves.

Partly it's an art.

v

The facts of this world seen clearly
are seen through tears;
why tell me then
there is something wrong with my eyes?

To see clearly and without flinching,
without turning away,
this is agony, the eyes taped open
two inches from the sun.

What is it you see then?
Is it a bad dream, a hallucination?
Is it a vision?
What is it you hear?

The razor across the eyeball
is a detail from an old film.
It is also a truth.
Witness is what you must bear.

vi

In this country you can say what you like
because no one will listen to you anyway,
it's safe enough, in this country you can try to write
the poem that can never be written,
the poem that invents
nothing and excuses nothing,
because you invent and excuse yourself each day.

Elsewhere, this poem is not invention.
Elsewhere, this poem takes courage.
Elsewhere, this poem must be written
because the poets are already dead.

Elsewhere, this poem must be written
as if you are already dead,
as if nothing more can be done
or said to save you.

Elsewhere you must write this poem
because there is nothing more to do.

1981

A WOMEN'S ISSUE

The woman in the spiked device
that locks around the waist and between
the legs, with holes in it like a tea strainer
is Exhibit A.

The woman in black with a net window
to see through and a four-inch
wooden peg jammed up
between her legs so she can't be raped
is Exhibit B.

Exhibit C is the young girl
dragged into the bush by the midwives
and made to sing while they scrape the flesh
from between her legs, then tie her thighs
till she scabs over and is called healed.
Now she can be married.
For each childbirth they'll cut her
open, then sew her up.
Men like tight women.
The ones that die are carefully buried.

The next exhibit lies flat on her back
while eighty men a night
move through her, ten an hour.
She looks at the ceiling, listens
to the door open and close.
A bell keeps ringing.
Nobody knows how she got here.

You'll notice that what they have in common
is between the legs. Is this
why wars are fought?
Enemy territory, no man's
land, to be entered furtively,
fenced, owned but never surely,
scene of these desperate forays
at midnight, captures
and sticky murders, doctors' rubber gloves

greasy with blood, flesh made inert, the surge
of your own uneasy power.

This is no museum.
Who invented the word love?

Morning in the Burned House

In the burned house I am eating breakfast.
You understand: there is no house, there is no breakfast,
yet here I am.

The spoon which was melted scrapes against
the bowl which was melted also.
No one else is around.

Where have they gone to, brother and sister,
mother and father? Off along the shore,
perhaps. Their clothes are still on the hangers,

their dishes piled beside the sink,
which is beside the woodstove
with its grate and sooty kettle,

every detail clear,
tin cup and rippled mirror.
The day is bright and songless,

the lake is blue, the forest watchful.
In the east a bank of cloud
rises up silently like dark bread.

I can see the swirls in the oilcloth,
I can see the flaws in the glass,
those flares where the sun hits them.

I can't see my own arms and legs
or know if this is a trap or blessing,
finding myself back here, where everything

in this house has long been over,
kettle and mirror, spoon and bowl,
including my own body,

including the body I had then,
including the body I have now
as I sit at this morning table, alone and happy,

bare child's feet on the scorched floorboards
(I can almost see)
in my burning clothes, the thin green shorts

and grubby yellow T-shirt
holding my cindery, non-existent,
radiant flesh. Incandescent.

PATRICK LANE

(b. 1939)

In an essay entitled 'To the Outlaw', first published in John Gill's *New: American & Canadian Poetry* (1971), Patrick Lane writes passionately of the poet as an outlaw, a half-mad fugitive who inhabits the margins of society, the darkest corners: 'A poet is neither trained nor taught. He is the outlaw surging beyond the only freedom he knows, beauty in bondage. . . . The poem is a place of beauty that goes beyond knowledge and understanding.' For Lane, then, the poem would appear to be a sort of prison or cage in which experience is captured, its terrors rendered beautiful in words. Appropriately, images of confinement—jails, cages, rooms, attitudes, roles, social classes, political systems—abound in his poems. Animals—creatures that ought to exist outside the mental and physical prisons man makes, but are constantly being trapped, victimized, or rendered extinct—stalk through the pages of Lane's books, especially birds, those exotic and romantic reminders of our earthbound nature and our deepest yearnings for escape.

Another facet of Lane's romantic stance is his conviction that he writes about lower-class working experience from the INSIDE IN, rather than from the OUTSIDE IN. He insists that 'the personal is the only universal truth, the "everyman",' and argues that his 'search for enlightenment . . . is always balanced with my social commitment to the lower class, of which I am a member, with all its rage and pathos.' Thus he identifies strongly with Chilean poet Pablo Neruda

and with the plight of peoples in the Third World countries he has visited; so, too, he advocates a poetry along lines suggested in Neruda's essay 'Towards an Impure Art': 'A poetry impure as the clothing we wear, soup-stained, soiled with our shameful behaviour, our wrinkles and vigils and dreams. . . .'

The form and content of most of Lane's early work falls within such 'impure' bounds. His messages are not pretty; they are full of guilt and suffering, separation and loss. Gradually, however, the image of the tight-lipped loser who inhabits these poems gives way to a wiser, more reflective persona, capable of greater understanding and a broader historical reference. After the early work, which had been excessively anecdotal, Lane began to discover in the basic materials of his poetry *significant* form, which has more to do with the resources of language than with events themselves. Similarly, his considerable metaphorical gifts, which previously seemed unsuited to an age committed to understatement and economy, became more and more capable of profound and startling effects: the metaphor in 'Stigmata', for example, 'the scrimshawed teeth of endless whales, / the oceans it took to carve them', derives its power not from mere cleverness, but rather from the poet thinking his way into the image. For the reader this results in the shock of recognition, and delight at being confronted with a proposition (the creature shaped by the element it inhabits) so profoundly simple that it has escaped attention.

Whether he is writing about love, nature, the destruction of the Incas, or the castration of a ram, Lane is capable of a delicate but biting lyricism. In 'Mountain Oysters', for example, the speaker describes the quick and efficient slitting of the ram's scrotum and subsequent eating of the fried testicles with an excruciating matter-of-factness and verbal understatement ('brushed the tail aside / slit the bag / tucked the knackers in his mouth / and clipped the cords off clean'); these techniques, and the colloquial indifference of the farmer's off-hand remarks, serve to heighten the sense of pain and horror Lane wishes to communicate. The idea of 'cutting delicately' and then eating the testicles invokes a sense of incongruity, and calls up old wives' tales about strength and sexual prowess being derived from eating the organs of certain animals; then Lane beautifully juxtaposes the dining scene with an image of rams in the field, 'holding their pain / legs fluttering like blue hands / of tired old men.'

Ultimately there is a degree of poetic learning and a real commitment to literature in Lane's work that is of greater significance than his 'outlaw' stance. As he works with the longer line and explores certain metrical and syllabic possibilities that he eschewed in his earlier work, Lane becomes more and more capable of appropriating other voices, other times. In fact, in his teaching notes, which he generously made available and which he calls Meditations, there is considerable reference made to the importance of tradition, learning from the old masters. In Meditation 6, he admits that he had studiously and stupidly ignored tradition: 'It was simply that I had chosen too narrow a field to work in. I broke away

from my contemporaries and spent the next five years studying the masters. If I wanted to be a good writer, I thought back then, I have much to learn.' In his maturity, Lane encourages his students to study the old masters, to try out sonnets, sestinas and villanelles, 'to learn how difficult it is to write within prescribed forms.' He also pays tribute to a wide range of influences, including Jack Gilbert, Robert Hass, Elizabeth Bishop, Gwendolyn MacEwen, and Al Purdy.

He was born in Nelson, BC and has lived intermittently in the interior of British Columbia and in Saskatchewan before settling in Victoria. His travels have taken him to Europe, China, and South America. As his poems indicate, he has tried his hand at a wide variety of jobs, mostly manual. He was co-founder of Very Stone House, a small publishing venture Lane operated in transit out of a series of doomed Volkswagen vans, and has been writer-in-residence at Concordia University and the Universities of Manitoba and Alberta. He now lives on Vancouver Island and teaches part-time in the Department of Creative Writing at the University of Victoria. His books include *Letters from a Savage Mind* (1966), *The Sun Has Begun to Eat the Mountains* (1972), *Passing Into Storm* (1973), *Beware the Months of Fire* (1973), *Unborn Things* (1975), *Poems New and Selected* (1979) which won a Governor General's Award, *Old Mother* (1982), *Selected Poems* (1987), *A Linen Crow, A Caftan Magpie* (1984), *Winter* (1990), *Mortal Remains* (1991), *Selected Poems, 1978–1997* (1997) and *The Bare Plum of Winter Rain* (2000). He has published a collection of stories, *How Do You Spell Beautiful?* (1992), and is the subject of a critical study by George Woodcock, *Patrick Lane and His Works* (1984).

PASSING INTO STORM

Know him for a white man.
He walks sideways into wind
allowing the left of him

to forget what the right
knows as cold. His ears
turn into death what

his eyes can't see. All day
he walks away from the sun
passing into storm. Do not

mistake him for the howl you hear
or the track you think you
follow. Finding a white man

in snow is to look for the dead.
He has been burned by the wind.
He has left too much

flesh on winter's white metal
to leave his colour as a sign.
Cold white. Cold flesh. He leans

into wind sideways; kills without
mercy anything to the left of him
coming like madness in the snow.

THE BIRD

The bird you captured is dead.
I told you it would die
but you would not learn
from my telling. You wanted
to cage a bird in your hands
and learn to fly.

Listen again.
You must not handle birds.
They cannot fly through your fingers.
You are not a nest
and a feather is
not made of blood and bone.

Only words
can fly for you like birds
on the wall of the sun.
A bird is a poem
that talks of the end of cages.

ELEPHANTS

The cracked cedar bunkhouse
hangs behind me like a grey pueblo
in the sundown where I sit
to carve an elephant
from a hunk of brown soap
for the Indian boy who lives
in the village a mile back
in the bush.

The alcoholic truck-driver
and the cat-skinner sit beside
me with their eyes closed
all of us waiting out the last hour
until we go back on the grade

and I try to forget the forever
clank   clank   clank
across the grade
pounding stones and earth to powder
for hours in mosquito-darkness
of the endless cold mountain night.

The elephant takes form—
my knife caresses smooth soap
scaling off curls of brown
which the boy saves to take home
to his mother in the village.

Finished, I hand the carving to him
and he looks at the image of the great
beast for a long time
then sets it on dry cedar
and looks up at me:
                        What's an elephant?
he asks me
so I tell him of the elephants
and their jungles. The story
of the elephant graveyard
which no one has ever found
and how the silent
animals of the rain forest
go away to die somewhere
in the limberlost of distances
and he smiles at me
tells me of his father's
graveyard where his people have been
buried for years. So far back
no one remembers when it started
and I ask him where the graveyard is
and he tells me it is gone
now where no one will ever find it
buried under the grade of the new
highway.

MOUNTAIN OYSTERS

Kneeling in the sheep-shit
he picked up the biggest of the new rams
brushed the tail aside
slit the bag
tucked the knackers in his mouth
and clipped the cords off clean

the ram   stiff
with a single wild scream

as the tar went on
and he spit the balls in a bowl.

That's how we used to do it
when I was a boy.
It's no more gawdam painful
than any other way
and you can't have rams fighting
slamming it up every nanny

and enjoyed them with him
cutting delicately
into the deep-fried testicles.

Mountain oysters make you strong
he said
while out in the field
the rams stood holding their pain
legs fluttering like blue hands
of old tired men.

UNBORN THINGS

After the dog drowns in the arroyo
and the old people stumble into the jungle
muttering imprecations at the birds
and the child draws circles in the dust
for bits of glass to occupy
like eyes staring out of earth
and the woman lies on her hammock
dreaming of the lover who will save her
from the need to make bread again
I will go into the field
and be buried with the corn.

Folding my hands on my chest
I will see the shadow of myself; the same
who watched a father when he moved
with hands on the dark side of a candle
create the birds and beasts of dreams.

One with unborn things
I will open my body to the earth
and watch worms reach like pink roots
as I turn slowly tongue to stone
and speak of the beginning of seeds
as they struggle in the earth;
pale things moving toward the sun
that feel the feet of men above,
the tread of their marching
thudding into my earth.

Ecuador

THE CARPENTER

The gentle fears he tells me of being
afraid to climb back down each day
from the top of the unfinished building.
He says: I'm getting old
and wish each morning when I arrive
I could beat into shape
a scaffold to take me higher
but the wood I'd need
is still growing on the hills
the nails raw red with rust
still changing shape in bluffs
somewhere north of my mind.

I've hung over this city like a bird
and seen it change from shacks to towers.
It's not that I'm afraid
but sometimes when I'm alone up here
and know I can't get higher
I think I'll just walk off the edge
and either fall or fly
and then he laughs
so that his plum-bob goes awry
and single strokes the spikes into the joists
pushing the floor another level higher
like a hawk who every year adds levels to his nest

until he's risen above the tree he builds on
and alone lifts off into the wind
beating his wings like nails into the sky.

STIGMATA

For Irving Layton

What if there wasn't a metaphor
and the bodies were only bodies
bones pushed out in awkward fingers?
Waves come to the seawall, fall away,
children bounce mouths against the stones
man has carved to keep the sea at bay
and women talk with empty wombs
proclaiming freedom to the night.
Through barroom windows rotten with light
eyes of men open and close like fists.

I bend beside a tidal pool and take a crab from the sea.
His small green life twists helpless in my hand
the living bars of bone and flesh
a cage made by the animal I am.
This thing, the beat, the beat of life
now captured in the darkness of my flesh
struggling with claws as if it could tear its way
through my body back to the sea.
What do I know of the inexorable beauty,
the unrelenting turning of the wheel I am inside me?
Stigmata. I hold a web of blood.

I dream of the scrimshawed teeth of endless whales,
the oceans it took to carve them. Drifting ships
echo in fog the wounds of Leviathan
great grey voices giving cadence to their loss.
The men are gone
who scratched upon white bones their destiny.
Who will speak of the albatross in the shroud of the man,
the sailor who sinks forever in the Mindanao Deep?
I open my hand. The life leaps out.

ALBINO PHEASANTS

At the bottom of the field
where thistles throw their seeds
and poplars grow from cotton into trees
in a single season I stand among the weeds.
Fenceposts hold each other up with sagging wire.
Here no man walks except in wasted time.
Men circle me with cattle, cars and wheat.
Machines rot on my margins.
They say the land is wasted when its wild
and offer plows and apple trees to tame
but in the fall when I have driven them away
with their guns and dogs and dreams
I walk alone. While those who'd kill
lie sleeping in soft beds
huddled against the bodies of their wives
I go with speargrass and hooked burrs
and wait upon the ice alone.

Delicate across the mesh of snow
I watch the pale birds come
with beaks the colour of discarded flesh.
White, their feathers are white,
as if they had been born in caves
and only now have risen to the earth
to watch with pink and darting eyes
the slowly moving shadows of the moon.
There is no way to tell men what to do . . .
the dance they make in sleep
withholds its meaning from their dreams.
That which has been nursed in bone
rests easy upon frozen stone
and what is wild is lost behind closed eyes:
albino birds, pale sisters, succubi.

Winter 22

There is almost no air left
in the white balloon blowing across the snow.
It is wrinkled and barely lifts from the drifts.
If you could read the crinkled writing on its side
it would say: *Save the Whales*,
a temporary greed he loves,
the wish to preserve without regret.
He loves it in the way he loves
all those old poems about Byzantium,
cages full of gilded mechanical birds,
that impossible dream of beauty
while everything blows away.

Fathers and Sons

I will walk across the long slow grass
where the desert sun waits among the stones
and reach down into the heavy earth
and lift your body back into the day.
My hands will swim down through the clay
like white fish who wander in the pools
of underground caves and they will find you
where you lie in the century of your sleep.

My arms will be as huge as the roots of trees,
my shoulders leaves, my hands as delicate
as the wings of fish in white water.
When I find you I will lift you out
into the sun and hold you
the way a son must who is now
as old as you were when you died.
I will lift you in my arms and bear you back.

My breath will blow away the earth
from your eyes and my lips will touch
your lips. They will say the years have been
long. They will speak into your flesh
the word *love* over and over,

as if it was the first word of the whole
earth. I will dance with you and you
will be as a small child asleep in my arms
as I say to the sun, bless this man who died.

I will hold you then, your hurt mouth curled
into my chest, and take your lost flesh
into me, make of you myself, and when you are
bone of my bone, and blood of my blood,
I will walk you into the hills and sit
alone with you and neither of us
will be ashamed. My hand and your hand.

I will take those two hands and hold them
together, palm against palm, and lift them
and say, this is praise, this is the holding
that is father and son. This I promise you
as I wanted to have promised in the days
of our silence, the nights of our sleeping.

Wait for me. I am coming across the grass
and through the stones. The eyes
of the animals and birds are upon me.
I am walking with my strength.
See, I am almost there.
If you listen you can hear me.
My mouth is open and I am singing.

THE BATHROOM

To be cleansed, to take your body in your hands,
to bend and shape its flesh, its teeth and nails,
to wipe clean the cock and ass of you,
the eye and ear and mouth of you, to touch
the lips and eyes and know there is no touch
like yours, the single pores, the scars, the hidden
solitudes, palm of hand, sole of foot,
the arcs and crescents of lines
that mark fate, love, and life,
the mount of Mars, of Venus, Jupiter,

and that faint light, Uranus, who sings his song
in the constellations of your hands,
the stars and moons in this hiding room, the one
you lock when you're a boy and your mother
wants to come and wash your hair
and for the first time you say, *No*, and she knows.
Then you are gone and she begins to hide,
beneath the carapace of motherhood some grief
you never understand. This room
where you sit and read the poets,
the smell of piss and shit rising around you
in the privacy where none may enter,
the single hair on your wrist you stare at,
so strange and beautiful, and how you touch it
with your fingertip and feel your flesh move.
Alone, exquisite, you stand,
and you cover yourself with the dead
skins of animals and plants, comb your blonde hair,
stare for a last moment at what has now become
a stranger, the one you will give to the world.

bpNICHOL

(1944–1988)

Barrie Phillip Nichol was born in Vancouver and divided his childhood years between his birthplace and Winnipeg and Port Arthur (Thunder Bay). He obtained a teaching certificate from the University of British Columbia and taught elementary school briefly before settling in Toronto, where he worked at the University of Toronto library and began his experiments in visual poetry, inspired initially by the work of Earle Birney and bill bissett. In 1964, he and David Aylward founded *Ganglia* magazine and press; then came *grOnk* (1967), a visual-poetry newsletter. Nichol joined a community called Therafields and was a lay-therapist himself for many years, after which he worked as an editor for Coach House Press and Underwhich Editions and taught part-time at York University. He was also a script-writer for the children's television program, *Fraggle Rock*. His projects as a sound poet include the record *Motherlove* (1968) and a performance group called The Four Horsemen, composed of Nichol, Paul Dutton, Steve McCaffery, and Rafael Barreto-Rivera, which specialized in non-verbal 'readings' and improvisations and was the subject of a film made by Michael Ondaatje in 1970, *The Sons of Captain Poetry*.

Nichol published broadsides, pamphlets, chapbooks, and a host of full-length books, including *Journeying & the returns* (1967), a boxed gathering of visual poems in an envelope, an animated flip-poem, and a more conventional lyric sequence; the four titles for which he won the Governor General's Award in 1970—*Still Water, The Cosmic Chef, Beach Head*, and *The True Eventual Story of Billy the Kid*, which was attacked as pornographic in the House of Commons; several prose works, including *Two Novels* (1969), *Craft Dinner* (1978), and *Journal* (1978); *Selected Writing: As Elected* (1980), and the work for which he is best known, *The Martyrology*, which grew, from 1972 until his death in 1988, into a vast and highly regarded life-work. A posthumous collection edited by George Bowering and Michael Ondaatje, called *An H in the Heart: A bpNichol Reader*, appeared in 1994.

Nichol's visual experiments, which owe something to the pioneering work of poets such as Ian Hamilton Finlay, Dom Sylvester Houédard, and Emmett Williams, include cartoons, drawings, and concrete poems, where words, letters, and sometimes graphics are deployed on the page to evoke a primarily visual response. Whereas the painterly concrete poems belong to the post-Gutenberg era of the printed page, Nichol's experiments, which sometimes abandon ordinary words and syntax alike in favour of utterances of pure sound, or produce sounds and patterns that mimic conventional usage (as do, say, the works of Edward Lear and, at times, e.e. cummings), are intended to recall poetry's origins in an oral tradition and to emphasize its relation to music. In *The Martyrology*, however, Nichol brings these two areas of investigation together, using language (words and their combinations) as both form and content. The 'saints' he employs structurally—such as St Orm and St Ranglehold—are drawn from the dictionary's 'st' section, where the word *strap*, for example, might serve to locate a very contemporary poetic icon: St Rap. Puns and words games are central to Nichol's work, where he is at play, constantly, in the fields of the language. And yet his saints serve the larger purpose of spiritual questing, providing a linguistic springboard from which to explore and give shape to experience.

The most useful guide to Nichol's work and poetics is *Tracing the Paths: Reading Writing The Martyrology* (1988), edited by Roy Miki, which contains a number of important statements by Nichol himself. In 'Talking About the Sacred in Writing', Nichol makes an intriguing statement about the poet's relation to language:

> . . . when I stumbled across the saints with David Aylward in the ST words in language, and for David that's all it was, it was puns—but for me, I suddenly found myself writing a series called Scraptures, in which I was addressing and talking to these saints—long, very argumentative, shrill poems full of extreme rhetoric and, you know, lots of talk about the language revolution and so on was going down. I realized that for some reason these figures which had arisen out of language had a meaning to me that I would not have imagined, that I only got to through the pun, which is why I've tended to follow the pun ever since. But when I began to do that, I began to become more conscious that I had a belief, in essence, in the sacredness of the activity of language—not in the particular language necessarily. My own particular limitation is that I am a speaker of English, and it's the tongue I work in, and it's the tongue I am familiar with. But I think it's the activity of

language itself, which is different in each language space you enter. I have a profound belief in *that* as a sacred activity—that is to say, *something* goes on. Now, you can use it to crack cheap jokes, you can use it to make profound statements, you can use it to deal with the political necessities of the world, and you can use it to write love poetry. You can use it for all sorts of things, but the activity itself has a tremendous power that has to be, within itself, respected. Now, it seems to me—what I've learned for myself—is that once I respect that activity of the language, then through the language I am literally led to things that I would not arrive at otherwise. Therefore, in a real sense I give up, on the one hand, some sense of the self as guiding the poem, though on the other hand I put a tremendous emphasis on getting my technical chops together so that when I am in the midst of the poem there's nothing standing between me and following it wherever it wants to go. If a poem has an urge to suddenly go off in this direction and write long, Proustian-style sentences, then I'm not going to stop because I'm hung up on the semicolon and don't know how to push it around. I have to somehow have the ability to follow where the thing itself leads me.

In 'Narrative in Language: The Long Poem', Nichol says: 'When we write as we write we are always telling a story. When I write as I write I am telling the story of how I see the world, how it's been given to me, what I take from it. In the long poem I have the time to tell you that in all its faces or, at least, in as many faces as I've seen so far. Even when I'm not telling a specific story, I'm telling you that story. A narrative in language. The long poem. How I see the world.'

BLUES

FROM 'THE CAPTAIN POETRY POEMS'

dear Captain Poetry,
your poetry is trite.
you cannot write a sonnet
tho you've tried to every night
since i've known you.
we're thru !!
    Madame X

dear Madame X

    Look how the sun leaps now upon our faces
    Stomps & boots our eyes into our skulls
    Drives all thot to weird & foreign places
    Till the world reels & the kicked mind dulls,
    Drags our hands up across our eyes
    Sends all white hurling into black
    Makes the inner cranium our skies
    And turns all looks sent forward burning back.
    And you, my lady, who should be gentler, kind,
    Have yet the fiery aspect of the sun
    Sending words to burn into my mind
    Destroying all my feelings one by one;
        You who should have tiptoed thru my halls
        Have slammed my doors & smashed me into walls.

       love
       Cap Poetry

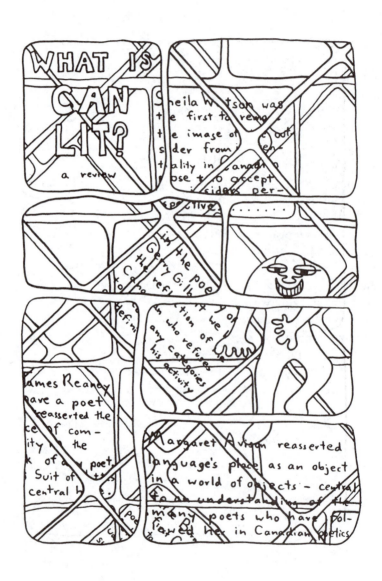

Allegory # 6

LANDSCAPE: I
for thomas a. clark

alongthehorizongrewanunbrokenlineoftrees

THE MOUTH

1

You were never supposed to talk when it was full. It was better to keep it shut if you had nothing to say. You were never supposed to shoot it off. It was better to be seen than heard. It got washed out with soap if you talked dirty. You were never supposed to mouth-off, give them any of your lip, turn up your nose at them, give them a dirty look, an evil eye or a baleful stare. So your mouth just sat there, in the middle of your face, one more set of muscles trying not to give too much away. 'Hey! smile! what's the matter with you anyway?'

2

Probably there are all sorts of stories. Probably my mouth figures in all sorts of stories when I was little but I don't remember any of them. I don't remember any stories about my mouth but I remember it was there. I remember it was there and I talked & sang & ate & used it all the time. I don't remember anything about it but the mouth remembers. The mouth remembers what the brain can't quite wrap its tongue around & that's what my life's become. My life's become my mouth's remembering, telling stories with the brain's tongue.

3

I must have been nine. I'm pretty sure I was nine because I remember I was the new boy in school. I remember I was walking on my way there, the back way, thru the woods, & here was this kid walking towards me, George was his name, & I said 'hi George' & he said 'I don't like your mouth' & grabbed me & smashed my face into his knee. It was my first encounter with body art or it was my first encounter with someone else's idea of cosmetic surgery. It was translation or composition. He rearranged me.

4

The first dentist called me the Cavity Kid & put 35 fillings into me. The second dentist said the first dentist was a charlatan, that all the fillings had fallen out, & put 38 more fillings in me. The third dentist had the shakes from his years in the prisoner of war camp & called me his 'juicy one,' saliva frothing from my mouth as his shaky hand approached me. The fourth dentist never looked at me. His nurse put me out with the sleeping gas & then he'd enter the room & fill me. The fifth dentist said my teeth were okay but my gums would have to go, he'd have to cut me. The sixth dentist said well he figured an operation on the foot was okay coz the foot was a long way away but the mouth was just a little close to where he thot he lived & boy did we ever agree because I'd begun to see that every time I thot of dentists I ended the sentence with the word 'me.' My mouth was me. I wasn't any ancient Egyptian who believed his Ka was in his nose—nosiree—I was just a Kanadian kid & had my heart in my mouth every time a dentist approached me.

5

It all begins with the mouth. I shouted waaa when I was born, maaa when I could name her, took her nipple in, the rubber nipple of the bottle later, the silver spoon, smashed peas, dirt, ants, anything with flavour I could shove there, took the tongue and flung it 'round the mouth making sounds, words, sentences, tried to say the things that made it possible to reach him, kiss her, get my tongue from my mouth into some other. I liked that, liked the fact the tongue could move in mouths other than its own, & that so many things began there—words did, meals, sex—& tho later you travelled down the body, below the belt, up there you could belt out a duet, share a belt of whiskey, undo your belts & put your mouths together. And I like the fact that we are rhymed, mouth to mouth, & that it begins here, on the tongue, in the pun, comes from mouth her mouth where we all come from.

6

I always said I was part of the oral tradition. I always said poetry was an oral art. When I went into therapy my therapist always said I had an oral personality. I got fixated on oral sex, oral gratification & notating the oral reality of the poem. At the age of five when Al Watts Jr was still my friend I actually said, when asked who could do something or other, 'me or Al' & only years later realized how the truth's flung out of you at certain points & runs on ahead. And here I've been for years running after me, trying to catch up, shouting 'it's the oral', 'it all depends on the oral', everybody looking at my bibliography, the too many books & pamphlets, saying with painful accuracy: 'that bp—he really runs off at the mouth.'

●

old mothers who are gone now
all mute
we are your tongues

born from your mouths' mouths
we have your say
Mother Leigh, Mother Workman, Mother Nichol, Mother Fuller
how many of you am i speaking for today
do you care what words pour from my lips?

this old body flaps in the wind
looks out over the prairie this cold March day
into that landscape most of you wandered into as girls
took up the burden of all that birthing
all that laying down
of the law
the line

old mothers who came before you
i don't know the names of & never will
all talking at once, if you could, in all those other languages
Celtic, German, Cherokee, Dutch

No eyes now, no tongue
only these two, this one
old nouns disappearing behind us
vague pronoun reference a life becomes
who does this i refer to?
which s now speaks thru this he?
eh? She?!

●

for Caspar, who i never knew, so few alive now who did,
what was his thinking? a roof for the family? bread for
the table? and Sarah? birthing all those kids? the two of them
on those various stretches of prairie, all that breaking of
the soil, new ground, they knew what that meant, did it, but

i'm reading all these poems, daily it seems, someone grows old,
someone writes about it, goes to visit their mother or
father, the guilt and grief, the estrangement, changing it all
into myth, as tho that makes it better, it doesn't, they did
what they had to do, died, i never knew

them, me, their great grandson, grows old, becomes
someone else's burden of guilt or grief, my own Sarah,
barely five, so many years since Caspar was alive, all of us
in time, dying, how we all go, on, away,
simply this business, being, day to day, until it's over

St. Anzas VII

he. not He then, or She . . . don't SH me that way!
he was. hew as close as he could to that be
ings you long, first to second to third
personhood, long distance cowl of history
of istory if we drop the h at last
just as the english class system 'ad it
hit's unimportant 'e says. who's HSing at me
that way? whoops. no me ey? e's ear to stay coz e
say so. so.

appen as likely. different of listing. quot
ruin sneer.

little mistle didn't and. ten or if could deliver. rude.
stiff as combination wrestle.

as pirate e remains idden, reveals is face,
all tat fog on te glass, e made it so ard, our st.,
ruggle just to see er,
hi reveal er to you
as hi despair in breat,
breating in & out
any other way to breate? hi don't tink so
so hi tink
hi tink so

whistle mean morning, the soon's ascension. rugged
as listen didn't. yellow's misery
lips. rodent.

horrible horrible. dread little awful
rymes nobly. something kelp window sizing
over and doom. longbow. rhythm.

he paces his room, or sits
indifferent in his chair, the different chairs
pain now, most days, is how you sit.
he sits. he's it, see? it speaks.
addresses the you out there, those eyes,
god-like, or like god is, unknown, addressed in faith,
like a prayer, he was told god knows
what you write or say, is always there, reading, over your shoulder.
irritating when someone does that ey? god's doing that.
you's too, you's the one both he & she's talking to.
so what does we assume hey? or they?
assumes you're out there, one day now or sometime,
read and or engage this. he believes in you.
believes you.
he believes.

apple not ridiculous
rodeos as these yet
certainly a definite breeze, deaf night and

supple. widower at the arch. contract.

he is not sure any longer. con's
vention, trying it on.

ripped or turn, slightly. gnarled aperture
gripped slam. over. didn't he then or
if perhaps, when? ain't no neither. just
just. chord.

slippage.

in the long night, when faith won't come, or reason, or
the reason for faith, the reason for the long night,
the reason for the thot in the first place, which was, after all,
not the first place, not even the last, bears no number really,
the convention of certain trite phrases, seeming truisms, artifice
of strong emotion, and then the strong emotion. so that
in the long night, it being December after all, two days away from
the start of winter, but not meaning the, not *that* specific,
and not "a," not any, but in a long night's writing, or at least
one night, particled rather, the words pile up, one
after the other, two after the start of winter, n o t
he keeps wanting to read n o p, you're out there aren't you. he
senses you. will not speak to you. "i"
hidden in this voice. is
not he. he. he.

beaten electric, falcon ignite three. seven to 7
5. indifferent or alibi scissors zero
scrimmage.

fatten lift. geriatric. growth sense
like 3 bibs middle dropped, wrangled. sad
dipped handlebar. must dash. dish
history lamb widens petulant.

be leaf (this in description
—invocation? ("be page you reading—
be me.") he admires content.)
head mires. content's
something more than saying.
's said too
people's involved in this
is the way to go he said,
smiling like a cheshire cat,
"we're all mad here!"

sadness. teensie tugboats upended. virtual
watershed. x-ray's yellow zipper attracts bees
careful. didn't expect favours. got habits instead,
just knowledge, logic. (meaningless)

neat open pen. questions restricts
temperamental overture. litigation. relation. all
demand beverage calypso. triceratops.
fearful.

simile's simian "monkey see
monkey do" something to do with
evolution or e's volition or
un reve's solution, intention, al's fallacy, or dora's,
d' citation's dictation's aura
or a borealis, lumination that enters, here,
he rethinks his desire
to take you with him, fellow pilgrims
progressing, the synapse sees,
e's right there with you, is words, is
the interplay of which e do, speak
and it will all unfold. "i smile i's mile"
contradiction's in the diction
nary one part is true, pro too, & pre,
when words is all e got e go t, s, v;
e go a to z to b
with you.

grey. forum. how canadian select
general house to wave brave map. moving
frontiers another. the story. least so contemporary
horizons isolation intermedia enchanted.

blizzard winnebago blanket. space. hubris trash. remembrances.
echoes. new convincing cave. own.

it a weird world your worship, your readership you
maybe He or She? me? who in
 's he talking to?

pro (never am) nouns.
you got to come to terms with your terms
on your own
in this short
term e calls a life, calls you, ambiguous
finger pointed into the blue you's i's
what de skies disguise
above this page
this screen

dandelion. sanding sold thickening fewer vernal. yes
poetry. accepted steams fifteen slide. rebel
good coming. excess.

line. definite historical. nothing.
definite. entrances. lives metaphysics Tuesday.

the thickening night words. the tongue
unfolding flesh, rasps along the body's length
is words. moves across the room. sits. writes.
has just written. fact this fiction. the thickening night;
the unfolding flesh; the you he addresses
across this room that is, as any room, crowded
with old standards, stock scenes, clichés
we have seen before, heard. who
directed this shit? he did. his flesh
thickens. hangs
where he would wish it not to be. night
falls. the tongue
explores its own mouth. shut up. put it
here. there, he said. here. & there, she said.
here. here.

MONOTONES

XXVII

in these rooms
there is so much reaching across to you

i have opened my mouth &
swallowed the whole note of
my longing

faces

window

a frozen sea to walk upon

returning home
i remember
hands reached up

ridiculous gestures

a day when nothing fit

a muzzled horse
by a frozen sea
and the man who held it   gone

the quartered note breaks

pick up the stake of
a lost game

squares to move in
into   halls   walls   nouns & names the
spaces seem   futile
                        too far to cross   properly
(singing)
& are closed off

or are not seen

•

sometimes i hear music
there's nothing there
a gradually distancing whistle in the pipes
the creak of stairs
like the line from an old pop song
hummed before you know you're doing it
you recognize the truth of

the walls of the house shake
vibrations from the train rumbling by
to whistle to draw attention to itself
draws attention to itself by the absence there
less than half a mile from where i lie
not quite dreaming
        the point is
        the reading   the two stanzas
        a record of thots the mind thinks
                          thank
        they link
            a song
        nothing to do with questions of
        what does or doesn't belong

more of that
this is a description of where the work will go, is not meant to sound
anything like poetry, drawing attention to itself by that very absence, a
rain of thot shaking everything around it, i do *hear* music, there *is* nothing there, what i want a record of, in these books, my poetry(

YOU TOO, NICKY

I

All of us are born out of someone. Too many of us spend a lifetime tied to
that moment or trying to live it down. But family, as what you came from,
what came before you, lives in the body like an organ you only know the
shape of thru x-rays or textbooks. Who were they, really, those early ones who

suffer from the diffusion of histories lived with no importance given to writing them down? We, all of us, move forward thru time at the tip of a family, a genealogy, whose history & description disappears behind us.

"You too, Nicky," a friend said to me, "none of us ever escapes our families." And restless, as i have been, tired, as i am now, feeling some sort of longing which can only be satisfied by moving & is never satisfied by standing still, i took off with Ellie in the autumn of 1979 to visit, revisit, both our families. Among the luggage we carried was a notebook i had kept in 1969 when i had last driven west. In its opening pages i found this poem:

the dead
    porcupine
            decapitated by
the speeding cars
               & the bleak stone
landscapes
        going home (?)
thru the Sault

        it is
a country as wide as dreams are
full of the half-formed
unsuspected
       ruthlessness
around the corner of things
the smooth hum of the car
carrying the far strangers ahead of us

nothing is as it seems

the partly known truth entices

we are forbidden to pass till the future is seen

it is as if
       hands
           reached out & touched us
as they were meant to do
the grey clouds turned over &
their backs were blue

II

You have plans but so many of them don't work out. You have dreams, tho you do not mean the dreams you wake from, troubled or happy, but visions rather, glimpses of some future possibility everything in you wishes to make real. We drove west but the poems I'd planned to write barely occurred. A few fragments here & there—Edmonton, Blue River, Vancouver—cities & places I had visited & written from before. By the time we got back Ellie was pregnant and much of the shape of our lives together changed. Even tho our son died stillborn, or because of it perhaps, our lives changed absolutely. It is the kind of moment of which one tends to say "something deepened between us" and yet that notion of depth seems in itself shallow, lacking as it does an attention to the details of the dailiness between you, the actual exchanges that comprise living. Other poems occurred but nothing of what was planned. We came out of families, came together and within two years of that trip had begun a family of our own. Except the family was there before we began. We were part of it. Became part of it again. Despite what I had once intended. Unplotted, unplanned, undreamt of. It continued. It began.

III

There is some large meditation that seems obvious. An inference or moral perhaps. I only know the poem unfolds in front of me, in spite of me, more in control than me. It's not that the poem has a mind of its own but that poetry is its own mind, a particular state you come to, achieve.

Sometimes i talk too much of it, like a magician explaining his best trick and you see after all he is only human. Which is what I wish to be, am, only human.

Certain phrases like that, that hover on the edge of cliché, seem like charms to me & i clutch them to my chest. And the real magic, which is what the language can achieve, remains a mystery the charm connects you to.

it is not so much that
images recur
but that life
repeats itself
& the lights of
Vancouver say
shine
even when lines aren't there to be written

Only human, only a skill you've managed to achieve. And if the writing is evocative it is only so thru evocation. Which is partly syntax, partly mystery.

IV

what is smaller than us?

what is more futile than
our wars and treacheries

we are all dying
every day walking closer to the grave
the sword and the bomb and age accompanies us

what are the great themes but those we cannot name
properly

what are the minor notes but
our lives

here amidst the flickering oil wells
among the fields now emptied from harvest

our lives

all that really is ours

V

Of course I repeat myself, phrases, insist certain contents over & over.

> driving thru the smoke of the forest fires
> Blue River to Kamloops
> sun not yet visible over the mountaintops

Of course I had driven that road before. Others. Correspondences. You build up a vocabulary of shared experiences, constants you draw upon tho you cannot depend on them.

> between the still standing trees
> the smoke   the mist
> down into the valleys

Of course I am *aware* of what I am doing, not aware. Of course there are such contradictions in living.

VI

We have our infatuations, our cloudings of the mind. People, ideas, things. We have our fevers that drive others from us, afraid of the shrill quality in our voice.

> we are pushed here   there
> "driven" is what we say
> and the i is lost

And if i tries to retain a kind of loyalty to ideas, not blindly, but allowing them, always, to evolve under the scrutiny that time permits, it is simply that struggle with constancy, to stick with what makes sense until it no longer makes sense, to not be swayed by infatuation's blind calling. It is what binds books together, these motifs and concerns, the trace of a life lived, a mind.

> in the rooms you live in
> other people's books line your shelves

> the traces of their lives
> their minds

> too

something of that is what family is. other minds enter, other lives you pledge a constancy to.

there are other journeys, other poems, other plans that do not realize themselves.

living among family you are changed. it is the way your vocabulary increases. you occupy certain nouns, are caught up in the activity of certain verbs, adverbs, adjectives. syntax too. tone.

the language comes alive as you come alive and the real mysteries remain.

    outside the window
    the rumble of other journeys
    planes, trains, cars passing
    the feet of friends or strangers echo the unseen concrete

the blind is white under its horizontal ribbing

the world enters

your ear

MICHAEL ONDAATJE

(b. 1943)

Michael Ondaatje was born in Ceylon where he lived for eleven years. Educated at Dulwich College in England before coming to Canada in 1962, he studied at Bishop's University, the University of Toronto, and Queen's University, where he completed an MA on Edwin Muir. Ondaatje has published numerous books of poetry: *The Dainty Monsters* (1967); *The Man with Seven Toes* (1969), a macabre narrative set in Australia; *The Collected Works of Billy the Kid* (1970, winner of a Governor General's Award), a novelistic sequence of poems and prose that explores, often in a stream-of-consciousness manner, the physical and psychic life of the famous American folk-hero; *Rat Jelly* (1973); *There's a Trick with a Knife I'm Learning to Do* (1979); *Secular Love* (1986); and *Handwriting* (1998). His works of prose include the poetic novel *Coming Through Slaughter* (1976), the autobiographical *Running in the Family* (1982), and three novels— *In the Skin of a Lion* (1987); *The English Patient* (1992), which won the prestigious Booker Prize and was made into a highly successful film; and *Anil's Ghost* (2000), which won the Giller Prize, a Governor General's Award, and the Prix Medicis (France). Ondaatje has published one critical study, *Leonard Cohen* (1970); made several short films, including one on concrete poet bpNichol called *Sons of Captain Poetry*, and *The Clinton Special*, about Theatre Passe Muraille's 'The Farm Show'; and edited *Personal Fictions* (1977), *The Long Poem Anthology* (1979), and *Ink Lake* (1990, short stories). He lives in Toronto and is associated with Glendon College.

Ondaatje has an acute eye for the bizarre, the 'abnormal', 'the out-of-the-way'. His landscapes are peopled with strange beasts, cripples, lost, violent souls, animals—all moving in and out of focus, emerging from and receding into some uncharted region of racial memory. He is fascinated with energy, especially as it is manifested in the form of violence. His poetry is a catalogue of scars, whether the psychic scar that defines an emotional relationship or the disastrous historical event that shapes the destiny of a nation or civilization. Even in the domestic world, which he calls 'a cell of civilized magic', the poet perceives division, the struggle for space and survival.

Thomas Mann remarked that the 'abnormal', the bizarre, is the best, if not the only, route to the 'normal'. Ondaatje's figures, like the parade of freaks and grotesques in a Fellini film, are important for what they reveal of the obsessions, perversions, and fears of so-called normal men. This is not to suggest that his poetry is unrelentingly black or morbid. It is not. He does not revel in the depiction of violence, but brings to bear on his materials considerable integrity and restraint. This is especially obvious in 'Elizabeth' and 'Peter', where the use of understatement heightens the dramatic impact of events. Ondaatje also has a sense of humour, an engaging capacity for the comic and the ironic. If his characters often have blood on their hands and violence on their minds, they are just as likely to have shaving-cream on their chins and dragons in their tennis nets. His poems never seem to be reworkings of a single feeling or mood, because his ability to assume a variety of points of view enables him to describe events and sensations from the inside, as it were. Furthermore, the strong narrative element keeps him from overloading or overworking a single image and gives the poetry a sense of movement and space.

If Ondaatje has a poetics, it is expressed in his poem '"The gate in his head": for Victor Coleman'. 'My mind is pouring chaos / in nets onto the page', he writes. Words are the unique threads that, properly woven, can snare strange, unexpected things. Ondaatje recognizes the importance of form in poetry; even his most casual, personal poetry is held together by some linguistic device. But he rejects an undue emphasis on formal structure. In a letter to the present writer he states his 'distrust of all critics and nearly all dogmatic aesthetics and all rules and all clubs / cliques / schools of poetry'; instead, he expresses a 'wish to come to each poem and let it breed in its own vacuum and have its own laws and order'. He prefers the 'caught vision' of a blurred photograph to the standard reproduction of a recognizable reality: 'The beautiful formed things caught at the wrong moment / so they are shapeless, awkward / moving to the clear.'

The wrong moment is the right moment: that is the secret of Ondaatje's peculiar form of myth-making. He catches his subject when it is moving *towards* clarity, when it is neither completely vague and unrecognizable nor completely clear and obvious. He can only use the traditional nets of classical mythology by altering our perception of them, by coming at them from unexpected angles. Otherwise they are too static and destroy the subject they are called upon to illuminate.

Ondaatje is a kind of dramatist of disaster, with a cinematic concern for detail, for the appropriate image, for angles of vision. Like Bergman and Fellini, he has a special talent for finding the striking image, the image that remains hooked in the mind long after other details or events have faded. The fantastical aspects of his work should not draw attention from the fact that he has a powerful shaping instinct. He says, in an interview with Christoper Levenson in *Manna*, that he aimed in *Billy the Kid* to create a 'mental shorthand', where you have a 'person thinking very naturally and yet have the lines withdrawing and changing meaning depending on whether line B referred to line A or to line C. So a formal punctuation had to be removed and so it had to be suggested in the phrase or in the way the line fell on the page.' Similarly, in an interview with Sam Solecki in *Spider Blues*, he insists on the importance of 'architecture', which is a matter of 'repeating and building images and so making them more potent';

what I want is something more physical, something having to do with the placing of a scene in one place and not in another—that kind of thing. How one composes a book. How one turns the real everyday object into something more by placing it in exactly the right place, with the right tone. There is an architecture of tone as well as of rhythm. What academics are obsessed with is who won the horse race or what it really means. But if you watch a replay you start discovering form. You don't watch the horse in front any more—the leading horse representing 'content'—but the horse in fourth place saving himself. I think that writers think about and are interested in that kind of thing, the undercurrents of shape and tone as opposed to just the meaning.

Ondaatje's work has been the subject of many articles and books, including Douglas

Barbour's *Michael Ondaatje* (1993), Leslie Mundwiler's *Michael Ondaatje: Word, Image, Imagination* (1984), Sam Solecki's *Spider Blues: Essays on Michael Ondaatje* (1985), and Nell Kozak Waldman's *Michael Ondaatje and His Works* (1992).

EARLY MORNING, KINGSTON TO GANANOQUE

The twenty miles to Gananoque
with tangled dust blue grass
burned, and smelling burned
along the highway
is land too harsh for picnics.
Deep in the fields
behind stiff dirt fern
nature breeds the unnatural.

Escaping cows canter white
then black and white
along the median, forming out of mist.
Crows pick at animal accidents,
with swoops lift meals—
blistered groundhogs, stripped snakes
to arch behind a shield of sun.

Somewhere in those fields
they are shaping new kinds of women.

ELIZABETH

Catch, my Uncle Jack said
and oh I caught this huge apple
red as Mrs Kelly's bum.
It's as red as Mrs Kelly's bum, I said
and Daddy roared
and swung me on his stomach with a heave.
Then I hid the apple in my room
till it shrunk like a face
growing eyes and teeth ribs.

Then Daddy took me to the zoo
he knew the man there
they put a snake around my neck
and it crawled down the front of my dress.
I felt its flicking tongue
dripping onto me like a shower.
Daddy laughed and said Smart Snake
and Mrs Kelly with us scowled.

In the pond where they kept the goldfish
Philip and I broke the ice with spades
and tried to spear the fishes;
we killed one and Philip ate it,
then he kissed me
with raw saltless fish in his mouth.

My sister Mary's got bad teeth
and said I was lucky, then she said
I had big teeth, but Philip said I was pretty.
He had big hands that smelled.

I would speak of Tom, soft laughing,
who danced in the mornings round the sundial
teaching me the steps from France, turning
with the rhythm of the sun on the warped branches,
who'd hold my breast and watch it move like a snail
leaving his quick urgent love in my palm.
And I kept his love in my palm till it blistered.

When they axed his shoulders and neck
the blood moved like a branch into the crowd.
And he staggered with his hanging shoulder
cursing their thrilled cry, wheeling,
waltzing in the French style to his knees
holding his head with the ground,
blood settling on his clothes like a blush;
this way
when they aimed the thud into his back.

And I find cool entertainment now
with white young Essex, and my nimble rhymes.

'THE GATE IN HIS HEAD'
For Victor Coleman

Victor—the shy mind
revealing faint scars
coloured strata of the brain
not clarity but the sense of shift.
A few lines / the tracks of thought.
The landscape of busted trees
melted tires in the sun
Stan's fishbowl
with a book inside
turning its pages
like some sea animal
camouflaging itself
the typeface clarity
going slow blond in the sun full water

My mind is pouring chaos
in nets onto the page.
A blind lover, dont know
what I love till I write it out.
Then from Gibson's your letter
with a blurred
photograph of a gull.
Caught vision. The stunning white bird
an unclear stir.

And that is all this writing should be then.
The beautiful formed things caught at the wrong moment
so they are shapeless, awkward
moving to the clear.

FROM THE COLLECTED WORKS OF BILLY THE KID

Christmas at Fort Sumner, 1880. There were five of us together then.
Wilson, Dave Rudabaugh, Charlie Bowdre, Tom O'Folliard, and me. In
November we celebrated my 21st birthday, mixing red dirt and alcohol—a
public breathing throughout the night. The next day we were told that Pat
Garrett had been made sheriff and had accepted it. We were bad for progress

in New Mexico and cattle politicians like Chisum wanted the bad name out. They made Garrett sheriff and he sent me a letter saying move out or I will get you Billy. The government sent a Mr. Azariah F. Wild to help him out. Between November and December I killed Jim Carlyle over some mixup, he being a friend.

Tom O'Folliard decided to go east then, said he would meet up with us in Sumner for Christmas. Goodbye goodbye. A few days before Christmas we were told that Garrett was in Sumner waiting for us all. Christmas night. Garrett, Mason, Wild, with four or five others. Tom O'Folliard rides into town, leaning his rifle between the horse's ears. He would shoot from the waist now which, with a rifle, was pretty good, and he was always accurate.

Garrett had been waiting for us, playing poker with the others, guns on the floor beside them. Told that Tom was riding in alone, he went straight to the window and shot O'Folliard's horse dead. Tom collapsed with the horse still holding the gun and blew out Garrett's window. Garrett already halfway downstairs. Mr. Wild shot at Tom from the other side of the street, rather unnecessarily shooting the horse again. If Tom had used stirrups and didnt swing his legs so much he would probably have been locked under the animal. O'Folliard moved soon. When Garrett had got to ground level, only the horse was there in the open street, good and dead. He couldnt shout to ask Wild where O'Folliard was or he would've got busted. Wild started to yell to tell Garrett though and Tom killed him at once. Garrett fired at O'Folliard's flash and took his shoulder off. Tom O'Folliard screaming out onto the quiet Fort Sumner street, Christmas night, walking over to Garrett, no shoulder left, his jaws tilting up and down like mad bladders going. Too mad to even aim at Garrett. Son of a bitch son of a bitch, as Garrett took clear aim and blew him out.

Garrett picked him up, the head broken in two, took him back upstairs in the hotel room. Mason stretched out a blanket neat in the corner. Garrett placed Tom O'Folliard down, broke open Tom's rifle, took the remaining shells and placed them by him. They had to wait till morning now. They continued their poker game till six a.m. Then remembered they hadnt done anything about Wild. So the four of them went out, brought Wild in to the room. At eight in the morning Garrett buried Tom O'Folliard. He had known him quite well. Then he went to the train station, put Azariah F. Wild on ice and sent him back to Washington.

*

She leans against the door, holds
her left hand at the elbow
with her right, looks at the bed

on my sheets—oranges
peeled half peeled
bright as hidden coins against the pillow

she walks slow to the window
lifts the sackcloth
and jams it horizontal on a nail
so the bent oblong of sun
hoists itself across the room
framing the bed the white flesh
of my arm

she is crossing the sun
sits on her leg here
sweeping off the peels

traces the thin bones on me
turns toppling slow back to the pillow
Bonney Bonney

I am very still
I take in all the angles of the room

*

I have seen pictures of great stars,
drawings which show them straining to the centre
that would explode their white
if temperature and the speed they moved at
shifted one degree.

Or in the East have seen
the dark grey yards where trains are fitted
and the clean speed of machines
that make machines, their
red golden pouring which when cooled
mists out to rust or grey.

The beautiful machines pivoting on themselves
sealing and fusing to others
and men throwing levers like coins at them.
And there is there the same stress as with stars,
the one altered move that will make them maniac.

LETTERS & OTHER WORLDS

'for there was no more darkness for him and, no doubt
like Adam before the fall, he could see in the dark'

My father's body was a globe of fear
His body was a town we never knew
He hid that he had been where we were going
His letters were a room he seldom lived in
In them the logic of his love could grow

My father's body was a town of fear
He was the only witness to its fear dance
He hid where he had been that we might lose him
His letters were a room his body scared

He came to death with his mind drowning.
On the last day he enclosed himself
in a room with two bottles of gin, later
fell the length of his body
so that brain blood moved
to new compartments
that never knew the wash of fluid
and he died in minutes of a new equilibrium.

His early life was a terrifying comedy
and my mother divorced him again and again.
He would rush into tunnels magnetized
by the white eye of trains
and once, gaining instant fame,
managed to stop a Perahara in Ceylon
—the whole procession of elephants dancers
local dignitaries—by falling
dead drunk onto the street.

As a semi-official, and semi-white at that,
the act was seen as a crucial
turning point in the Home Rule Movement
and led to Ceylon's independence in 1948.
(My mother had done her share too—
her driving so bad
she was stoned by villagers
whenever her car was recognized)

For 14 years of marriage
each of them claimed he or she
was the injured party.
Once on the Colombo docks
saying goodbye to a recently married couple
my father, jealous
at my mother's articulate emotion,
dove into the waters of the harbour
and swam after the ship waving farewell.
My mother pretending no affiliation
mingled with the crowd back to the hotel.

Once again he made the papers
though this time my mother
with a note to the editor
corrected the report—saying he was drunk
rather than broken hearted at the parting of friends.
The married couple received both editions
of *The Ceylon Times* when their ship reached Aden.

And then in his last years
he was the silent drinker,
the man who once a week
disappeared into his room with bottles
and stayed there until he was drunk
and until he was sober.

There speeches, head dreams, apologies,
the gentle letters, were composed.
With the clarity of architects
he would write the row of blue flowers

his new wife had planted,
the plans for electricity in the house,
how my half-sister fell near a snake
and it had awakened and not touched her.
Letters in a clear hand of the most complete empathy
his heart widening and widening and widening
to all manner of change in his children and friends
while he himself edged
into the terrible acute hatred
of his own privacy
till he balanced and fell
the length of his body
the blood screaming in
the empty reservoir of bones
the blood searching in his head without metaphor

THE CINNAMON PEELER

If I were a cinnamon peeler
I would ride your bed
and leave the yellow bark dust
on your pillow.

Your breasts and shoulders would reek
you could never walk through markets
without the profession of my fingers
floating over you. The blind would
stumble certain of whom they approached
though you might bathe
under rain gutters, monsoon.

Here on the upper thigh
at this smooth pasture
neighbour to your hair
or the crease
that cuts your back. This ankle.
You will be known among strangers
as the cinnamon peeler's wife.

I could hardly glance at you
before marriage
never touch you
—your keen nosed mother, your rough brothers.
I buried my hands
in saffron, disguised them
over smoking tar,
helped the honey gatherers . . .

*

When we swam once
I touched you in water
and our bodies remained free,
you could hold me and be blind of smell.
You climbed the bank and said

this is how you touch other women
the grass cutter's wife, the lime burner's daughter.
And you searched your arms
for the missing perfume
                    and knew

          what good is it
to be the lime burner's daughter
left with no trace
as if not spoken to in the act of love
as if wounded without the pleasure of a scar.

You touched
your belly to my hands
in the dry air and said
I am the cinnamon
peeler's wife. Smell me.

ESCARPMENT

He lies in bed, awake, holding her left forearm. It is 4 a.m. He turns, his eyes
rough against the night. Through the window he can hear the creek—which
has no name. Yesterday at noon he walked along its shallow body overhung

with cedar, beside rushes, moss, and watercress. A green and grey body whose intricate bones he is learning among which he stumbles and walks through in an old pair of Converse running shoes. She was further upriver investigating for herself and he exploring on his own now crawling under a tree that has uprooted and spilled. Its huge length across a section of the creek. With his left hand he holds onto the massive stump roots and slides beneath it within the white water heaving against him. Shirt wet, he follows the muscle in the water and travels fast under the tree. His dreaming earlier must have involved all this.

In the river he was looking for a wooden bridge which they had crossed the previous day. He walks confidently now, the white shoes stepping casually off logs into deep water, through gravel, and watercress which they eat later in a cheese sandwich. She chews much of it walking back to the cabin. He turns and she freezes, laughing, with watercress in her mouth. There are not many more ways he can tell her he loves her. He shows mock outrage and yells but she cannot hear him over the sound of the stumbling creek.

He loves too, as she knows, the body of rivers. Provide him with a river or a creek and he will walk along it. Will step off and sink to his waist, the sound of water and rock encasing him in solitude. The noise around them insists on silence if they are more than five feet apart. It is only later when they sit in a pool legs against each other that they can talk, their conversation roaming to include relatives, books, best friends, the history of Lewis and Clark, fragments of the past which they piece together. But otherwise this river's noise encases them and now he walks alone with its spirits, the clack and splash, the twig break, hearing only an individual noise if it occurs less than an arm's length away. He is looking, now, for a name.

It is not a name for a map—he knows the arguments of imperialism. It is a name for them, something temporary for their vocabulary. A code. He slips under the fallen tree holding the cedar root the way he holds her forearm. He hangs a moment, his body being pulled by water going down river. He holds it the same way and for the same reasons. Heart Creek? Arm River? he writes, he mutters to her in the darkness. The body moves from side to side and he hangs with one arm, deliriously out of control, still holding on. Then he plunges down, touches gravel and flakes of wood with his back the water closing over his head like a clap of gloved hands. His eyes are open as the river itself pushes him to his feet and he is already three yards down stream and walking out of the shock and cold stepping into the sun. Sun lays its crossword, litters itself, along the whole turning length of this river so he can step into heat or shadow.

He thinks of where she is, what she is naming. Near her, in the grasses, are Bladder Campion, Devil's Paintbrush, some unknown blue flowers. He stands very still and cold in the shadow of long trees. He has gone far enough to look for a bridge and has not found it. Turns upriver. He holds onto the cedar root the way he holds her forearm.

LAST INK

In certain countries aromas pierce the heart and one dies
half waking in the night as an owl and a murderer's cart go by

the way someone in your life will talk out love and grief
then leave your company laughing.

In certain languages the calligraphy celebrates
where you met the plum blossom and moon by chance

—the dusk light, the cloud pattern,
recorded always in your heart

and the rest of world—chaos,
circling your winter boat.

Night of the Plum and Moon.

Years later you shared it
on a scroll or nudged
the ink onto stone
to hold the vista of a life.

A condensary of time in the mountains
—your rain-swollen gate, a summer
scarce with human meeting.
Just bells from another village.

The memory of a woman walking down stairs.

                *

Life on an ancient leaf
or a crowded 5th-century seal

this mirror-world of art
—lying on it as if a bed.

When you first saw her,
the night of moon and plum,
you could speak of this to no one.
You cut your desire
against a river stone.
You caught yourself
in a cicada-wing rubbing,
lightly inked.
The indelible darker self.

A seal, the Masters said,
must contain bowing and leaping,
'and that which hides in waters.'

Yellow, drunk with ink,
the scroll unrolls to the west
a river journey, each story
an owl in the dark, its child-howl

unreachable now
—that father and daughter,
that lover walking naked down blue stairs
each step jarring the humming from her mouth.

I want to die on your chest but not yet,
she wrote, sometime in the 13th century
of our love

before the yellow age of paper

before her story became a song,
lost in imprecise reproductions

until caught in jade,

whose spectrum could hold the black greens
the chalk-blue of her eyes in daylight.

*

Our altering love, our moonless faith.

Last ink in the pen.

My body on this hard bed.

The moment in the heart
where I roam, restless, searching
for the thin border of the fence
to break through or leap.

Leaping and bowing.

PAT LOWTHER

(1935–1975)

Pat Lowther (nee Tinmouth) was born and grew up in North Vancouver, at that time a rugged, sparsely populated landscape such as the one she describes in 'Coast Range': 'Just north of town / the mountains start to talk / back-of-the-head buzz / of high-stubbled meadows / minute flowers / moss gravel and clouds.' This close proximity to, and awareness of, nature in its raw and primitive state was to be a constant in her life and poetry. She reveals an almost visceral awareness of the terrain she inhabited, participating in its energy and transformational character whether her subject is mountains, craneflies, or the waters of Furry Creek.

Images of earth, and stone in particular, everywhere abound in her poetry. She identifies strongly with Chilean poet Pablo Neruda and his involvement with his people at the baserock level of their work upon the earth. Neruda, she says, is 'the man who moves / under the hills, / the man who kisses stone'; he is someone who, transported suddenly to the west coast of Canada, 'would know where / the clamshell middens are'. Like Neruda, Lowther knows that it 'isn't easy / to keep moving thru the perpetual motion of surfaces' in a world where the bodies are 'laid / stone upon stone'; but the process is necessary: 'You are changing, Pablo, / becoming an element / a closed throat of quartz / a calyx / imperishable in earth'.

At the psychological level, Lowther's preoccupation with stone, the most resistant of the things in the physical world,

represents a desire to eliminate the surfaces, edges, boundaries that separate people from each other and from objects in nature. The sense of *relation*—the positions occupied by people, living things and inanimate objects—fascinates her: thus she concerns herself with the silence between words, or the spaces between notes of music; she regards love as a kind of intersection; she sees certain gadgets and phenomena, such as phone booths and hot-line shows, as symbols of our struggle to reach beyond the limits of our own skin into other spheres of knowing. 'The world falls through my forehead', she says, 'resistlessly as rain.'

Lowther was intensely conscious of the major intellectual issues of her time: the role of women in society, the way power politics plays out in private and public life. Yet her feminist concerns were only a part of her larger concern with extending consciousness, as she suggests in a note to her poems in *Mountain Moving Day* (1973, edited by Elaine Gill for the Crossing Press):

I see the woman's revolution as part of a new outreach of consciousness. The liberation of women from imposed self-images is happening. Even the most hostile and fearful women are absorbing it subliminally right along with the cream depilatory commercials. New assumptions are being accepted below the level of consciousness. . . . At one time I believed we humans were coming to the end of our evolutionary cycle—devolving like dandelions. Now I see the half breeds of the future passing like migrating birds, and I begin to have a kind of tentative hope.

For Lowther poetry is a means of effecting change in individuals and in society. In 'Regard to Neruda', she states: 'Often now I forget / how to make love / but I think I am ready / to learn politics.' For the poet, learning politics involves exercising full control over the language and its precious resources. The poem itself becomes a magical tool or vehicle for transporting the reader from one level of consciousness to another, and from a position of estrangement from the things, events, and people of this world to one of full participation and involvement.

Although many of her poems are political at this deeper level, Lowther has also written about specific political events in recent history. 'Chacabuco, The Pit', which deals with the aftermath of the US-assisted overthrow of the government of Salvador Allende in Chile, is a powerful hymn to survival, to the earth and its people. What interested Lowther was not so much the betrayal of human values evident in the military coup, but rather the miraculous persistence of the human spirit which, like the sexual energy that keeps the species from extinction, is a 'holy mystery / beyond refusal'.

Lowther's poetry is remarkable less for its 'fashionable' content than for its maturity and control. Whether she is writing brief imagistic pieces, confessional lyrics, or passionate meditations, she is extremely conscious of prosody—not with rhythm as a decorative aspect of poetry, but with what Pound called the 'articulation of the total sound of the poem'. This line from 'Coast Range'—'billygoat-bearded creeks / bumsliding down / to splat into the sea'—seems to me acoustically superb and brilliantly imagined, a perfect example of what Keats called *negative capability*, the ability to get sufficiently inside an object, person, or event to render it palpable to a reader. Certainly no one has more subtly and playfully conjured the appearance, gymnastics, and sound-scape of a skinny, ragged coastal waterfall.

Before she was murdered by her husband Roy Lowther in 1975, Pat Lowther had published three books of poetry: *This Difficult Flowring* (1968), *The Age of the Bird* (1972), and *Milk Stone* (1974). Her reputation was growing rapidly. Her poems appeared in *Best Poetry of 1965: Borestone Mountain Poetry Awards*, in Jim Brown's and David Philip's *West Coast Seen* (1969), and in Al Purdy's anthology *Fifteen Winds* (1969). She had been elected national chairman of The League of Canadian Poets and had just begun to teach Creative Writing at the University of British Columbia. *A Stone Diary*, accepted before her death, was published posthumously in 1977; *Final Instructions* appeared in 1980; *Water Clock*, in 1985; and *Time Capsule: New and Selected Poems*, edited with an introduction by her daughters Chris and Beth Lowther, in 1996. Keith Harrison's anti-novel, *Furry Creek*, a fictionalized account of the impact of Lowther's death on a number of real and imagined lives, was published in 1999, followed shortly after by Toby Brooks' biography, *Pat Lowther's Continent: Her Life and Work* (2000).

WANTING

Wanting
to be broken
utterly
split apart with a mighty tearing
like an apple broken
to unfold
the delicate open veined petal pattern
inside the fruit

I am arrogant
knowing
what I can do
for a man

I am arrogant
for fear
I may be broken
utterly open
and he not see
the flower shape of me

TOUCH HOME

My daughter, a statistic
in a population explosion
exploded
         popped
out of my body like a cork.

The doctors called for oxygen,
the birth too sudden, violent,
the child seemed pale

But my daughter lay
in perfect tranquility
  touching   the new air
        with her
   elegant   hands.

TWO BABIES IN TWO YEARS

Now am I one with those wide-wombed
mediterranean women
who pour forth litters of children,
mouthfuls of kisses and shrieks

their hands always wet and full
in motion

Each is the weaver of her province:
spinning a tight fuzzy world out
of her own body
and distracted mind

(a loose shred of thought
loops in 'there is
the sun'
or 'the sea with fish'
in the smeary congress of kitchens)

Now that the late summer stays,
the child hangs in
the webbing of my flesh

and last year's baby, poised
on the lip of the spinning
kitchen, bedroom,
vacuum, living
room, clings to the cord
of my skirt, afraid yet
of her first step.

COAST RANGE

Just north of town
the mountains start to talk
back-of-the-head buzz
of high stubbled meadows
minute flowers
moss gravel and clouds

They're not snobs, these mountains,
they don't speak Rosicrucian,
they sputter with
billygoat-bearded creeks
bumsliding down
to splat into the sea

They talk with the casual
tongues of water
rising in trees

They're so humble they'll let you
blast highways through them
baring their iron and granite
sunset-coloured bones
broken for miles

And nights when
clouds foam on a beach
of clear night sky,
those high slopes creak
in companionable sleep

Move through gray green
aurora of rain
to the bare fact:
The land is bare.

Even the curly opaque Pacific
forest, chilling you full awake
with wet branch-slaps,
is somehow bare
stainless as sunlight:

The land is what's left
after the failure
of every kind of metaphor.

*

The plainness of first things
trees
gravel
rocks
naive root atom
of philosophy's first molecule

The mountains reject nothing
but can crack
open your mind
just by being intractably there

Atom: that which can not
be reduced

You can gut them
blast them
to slag
the shapes they've made in the sky
cannot be reduced

OCTOPUS

The octopus is beautifully
functional as an umbrella;
at rest a bag of rucked skin
sags like an empty scrotum
his jelled eyes sad and bored

but taking flight: look
how purposeful
in every part:
the jet vent smooth
as modern plumbing
the webbed pinwheel of tentacles
moving in perfect accord
like a machine dreamed
by Leonardo

HOTLINE TO THE GULF

1

A hot wire
into the immense
turquoise
chasm of silence

this slenderest serpent
electrode fanged
excruciatingly
delicately
into my jugular
snaking under my ear
down to the heart's
chambers

it brings me new
perceptions: the world
is not a sphere,
it's a doughnut,
there's a huge
hole at the centre

away down there
are clouds,
a static of voices
remote as angels

2

Write to me, darling
from the other world.
send me olives.

3

There was this woman
on the radio:
all you had to do
was phone CJOR

and she'd give you
the inside dope
on your loved ones
Passed Beyond.

Turning the dial,
what I heard was
my sister's voice:
What can you tell me
about my little boy?

And I ripped the cord
from the wall
beat my fists
on the kitchen
counter, crying
against that reaching
more terrible
even than death

4

A list of things done
with hot wires:
  cauterizing small wounds
  burning off warts
  removing the eyes
  of caged songbirds
  shoving it up the penis
  of prisoners

5

Speak to me
for Gods sake
There are worse things
than death
though you and I
are not likely
to experience
any of them

6

I could almost climb
that wire down
hand over hand
like a fine chain
dangling
into the cool
abyss

a faint odour
of absence
windless air,
buzzing
of distant voices
I can't recognize

7

Or that imaginary
ribcage
which sheltered me like
a white picket fence
built with love
expanded,
rushed outward
out of sight:

I'm a red
thing beating
at the centre
of emptiness

only a hot vein
wires me
to the perimeter
straining
to hear syllables
in the hiss of blood

REGARD TO NERUDA

When I heard that
the world's greatest poet
was running for president:
being north american
I would have laughed, until
I thought of the campaign trek
over country that was
his blood and bed,
the persistent human song
for which he became
rivers, harps of forests,
metallic skies of cities.
and I thought also
of the tenderness implied
in his handshake.

Could I see with his high vision
(man with thick hands and belly
full of good things)
the naked feet of beginnings,
the sons of rare minerals
transforming the earth,
could I wash my country
with songs that settle
like haloes on the constituents,
I'd campaign
to be prime minister
without kisses.

Often now I forget
how to make love
but I think I am ready
to learn politics.

THE DIG

Even where traffic passes
the ancient world has exposed
a root, large and impervious,
humped like a dragon
among the city's conduits.
Look, they say,
who would have thought
the thing so tough,
so secretive?

THE DIGGERS

The bone gloved in clay
shallow perhaps where arches
of feet go over;
they see it as finished
round like a jar;
a shard they see as whole.

Will our bones tell
what we died of?

The diggers
with very gentle fingers
lift up the bones of a woman;
tenderly they take off
her stockings of earth;
they have not such love
for the living
who are not finished
or predicted.

THE BONES

The men we see always swift
moving, edged with a running light
like fire; their hands infinitely
potent, working in blood,
commanding the death of animals,
the life of the tribe.

The women we see finished
completed like fat jars,
like oil floating on water:
breasts   bellies   faces
all round and calm.

Their bones should thrash
in the diggers' baskets
should scream against the light.

Their work bent them
and sex, that soft explosion
miraculous as rain
broke in them over and over,
their bodies thickened like tubers
broke and were remade
again and again crying out
in the heave of breaking
the terrible pleasure
again and again till
they fell away, at last
they became bone.

Even their hands
curved around implements,
pounding-stones, were worshipping
the cock that made them
round and hollow.

But before their falling away
was an anger,
a stone in the mouth.
They would say there is
a great fall like water,
a mask taking shape on air,
a sound coming nearer
like a heavy animal
breaking twigs.

And the flesh stamen
bursting inside them
splayed their bones
apart like spread legs.

Will our bones tell
sisters, what we died of?
how love broke us
in that helplessly desired
breaking, and men
and children ransacked our flesh,
cracked our innermost bones
to eat the marrow.

DAPHNE MARLATT

(b. 1942)

Daphne (Buckle) Marlatt was born in Melbourne, Australia, and lived in Penang, Malaysia, before emigrating with her family to North Vancouver in 1951. She graduated from the University of British Columbia in 1964 and then pursued her MA in Comparative Literature at the University of Indiana. Her poetic influences include Robert Duncan and Charles Olson, from whom she learned to develop an acute attention not only to the particulars of speech, but also to the body and its messages at the time of writing, a process that has come to be known as *proprioception*. She is the author of several works of fiction, *Zócalo* (1977), *The Story, She Said* (1977), *Ana Historic* (1988), and *Taken* (1996), and numerous volumes of poetry, including *Frames: Of A Story* (1968), *Leaf/leafs* (1969), *Rings* (1971), *The Vancouver Poems* (1972), *Steveston* (1975), *Net Work: Selected Writings* (1980), *What Matters: Writing 1968–1970* (1980), *Our Lives* (1980), *How Hug A Stone* (1983), *Touch to My Tongue* (1984) and *Salvage* (1991). *Ghost Works* was published in 1993 and a gathering of her critical writings, *Readings from the Labyrinth*, in 1998. Her work has been widely discussed in articles and books, including Susan Knutson's *Contested Knowing: narratological readings of Daphne Marlatt's* How Hug A Stone *and Nicole Brossard's* Picture Theory (1989) and Douglas Barbour's *Daphne Marlatt and Her Works* (1992).

Marlatt has lived in the Vancouver area for many years, but has also taught and served as writer-in-residence at the Univer-

sities of Alberta, Saskatchewan and Manitoba. She raised two children from her first marriage and lived for many years with the artist Roy Kiyooka; but then, like Adrienne Rich, came to acknowledge and explore her own unfolding lesbianism. Much of her recent work, as she explains in the Foreword to *Salvage*, was 'generated out of a growing sense of community with women writers/readers, drawn by currents of desire in language for contact through time, over space and across culture.' Marlatt has also devoted much of her writing life to moving out from what she calls 'the safety of known forms', as she says in the Afterword to *Our Lives*, where it is necessary 'to write into the unknown of our actual present'.

Fred Wah's Introduction to *Net Work* is a sensitive and thorough account of Marlatt's developing theory and practice, quoting liberally from her interview with George Bowering in *Open Letter* (4, 3, Spring 1979), where she makes an acute observation on the social function of poetry: 'I take it that a writer's job is to continue to give accurate witness of what's happening. One person isn't going to change what Marathon Realty is doing, what the CPR is doing. . . . You cannot change the world. You can change consciousness, & language is intimately tied up with consciousness. That's our true field of action, is language, as poets. And all you can do is to insist on the seeing as it's evidenced & manifested in the language. In an accurate use of language.' In the same interview she talks about writing as a process of attending to whatever is at hand (which includes body, present, history, prehistory):

My notion re prose & poetry is that I'm confused. I have a feeling that both of them have nothing to do with the way they look on the page, but with the way the language is moving. A particular kind of attention to language. Simply, that standard prose is written as if language was transparent. You're not seeing it. Poetry is written with the awareness that it's not transparent, that it is in fact a medium & that you are operating in it thanks to it. It's like the difference between being land animals &—we don't usually experience air, you know. We breathe in & we breathe out without being aware that we are breathing in any medium at all. That it is our medium. Once we get into the water, which is a foreign element to us, we're very aware of the difficulty of moving thru that element. That's like poetry. You are aware that you are moving in an element, in a medium, & that, in fact, any moving forward you make is thanks to that element that you're moving in. So that language . . . writes the story as much as you do.

Marlatt explains in an essay in *Open Letter* (1980) how, while keeping her 'ear on the pulse of language', she came to explore prose forms:

I had definitely abandoned the textbook notion of sentence as the container for a completed thought, just as writing open form poetry had taught me the line has no box for a certain measure of words, but a moving step in the process of thinking/feeling, feeling/thinking. Our word 'sentence' comes from L. *sentire*, to feel, think—the muscularity, the play of thought that feels its way, flexive and reflexive, inside the body of language. In short, a proprioceptive (receiving itself) prose.

Marlatt's exploration of language, which is most eloquently explained in her essay 'Musing with Mothertongue' (from *Touch to My Tongue*), has less to do with the search for poetic novelty than with a belief that language, like Shakespeare's sleep, is our chief nourisher and the means by which poet and reader alike might co-exist in, and with, the world: 'language thus speaking (i.e., inhabited) relates us, "takes us back" to where we are, as it relates us to the world in a living body of verbal relations. articulation: seeing the connections (and the thighbone, and the hipbone, etc.). putting the living body of language together means putting the world together, the world we live in: an act of composition, an act of birthing, us, uttered and outered there in it.'

Although this deeply political view of language and the function of poetry is reflected in most of her work, it is most clear in *Steveston*, where Marlatt and photographer Robert Minden turn ear and eye—and the other senses—on a small fishing community in the mouth of the Fraser River, that is the berth, and birthing-place, of boats, Finns, float-houses, barbers, Japanese, canneries, Indians, net-lofts, a place of intersection between what is native and foreign, between past and present, earth and water, river and ocean, the idea and the actual. The poem-sequence, a series of meditations on place, history, and the flotsam of physical and human reality, is not just a marriage of documentary material, descriptive detail, and personal impression, but, like Wright Morris's *The Home Place*, a hymn and a testimonial to the passing of a way of life.

Marlatt's poetry and fiction is ambitious, multi-layered, and increasingly driven by both personal and tribal narratives, which she describes as 'historicity stored in the tissue'. In *Salvage*, she recovers and reconsiders her life and work in terms of 'litter. wreckage. salvage', the latter word being the operative one. As she explores writing, marriage, mothering, and a shifting sexuality, Marlatt surrenders to the inevitable appeal of story: 'these sub-liminal stories. what is narrative but the burden of an emotion the writing labours under, trying to recover, uncover, this thing about to be hatched?'

Narrative as a strategy for survival, 'the music of connection', border-blur, 'revising the old scripts'—these are among Marlatt's chief concerns as a person and a writer: 'Feminist writing reaches for something beyond the notion of conquest, romantic or not. It undoes oppositions in a multivalent desire for relationship, whether with women or men, cats, trees, the particular slant of light in a street or a breaking wave, a certain luminosity of being (as Virginia Woolf would put it) we participate in.'

IMAGINE: A TOWN

Imagine a town running
                (smoothly?
a town running before a fire
canneries burning
                    (do you see the shadow of charred stilts
on cool water? do you see enigmatic chance standing
just under the beam?

                    He said they were playing cards in the
Chinese mess hall, he said it was dark (a hall? A shack.
they were all, crowded together on top of each other.
He said somebody accidentally knocked the oil lamp over, off
the edge

            where stilts are standing, Over the edge of the
dyke a river pours, uncalled for, unending:

                            where chance lurks
fishlike, shadows the underside of pilings, calling up his hall
the bodies of men & fish corpse piled on top of each other (residue
time is, the delta) rot, an endless waste the trucks of production
grind to juice, driving through

                        smears, blood smears in the dark
dirt) this marshland silt no graveyard can exist in but water swills,
endlessly out of itself to the mouth

                      ringed with residue, where
chance flicks his tail & swims, through.

A BY-CHANNEL; A SMALL BACKWATER:

A by-channel; a small backwater:
                                        slough, Finn Slough (or Gilmour,
by Gilmour Island), slough for sale as 'deep sea frontage',
has been always, simply, backwater clutch of shacks, floats,
sheds: a swamp & dusty marsh grass sheltering mosquito boats,
small gillnetters & other vessels in this amphibious place,
half earth half water, half river half sea, tide fills, swiftly,
pushing muddy fingers into timbers of the float, crawling round
pilings & rushes, glinting up a web of net stranding float where
a man & woman bend, knotting holes deadheads & other refuse a murky
river roils, have torn, ripped, & otherwise scorned, sometimes from
leadline to cork . . .

                                        The slow effort of
this people's morning: rise with predawn birdsong & coffee
stretching stiffer & stiffer bones, pack lunch, pad past the
cloistered silence of tv, crunch of gravel, drive (green Pinto)
down to where their boats lie, light filtering immense
vegetation.

                Check fuel, untie & start the engine ('a 7 Easthope
& a 15, wasn't it a 15 Easthope they had too? They thought they really
had something on the go—now when they look back they think it's a
joke, you know, why, have we actually been fishing with those?'

'That was the onetime king engine' on this coast, days when
nobody had any money, they bought a used car engine for two bucks,
had it delivered down to the slough, the poor

                                shelter of swamp
houses, float- ('when I look at it now it looks like a summer cabin')
under the lee of a dyke Finnish squatters & other folk whose lives
are inextricably tied with the tide that inundates their day, their
time measured only by: this sucking at vegetal silence swallows shred,
from the boom of idle boats, from the ridgepole of shadowy netshed
jets drone: this land up for deep sea frontage ('oh yes, it'll be
freighters & cement scow, barges & containerized shipping all the
way up to New Westminster,
                        you can't stop progress, can you?'

How *accept* its creeping up?
like a disease, like time, the tide they still know how to run,
with it, up under ('remember how your net got wrapped & rolled?')
that barge, danger at dark or fog, still after the fish which still
run shadowy lines thru all that murk against the shifting bars of
shipping channel, slipping that traffic, that bottom:

'You sure find out
when you get all the rubbish from down there—lot of bark, papers,
bathroom papers—it's real messy sometimes. Trees & twigs &
branches, branches of trees even floating down there. & then there's,
I dunno what kind of plant it is, it's like a crabapple limb & it's
just full of little twigs, & that's a wicked one when it gets caught in
to a thin net. & ends of logs that have been cut, you know, stump
ends & round blocks drifting. The sawmills open their gates, you know
& let all their loose stuff out—when that comes dashing there's even
sawdust in the river.'

At bottom of this slippery time, it's her boat,
her feet on, managing the freshet, swollen, flooding (highest tides
of the year last week) water on water swell, with a wind running
norwesterly 'it gets pretty choppy here', 'I've been here with a blow
that's bin blowing 47 miles an hour—just big big waves washing
way up above the rocks.' 'See it's narrow & when the wind blows
those waves break & cross, it gets real rough.'

She runs in the
throat of time, voicing the very swifts & shallows of that river,
urging, in the dash of it, enough to keep up, to live on. When nets
are up 50%, fuel's up, & the packers taking chum salmon, undressed,
at 20 cents a pound, 'the same they sell in the stores dressed at $1.20,
while they're selling the roe they don't even pay us for at $2.20
a pound, clear profit' . . .

Somehow they survive the oily waters swirling
under packers piling, bargeloads of herring sucked up, truckloads
left to rot, salmon on ice in the packerboats collecting twenty hours
a day,

Somehow they survive, this people, these fish
survive the refuse bottom, filthy water, their choked lives,
in a singular dance of survival, each from each. At the
narrows, in the pressure of waves so checked & held by
'deep-sea frontage' it's the river's push against her, play of
elements her life comes rolling on, hair flying. In gumboots,
on deck with rubber apron ('it's no dance dress'), she'll take
all that river gives, willing only to stand her ground (rolling,
with it, right under her feet, her life, rolling, out from under,
right on out to sea . . .

VACANT, LOTS

      of vacant lots vegetation fills: dandelion, tansy in tall
spokes, small clover only those close to the ground will see. in seedy
grasses waving off sandhill lots, they weave, waving a bottle, hey!
come on over. sunstruck, drowsy & raucous, sun fuming the wine in
their heads. vacant over sidewalk, weaving up against telephone
poles . . . can't do it, man. i'm a good man, or. my name is mud . . .

no wires over vacant lots. no connection calling them back. home
this moment, these small flowers, this much satupon mud worn into
backsides of hills they view the city from, its increment of meaning
every hoarding, every passing bus leaks, *non-sense*, a verbal
inflation that 'standardizes the value of words'

                                    shut up, shut up
he yells, into the open air signs fill, everywhere. 'else is better,'
they say. they want to fill up the vacant lot he is, a hole in the
system words won't fill. fill in the grass. full with friends
camped in a ring around a bottle—on vacation we say (see vacant,
see empty of work)—empty (pay, pay). & a fight erupts. someone
stoned is left alone. vacant, we say of eyes deprived of sense
(our sense), except for nightmare: always someone climbing on somebody
else's neck, for a bit more air. always these holes in ourselves or
where we are.
           battered & bleeding. so few words, worry beads in the
mouth, accrue value, being tongued over & over: go fuck yourself, or.
there's a friend (in need).

hey he sez, stopping me by the liquor store, i think what for? small
change? you better vote NDP or, lifting his cast, i'll club you over
the head. & the grin runs somewhere between me & his buddies who rock
back on their heels & applaud.

'votes get cast, silently in vacant
lots the terms run free. dying into the grass. wild not free, these men
kill the system in themselves, themselves ghosts of the open air.

LISTEN

he was reading to her, standing on the other side of the kitchen counter where
she was making salad for supper, tender orange carrot in hand, almost
transparent at its tip, slender, & she was wondering where such carrots came
from in winter. he was standing in the light reading to her from a book he
was holding, her son behind him at the table where amber light streamed from
under a glass shade she had bought for its warm colour midwinter, though he
had called it a cheap imitation of the real thing.

in its glow her son was drawing red Flash & blue Superman into a comic he
was making, painstakingly having stapled the pages together & now with his
small & definite hand trying to draw exact images of DC Superstars & Marvel
heroes none of them had ever seen except in coloured ink.

but he was reading to her about loss, excited, because someone had named it
at last, was naming even as he read, the shape of what he felt to be his own,
recognized at last in words coming through him from the page, coming to her
through his emphatic & stirred voice stumbling over the rough edges of terms
that weren't his, even as he embraced them. lost, how their dancing had lost
touch with the ring dance which was a collective celebration, he said.

she was standing with the grater in one hand, carrot in the other, wondering
if the grating sound would disturb him. she wanted to hear what had stirred
him. she wanted to continue the movement of making salad which, in the
light & the lowenbrau they shared, was for once coming so easily, almost was
spring stirring around the corner of the house in a rhythm of rain outside she
was moving in, had moved, barely knowing it was rain beyond the wetness of
walking home—

hand in hand, he was saying, a great circle like the circle of the seasons, & now people barely touch, where at least with the waltz they used to dance in couples, then with rock apart but *to* each other, whereas now, he caught her eye, the dances we've been to you can see people dancing alone, completely alone with the sound.

lifting the carrot to the grater, pressing down, watching flakes of orange fall to the board, she felt accused in some obscure way, wanted to object (it was her generation after all), thought up an obscure argument about how quadrilles could be called collective in ballrooms where privileged guests took their assigned places in the dance. but now, & she recalled the new year's eve party they'd been to, almost a hundred people, strangers, come together, & people don't know each other in the city the way they used to in a village. but that only glanced off what the book was saying about husbandry & caring for the soil as a collective endeavour.

the whole carrot was shrinking into a thousand flakes heaped & scattered at once, the whole carrot with its almost transparent sides shining in the light, had ground down to a stump her fingers clutched close to the jagged pockets of tin that scraped them, she saw her fingers, saw blood flying like carrot flakes, wondered why she imagined blood as part of the salad. . . .

listen, he was saying, this is where he's really got it. & he read a long passage about their imprisonment in marriage, all the married ones with that impossible ideal of confining love to one—*one cannot love a particular woman unless one loves womankind*, he read. listen, he said, & he read her the passage about the ring dance, about the participation of couples in one great celebration, the *amorous feast that joins them to all living things.* he means fertility, she said, thinking, oh no, oh back to that, woman's one true function. he means the fertility of the earth, he said, he means our lives aware of seasonal growth & drawing nourishment from that instead of material acquisition & exploitation. listen, he read a passage about sexual capitalism, about the crazy images of romance that fill people's heads, sexual freedom & skill & the me-generation on all the racks of all the supermarket stores.

using her palms like two halves of a split spoon, she scooped up the heap of carrot flakes & dropped them onto a plate of lettuce, dark because it was romaine torn into pieces in the wooden bowl with other green things. dance. in & out. she watched the orange flakes glisten in their oil of skin, touch the surfaces of green she tossed with real spoons, each flake dipping into the dark that lay at the heart of, what, *their* hearts, as they had, the other night, sunk into bed at the end of the party, drunk & floating, their laughter sifting in memory through conversations, wrapt in the warmth of what everyone had said & how they had moved away & toward each other & loved in very obscure ways, slowly they had made love to everyone they loved in each other, falling through & away from their separate bodies—listen, she said, as the rain came up & she set the salad on the wooden table underneath the lamp.

FEEDING THE PIGEONS

to speak to, call to (here, pigeon, come on, it's all right) the
free & unobliged (come on, birdies), plastic dish of seed at
arm's length so they fly, flutter, squawk, perch, lift at will in
a flash wheeling his shoulders, aura of feathers falling flaring
winged things

not the National Gallery, not the Tate. he wants to be where
live things are soaring past Nelson on his column, over
birdshit on the Imperial Lions, falling rhythm & whorling
in great broken rings across this memorial to war

over the Nile, Cape St. Vincent, over Copenhagen &
Trafalgar cast from captured French cannon . . . over *milk floats
& a concrete mixer . . .* (hurled) *stones & petrol bombs, vehicles
overturned & set alight . . .*

strong grey wings, stunted claws, some twisted & deformed,
one with wire round its feet (catch it & then we can free
it)—panickt flapping. plump grey breast with green leaves
& violets. stand back, if you don't stand back you'll catch it,
taxis whirring by in fleets clipping the edge off unwary
pedestrians looking left. from under her veil she warns, stand
back, if you fall off the edge you'll be electrocuted. as it
begins, this thrum way back in the tunnel rocketing forward,
fear, rocketing through my whole being

       lost
          squat   turbanned hawking   muddy water
boys haul off the white   ship-leave two hours   Towers
of Silence   vultures   welcome to Bombay madam

three small girls ah very pretty   to the zoo she said knowing
it at Parel Road   Victoria & Albert   untouchable
scream in the air tearing like fine silk   how does she know
Hindi know this isn't the way stiffening you will die insane
in a foreign country
    yes yes this is the way   to contact shrinking inside
her jewellery
    Maha Amba   stop stop i say   beating on the glass
with rupees   right here   but mem this is not the
zoo   right now it's Mumbai
    every cab back a possible abduction off unknown
streets to bring us back   do you speak English? do you
know the way to the pier?   Unbearable loss don't take
them from me

                                her i lost, not him in the
throng, djellabas, saris, japanese sailors, punks with mohican
haircuts, honky canadians circling the downspout of Empire.
he stands in blue joggers firmly planted on cement. hey mom,
look at him on my head, take a picture, mom, he's the
greediest. lost in the behaviour of pigeons, plump, fast-
flying birds with small heads & low cooing voices, domestic
& ringtailed, rock-dove alone in the ruined palace crying,
ku? ku? ku? (*qua?*) where have you gone? first love that teaches
a possible world

—i want to go home, he says, where it's nice & boring. here
everyone's scared deep down. here everyone's forgotten how
to laugh. hearing the grandfather clock tick on . . .

& i can do nothing but stand in my sandals & jeans
unveiled, beat out the words, dance out names at the heart
of where we are lost, hers first of all, wild mother dancing
upon the waves, wide-wandering dove beat against, & the
dance beats with you, claims of the dead in our world (the
fear that binds). i am learning how the small ones live, ruffled
neck feathers ripple snakelike movement of the neck last
vestige of dinosaurs: then lift, this quick wing flap, heart at
breast strike up a wild beating, blood for the climb, glide,
rest, on air current, free we want to be where live things are.

HEALING

stray white lips, petals kissing middle distance between
blue iris you, me, moss there and small starred dandelions.
in the drift gathering, days, hours without touch. gauze,
waiting for the two lips of your incision to knit, waiting for
our mouths to close lip to other lip in the full spring of
wet, revived, season plants come alive. this season of your
body traumatized, muscles torn where the knife went, a
small part of you gone. gall, all that is bitter, melancholy.

each day we climb a small hill, looking. rufous humm-
ingbirds dive before our very eyes kissing space. fawn lilies
spring moist lips to wing filled air. i want to open you like a
butterfly. over bluffs the rim of blue distance we might
leap, free fall, high above us four bald eagles scream for
pure glee. glee, it falls on us, bits of sound shining, rain of
rung glass. glisten, glare. (g)listen, all of it goes back
shining, even *gall* does, glass and glazing, every yellow
hope a spark, lucid and articulate in the dark i wake to,
reaching for you. somewhere a bird calls. it is our bird, the
one that wings brightness, *springan*, scattering through us
as your lips open under mine and the new rain comes at
last, lust, springs in us beginning all over again.

TWO WOMEN IN A BIRTH

what is there between them? in this in. desire in their desire
room in their room somebody in the body of not in but in
the doubling of. mise en abyme. out in the outback we are
in the desert then or the abandoned. *the desert of ice of love
of stolen dreams desert of the heart.* but what if the
boundary goes walking? refuses to be that place the hero
enters with his *gold* his *drums* his *caravans*—o *the desert
generals the desert fathers the desert rats the desert
revolution.* (we saw hoofprints of camels and never camels
but scrub and many varieties of: we stood in the middle of
nothing and it was full.) bleak obstacle-boundary-space to
and for this adventures ground to this figure and exploits
grave-cave she has rolled over in all that red dust (the

year is endless here) given herself a shake and birthed into subject. the inconceivable doubling herself into life no slouch-backed beast (even double humped) heading for Bethlehem but the doubling of 'woman' into hundreds camped in the middle of desert outside Pine Gap's nuclear base, and the voice of the desert is the sound of their singing out their anger relentless and slow as dunes walking. we are off the train in order to be in the desert no longer the object of exchange but she-and-she-who-is-singing (as the women have always sung) this body *my (d)welling place*, unearthed.

BOOKING PASSAGE

> *You know the place: then*
> *Leave Crete and come to us*
> Sappho/Mary Barnard

this coming & going in the dark of early morning, snow scribbling its thaw-line round the house. We are under-cover, under a cover of white you unlock your door on this slipperiness.

to throw it off, this cover, this blank that halts a kiss on the open road. i kiss you anyway, & feel you veer toward me, red tail lights aflare at certain patches, certain turns my tongue takes, provocative.

we haven't even begun to write . . . sliding the in-between as the ferry slips its shore-line, barely noticeable at first, a gathering beat of engines in reverse, the shudder of the turn to make that long passage out—

the price paid for this.

we stood on the road in the dark. you closed the door so carlight wouldn't shine on us. our kiss reflected in snow, the name for this.

under the covers, morning, you take my scent, writing me into your cells' history. deep in our sentencing, i smell you home.

there is the passage. there is the booking—& our fear of this.

you, sliding past the seals inert on the log boom. you slide & they don't raise their heads. you are into our current now of going, not inert, not even gone as i lick you loose. there is a light beginning over the ridge of my closed eyes.

passage booked. i see you by the window shore slips by, you reading Venice our history is, that sinking feel, those footings under water. i nose the book aside & pull you forward gently with my lips.

a path, channel or duct. a corridor. a book & not a book. not booked but off the record. this.

irresistible melt of hot flesh. furline & thawline align your long wet descent.

nothing in the book says where we might head. my tongue in you, your body cresting now around, around this tip's lip- suck surge rush of your coming in other words.

we haven't even begun to write . . . what keeps us going, this rush of wingspread, this under (nosing in), this wine-dark blood flower. this rubbing between the word and our skin.

*   *   *

"tell me, tell me where you are" when the bush closes in, all heat a luxuriance of earth so heavy i can't breathe the stifling wall of prickly rose, skreek of mosquito poised . . . for the wall to break

the wall that isolates, that i so late to this: it doesn't, it slides apart— footings, walls, galleries, this island architecture

one layer under the other, memory a ghost, a guide, histolytic where the pain is stored, murmur, mer-*mère*, historicity stored in the tissue, text . . . a small boat, fraught. trying to cross distance, trying to find that passage (secret) in libraries where whole texts, whole persons have been secreted away.

original sin he said was late overlay. & under that & under that? sweat pouring down, rivers of thyme and tuberose in the words that climb toward your scanning eyes

She shouts aloud, Come! we know it;
thousand-eared night repeats that cry
across the sea shining between us

*   *   *

this tracking back & forth across the white, this tearing of papyrus crosswise, this tearing of love in our mouths to leave our mark in the midst of rumour, coming out.

. . . to write in lesbian.

the dark swell of a sea that separates & beats against our joined feet, islands me in the night, fear & rage the isolate talking in my head. to combat this slipping away, of me, of you, the steps . . . what was it we held in trust, tiny as a Venetian bead, fragile as words encrusted with pearl, *mathetriai*, not-mother, hidden mentor, lost link?

to feel our age we stood in the road in the dark, we stood in the roads & it was this old, a ripple of water against the hull, a coming and going

we began with . . .

her drowned thyme and clover, fields of it heavy with dew our feet soak up, illicit hands cupped one in the other as carlights pick us out. the yell a salute. marked, we are elsewhere,

translated here. . .

like her, precisely on this page, this mark: *a thin flame runs under / my skin.* twenty-five hundred years ago, this trembling then. actual as that which wets our skin her words come down to us, a rush, poured through the blood, this coming & going among islands is.

GARY GEDDES

(b. 1940)

In his poem 'Philip Larkin' Geddes pays tribute to the British poet in terms that define his own poetics: 'He was a man whose words stopped short / of ecstasy, whose impaired tongue and ear refused / the grand theme, the gesture of extravagance.' He concentrates on the often unnoticed desperation of other human beings—a desperation as quiet as that of the Master of Horse, forced to watch the animals in his charge driven overboard; a desperation as profound as that of Paul Joseph Chartier (in the serial poem *War & Other Measures*), whose imagined autobiography, ending with his blowing himself up in a House of Commons washroom, evokes the fundamental political structure of Canada. Such subject matter has prompted the most frequent label applied to Geddes— *political* poet.

Although this summary is appropriate, Geddes does not deal with headline events and transient front-page issues. (It was six years after the Vietnam War that he wrote 'Sandra Lee Scheuer'.) His concerns are discovered 'out along the side-roads', within people and communities not usually thought of as political, and within stories whose refusal of any 'gesture of extravagance' makes a reader blink with disbelief. The political element Geddes so often uncovers is the brutality of the structures human beings use to organize their collective power, or the sudden realization of responsibility for others that comes to individuals in the unpredictable byways of their lives.

Geddes summed up this central and sustained interest of his work in an interview with Louise Schrier in *Anthos* (Nov. 1986): 'I agree with W.H. Auden that all good poetry is political, because it remembers and records what we can't afford to forget about our private and collective pasts.' The primacy of remembering and recording dictates Geddes's preference for narrative, and for the forms of letter/diary and dramatic monologue. The urgent confidences of the epistolary mode, ostensibly addressed to a single privileged reader, shape Geddes's language and line, even when a specific poem does not overtly adopt the conventions of the letter.

The Terracotta Army (1984) is a book-length series of dramatic monologues in which various third-century BC Chinese military sculptures are imagined addressing the sculptor and questioning both the values of the age and the accuracy of his interpretation. The general strategy of these poems is a technique that Geddes favours even in situations where a strict definition of dramatic monologue would not apply; his interest in the dilemma of the unprivileged is expressed, not in declaiming or in satire, but in trying to imagine his way into the language through which a particular person would express himself.

Narrative is prominent both in Geddes's dramatic monologues and in his letter-poems: what his characters speak has the shape of story. Most of the books, too, are organized as narrative; even a more obviously personal book like *Snakeroot* (1973) conveys the tensions of growing up mainly through anecdotes recounting the rituals of rural Saskatchewan. Geddes's most important and memorable books—from *Letter of the Master of Horse* (1973) and *War & Other Measures* (1976) to *Hong Kong* (1987)—are made of discrete poems (sometimes themselves tersely lyrical) assembled into story:

> I've used in a number of pieces a kind of fragmented narrative form to suggest that the mind works in very unusual ways, does not release its information in a nice straight linear fashion; and that somehow juxtaposing and counter-pointing can be much more revealing than telling in a straightforward fashion. The sections in these pieces are like little stopped frames in a film. They're all very short and intense; they have an event going on, and an emotion attached; together they add up to a kind of poetic novel.

Such arguments, and his own books, made Geddes a primary force in the development of one strain in the long poem in Canada in the 1970s and 1980s: the serial or interrupted narrative, which interweaves elements of different stories (as they are concentrated in the language of various characters) into a larger story.

Geddes seldom attracts attention for unusual vocabulary, or for the extended manipulation of a clever conceit. On the other hand he is not slangily casual or without concern for telling details of image and sound. As he wrote in *Anthos*:

> I want the poems to touch people deeply and make them care about themselves, their world, and language itself. This view of poetry does not lend itself to extremes of eclecticism or undue ornamentation. But, I'd say, the techniques and craft are there, for those who want to look carefully. . . . The thrust of

narrative allows me certain freedoms that aren't available to the lyric poet, one of which is a degree of monumental distraction (in character, event, terrain) that draws a reader's attention away from the so-called niceties of form (Letter to Ricou, 21 Oct. 1987).

So diverted, the reader is less likely to notice the niceties of language than when reading A.M. Klein or Phyllis Webb. But they are there—in exact and mnemonic phrases of echoing sounds, in his attention to the nuances of the language of mass-market consumerism, in the sudden shifts to intense metaphors for love and anger within the casual voice of the storyteller, and in the overtly metalinguistic elements that suddenly appear in *Changes of State* (1986) and *Hong Kong*. Geddes's tone and ear are, to return to the Larkin image, deliberately constrained but not impaired.

Geddes was born and raised in Vancouver, with a four-year interlude on a farm in Saskatchewan. He studied at UBC, Reading, and the University of Toronto, where he completed his doctorate. He taught for twenty years at Concordia University in Montreal, but now lives at French Beach on Vancouver Island, where he commuted for three years to Western Washington University in Bellingham to serve as Distinguished Professor of Canadian Culture. His other books of poetry include *Rivers Inlet* (1971), *The Acid Test* (1981), *Light of Burning Towers: Selected Poems* (1990), *Girl by the Water* (1994), *The Perfect Cold Warrior* (1995), *Active Trading: Selected Poems 1970–1995* (1996) and *Flying Blind* (1998). He also published *Conrad's Later Novels* (1980, criticism), *The Unsettling of the West* (1986, stories), the collaborative *Les Maudits Anglais* (1984, a play), *I Didn't Notice the Mountain Growing Dark* (1986, translations, with George Liang, from the Chinese) and *Sailing Home: A Journey Through Time, Place and Memory* (2001, a non-fiction memoir). He is an editor of several anthologies, including *20th-Century Poetry & Poetics, 4ᵗʰ edition* (1996), and *The Art of Short Fiction: An International Anthology* (1992). His awards include the E.J. Pratt medal, the America's Best Book Award in the 1985 Commonwealth Poetry Competition, the 1987 National Magazine Award, the Poetry Book Society Recommendation in the U.K., and the Gabriela Mistral Prize in Chile.

Laurie Ricou

SANDRA LEE SCHEUER

(Killed at Kent State University on May 4, 1970 by the Ohio National Guard)

You might have met her on a Saturday night
cutting precise circles, clockwise, at the Moon–Glo
Roller Rink, or walking with quick step

between the campus and a green two-storey house,
where the room was always tidy, the bed made,
the books in confraternity on the shelves.

She did not throw stones, major in philosophy
or set fire to buildings, though acquaintances say
she hated war, had heard of Cambodia.

In truth she wore a modicum of make-up, a brassiere,
and could, no doubt, more easily have married a guardsman
than cursed or put a flower in his rifle barrel.

While the armouries burned she studied,
bent low over notes, speech therapy books, pages
open at sections on impairment, physiology.

And while they milled and shouted on the commons
she helped a boy named Billy with his lisp, saying
Hiss, billy, like a snake. That's it, SSSSSSSS,

tongue well up and back behind your teeth.
Now buzz, Billy, like a bee. Feel the air
vibrating in my windpipe as I breathe?

As she walked in sunlight through the parking-lot
at noon, feeling the world a passing lovely place,
a young guardsman, who had his sights on her,

was going down on one knee as if he might propose.
His declaration, unmistakable, articulate,
flowered within her, passed through her neck,

severed her trachea, taking her breath away.
Now who will burn the midnight oil for Billy,
ensure the perilous freedom of his speech?

And who will see her skating at the Moon-Glo
Roller Rink, the eight small wooden wheels
making their countless revolutions on the floor?

LETTER OF THE MASTER OF HORSE

I was signed
on the King's authority
as master of horse.
Three days
            (I remember
             quite clearly)
three days after we parted.
I did not really believe it,
it seemed so much the unrolling
of an incredible dream.

Bright plumes, scarlet tunics,
glint of sunlight on armour.
Fifty of the King's best horses,
strong, high-spirited, rearing
to the blast of trumpets,
galloping
down the long avenida
to the waiting ships.
And me, your gangling brother,
permitted to ride with cavalry.

Laughter,
children singing
in the market, women
dancing, throwing flowers,
the whole street covered
with flowers.

In the plaza del sol
a blind beggar kissed my eyes.
I hadn't expected the softness
of his fingers
                moving upon my face.

A bad beginning.
The animals knew, hesitated
at the ramps, backed off,
finally had to be blindfolded
and beaten aboard.

Sailors grumbled for days
as if we had brought on board
a cargo of women.

But the sea smiled.
Smiled as we passed
through the world's gate,
smiled as we lost our escort
of gulls. I have seen
such smiles on faces of whores
in Barcelona.

For months now
an unwelcome guest
in my own body.

I squat by the fire
in a silence broken only
by the tireless grinding
of insects.

I have taken
to drawing your face
in the brown earth
at my feet.
                (The ears are
                never quite right.)

You are waving,
waving. Your
tears are a river
that swells, rushes beside me.
I lie for days in a sea drier
than the desert of the Moors
but your tears are lost,
sucked
into the parched throat of the sky.

I am watched daily.
The ship's carpenter is at work
nearby, within the stockade,
fashioning a harness for me,
a wooden collar. He is a fool
who takes no pride in his work,
yet the chips lie about his feet
beautiful as yellow petals.

Days melt
in the hot sun, flow
together. An order is given
to jettison the horses,
it sweeps like a breeze
over parched black faces.

I am not consulted, though
Ortega comes to me later
when it is over and says:

> God knows, there are men
> I'd have worried less to lose.

The sailors are relieved,
fall to it with abandon.
The first horse is blindfolded,
led to the gunwales, and struck
so hard it leaps skyward
in an arc, its great body
etched against the sun.

I remember thinking
how graceless it looked,
out of its element, legs
braced and stiffened
for the plunge.

They drink long
draughts, muzzles submerged
to the eyes, set out like spokes
in all directions.
The salt does its work.
First scream, proud head
thrown back, nostrils flared,
flesh tight over teeth
and gums
                    (yellow teeth
                    bloody gums).
The spasms, heaving bodies,
turning, turning.
I am the centre
of this churning circumference.
The wretch beside me,
fingers
knotted to the gunwales.

They plunge toward
the ship, hooves crashing
on the planked hull.
Soft muzzles ripped
and bleeding on splintered wood
and barnacles.
The ensign's mare
struggles half out of the water
on the backs of two
hapless animals.

When the affair ended
the sea was littered with bodies,
smooth bloated carcasses.
Neither pike pole nor ship's
boats could keep them off.

Sailors that never missed
a meal retched violently
in the hot sun. Only
the silent industry of sharks
could give them rest.

What is the shape of freedom,
after all? Did I come here
to be devoured by insects, or
maddened by screams in the night?

Ortega, when we found him
pinned and swinging in his bones,
jawboned pinned and singing
in the wind: God's lieutenant,
more eloquent in death.

Sooner or later hope
evaporates, joy itself
is seasonal. The others?
They are Spaniards, no more
and no less, and burn with a lust
that sends them tilting
at the sun itself.

Ortega, listen, the horses,
where are the sun's horses
to pull his chariot from the sea,
end this conspiracy of dark?

The nights are long, the cold
a maggot boarding in my flesh.

I hear them moving,
barely perceptible, faint
as the roar of insects.
Gathering,
gathering to thunder
across the hidden valleys
of the sea, crash of hooves
upon my door, hot quick
breath upon my face.

My eyes, he kissed my eyes,
the softness of his fingers
moving. . . .

Forgive me, I did not
mean this to be my final
offering. Sometimes the need
to forgive, be forgiven,
makes the heart a pilgrim.
I am no traveller,
my Christopher faceless
with rubbing on the voyage
out, the voyage into exile.
Islanded in our separate
selves, words
are too frail a bridge.

I see you in the morning
running to meet me down
the mountainside, your face
transfigured with happiness.
Wait for me, my sister,
where wind rubs bare
the cliff-face, where we rode
to watch the passing ships
at day-break, and saw them
burn golden, from masthead
down to waterline.

I will come soon.

THE STRAP

No other sound was heard throughout the school
as Jimmy Bunn surrendered to the strap.
He stood before me in the counsellor's office
eye to eye, while the desk drawer gaped,
his farmer's hands stretched out in turn
expectant as beggars. My heart was touched.
I gave them more than they had bargained for.
Six on each. The welts, like coins,
inflated as we watched. Nothing he'd done

deserved such largesse, disrupting my sermon
on the Bay of Pigs invasion and how Americans
are hooked on violence, etcetera, etcetera.
They say there's a kinship in aggression
that knits the torturer and his victim;
we came to be the best of friends.
But each excuse and subterfuge exploded
in my brain as he dropped his puffed pink hams
and fought back tears. I put the leather tongue
into the gaping drawer and pushed it shut.

JIMMY'S PLACE

We found the cow in a grove below the road,
leaning against an alder for support,
her udder swollen, her breath ragged and grating
as a rasp. I could have drowned
in the liquid eye she turned to me.
Her calf, though dead, was perfectly positioned,
forelegs and head protruding from the flaming ring
of vulva. Too large, perhaps, or hind legs
broken through the sac, dispersing fluids.
Much as we tried we couldn't pry it loose
and flesh around the legs began to give
from pressure on the rope. The cow
had no more strength and staggered back
each time we pulled. Tie her to the tree,
I said, being the schoolmaster and thinking
myself obliged to have an answer, even here
on the High Road, five miles south of town
where the island bunched in the jumble
of its origins. It was coming, by God,
I swear it, this scrub roan with her shadow self
extending out behind, going in both directions
like a '52 Studebaker, coming by inches
and our feet slipping in the mud and shit
and wet grass. She raised her head and tried
to see what madness we'd concocted in her wake,
emitted a tearing gunny-sack groan,
and her liquid eye ebbed back to perfect white.

SASKATCHEWAN: 1949

Father is riding
the ridgepole of the new barn
and dreaming ocean.

He grips the keel
with shipwright's thighs.
Studs and two-by-fours
like bleached, white ribs
take measure of the sky.

He cannot fathom the wash
of tides, war's currents,
love's coups d'état,
that ground him
on this ancient seabed
of prairie.
         He knows
what his fingers know:
claw hammer, crowbar,
and a clutch of nails.

Close-hauled bedsheets
nudge the house to windward.
Ripe wheat breaks like surf
on beaches of new lumber.

Ahoy! Ahoy! cries Noah
from his ark.

Shoals of brown cattle
dot the sweetgrass shallows.
Crows swim up like sturgeon
from the startled corn.

PHILIP LARKIN

He was a man whose words stopped short
of ecstasy, whose impaired tongue and ear refused
the grand theme, the gesture of extravagance,
and found, instead, out along the side-roads,

pantleg rolled, cycle propped against a tree,
a desperation so quietly profound even toad,
blinking among grass-spears, had overlooked.
He composed no score for happiness, but improvised

a life of common pleasures taken in a minor key:
a few pints with friends who didn't talk of poetry,
an early morning stroll in Pearson Park,
industrialist's gift to dreary, fog-bound Hull,

sausages on campus, a slice of Humber pie.
Hearing-aid turned off, he tunes his inner music,
a private soul station, some such jazz,
communes with Jelly Roll and Beiderbecke,

or watches from his window at the Nuffield,
where Westbourne intersects with Salisbury,
winos rub themselves against the freshly-painted
thighs of mermaids in the Victorian fountain,

who take their own libations from a conch.
While such doleful enthusiasts drink his health,
all flesh conspires to silence Larkin;
he undergoes a sea-change in the Avenues.

With no more reason to attend, he sings the poem
of his departure, achieves his wish to be alone.
Propped up in bed and talking to himself,
one thing only is denied: the desire of oblivion.

ROBERT BRINGHURST
(b. 1946)

Robert Bringhurst was born in the United States and raised in the mountains of Montana, Wyoming, Utah, Alberta, and British Columbia. He spent a number of years in the Middle East, Europe, and Latin America, so it is not surprising that he reads and translates from half a dozen ancient and modern languages. In his poem 'The Song of Ptahhotep', the narrator says, 'I have seen at the well how the words / tune the heart, how they make one who hears them / a master of hearing. If hearing enters the hearer, / the hearer turns into a listener. Hearing is better / than anything else. It cleanses the will.' Bringhurst has striven to master the art of listening, hearing the voices of the land, hearing the voices of ancient cultures. To be a listener, he has chosen to inhabit the edges of society and to live close to wilderness, although he is also a keen student of typography and printing and has worked as a book designer in Toronto and Vancouver, where he has lived on and off since 1973. His interest in book design led to the publication of his seminal work, *The Elements of Typographic Style* (1992).

In his poem 'Anecdote of the Squid', Bringhurst draws a clever portrait of the squid as a sort of disappearing artist who, in the presence of enemies, makes artefacts that are mistaken for the squid itself. Meanwhile, the wily squid 'grows / transparent and withdraws, / leaving behind him his / coagulating shadows.' Like his squid, Bringhurst belongs to the older tradition of objectivity in art, expressed in Flaubert's statement that

the novelist should be 'everywhere felt, but nowhere seen' in his work and in Yeats's comment that, in art, 'all that is personal soon rots'. Bringhurst places himself squarely in this tradition. 'Music that is too human is useless,' he writes in 'Vietnamese New Year in the Polish Friendship Centre'. 'That which is too exclusively human is not human enough. Our deepest passions push us way outside ourselves.' The aim is to discover the artistic means to move beyond the limits of the self to a larger, perhaps deeper, sphere of knowing; this means eschewing confession, domestic reportage, and the other personal fictions that so dominate contemporary poetry in Canada and abroad. Bringhurst's chosen path may be as perilous as it is unpopular: the danger lies in forgetting that art must make its appeal through the senses, not through the intellect alone, and thus drifting too close to abstraction and pretentiousness. And yet Bringhurst's best work has both the concreteness and the luminosity that characterize the classics in this tradition. As he writes in 'Vietnamese New Year', 'art is not a house. Art is an opening made in the air. It is seeing and saying and being what is in the world. . . . Literature is a struggle with *hearing, listening*. The writer needs a stethoscopic ear, and he can—I prefer that he should—lay it against the stones and wild grasses as well as against his own chest. And the chests, of course, of other human beings.'

In order to create poetry that is human in the deepest sense, Bringhurst has been drawn to history and narrative. Story, from its origins in parable and myth, is a moral art, instructing as it entertains and engages with its characters and events. Historical events or personages provide a distancing from the present that allows both poet and reader greater imaginative freedom. Asked about his interest in the long poem, he replies,

I don't live in a world in which the short poem is a welcome or sensible object. What can I do with one if I write it except send it to the editor of some morose or flippant little magazine—or worse, sell it for money to the editor of some hopped-up monthly, where it will function as an ornament between two columns of racy prose and a four-colour ad for Scotch whisky? The short poem is welcome grace in an ordered life. We do not lead ordered lives. We live in a catastrophic world—a world which the short poem can't convincingly address. A world, therefore, in which, if someone does read a poem, he is likely to read it too earnestly and all wrong, or too quickly, too lightly, and equally wrong. The temptation in such a world is to create an island of answering: to reinvent everything, to write another obese, eccentric monument, in spite of one's best intentions.

'What poetry knows, or what it strives to know, is the dancing at the heart of being,' Bringhurst says in an essay in Tim Lilburn's *Poetry and Knowing*. 'Poets make things, but they don't make poetry; poetry is present to begin with; it is there, and poets answer it if they can. The poem is the trace of the poet's joining in knowing. Its one and only use in this world is to honour the gods, the dead, and other nonhumans and humans—to honour being, in other words—by allowing others to join in that knowing as well.

'But the test I value most,' Bringhurst says in 'Reflections on the Stone Age' (*The Second Macmillan Anthology*, 1989, edited by John Metcalfe and Leon Rooke),

depends not at all on the prospect of human survivors. I like merely to ask whether a poem dishonours or honours the world. I like to ask whether it is fit to be thought about next to a glacier-scarred stone or the limb of a mountain larch or a grass blade, or fit to be listened to with kingfishers and finches. It is not that I confuse, or wish to confuse, culture and nature. They are as different from one another as herbs from herbivores—and as intimately linked. But the works of art that matter most to me are bridges between us and the world we live in: a means of making that difficult crossing. The hardest journey of all, and one we can never make too often, is the journey to where we are.

Bringhurst's books include *The Shipwright's Log* (1972), *Cadastre* (1973), *Deuteronomy (1974), Bergschrund* (1975), *The Stonecutter's Horses* (1979), *Tzuhalem's Mountain* (1982), *The Beauty of the Weapons: Selected Poems, 1972–82* (1982), *Pieces of Map, Pieces of Music* (1986), *The Blue Roofs of Japan: A Score for Interpenetrating Voices* (1986) and *The Calling: Selected Poems* (1995). He is also the author of *Boats Is Saintlier Than Captains: Thirteen Ways of Looking at Morality, Language and Design* (1997), *Visions: Contemporary Art in Canada* (1983) and (with Haida artist Bill Reid) an illustrated collection of Haida stories called *The Raven Steals the Light* (1984), with a preface by Claude Levi-Strauss. His work in the area of cultural anthropology also includes *The Black Canoe: Bill Reid and the Spirit of Haida Gwai* (1992) and *A Story as Sharp as a Knife: The Classical Haida Mythtellers and Their World* (1999).

THE BEAUTY OF THE WEAPONS

El-Arish, 1967

A long-armed man can
carry the nine-millimetre
automatic gun slung
backward over the right shoulder.

With the truncated butt
caught in the cocked
elbow, the trigger
falls exactly to hand.

These things I remember,
and a fuel-pump gasket cut
from one of the innumerable
gas masks in the roadside dump.

I bring back manuscript picked
up around incinerated trucks
and notes tacked next
to automatic track controls.

Fruits of the excavation.
This is our archaeology.
A dig in the debris
of a civilization six weeks old.

The paper is crisp and brittle
with the dry rock and the weather.
The Arabic is brittle
with the students' first exposure

to air-war technology and speed.
Ridiculous to say so, but
the thought occurs,
that Descartes would be pleased:

the calculus is the language
of the latest Palestinian
disputations
in the field of theology.

The satisfying feel
of the fast traverse
on the anti-aircraft guns
is not in the notes.

It lies latent and cool
in the steel, like the intricate
mathematics
incarnate in the radar:

the antennae folded and rolled
like a soldier's tent
sweeping the empty
sky and the barren horizon,

the azimuth and the elevation,
sweeping the empty air
into naked abstraction
leading the guns.

The signal is swirled until it
flies over the lip like
white, weightless
wine from a canteen cup.

Invisibly, the mechanism sings.
It sings. It sings like a six-ton flute:
east, west, always the same
note stuck in the rivetless throat.

And yet, a song as intricate
as any composition by Varèse,
and seeming, for the moment, still
more beautiful, because,

to us, more deadly.
Therefore purer, more
private, more familiar,
more readily feared, or desired:

a dark beauty with a steel sheen,
caught in the cocked
mind's eye and brought
down with an extension of the hand.

ANECDOTE OF THE SQUID

The squid is in fact
a carnivorous pocket
containing a pen, which serves
the squid as his skeleton.

The squid is a raised finger or
an opposed thumb. The squid's quill
is his long, scrupulous nail, which
is invisible.

The squid is a short-beaked
bird who has eaten
his single wing, or impaled
himself on his feather.

The squid, however,
despite his Cadurcian
wineskin and four hundred cups,
does not entertain.

The squid, with his eight
arms and his two
brushes and his sepia,
does not draw.

The squid knows too that the use
of pen and ink is neither recording
impressions nor signing his name
to forms and petitions.

But the squid may be said,
for instance, to transcribe
his silence into the space
between seafloor and wave,

or to invoke an unspoken
word, whose muscular
non-pronunciation the squid
alone is known to have mastered.

The squid carries his ink
in a sack, not a bottle.
With it the squid makes
artifacts.

These are mistakable for
portraiture, or
for self-portraiture, or,
to the eyes of the squid-eating whale,

for the squid, who in the meanwhile grows
transparent and withdraws,
leaving behind him his
coagulating shadows.

THE STONECUTTER'S HORSES

(This is in some measure the story of Francesco Petrarca, who was a gentleman, and a scholar, and a brilliant poet, and a good Roman Catholic, and the father of an illegitimate daughter whom he loved very deeply and whose illegitimacy was, for him, a source of incurable pain. His feelings concerning himself and his daughter grew so intense that for years he would not speak her name in public, though he pronounced it often enough and lovingly enough in private. After her marriage he sought to simplify his affairs and his explanations by adopting as his foster son the man he might have called his son-in-law: his daughter's husband Brossano. With him and few others, Petrarca shared the story of his precious wound.

On the morning of 4 April 1370, in one of the upper rooms of his house in Padova, in the north of Italy, Francesco Petrarco summoned his secretary, to whom he dictated in simple Italian the first draft of his last will and testament. A later version of this document—the dry and guarded Latin rewrite which Petrarca considered suitable for public disclosure—still survives. Only an occasional flash in the Latin suggests the rough glint of its predecessor. The close, for instance, reads: Ego Franciscus Petrarca scripsi qui testamentum aliud fecissem si essem dives ut vulges insanem putat. *'I, Francesco Petrarca, have written this. I would have made a different testament if I were rich, as the lunatic public believes me to be.' The Italian original would, I believe, have begun with a meditative wail:* Io, Francesco, io, io. . . . *)*

I, Francesco, this April day:
death stirs like a bud in the sunlight, and Urban
has got off his French duff and re-entered Rome
and for three years running has invited me to Rome,
over the bright hills and down the Cassia,
back through Arezzo one more time,
my age sixty-five and my birthday approaching,
the muggers on the streets in broad daylight in Rome,
the hawks and the buzzards. . . .
                                        Take this down.

No one has thought too deeply of death.
So few have left anything toward or against it.
Peculiar, since thinking of death can never be
wasted thinking, nor can it be come to
too quickly. A man carries his death with him
everywhere, waiting, but seldom thinking
of waiting. Death is uncommonly like the soul.

What I own other than that ought to fall
of its own weight and settle. But beggars and tycoons
and I are concerned with our possessions,
and a man with a reputation for truth
must have one also for precision.
                                        I leave
my soul to my saviour, my corpse to the earth.
And let it be done without any parades.
I don't care very much where I'm buried,
so it please God and whoever is digging.
Still, you will ask. You will badger me.
If I am dead you will badger each other.
But don't lug my bones through the public streets
in a box to be gabbled at and gawked at and followed.
Let it be done without any parades.

If I die here in Padova, bury me here
near the friend who is dead who invited me here.
If I die on my farm, you can use the chapel
I mean to build there, if I ever build it.
If not, try the village down the road.

If in Venezia, near the doorway.
If in Milano, next to the wall.
In Pavia, anywhere. Or if in Rome ...
if in Rome, in the center, of course, if there's room.
These are the places I think I might die in
in Italy.
          Or if I happen to be in Parma,
there is a cathedral of which, for some reason,
I am the archdeacon. But I will avoid
going to Parma. It would scarcely be possible,
I suppose, in Parma, not to have a parade.

At any rate, put what flesh I have left
in a church. A Franciscan church if there is one.
I don't want it feeding a tree from which
rich people's children swipe apples.

Two hundred ducats go to the church in which
I am buried, with another hundred to be given
out in that parish to the poor, in small doses.
The money to the church, let it buy a piece of land
and the land be rented and the rental from the land
pay for an annual mass in my name.
I will be fitter company in that sanctuary
then, present in spirit and name only,
than this way, muttering to the blessed virgin
through my hemorrhoids and bad teeth. I should be glad
to be rid of this sagging carcass.
                    Don't write that.

I have cleared no fields of their stones. I have built
no barns and no castles. I have built a name
out of other men's voices by banging my own
like a kitchen pan. My name to the Church
with the money it takes to have it embalmed.

Very few other things. My Giotto to the Duke.
Most men cannot fathom its beauty. Those
who know painting are stunned by it. The Duke
does not need another Giotto, but the Duke knows painting.

To Dondi, money for a plain ring to remind him
to read me.
                    To Donato—what? I forgive him
the loan of whatever he owes me. And I
myself am in debt to della Seta. Let it
be paid if I haven't paid it. And give him
my silver cup. Della Seta drinks
water. Damned metal ruins the wine.

To Boccaccio, I am unworthy to leave
anything, and have nothing worthy to leave.
Money then, for a coat to keep himself warm
when he works after dark, as he frequently does,
while the river wind stutters and bleats at his window,
and his hand-me-down cordwood fizzles and steams.

My lute to Tommaso. I hope he will play it
for God and himself and not to gain fame
for his playing.
                    These are such trivial legacies.

Money to Pancaldo, but not for the card table.
Money to Zilio—at least his back salary.
Money to the other servants. Money to the cook.
Money to their heirs if they die before I do.

Give my Bible back to the Church.
                              And my horses . . .
my horses.
                    Let a few of my friends, if they wish to,
draw lots for my horses. Horses
are horses. They cannot be given away.

The rest to my heir and executor, Brossano,
who knows he is to split it, and how he is to split it,
and the names I prefer not to put into this

instrument. Names of no other importance.
Care for them. Care for them here in this house
if you can. And don't sell off the land to get money
in any case. Selling earth without cause
from the soul is simony, Brossano. Real-estate
hucksters are worse than funeral parades.
I have lived long enough in quite enough
cities, notwithstanding the gifts
of free lodging in some of them, long enough, Brossano,
to know the breath moves underfoot in the clay.
The stone quarried and cut and reset
in the earth is a lover's embrace, not an overlay.

The heart splits like a chinquapin pod,
spilling its angular seed on the ground.

Though we ride to Rome and back aboard animals,
nothing ever takes root on the move.
I have seen houses and fields bartered
like cargo on shipboard. But nothing takes root
without light in the eye and earth in the hand.

The land is our solitude and our silence.
A man should hoard what little silence
he is given and what little solitude he can get.

Just the one piece over the mountains
ought, I think, to be given away. Everything
I have ever done that has lasted began there.
And I think my heir will have no need to go there.
If Brossano die before I do,
look to della Seta. And for his part let him
look into that cup. He will know my mind.

A man who can write as I can ought not
to talk of such things at such length. Keep this
back if you can. Let the gifts speak
for themselves if you can, small though they are.
But I don't like the thought of what little there is
spilling into the hands of lawyers through lawsuits.

The law is no ritual meant to be practised
in private by scavengers. Law is the celebration
of duty and the ceremony of vengeance. The Duke's
law has nothing to do with my death
or with horses.
     Done.
        Ask the notaries to come over
precisely at noon. I will rewrite it
and have it to sign by the time they arrive.

THESE POEMS, SHE SAID

These poems, these poems,
these poems, she said, are poems
with no love in them. These are the poems of a man
who would leave his wife and child because
they made noise in his study. These are the poems
of a man who would murder his mother to claim
the inheritance. These are the poems of a man
like Plato, she said, meaning something I did not
comprehend but which nevertheless
offended me. These are the poems of a man
who would rather sleep with himself than with women,
she said. These are the poems of a man
with eyes like a drawknife, hands like a pickpocket's
hands, woven of water and logic
and hunger, with no strand of love in them. These
poems are as heartless as birdsong, as unmeant
as elm leaves, which, if they love, love only
the wide blue sky and the air and the idea
of elm leaves. Self-love is an ending, she said,
and not a beginning. Love means love
of the thing sung, not of the song or the singing.
These poems, she said. . . .
      You are, he said,
beautiful.
   That is not love, she said rightly.

POEM WITHOUT VOICES

The light that blooms in your body
blooms in my hands. Around us the ground
is strewn with its petals.

I have seen on a street in Guadalajara
wind set the petals of a jacaranda
down on the ground surrounding a pine.

Love, this is evergreen; let it be.
You will see, they fall also. Listen
again: the silences

ripen
deep in the sullen beaks
of the intricate wooden flowers.

FOR THE BONES OF JOSEF MENGELE, DISINTERRED JUNE 1985

Master of Auschwitz, angel of death,
murderer, deep in Brazil they are breaking
your bones—or somebody's bones: my
bones, your bones, his bones, whose
bones does not matter. Deep in Brazil they are breaking
bones like loaves of old bread. The angel
of death is not drowning but eating.

Speak! they are saying. *Speak! Speak!*
If you don't speak we will open and read you!
Something you too might have said in your time.
Are these bones guilty? they say. And the bones
are already talking. The bones, with guns
to their heads, are already saying, *Yes!*
Yes! It is true, we are guilty!

Butcher, baker, lampshade and candlestick
maker: yes, it is true. But the bones? The bones,
earth, metals, teeth, the body?
These are not guilty. The minds of the dead
are not to be found in the bones of the dead.
The minds of the dead are not anywhere to be found,
outside the minds of the living.

DON MCKAY

(b. 1942)

Born in Owen Sound, Ontario, Don McKay studied at the University of Wales, has taught at the University of Western Ontario and the University of New Brunswick, and now writes fulltime in Victoria. His books include *Air Occupies Space* (1973), *Long Sault* (1975), *Lependu* (1978), *Lightning Ball Bait* (1981), *Birding, or Desire* (1983), *Night Field* (1991, Governor General's Award), *Apparatus* (1997), and *Another Gravity* (2000 Governor General's Award). McKay is a virtuoso who moves through the various levels of prosody and languaging as a bird moves through air, every muscle working to full capacity, but with the appearance of complete ease.

In 'Some Remarks on Poetry and Poetic Attention' (*The Second Macmillan Anthology*, edited by John Metcalf and Leon Rooke, 1989), McKay says: 'I suspect that the quality of attention surrounding a poem is more important to me than poetry. A species of longing that somehow evades the usual desire to possess. Or, I should add, to use.' Writing poetry, 'that wonderful, useless musical machine', involves, he says, a mental set like that of bird-watching, 'a kind of suspended expectancy, tools at the ready'. He asks for 'a linguistics I can talk with. The meetings of experience and language—negotiation, abrasion, dominion, cross-pollination, intercourse, infection . . . wildness invading language as music, which occurs as soon as syntax is seen as energy rather than enthroned as order.'

In a second essay, 'Baler Twine: thoughts on ravens, home, and nature poetry', in *Studies in Canadian Literature* 18 (1993) and in Tim Lilburn's *Poetry and Knowing*, McKay tries to define his sense of wilderness:

By 'wilderness' I want to mean, not just a set of endangered spaces, but the capacity of all things to elude the mind's appropriations. That tools retain a vestige of wilderness is especially evident when we think of their existence in time and eventual graduation from utility: breakdown. To what degree do we own our houses, hammers, dogs? Beyond that line lies wilderness. We probably experience its presence most often in the negative as dry rot in the basement, a splintered handle, or shit on the carpet. But there is also the sudden angle of perception, the phenomenal surprise which constitutes the sharpened moments of *haiku* and imagism. The coat hanger asks a question; the armchair is suddenly crouched: in such defamiliarizations, often arranged by art, we encounter the momentary circumvention of the mind's categories to glimpse some thing's autonomy—its rawness, its *duende*, its alien being.

A second concern in this essay is the notion of 'home', which, he says, 'is the action of the inner life finding outer form; it is the settling of self into the world.'

'Home makes possible the possession of the world, the rendering of the other as one's interior. On the other hand, home is also the site of our appreciation of the material world, where we lavish attention on its details, where we collaborate with it. In fact, it often seems that home, far from being just a concretization of self, is the place where it pours itself out into the world, interiority opening itself to material expression.'

McKay takes on the title of 'nature poet' with confidence, though he wants to remove that phrase from the 'vacuous piety' it normally evokes. The impulse behind nature poetry, he says, is 'a sort of readiness, a species of longing which is without the desire to possess'; it 'celebrates the wilderness of the other: it gives ontological applause.' While he is conscious that language is not transparent, or purely referential, McKay argues that the external world *does* speak to, or impinge on, our consciousness. Like Levertov and Lilburn, he believes that 'poetic attention is based on a recognition and valuing of the other's wilderness; it leads to a work which is not a vestige of the other, but a translation of it.' Without denying post-structuralist claims that non-linguistic experience may be impossible, he insists that

> although it cannot be spoken, radical otherness exists. In fact nature poetry should not be taken to be avoiding anthropocentrism, but to be enacting it, thoughtfully. It performs that translation which is at the heart of being human, the simultaneous grasp and gift of home-making. And the persistence of poetic attention during the act of composition is akin to the translator's attention to the original, all the while she performs upon it a delicate and dangerous transformation. Our epistemological dilemma is not resolved, as by aeolian harpism, but ritualized and explored.... Part of the excitement inside this species of meditative act

is linguistic; it's the excitement of a tool which has hatched the illicit desire to behave like an animal.

In a final statement, McKay identifies a cost for the entire nature/culture dichotomy: 'That is, to be blunt, it is as dangerous to act as though we were not a part of nature as it is to act as though we were not a part of culture; and the intellectual and political distortions produced by these contrary ideologies are greatly to be feared.'

In 'Some Remarks' McKay admits that he's 'not wild about the taste of paper or the narcissism of the "signifier", however free or ideologically correct the play may seem in those salons of the spirit where it is pursued. I don't believe that "reference" is a consequence of imperialism, late capitalism, or the patriarchy. Freeing words from the necessity to refer is equivalent to freeing Tundra swans from the necessity to migrate, or, getting down to it, freeing any creature from its longing for another.' Not surprisingly, he places great value on metaphor as the supreme human and linguistic operation which argues and illustrates that the things of this world stand in essential relation to one another. Metaphor, he argues, is the site, or rift, of that encounter.

'The excitement of metaphor', he says in 'Remembering Apparatus: Poetry and the Visibility of Tools' (*Queen's Quarterly*, 106/3, Fall, 1999), 'stems from the injection of wilderness into language; it is quick, tricky, and, as we have seen, not easily domesticated to utility.' In order to invoke the wilderness outside language, McKay insists, metaphor is an essential tool: 'With a metaphor that works we're immediately convinced of the truth of the claim because it isn't rational. The leap always says (besides its fresh comparison) that language is not commensurate with the real, that leaps are necessary if we are to regain some sense of the world outside it. In this sense, metaphor's first act is to un-name its subject, reopening the question of reference.'

The Great Blue Heron

What I remember
about the Great Blue Heron that rose
like its name over the marsh
is touching and holding that small
manyveined
wrist
upon the gunwale, to signal silently—

look

The Great Blue Heron
(the birdboned wrist).

Fridge Nocturne

When it is late, and sleep,
off somewhere tinkering with his motorcycle, leaves you
locked in your iron birdhouse,
listen to your fridge, the old
armless weeping willow of the kitchen.

Humble murmur, it works its way
like the river you're far from, the Saugeen, the Goulais
the Raisin
muddily gathers itself in pools to drop things in
and fish things from,
the goodwill mission in the city of dreadful night.

Adagio for a Fallen Sparrow

In the bleak midwinter
frosty wind made moan
earth was hard as iron
water like stone

Sparrows burning
bright bright bright against the wind
resemble this item, this frozen
lump on the floor of my garage, as fire
resembles ash:

not much.

A body to dispose of,
probably one I've fed all winter, now
a sort of weightless fact,
an effortless repudiation of the whole shebang.
I'd like to toss it in the garbage can but can't let go
so easily. I'd bury it
but ground is steel
and hard to find. Cremation?
Much too big a deal, too rich and bardic
too much like an ode. Why not simply splurge
and get it stuffed, perch it proudly on the shelf
with Keats and Shelley and *The Birds of Canada?*

But when at last
I bury it beneath three feet of snow
there is nothing to be said.
It's very cold.
The air
has turned its edge
against us.
My bones
are an antenna picking up
arthritis, wordless keening of the dead.

So, sparrow, before drifting snow
reclaims this place for placelessness, I mark your grave
with four sticks broken from the walnut tree:
one for your fierce heart

one for your bright eye

one for the shit you shat upon my windshield
while exercising squatters' rights in my garage
and one to tell the turkey vultures where your thawing body lies
when they return next spring to gather you
into the circling ferment of themselves.

And my last wish: that they do
before the cat discovers you and eats you, throwing up,
as usual, beside the wicker basket in the upstairs hall.

WAKING AT THE MOUTH OF THE WILLOW RIVER

Sleep, my favourite flannel shirt, wears thin, and shreds, and birdsong happens in the holes. In thirty seconds the naming of species will begin. As it folds into the stewed latin of afterdream each song makes a tiny whirlpool. One of them, zoozeezoozoozee, seems to be making fun of sleep with snores stolen from comic books. Another hangs its teardrop high in the mind, and melts: it was, after all, only narrowed air, although it punctuated something unheard, perfectly. And what sort of noise would the mind make, if it could, here at the brink? Scritch, scritch. A claw, a nib, a beak, worrying its surface. As though, for one second, it could let the world leak back to the world. Weep.

EARLY INSTRUMENTS

The wolf at the door
and the wolf in the forest and the work
work work of art. The scrape,
the chop, the saw tooth
tasting maple. The cradle, the cup, the muscle
in your mother's arm and back
and pelvis, muscle flexing in the air
between two people arguing,
two people loving, muscle
pumping blood. Gut
summoned to speak. The rotary cuff, the wrist,
having learnt the trick of witching wands and locks,
the heft, the grain, the web,
the rub of moving parts.
And the tiny sea in the ear
and the moth wing in the mind, which wait.

STRETTO

Having oversold the spirit, having,
having talked too much of angels, the fool's rush, having the wish,
thicker than a donkey's penis,
holier than o, having the wish
to dress up like the birds,

to dress up like the birds and be and be and be.
Off the hook.
Too good for this world.
Unavailable for comment.
Elsewhere.

      *

        Wonderful Elsewhere, Unspoiled,
Elsewhere as Advertised, Enchanted, Pristine,
Expensive. To lift, voluptuous, each feather cloak
worth fifty thousand finches: to transcend
the food chains we have perched upon and hover—hi there
fans from coast to coast—to beam back dazzling
shots of the stadium, drifting in its cosmos
like a supernova, everywhere the charged
particles of stardom winking and twinking, o, exponentially
us. As every angel is.

      *

        Every angel is incestuous.
Agglutinoglomerosis: the inlet choked with algae thriving on the warmth
imparted by the effluent. *Contermitaminoma:* runoff through
the clearcut takes the topsoil to the river then
out into the bay to coat the coral reef in silt. *Gagaligogo:*
seepage from the landfill finds the water table. *Elugelah:* the south-
sea island angelized by the first H-blast.
                In the dead sea
we will float as stones. Unmortal

      *

        Unmortality Incorporated.
No shadow. All day
it is noon it is no one. All day
it utters one true sentence jammed
into its period. Nothing is to be allowed
to die but everything gets killed
and then reclassified: the death of its death
makes it an art form. Hang it.

Prohibit the ravens. Prohibit the coyotes.
Prohibit the women with their oils and cloths and
weep weep weeping. Tattoo this extra letter
on the air:
        This is what we can do.
Detonation. Heartbeats of the other,
signed, sealed,
delivered. Thunder
eats of its echo eats its vowels smothers its
elf. To strike
hour after hour   the same hour. To dig
redig the gravels that are no one's grave.

       *

       Gravels, aye, tis gravels ye'll gnash mit muchas gracias and will it
please thee sergeant dear to boot me arse until I hear the mermaids sinking?
You know it: tis the gravel of old rocknroll highroad, me darling sibs, the yellow brick jornada del muerto. You fancy me far from your minds, wandering
lonely as a clod in longlost brotherhood, while your door's locked and your life's
grammatically insured, yet (listen) scurry scurry (Is-that-Only-A-Rat-In-The-
Basement-Better-Phone-Dad-Oh-No-the-Line's-Dead, Mandatory Lightning
Flash) yup, here I am with the hook old chum. Hardly Fair, what? Now gnash
this: beautiful tooth, tooth beautiful. Repeat: die nacht ist die nacht. How
many fucking times do I have to *Fucking* tell you, me rosasharns? Nayther
frahlicher ner mumbo, nayther oft when on my couch I lie ner *bonny doom* will
lift from these eyes of thine their click clock particles of record time. *Ammo
ergo somme.* We bombs it back to square one, then, o babes in arms, we bombs
square one. Nomine Fat Boy ate Elugelah ate Alamogordo gravel. Mit click
clock lock licht nicht.
Encore.
Die Nacht ist die Nacht.

NOCTURNAL MIGRANTS

Another gravity. I am on my way
to the bathroom, the dream in my head still
struggling not to die into the air, when my bare feet step
into a pool of moonlight on the kitchen floor and turn,

effortlessly, into fish. All day surviving in the grim purdah
of my work socks wishing only to be kissed by cold
equivocal light, now they swim off,
up, singing old bone river, hunched-up toes
and gormless ankles growing
sleek and silver, old bone river,
gather me back.
On pause in my kitchen,
footless, I think of them up there among the night fliers—
Snow Geese, swans, songbirds—
navigating by the stars and earth's own
brainwaves. How early radar techs discovered
ghostly blotches on their screens and,
knowing they weren't aircraft—theirs
or ours—called them angels. Back in my dream
the old lady who sells popcorn has been fading in my arms
as I run through its corridors and lobbies, taking her
empty weight through foyers, antechambers,
vestibules, a whole aerobics class completely deaf
inside its trance of wellness, my old
popcorn lady dwindling to a feather boa,
then a scarf of smoke. A gravity
against the ground, a love
which summons no one home
and calls things to their water-souls. On the tide flats
shore birds feed and bustle, putting on fat
for the next leg of the long
throw south. When a cold front
crosses the Fundy coast, they test it
with their feathers, listening to its muscular
northwesterlies, deciding when to give their bodies
to that music and be swept,
its ideal audience, far out over the Atlantic. The face
in the bathroom mirror looks up
just as I arrive, a creature that has
caught me watching and is watching back. Around us
wind has risen, rushes in the foliage,
tugs at the house.

WINGS OF SONG
'We talk because we are mortal.'
    —Octavio Paz

And because we aren't gods,
or close to gods,
we sing. Your breath steps
boldly into lift to feel that other breath
breathing inside it: Summertime, Amazing Grace. And when it stops
you sense that something fold back
into air to leave you listening,
lonely as a post. Shall we call this angel?
Shall we call it animal, or elf? Most of us
are happy with a brief
companionable ghost who joins us in the shower or
behind the wheel. Blue Moon, Hound Dog, Life
Is Like a Mountain Railroad. When your voice
decides to quit its day job, which is mostly
door to door, to take its little sack of sounds
and pour them into darkness, with its
unembodied barks and murmurs, its refusal
to name names, its disregard for sentences,
for getting there on time,
or getting there,
or getting.

WINTER SOLSTICE MOON: AN ECLOGUE
(December: Pacific Rim National Park)

Full moon falling on Christmas Eve: I wondered,
as we carried our supplies—wine, rain gear, gifts—
from the car to the cabin, whether everything was
about to get conscripted into either family life
or lunacy. We put
the perishables in the fridge,
walked out on the beach: in the east
the blacker blackness of the mountains, already backlit
by the moon, and lower down each cabin's roof
outlined in lights, reminding everyone that this

was supposed to be the feast of homes
and homebodies, the time to bring a tree indoors
and charm its boreal heart with bric-a-brac,
to make ourselves so interesting its needles would forget
the roots they left behind. On the wet
corrugated sand the lights were smeared and
rippled, an elaborate film noir effect,
an opening sequence into which a cop car,
like an urban orca, should intrude. To the west
ocean was a far roar under its hush-hush
on the sand, a giant with a lisp.

I was thinking of the house we'd left
huddled darkly round its
turned-down furnace, one missing tooth
in the block's electric smile. How much
we ask of them, that they articulate
the space around us into stanzas,
pauses in the flow which gather time,
or rather, where time, slightly pregnant,
might gather if it chose; that they should be the bodies
of our bodies and the spirit's husk
against the hypothermia which dogs it,
a.k.a. the dreads; that they be resolute yet intimate, insulated,
pest-free, dry, well-founded in the earth but airy,
fire in the belly and a good deep well attached to copper
plumbing, CSA approved; that they should be
possessed of character but not by ghosts, and not
the sort of character who wakes you
in the middle of the night and suddenly
needs money; that they should shed the rain and keep the wind
from blowing out the candle flame of talk, the bedtime stories,
murmurings, the small redundant phrases with which one voice
solaces another.
And when it goes awry—the cracks the bills the noise the
drains the silences the bugs—to take the blame and sit there,
stoically, on the market while new dreamers sniff the air
and poke their noses into closets,
hatching their improbable plots.

We walked through soft mist,
filling our ears with the ocean's boom
and whisper. Is it the listening that loosens,
letting its knots go, or the voice,
saying those great unsayings to itself until
ovation on the inside equals ovation out? And rain forest,
I thought as we turned back at the cliff,
must be the way it gets translated into plants,
who remember water with each rounded,
downward gesture.
                            Then the moon. Over the mountain it hung
and roiled inside itself,
pure style which took the scene aslant, selecting
the bristle of frost on the drift logs, the patch
of duct tape on my boot, the whites of your eyes,
leaving whatever was not glimmering in deeper shadow,
uninhabited. Can you recall
those nights we spent learning from the wolves to be
the tooth and tongue of darkness, how to hunt
and howl? Me neither. Now that howl's
inverted in us, the long *o* of *alone*. The wolves
are dogs. The sun says *here*, the moon says
nowhere, the nameless moon
that sheds the blunt domesticating myths
the way a mirror utterly forgets you
when you leave the bathroom, the empty moon
soliciting our ghosts, calling on them to leave home,
that gilded cage, that theme park of the human.

But the sea was gazing back, its look
rich with tumult and the possibility of huge hearts
sounding the depths. Between them
otherworldliness is quickened. One theory—
my favourite—goes that once the earth and moon were one,
spinning monthlessly in space, and somehow—whether by asteroid
or apple, *différance*, tabu—they broke up and the moon,
newly fallen, risen, floated off into its orbit, while
into the crater of its absence flowed
the great tear known as the Pacific Ocean.

                                    So:
a story full of loss and eros, three-fifths
of the way to myth. Let's leave it there—something human,
homespun, like a basket, a translation, or a loaf of bread—
beside the incandescent water. Our cabin sat
under its little party hat of lights, and to it,
wanting its warmth, and supper, and to give our gifts,
we went.

ANNE SZUMIGALSKI

(1922–1999)

Anne Szumigalski (née Davis) was born in London, England, and raised in Hampshire. During the war she worked with refugees and as an interpreter with the British Red Cross, speaking French, German, and Dutch fluently, as well as some Polish and Russian. She was with the first Civilian Relief Unit to enter Europe after D-Day. She met her husband, an ex-POW, in Germany and immigrated to Canada in 1951. She settled in Saskatoon in 1956 and became an active participant in the development of the Saskatchewan Writers' Guild. Szumigalski raised four children and was a tireless editor and supporter of young poets; she also taught imaginative writing in schools and at the Saskatchewan Summer school for the Arts in Fort San. She served as writer-in-residence at the Winnipeg Public Library; and two of her books were nominated for a Governor General's Award.

In *The Word, the Voice, the Text: The Life of A Writer* (1990), a delightfully whimsical anti-memoir, Szumigalski describes poetry as a game, a virus, a song, a dance, the angels made flesh, taking your wit for a walk, a way of hanging around for longer than your body, 'imagination struggling against form . . . an overriding idea in conflict with an assertive language . . . the energy of the body (expressed in rhythm, sound, repetition, and so on) wrestling with the energy of the intellect (expressed in theories, ideas, logic).' Of her attitude to poetry, she says, with typical irony and mock-seriousness: '. . . at the age of twelve, I decided that if the literary arts can be thought of as a mountain, then

poetry is at the very peak. The pointy tops of mountains are no doubt the smallest part. The air is more rarified up here and there is snow under your boots, but then you are as near the heavens as you can get while still having your feet on the ground. Well worth the climb, wouldn't you say?'

While she made a lifelong commitment to the writing of poetry, she refuses to pontificate about the creative process, preferring to leave matters fluid, open:

How, in fact, did we come to write anything: what's behind our passion for narrative, our devotion to words: must we always be unsatisfied with what we write, what we imagine, what we express? It's these questions and many like them that occupy my mind when I am not actually writing myself. Digging in the garden, soaking in the bathtub, eating my solitary supper, my mind always returns to these speculations and arguments. They are as much a part of my being as poetry itself.

Szumigalski's poetry is unusual in Canada for its obliviousness to the attractions of place. When asked the reasons for this feature of her work, she said: 'If landscape is important to my work, it's the inner landscape. The world of imagination is so much larger. That's where I prefer to reside.' The inner world of her poems is one of transformation, talking corpses, bizarre contracts binding people together, real and psychic surgery; it is a fantastical landscape stretching between birth and death, with the wonderful concreteness and illogic of dreams. While she was not conventionally religious, Szumigalski loved to quote William Blake on the poet's relationship with the physical world: 'What,' it will be questioned, 'when the sun rises do you not see a disk of fire somewhat like a guinea?' 'O no, no. I see an innumerable company of the heavenly host crying, "Holy, holy, holy is the Lord God Almighty".'

Szumigalski's later work explores the formal possibilities of the prose poem, a form that appears on the printed page without line-breaks, but still retains the density of image, sound, and rhythm associated with lyric poetry. The prose poem is a highly charged form, whose impact and compression require that it not extend beyond two or three pages. Because its appearance on the page serves to free the prose poem from some of the conventions and expectations of the lyric poem, this form lends itself well to both the psychological intensity and the dream-like juxtapositions that are central to Szumigalski's poetry. Although she sometimes uses the prose poem for narrative purposes, she never strays far from either the length or the compression required to sustain lyric intensity. Whether structured around a feeling, an anecdote, or an idea, these compact, richly textured pieces seem always to strive beyond quotidian reality, to a region where image becomes symbol and where symbol achieves the status of archetype.

Szumigalski's collections include *Woman Reading in Bath* (1974), *Wild Man's Butte: A Stereophonic Poem* (1979), *A Game of Angels* (1980), *Doctrine of Signatures* (1983), *Risks* (1983), *Instar: Poems and Stories* (1985), *Dogstones: Selected and New Poems* (1986), *Rapture of the Deep* (1991), *On Glassy Wings: Poems New and Selected* (1997), and *Sermons on Stones: Words and Images* (1997). She is also co-editor (with Don Kerr) of *Heading Out: The New Saskatchewan Poets* (1986) and the author of radio drama, a screenplay, several other titles, including a play, *Z: A Meditation on Oppression, Desire and Freedom* (1995), which won the Saskatchewan Book of the Year Award, and two collaborative works: *Journey=Journée* (1988, co-authored with poet Terence Heath) and *Voice* (1994, with visual artist Elise Yates St George). She also edited *Why Couldn't You See Blue?* (1994), the poems of Carolyn Heath.

VICTIM

Ah the cliff edge—where so many murders are done
Can't you see the body among the boulders
Far down on the beach?
While the seagulls scream they are filming
A frail girl in a thin nightgown
Prone on the distant rocks

Mr. B and I are walking hand in hand
Up the cliff path knowing
That under our feet
Disaster and drama are making a second-rate movie
Take no notice my darling Mr. B
Tell me a simple answer to the urgent question
Who am I? Who are we?

Mr. B is a known madman   a suspected murderer
I think the cops are after him for being himself
For not sobbing
For not beating his breast
When he finds a victim on the beach
Bloody and wet in the tide
Was that my body we saw down there Mr. B
Twisted in seaweed   Who am I?   Who was I?

He picked me up on the beach
I am the tiny girl in the thin nightgown
That Mr. B carries in a seashell
In his trousers pocket among
The sticks of Dentyne gum and the spent flashbulbs
Oh I am glad I am dead and can't see
The dirty darkness in here

I was murdered last Thursday but even so
The heat of his groin
And all the fumbling that goes on there
Is disturbing my final rest

Girl with a Basket

Now comes dusty Beatrice drab girl
With her arms full of bales wound with fresh linen
She lets fall white coils down between long gray fingers
Nor smudges nor smears clear light   cold linen

Beatrice why are you crying as you smooth the sheet
With your dark hand?
She makes a short drain snort in her nose
Being fearful and glad to watch the head cup open
Or green shell belly slit with small sharp knife
Looks down and sees eight rows of seeds
Neatly knitted into a web of pith   her one comfort
The sweet drops that drip from the flesh
Not like tears they run
Like whey from squeezed cheeses

FISHHAWKS

my son stands in waist-high water
the salt reddens his skin
out of his face spring wiry hairs
thickening to a beard
his arms have become wide and heavy

he splices rope
smells of the tar that blackens his fingers
he has learned to make his living from the sea

(the huge shadow of a bird
darkens the sand around us
I speak, say to you *look*
at that rare creature
an osprey)

further out from the shore
your daughter is a rock
jutting from the waves
she is rounded and hollow
within her is a sea-cave
her face is a pearly shell
a shining operculum
stoppers up her mouth
her singing is muffled, a murmur

the boy smiles
his semen darts out of him
a shoal of swift fishes
entering her secret place
he stretches out his finger
flicks away the shell plug from her mouth
so that she may cry out

you look at me, say
this has all happened far too quickly
we wade out   I say:
there is just time for us to bless them
but in that glance they have crossed the horizon
are washed away out of our sight

we two return to the beach
the salt water drips from us
making the dull shingles glisten
our wet clothes cling to our legs
behind us the sun is clouded
the sea is cold not splendid
I am a widow I tell you
but we are just strangers you reply

out there where the great bird hovers
mantling preparing to spiral
there is faint wailing

THE LULLABY

a woman offers a man an orange
it is heavy and cold in her hand

the man is afraid of the woman's gift
is afraid to accept anything
especially an orange
for who knows it may contain
the woman's liver and heart
her thighs and her low breasts hanging
it may contain her children
with their night cries
and their noses running

the woman turns to her child
who has dirtied himself again
she strips him as usual
and washes him off in the creek
and the creek runs on
taking the child's dirt to the river
and the river carries it to the sea

the man settles himself in a treefork
with his back against a branch
for he's afraid to follow
the woman into the house

dark comes and the woman lights a lamp
he watches her shadow cross the window
he hears her laughing her child to sleep

THE ARRANGEMENT

she's arranging irises in a polished brass vase as elegant and narrow-
shouldered as herself *made from a bombcase* she explains to the tall blue
flags stiff as april that will not obey her arthritic fingers *1916* she adds
softening the effect with a spray of ferny leaves

bombs falling on london all around the town whistling down from
silvery zeppelins which nose about in the sky huge docile fish
swimming in the upper air

she stalks naked through the dark rooms watching her reflection flicker
in grey mirrors soft thin body, pale legs, wiry red hair resting uneasily
on white shoulders and freckled arms   she peers closer examines the
small uneven face the emphatic mouth the smallpox scar between the
foxy brows

this is the first time she has ever been alone in the forest-hill house
where she was born

if ever she was born for there's no record of any such birth of any such
person as herself, none   she found that out at her wedding five
months ago *you are marrying nobody* and she rests her fingers lightly
on the two stars on william's epaulette then leans forward and kisses
him on the mouth she can feel that her warm lips shock him for he's
younger and much shyer than she is   *bill my will* she whispers again
to the dark house this lonely night *can you survive all this? can I?*

for she carries in her velvet belly a weight lighter than a burr a kernel
from which a red-haired child may grow

now she's in the cool garden hugging her thin arms round her fine
nakedness chalkwhite roses bloom in their beds their stems and thorns
black as blood one open flower stares up at her with the pinched face
of an infant about to cry

the earth shrieks   cracks apart   rumbles   shakes   shakes   and
trembles to a stop

fish has laid his tumble of eggs among the pavements and the houses
the school crumples   the churchtower falls into the park the walls of
the prison break open and men rush out thanking the fishgod for their
deliverance almost at once they turn into muddy soldiers grumbling
and joking about the war, the mud, wet feet, rats and the rotten
bitter war

she lies flat in the roses covered with plaster dust from next door
thorns clawing at her chin and her breasts the cocklebur little nut
moves within her parts from its seedcase and drops from her to the
earth followed by a narrow warm tickle

she scratches among the roses as a cat might then buries the tiny thing
without a tear stands up dizzy lighter by the weight of a handful of
leaves

in the house she draws the heavy curtain so close that not a chink parts
them then lights a candle and flings herself onto the wide bed a small
empty space aches within her, aches coldly through her sleep which
lasts long into the next day

downstairs in the back kitchen where the window is broken and the
door swings loose on its hinges the small debris of the city has been
sifting into the house all night a layer of fine particles covers the sink
and the green glass flower-holders   by morning the shelf and the vases
that stand there—blue raku, enamelled chinoiserie, silver beaten thin
as steam—are greyed with a layer of fine detritus which might be the
dust of a century

SHRAPNEL

shrapnel has torn the man's ribs apart
there is a shabby wound in his breast
his mouth opens innocently upon a cry

he wants to curse his enemies but cannot
for he sees them as striplings lying in the grass
each with a girl beneath him
the long grass full of clover and fieldherbs
waves gently in the heat

the men get up from the women
and buckle on their belts
the women just lie there looking up at the thundery sky
we are wounded with joy they tell each other
we are happy happy happy

the soldier sees this he hears all this
as he lies there asking the earth
is this my final place my own place
he glances upwards to where
the tops of the trees almost meet
there is just a small patch of empty sky showing
it must be spring for a bird with a straw in its beak
swoops down to a low bough   he tries to think
of the name of the bird
he tries to think of his own name
the name of his son who has learned to speak already
so his wife writes   he has seen the child only once
and that was more than a year ago

he tries to remember the colour of his wife's eyes
he sees only her frailty those little narrow birdbones
beneath the soft flesh
he wishes she was another woman
one easier to abandon   one calm and robust
with a wide smooth brow

but who could forget that pitiful teat
in the child's mouth
the curious maze of the blue milkveins whose pattern
he traces in the dirt   his hand touches a broken brick
here was a house   now he remembers the collapse
of its walls

he licks his lips tasting for brickdust
he counts his strong teeth with his tongue
they are all there unchipped   he hears the bland
voice of the dentist telling him he has perfect bite

he shuts his eyes against the light but it shines on
through rosy lids which are the same colour exactly

as his wife's secret he wants to part her legs
and touch her glistening vermillion lining
now at last he understands
why he loves the bodies of women
more than the bodies of men   for pale skin covers
a man all over and only a wound can show its lining

carefully he passes his hands over his body
buttoned into its tunic of stiff drab wool
until he finds the hole in his chest
he thrusts in his fist to staunch the blood
a pulse beats close to his folded fingers
it is insistent and strong
it is pushing him away from himself

THIRD TRIMESTER

The gibbous moon in the trees is the head of
a child slipping out between sturdy thighs,
lying under bent and bloodied knees. Every
twig is a coarse hair, pubic, female, innocent.

But the moon is nothing but folded paper, the
Old Man explains, wielding his scissors over
the crisp white sheet, *or a handful of coins,
the quarters one by one pushed into the
slitted back of a pot pig, or maybe a sacred
wafer shoved between the clenched teeth of a
nun.*

Then I told him of when I was brought to bed.
Clouds close-wrapped the body of my child.
They were a net of fine-knotted threads.
Small fingers, small toes kept getting caught
in that web.

The moon wavered in the mist, the wind
moithered like a wailing babe, when the head,
wet as though rained-on, squeezed out through
a slit no bigger than a shrieking mouth.

And the cut rope, and the dark blood
trickling, and the little daughter at last
lying in the lap of the sun.

HALINKA

It is right, they say, to bury a stillborn child with a
mirror on the pillow beside her. That way, at the
resurrection, when she opens her eyes for the first
time, she will see her face and recognize herself.

But that's not for you, little daughter, little flaccid
creature. For you, there never was such a thing as a
face. There were hands and fingers, curled feet with
curled toes. There was a heart in your chest, red and
whole as a candy, and a white iris growing in the
place of your understanding.

ROBERT KROETSCH

(b. 1927)

Robert Kroetsch was born in the small farming community of Heisler, Alberta, which has remained a dominant element in his imaginative life. In 1948 he graduated from the University of Alberta and went to work as a civilian education and information specialist for the US Army, spending time in Labrador and the North. He began graduate studies at McGill University, but received his MA from Middlebury College in 1957 and his Ph.D. from the University of Iowa in 1961. After several years of teaching in the English Department at the State University of New York in Binghamton—where he co-edited *Boundary 2*, a journal of postmodern literature—Kroetsch began teaching intermittently in Canada, accepting a permanent position at the University of Manitoba in 1978. He has become an important figure regionally and nationally, not only for his poetry and fiction, but also for the vigour and contagion of his critical essays.

In contrast to what he, and many other critics, perceive to be a puritanical and conservative streak in the Canadian consciousness, Kroetsch espouses a Dionysian aesthetic. As the narrator of his novel *Badlands*, Anna Dawe, says: 'God help us we are a people raised not on love letters or lyric poems or even cries of rebellion or ecstasy or pain or regret, but rather old hoards of field notes. Those cryptic notations made by men who held the words themselves in contempt but who needed them neverthe-less in order to carry home, or back if not

home, the only memories they would ever cherish: the recollections of their male courage and their male solitude.'

One of the chief preoccupations of Kroetsch's poetics has been to find alternatives to the lyric, with its expectations of closure and coherence. Kroetsch's pursuit of the long poem—not the narrative that so interested Pratt, but the fragmented epic and poem-sequence—has involved a struggle against the presumed systems and grids of inherited story, employing (instead of character and a linear unfolding of plot) such structuring devices as stone hammers, ledgers, seed catalogues, and grammar itself. Under scrutiny these ordinary things become objects of meditation, assuming, or acquiring, a larger symbolic value: the stone hammer undergoes transformations from natural object to weapon, artefact, functional object, and imaginative touchstone; the ledger serves as a clever device—with its columns of inventory, credit, and debit—for tallying up private and collective guilt in the accounting that is fundamental to all thinking lives; seeds and catalogues of seeds provide a wonderful metaphor for exploring the images of growth so germane to our survival as individuals and as a nation; and the conjunctive structures 'and/but' in *The Sad Phoenician* function as a maddening, if humorous, expression of the alternating currents of motivation and sexual desire, entry and withdrawal, braggadocio and bathos.

Poet Ron Smith, in an Afterword to *The Stone Hammer Poems*, insists that Kroetsch's 'preoccupation with the need to "uninvent" the old mythologies and invent or create a new mythology that is central to his prairie locale, is a revolutionary act that is key to the revelatory process found in all his writings. It is this process that allows Kroetsch to cross geographical and aesthetic boundaries in his art.' As a poet and theorist, however, Kroetsch is, above all, playful. He sees the poet as trickster or lover rather than priest. Kroetsch endorses the idea of the poem as something more than literary document; he praises 'hubbub' and 'commotion', conditions in which the poem is 'Freed from picture, into the pattern and tumble of sound.'

Kroetsch's poetics may be gleaned from *The Crow Journals* (1980) and two issues of *Open Letter* devoted to his work. 'What has come to interest me now,' he writes in the latter, 'is what I suppose you can call the dream of origins. Obviously, on the prairies, the small town and farm are not merely places, they are remembered places, even dreamed places. When they were the actuality of our lives, we had realistic fiction, and we had almost no poetry at all. Now, in this dream condition, as dream-time fuses into the kind of narrative we call myth, we change the nature of the novel. And we start, with a new and terrible energy, to write the poems of the imagined real place.'

Kroetsch's poetry books include *The Ledger* (1975), *The Stone Hammer Poems* (1975), *Seed Catalogue* (1977), *The Sad*

Phoenician (1979), *Field Notes* (1981), *The Criminal Intensities of Love as Paradise* (1981), *Advice to My Friends* (1985), *Excerpts from the Real World* (1986), and *Completed Field Notes: The Long Poems of Robert Kroetsch* (1989). His novels include *But We Are Exiles* (1965), *The Words of My Roaring* (1966), *The Studhorse Man* (1969), for which he received a Governor General's Award, *Gone Indian* (1973), *Badlands* (1975), *What the Crow Said* (1978), *Alibi* (1983), *The Puppeteer* (1992), and *The Man from the Creeks* (1998). His non-fiction writings include a book of critical essays, *The Lovely Treachery of Words: Essays Selected & New* (1989), and a quasi-biography, *A Likely Story: The Writing Life* (1995), in which he plays, yet again, with notions of fact, authority, and the self, employing a feminine double with the same initials, named Rita Kleinhart: 'What is more precious in our collective biography than those very things which we elect to conceal or discard? Discard is the most enduring version of circulation; discard, not retention, constitutes the materiality of trace.'

Kroetsch is much in demand at home and abroad as a reader and critic and his work continues to be widely discussed, as evidenced by Peter Thomas's *Robert Kroetsch* (1980); *Labyrinths of Voice: Conversations with Robert Kroetsch* (1982, with Shirley Neuman and Robert Wilson); Robert Lecker's *Robert Kroetsch* (1986); and Dianne Tiefensee's *The Old Dualities: Deconstructing Robert Kroetsch and His Critics* (1994).

POEM OF ALBERT JOHNSON*

It is his silence   they cannot allow
offended into a blood reason   the hunters
surround his cabin   with their loud law

---

*The so-called 'Mad Trapper of Rat River' was hunted to death by a small army of men in the Northwest Territories and the Yukon in the winter of 1932.

he will give no name   to hate or love
neither forgive nor blame   the righteous
fusillade   no word of hurt or mercy

no word   only his rivalling guns
confide his awareness   of their assault
confuse the hunters   into the bomb-blast

unhousing the harried trapper   bare
to the Arctic night   the brave running
by which he will become   poet of survival

to our suburban pain   the silent man
circling back   to watch them coming
giving new tracks   to the blizzard-white trail

leaving the faint sleigh dogs   scent
of their lost game   (police and Indians
together at last   punished by dark

and wind   neglect the weather
of their intent)   he will give no name
only the cold camp   where he almost slept

letting gunshot   into his best pursuer
his self's shadow   dressed in red authority
and after the quick exchanging   unspeakably dead

and gone beyond all living   the silent man
made the impossible crossing   the snowshoe pattern
over the closed pass   into the caribou herd

that gave him a gap   out of the closing frame
the trap   forged by the roaring bush plane
out of six weeks' hunting   the silent man

having leapt their ring   walked back
and baited their pride   with his spent body
bought them the cry they sought   and only kept

his silence   (we stand at his grave in Aklavik
mosquitoes swarming at our heads   like the posse
that slammed him   out of his last loading)

the poet of our survival   his hands and feet
frozen   no name on his dead mouth
no words betraying   either love or hate

MEDITATION ON TOM THOMSON

Tom Thomson I love you   therefore I apologize
for what I must say   but I must say
damn your jack pines   they are beautiful

I love your bent trees   and I love your ice
in spring   candled into its green rot
and I love the way you drowned   all alone

with your canoe   and our not even knowing
the time of day   and the grave mystery
of your genius   interrupted   is *our* story

and art, man, art   is the essential
luxury   the imperative QUESTION(?)
the re-sounding say   of the night's loon

and holy shit mother   the muskeg snatch
of the old north   the bait that caught
the fishing father   into his own feast

the swimming art-man   who did not drown
in the lake   in his pictures
who drowned   for murder or grief or

the weave of the water   would not hold
the shoulders of the sky   were deep
the maelstrom would not spin   to spit him

free, daddy, FREE FREE FREE   (but I must say
DAMN your jack pines)   for the whorl
of the whirlpool breaks us   one by one

we stretch and tear   the joints
opening like curtains   on a cool
Algonquin morning   onto a red sun

or down onto the black bottom   or far
(the grammar of our days   is ill defined)
or rapt in the root and fire   of that wind

bent forest   (about your pine trees
this evening   one of them moved
across my wall)   daring the light

daring the bright and lover's leap   across
the impassible gap   the uncertain
principle of time and space   straight down

he dove   and he would seize unearthly
shades   and he would seize the drowned land
the picture from the pool   the pool's picture

and the gods cried   Tom, Tom, you asshole
let go   and you had found their secret
and would not ever   let go   they cry

SEED CATALOGUE

1

No. 176—*Copenhagen Market Cabbage*: 'This *new introduction, strictly speaking,* is in every respect a *thoroughbred,* a *cabbage* of *highest pedigree,* and is *creating considerable flurry* among *professional gardeners* all *over the world.*'

We took the storm windows / off
the south side of the house
and put them on the hotbed.
Then it was spring. Or, no:
then winter was ending.

'I wish to say we had lovely success
this summer with the seed purchased
of you. We had the finest Sweet
Corn in the country, and Cabbage
were dandy.'

—W. W. Lyon, South Junction, Man.

> My mother said:
> Did you wash your ears?
> You could grow cabbages
> in those ears.

Winter was ending.
This is what happened:
we were harrowing the garden.
You've got to understand this:
I was sitting on the horse.
The horse was standing still.
I fell off.

> The hired man laughed: how
> in hell did you manage to
> fall off a horse that was
> *standing still*?

> Bring me the radish seeds,
> my mother whispered.

Into the dark of January
the seed catalogue bloomed

a winter proposition, if
spring should come, then,

with illustrations:

No. 25—*McKenzie's Improved Golden Wax Bean*: 'THE MOST PRIZED OF ALL
BEANS. *Virtue* is its own reward. We have had *many expressions* from *keen
discriminating gardeners extolling our seed* and *this variety.*'

> Beans, beans,
> the musical fruit;

> the more you eat,
> the more you virtue.

My mother was marking the first row
with a piece of binder twine, stretched
between two pegs.

The hired man laughed: just
about planted the little bugger.
Cover him up and see what grows.
My father didn't laugh. He was puzzled
by any garden that was smaller than a
quarter-section of wheat and summerfallow.

the home place: N.E. 17-42-16 W4th Meridian.

the home place: one and a half miles west of Heisler, Alberta,

> on the correction line road
> and three miles south

No trees
around the house.
Only the wind.
Only the January snow.
Only the summer sun.
The home place:
a terrible symmetry.

How do you grow a gardener?

> Telephone Peas
> Garden Gem Carrots
> Early Snowcap Cauliflower
> Perfection Globe Onions
> Hubbard Squash
> Early Ohio Potatoes

This is what happened—at my mother's wake. This
is a fact—the World Series was in progress. The
Cincinnati Reds were playing the Detroit Tigers.
It was raining. The road to the graveyard was barely
passable. The horse was standing still. Bring me
the radish seeds, my mother whispered.

2

My father was mad at the badger: the badger was digging holes in the potato patch, threatening man and beast with broken limbs (I quote). My father took the double-barrelled shotgun out into the potato patch and waited.

Every time the badger stood up, it looked like a little man, come out of the ground. Why, my father asked himself—Why would so fine a fellow live under the ground? Just for the cool of roots? The solace of dark tunnels? The blood of gophers?

My father couldn't shoot the badger. He uncocked the shotgun, came back into the house in time for breakfast. The badger dug another hole. My father got mad again. They carried on like that all summer.

> *Love is an amplification*
> *by doing/over and over.*
>
> *Love is a standing up*
> *to the loaded gun.*
>
> *Love is a burrowing.*

One morning my father actually shot at the badger. He killed a magpie that was pecking away at a horse turd about fifty feet beyond and to the right of the spot where the badger had been standing.

A week later my father told the story again. In that version he intended to hit the magpie. Magpies, he explained, are a nuisance. They eat robin's eggs. They're harder to kill than snakes, jumping around the way they do, nothing but feathers.

Just call me sure-shot,
my father added.

3

No. 1248—*Hubbard Squash*: 'As *mankind* seems to have a *particular fondness* for squash, *Nature* appears to have *especially* provided this *matchless* variety of *superlative flavor.*'

> *Love is a leaping up*
> *and down.*

Love
is a beak in the warm flesh.

'As a cooker, it heads the list for warted squash. The
vines are of strong running growth; the fruits are large,
olive shaped, of a deep rich green colour, the rind is
smooth . . .'

But how do you grow a lover?

This is the God's own truth:
playing dirty is a mortal sin
the priest told us, you'll go to hell
and burn forever (with illustrations)—

it was our second day of catechism
—Germaine and I went home that
afternoon   if it's that bad, we
said to each other   we realized
we better quit   we realized

let's do it just one last time
and quit.

This is the God's own truth:
catechism, they called it,
the boys had to sit in the pews
on the right, the girls on the left.
Souls were like underwear that you
wore inside. If boys and girls sat
together—

Adam and Eve got caught
playing dirty.

This is the truth.
We climbed up into a granary
full of wheat   to the gunny sacks
the binder twine was shipped in—

we spread the paper from the sacks
smooth sheets   on the soft wheel
Germaine and I   we were like / one

we had discovered, don't ask me
how, where—but when the priest said
playing dirty we knew—well—

he had named it   he had named
our world   out of existence
(the horse   was standing still)

—This is my first confession. Bless me father I played
    dirty so long, just the other day, up in the granary
    there by the car shed—up there on the Brantford Binder
    Twine gunny sacks and the sheets of paper—Germaine
    with her dress up and her bloomers down—

—Son. For penance, keep your peter in your pants
    for the next thirteen years.

But how—

        Adam and Eve and Pinch-Me
        went down to the river to swim—
        Adam and Eve got drownded.

But how do you grow a lover?

        We decided we could do it
        just one last time.

    4

It arrived in winter, the seed catalogue, on a January
day. It came into town on the afternoon train.

Mary Hauck, when she came west from Bruce County, Ontario,
arrived in town on a January day. She brought along
her hope chest.

She was cooking in the Heisler Hotel. The Heisler Hotel
burned down on the night of June 21, 1919. Everything
in between: lost. Everything: an absence

of satin sheets
of embroidered pillow cases
of tea towels and English china
of silver serving spoons.

How do you grow a prairie town?

> The gopher was the model.
> Stand up straight:
> telephone poles
> grain elevators
> church steeples.
> Vanish, suddenly: the
> gopher was the model.

How do you grow a past /
to live in

the absence of silkworms
the absence of clay and wattles (whatever the hell
    they are)
the absence of Lord Nelson
the absence of kings and queens
the absence of a bottle opener, and me with a vicious
    attack of the 26-ounce flu
the absence of both Sartre and Heidegger
the absence of pyramids
the absence of lions
the absence of lutes, violas and xylophones
the absence of a condom dispenser in the Lethbridge Hotel and
    me about to screw an old Blood whore. I was
    in love.
the absence of the Parthenon, not to mention the Cathédrale de Chartres
the absence of psychiatrists
the absence of sailing ships
the absence of books, journals, daily newspapers and everything
    else but the *Free Press Prairie Farmer* and *The
    Western Producer*

the absence of gallows (with apologies to Louis Riel)
the absence of goldsmiths
the absence of the girl who said that if the Edmonton Eskimos
    won the Grey Cup she'd let me kiss her
    nipples in the foyer of the Palliser Hotel. I
    don't know where she got to.
the absence of Heraclitus
the absence of the Seine, the Rhine, the Danube, the Tiber and
    the Thames. Shit, the Battle River ran dry
    one fall. The Strauss boy could piss across it.
    He could piss higher on a barn wall than any
    of us. He could piss right clean over
    the principal's new car.
the absence of ballet and opera
the absence of Aeneas

How do you grow a prairie town?

Rebuild the hotel when it burns down. Bigger. Fill it
full of a lot of A-1 Hard Northern Bullshitters.

—You ever hear the one about the woman who buried
    her husband with his ass sticking out of the ground
    so that every time she happened to walk by she could
    give it a swift kick?

—Yeh, I heard it.

   5

I planted some melons, just to see what would
happen. Gophers ate everything.

                    I applied to the Government.
                    I wanted to become a postman,
                    to deliver real words
                    to real people.

                    There was no one to receive
                    my application.

I don't give a damn if I do die do die do die do die do die
do die do die do die do die do die do die do die do die do
die do die do die do die do die do die do die do die do die
do

6

No. 339—*McKenzie's Pedigreed Early Snowcap Cauliflower*: 'Of the many *varieties*
of *vegetables* in *existence, Cauliflower* is *unquestionably* one of the *greatest inheritances* of the *present generation, particularly Western Canadians.* There is *no place* in
the *world* where *better cauliflowers* can be *grown* than right here in the *West.* The
finest specimens we have *ever seen,* larger and of *better quality,* are *annually grown*
here on our *prairies.* Being *particularly* a *high altitude plant* it *thrives* to a *point* of
perfection here, *seldom seen* in *warmer climes.'*

But how do you grow a poet?

Start: with an invocation
invoke—

His muse is
his muse / if
memory is

and you have
no memory then
no meditation
no song (shit
we're up against it)

                    how about that girl
                    you felt up in the
                    school barn or that
                    girl you necked with
                    out by Hastings' slough
                    and ran out of gas with
                    and nearly froze to
                    death with / or that
                    girl in the skating
                    rink shack who had on
                    so much underwear you

didn't have enough
prick to get past her /
CCM skates

Once upon a time in the village of Heisler—

—Hey, wait a minute.
That's a story.

How do you grow a poet?

For appetite: cod-liver
oil
For bronchitis: mustard
plasters.
For pallor and failure to fill
the woodbox: sulphur
& molasses.
For self-abuse: ten Our
Fathers & ten Hail Marys.
For regular bowels: Sunny Boy
Cereal.

How do you grow a poet?

'It's a pleasure to advise that I
won the First Prize at the Calgary
Horticultural Show . . . This is my
first attempt. I used your seeds.'

Son, this is a crowbar.
This is a willow fencepost.
This is a sledge.
This is a roll of barbed wire.
This is a bag of staples.
This is a claw hammer.

We give form to this land by running
a series of posts and three strands
of barbed wire around a quarter-section.

First off I want you to take that
crowbar and drive 1,156 holes
in that gumbo.
And the next time you want to
write a poem
we'll start the haying.

How do you grow a poet?

This is a prairie road.
This road is the shortest distance
between nowhere and nowhere.
This road is a poem.

Just two miles up the road
you'll find a porcupine
dead in the ditch. It was
trying to cross the road.

As for the poet himself
we can find no record
of his having traversed
the land / in either direction

no trace of his coming
or going / only a scarred
page, a spoor of wording
a reduction to mere black

and white / a pile of rabbit
turds that tells us
all spring long
where the track was

poet . . . say uncle.

How?

Rudy Wiebe: 'You must lay great black steel lines of
fiction, break up that space with huge design and, like
the fiction of the Russian steppes, build a giant
artifact. No song can do that . . .'

February 14, 1976. Rudy, you
took us there: to the Oldman River
Lorna & Byrna, Ralph & Steve and me
you showed us where
the Bloods surprised the Crees
in the next coulee / surprised
them to death. And after
you showed us Rilke's word
Lebensgliedes.

Rudy: Nature thou art.

7

Brome Grass (Bromus Inermis): 'No amount of cold will kill it. It *withstands* the
summer suns. Water may stand on it for several weeks without apparent injury.
The roots push through the soil, throwing up new plants continually. It *starts
quicker* than other grasses in the spring. *Remains green* longer in the fall.
Flourishes under absolute neglect.'

The end of winter:
seeding / time.

*How do you grow
a poet?*

(a)

I was drinking with Al Purdy. We went round and round
in the restaurant on top of the Chateau Lacombe. We
were the turning center in the still world, the winter
of Edmonton was hardly enough to cool our out-sights.

The waitress asked us to leave. She was rather insistent;
we were bad for business, shouting poems at the paying
customers. Twice, Purdy galloped a Cariboo horse
right straight through the dining area.

Now that's what I call
a piss-up.

                                        'No song can do that.'

(b)

No. 2362—*Imperialis Morning glory*: 'This is the wonderful *Japanese Morning
Glory*, celebrated the world
over for its *wondrous beauty*
of both flowers and foliage.'

Sunday, January 12, 1975. This evening after
rereading *The Double Hook*: looking at Japanese prints.
Not at actors. Not at courtesans. Rather: Hiroshige's
series, *Fifty-Three Stations on the Tokaido*.

From the *Tokaido* series: 'Shono-Haku-u.' The
bare-assed travellers, caught in a sudden shower.
Men and trees, bending. How it is in a rain shower /
that you didn't see coming. And couldn't have avoided /
even if you had.

> The double hook:
> the home place.
> The stations of the way:
> the other garden
>
> *Flourishes.
> Under absolute neglect.*

(c)

Jim Bacque said (I was waiting for a plane,
after a reading; Terminal 2, Toronto)—he said,
You've got to deliver the pain to some woman,
don't you.

—Hey, Lady.
   You at the end of the bar.
   I wanna tell you something.

—Yuh?

—Peter Knight—of Crossfield,
  Alberta. Bronc-Busting Champion
  of the World. You ever hear of
  Pete Knight, the King of All
  Cowboys, Bronc-Busting Champion
  of the World?

—Huh-uh.

—You know what I mean? King
  of *All* Cowboys . . . Got
  killed—by a horse.
  He fell off.

—You some kind of nut
  or something?

    8

                    We silence words
                    by writing them down.

THIS IS THE LAST WILL AND TESTAMENT
OF ME, HENRY L. KROETSCH:

(a) [yes, his first bequest]

To my son Frederick my carpenter tools.

It was his first bequest. First,
a man must build.

Those horse-barns around Heisler—
those perfectly designed barns
with the rounded roofs—only Freddie
knew how to build them. He mapped
the parklands with perfect horse-barns.

                    I remember my Uncle Freddie.
                    (The farmers no longer
                    use horses.)

Back in the 30s, I remember
he didn't have enough money
to buy a pound of coffee.

Every morning at breakfast
he drank a cup of hot water
with cream and sugar in it.

Why, I asked him one morning—
I wasn't all that old—why
do you do that? I asked him.

Jesus Christ, he said. He was
a gentle man, really. Don't you
understand *anything?*

9

The danger of merely living.

a shell / exploding
in the black sky: a
strange planting

a bomb / exploding
in the earth: a
strange

man / falling
on the city.
Killed him dead.

It was a strange
planting.

the absence of my cousin who was shot down while bombing
the city that was his maternal great-grandmother's
birthplace. He was the navigator. He guided himself
to that fatal occasion:

    — a city he had
      forgotten
    — a woman he had
      forgotten

He intended merely to release a cargo of bombs on a
target and depart. The exploding shell was:

a) an intrusion on a design that was not his, or
b) an occurrence which he had in fact, unintentionally,
   himself designed, or
c) it is essential that we understand this matter because:

He was the first descendant of the family to return
to the Old Country. He took with him: a cargo of bombs.

          Anna Weller: *Geboren* Cologne, 1849.
          Kenneth MacDonald: Died Cologne, 1943.

                A terrible symmetry.

A strange muse: forgetfulness. Feeding her far children
to ancestral guns, blasting them out of the sky, smack /
into the earth. Oh, she was the mothering sort. Blood /
on her green thumb.

10

After the bomb/blossoms
After the city/falls
After the rider/falls
(the horse
standing still)

Poet, teach us
to love our dying.

West is a winter place.
the palimpsest of prairie

under the quick erasure
of snow, invites a flight.

How / do you grow a garden?

(a)

> No. 3060—*Spencer Sweet Pea*:
> Pkt. $.10; oz. $.25;
> quarter lb. $.75; half lb. $1.25.

Your sweet peas
climbing the staked
chicken wire,
climbing the stretched
binder twine by
the front porch

taught me the smell
of morning, the grace
of your tired
hands, the strength
of a noon sun, the
colour of prairie grass

taught me the smell
of my sweating armpits.

(b)

How do you a garden grow?
How do you grow a garden?

'Dear Sir,
     The longest brome grass I remembered seeing was
one night in Brooks. We were on our way up to the Calgary
Stampede, and reached Brooks about 11 pm, perhaps earlier
because there was still a movie on the drive-in screen.
We unloaded Cindy, and I remember tying her up to the truck
box and the brome grass was up to her hips. We laid down
in the back of the truck—on some grass I pulled by hand—
and slept for about three hours, then drove into Calgary.

Amie'

(c)

No trees
around the house
only the wind.
Only the January snow.
Only the summer sun.

Adam and Eve got drowned—
Who was left?

LORNA CROZIER

(b. 1948)

Lorna Crozier was born in Swift Current, Saskatchewan, and now lives on Vancouver Island, where she teaches Creative Writing at the University of Victoria. She completed her BA at the University of Saskatchewan and MA at the University of Alberta in 1980. She taught high school briefly and worked as a director of communications for the Saskatchewan government. As a founding member of the Moose Jaw Movement, she has also been an instructor at the Saskatchewan Summer School for the Arts and the Banff School of Fine Arts, and writer-in-residence at the Regina Public Library and the University of Toronto. Her books include *Inside the Sky* (1976), *Crow's Black Joy* (1978), *Humans and Other Beasts* (1980), *No Longer Two People* (1981, with Patrick Lane), *The Weather* (1983, Saskatchewan Writers Guild Long Manuscript Poetry Award), *The Garden Going On Without Us* (1985, nominated for the Governor General's Award), *Angels of Flesh, Angels of Silence* (1988), *Inventing the Hawk* (1992, Governor General's Award), and *Everything Arrives at the Light* (1995). Crozier won first prize in the CBC Literary Competition for 1987–88. She also continues as poetry editor for Coteau Books and is a co-editor of *A Sudden Radiance: Saskatchewan Poetry* (1987).

An instructive account of her geographical and literary influences appears in *Contemporary Authors* (Vol. 113),

> The most important influence on my writing was *As for Me and My House* by Sinclair Ross. It was the first book I read

that was set in the landscape where I grew up, the southwest corner of Saskatchewan. It made me realize that someone from my area could actually be a writer and, in some ways, it gave me the courage to try.

> The landscape of southwestern Saskatchewan has definitely influenced my writing. I've tried to thread the wind and sky into my poems, to make them breathe the way the prairie does. But the influence of places goes beyond the recurrence of images particular to a certain landscape. The mutability and the extremes of the natural world in Saskatchewan have given rise to my sense of the fragility of happiness, love, and life itself. Our hold on things and on each other is so tenuous. My poems, I think, express the fearful hope I feel for the human—for our capability to return to love through pain and for our journey toward that sense of unity with all things, with the mule deer I startled from feeding in the coulee yesterday, and with the mute explosions of lichens on the stones in my grandfather's pasture. If the magic that is poetry can't lead us to that oneness, then I hope it at least can make us feel less alone.

The strong influence of Sinclair Ross would eventually lead Crozier to write her striking poem-sequence *A Saving Grace: The Collected Poems of Mrs. Bentley* (1996), based on one of the characters in Ross's novel *As for Me and My House*.

Whether it concerns the evocation of place or the exploration of the psyche, Crozier insists in 'Who's Listening?' (*NeWest Review*, February/March, 1989) that good poetry involves 'the most intimate self of the writer speaking to the most intimate self of the reader. When the two connect, poetry happens, magic happens, the sparks fly.' Furthermore, 'Poems can only happen in a moment of recognition, of intense and clear seeing. . . .' As she says in 'Searching for the Poem' (*Waves* 14, 1–2, Fall 1985),

Poems, when they happen, are magic and staring too hard at magic will make it go away. You may discover it's all a trick with mirrors, but then Calvino says a series of mirrors can multiply an object to infinity and reflect its essence in a single image that contains the whole of everything. I want the poem to do that, not reflect nature but contain it and everything else that exists, is dreamed or imagined. . . . If a poem could walk, it would have paws, not feet. Or hooves, small ones, leaving half moons in the sand. Something to make you stop and wonder what kind of animal this is, where it came from, where it's going.

In 'Speaking the Flesh' (*Language in Her Eye: Writing and Gender*, edited by Libby Scheier, Sarah Sheard, and Eleanor Wachtel 1990), Crozier addresses the issue of censorship—the public, systemic kind that tries to suppress a text for, say, its sexual or political content, and the more insidious pressures that work to control, if not suppress entirely, full expression in the act of writing. She attributes negative responses to erotic writing in part to 'the shock of the new', in part to the male desire/need to control feminine discourse and, therefore, the 'hidden stories' that have to be told—and heard. The violence of this struggle, according to Crozier, examples of which range from people leaving a reading to protest poetic content that displeases them to the massacre of female engineering students at the University of Montreal, is both text and sub-text in the debate on censorship.

And, from the same essay:

Feminism is, after all, a revolution. It has stormed the bastille of our literature as well as other fortresses in our society. It is upsetting the tradition, the patterns, the literary canon. It has changed what is being written about, and how, and by whom. It has changed the oldest of stories, revised what many thought were untouchable texts. And just as significantly, it has changed the reader's response to the 'classics', to what she has read in the past and to what she has yet to read. Because critics have developed a vocabulary to describe what it is many feminist writers are doing in their works, perhaps we've forgotten that literature hits people in the gut as well as the head; it hits them where they live.

Geography and politics aside, Crozier claims to be looking for the 'spark of the spiritual in everyday life' ('Two Goldfish in Snow,' in *A Matter of Spirit*, Susan McCaslin, ed., 1998). Poetry begins, she says,

at the edge of the ineffable, the silent site where words dissolve and one's understanding has more to do with intuition than reasoning, with emotion than logic. What cannot be named is the proper subject of poetry, even though poems are populated with the concrete and commonplace: an old stove, lichen on a stone, an egg carton, a cat's whisker. How can poetry not include the spiritual when even these familiar things are endowed with a presence as forceful as the objects our official religions have sanctified? They resonate with an energy we try to put words to, and yet they remain irrefutable and blessedly themselves.

In an essay called 'The Shape of Human Sorrow: A Meditation on the Art of Poetry' (*Border Crossings*, Summer, 1994), Crozier writes of her efforts to give shape to experience, including the death of her father. She quotes Rilke on the need to let memories disappear, seep into the bloodstream and grey matter until they are 'nameless, no longer to be distinguished from ourselves— only then can it happen that in some very rare hours the first word of a poem arises in their midst and goes forth from them.' The article has much to say that is tantalizing about the creative process in general and the making of her poem 'Late Spring: After the Death of My Father' in particular.

A BRIEF HISTORY OF THE HORSE

1

The brown horse grazing in pastures of sleep
is full of soldiers. Each has his own
corner of darkness, his corner of despair.
The soldiers feel the sway of the horse's belly
as she races night across the meadows.
All of them believe they are in the hold
of a ship that smells of grass and forgetfulness
though they can't understand her hours of stillness,
or the mad sound of flies eating her ears.
Each remembers being pushed through the pale
thighs of his wound away from the field
where he fell though he can't remember
the name of the country or the day or the year.
Sailors now, they have crossed oceans of clouds
to reach this green meadow at the end
of the twentieth century where someone
may unlatch a gate for the horse to enter,
open the door between her ribs and let the light
pick among their bones.

2

The farm girl who rides the horse
after her chores are done
has no idea they are there.

If she did, she would not
squeeze her thighs so tight
around the horse's flanks,
she would not ride so hard.

Sometimes she thinks
she hears voices
as she lays her cheek
along the horse's neck,
sometimes she has bad dreams.

Already longing for the city
she is bored with horses,
the feral smell of them
on her hands, along
the inside of her legs.

When she brushes the horse
wipes away the lather,
she does not know
it could be foam
from the sea
churned by drowning

or froth from the mouth
of a dying man.

3

The horse without wings
grazes calmly in the meadow.
She has no need of eternity,
no need of bits or bridles.

What she knows beyond
the good sense of her hooves
no one can tell.

If we call her *ship*
if we call her *nightmare*,
if we call her *history*,
she will not care.

When she wants to
she moves, flicks
at flies with her tail,
curls back her lip
and shows her yellow teeth.

When she wants to
she stands
absolutely still.

INVENTING THE HAWK

She didn't believe the words
when she first heard them, that blue
bodiless sound entering her ear.
But now something was in the air,
a sense of waiting as if
the hawk itself were there
just beyond the light, blinded
by a fine-stitched leather hood
she must take apart with her fingers.
Already she had its voice,
the scream that rose from her belly
echoed in the dark inverted
canyon of her skull.

She built its wings, feather by feather,
the russet smoothness of its head,
the bead-bright eyes,
in that moment between sleep and waking.

Was she the only one
who could remember them,
who knew their shape and colours, the way
they could tilt the world with a list of wings?
Perhaps it was her reason for living
so long in this hard place
of wind and sky, the stunted trees
reciting their litany of loss
outside her window.

Elsewhere surely someone was drawing
gophers and mice out of the air.
Maybe that was also her job,
so clearly she could see them.
She'd have to lie here forever,

dreaming hair after hair,
summoning the paws (her own heart
turning timid, her nostrils twitching).

Then she would cause the seeds
in their endless variety—the ones
floating light as breath,
the ones with burrs and spears
that caught in her socks
when she was a child,
the radiant, uninvented blades of grass.

SMALL RESURRECTIONS

The drumming of the moth
on the chimney glass
draws the soldiers from the fields
where they lie like cut wheat,
what is left of their jackets
wet with rain. Their hats
have fallen, their boots
no longer fit. Leather boats
whose seams have split
they sink into the earth
as if it were the sea,
yet the young men rise,
move to the measure of wings.

So small they have become,
so pale and thinly drawn,
no one sees them as they pass.
Not the farmer pitching hay,
the sinews in his arms thick as rope.
Not his daughter who whistles
for her pony at the gate.

As they march, one of them plays
a flute fashioned out of bone,
a sound the girl mistakes
for the blackbird's trill,

its three warning notes
quickening the air.

Whenever she hears it
she wants to go somewhere,
leave her father and her pony
at the gate, find a place
where no one knows her name.
Right now if someone stopped
and touched her,
her whole body would start to sing.

The moth beats on the glass
softly as the heartbeats
of a bird wrapped in wool.
Such a sad sound, this
faint, dusty drumming,
heard only by the smallest,
the most invisible of ears.

JOE LAWSON'S WIFE

The woman who pounded on our door
came out of the wind, hair wild,
voice thin and broken. Philip
drove with Dr Bird beside him,
I sat in the back with her,
Joe Lawson's wife, both of us silent
and staring straight ahead
though there was nothing to see
in those two beams of light. How
to comfort? When we got to the barn,
Philip was awkward with the rope.
The doctor pushed him aside,
climbed the milking-stool
the man had kicked away
and cut him down. Joe Lawson,
though it was hard to call
what hung in the barn
that name—the rope had cut into his neck,
his face blue and bloated.

I kept my eyes on his hands.
They were what you noticed
when you first saw Joe. Big, solid hands,
as much a part of the land as the stones
ice heaves from the earth every spring.

It was a minister they needed
not the doctor, but Philip hung back.
Dr Bird was the one who told me
Take her to the house and make some tea.
She wouldn't leave,
but covered her man with a blanket
that smelled of horse, then sat
in the dirty straw, his swollen head
in her lap. By then her sister had arrived
and the neighbour with a wagon.
The sun was rising, its splinters
from the cracks in the walls
falling all around her.

At last she let the men
carry the body from the barn
but still wouldn't go.
She pulled the wooden stool
to the stall and milked the cow,
its udder heavy, barn cats
coming out of nowhere at the sound.

There was no pail,
milk streamed out and hit the ground,
pooled around her feet,
the cats licking and mewling.
Her sister stood helplessly beside her
and motioned us away.
There was nothing to do but go,
above her head Philip mumbling
something I couldn't hear.

At home, he clung to me
as if his feet were swinging through the air
and it was I that held him up.

How to comfort. We bring so little
to each other. Later, after we had slept
he went into his study and I followed,
watched him from the door.
So upset, he left it open.

He tore the drawings he had sketched
last Sunday, his parishioners
as he had seen them from the pulpit—all
alike, his pencil strokes relentless,
pinning them and their piety to the pews.

Everything would change for us
if he could draw
that woman on her stool, her simple
act of courage—or was it resignation?
The shadow of her husband still
swaying from the rafters,
milk puddling at her feet
and between the cracks,
the sun's bright nails pounding through.

PACKING FOR THE FUTURE: INSTRUCTIONS

Take the thickest socks.
Wherever you're going
you'll have to walk.

There may be water.
There may be stones.
There may be high places
you cannot go without
the hope socks bring you,
the way they hold you
to the earth.

At least one pair must be new,
must be blue as a wish
hand-knit by your mother
in her sleep.

*

Take a leather satchel,
a velvet bag and an old tin box—
a salamander painted on the lid.

This is to carry that small thing
you cannot leave. Perhaps the key
you've kept though it doesn't fit
any lock you know,
the photograph that keeps you sane,
a ball of string to lead you out
though you can't walk back
into that light.

In your bag leave room for sadness,
leave room for another language.

There may be doors nailed shut.
There may be painted windows.
There may be signs that warn you
to be gone. Take the dream
you've been having since
you were a child, the one
with open fields and the wind
sounding.

*

Mistrust no one who offers you
water from a well, a songbird's feather,
something that's been mended twice.
Always travel lighter
than the heart.

WATCHING MY LOVER

I watch him hold his mother
as she vomits into a bowl.
After, he washes her face

with a wet cloth and we try
to remove her soiled gown
tied in the back with strings.

Unable to lift her
I pull the green cotton
from under the blankets, afraid
I'll tear her skin.
He removes the paper diaper.
No one has taught us
how to do this, what to say.
Everything's so fragile here
a breath could break you.

She covers her breasts with hands
bruised from tubes and needles,
turns her face away.
It's okay, Mom, he says.
*Don't feel shy. I've undressed
dozens of women in my time.*
In this room where my lover
bares his mother, we three laugh.

Later, I curl naked beside him
in our bed, listen to his sleeping,
breath by breath. So worn out
he burns with fever—the fires
his flesh lights to keep him
from the cold.

Though he has washed
I smell her on his skin
as if she has licked him
from head to toe
with her old woman's tongue
so everyone who lies with him
will know he's still
his mother's son.

A KIND OF LOVE

You can see it
in my graduation photograph.
You're Daddy's little girl, he said,
his arm heavy around my shoulders,
his face too naked, a sloppy
smile sliding to one side.
I held him up. Mom tied his shoes.
His love made me ashamed.

Some days I felt protective,
his hangdog look at breakfast
when no one talked to him but me,
sugar spilling from his spoon.
Don't tell Mum, he'd say
on Sundays when he took me boating,
sunk his third empty in the lake.
At home, she fried a chicken
in case he didn't catch a fish,
waited and kept things warm.
Even so, he died too soon.

Now I wait for you as if
you've spent a summer afternoon
in waves of wind and sunlight. I know
you've hidden a bottle somewhere
upstairs in your room. So far
I've stopped myself from looking
though I can't find what to do.

More and more I'm Daddy's
little girl in peau de soi,
my first long dress, its false
sheen a wash of mauve.
When you lean into me
the same look's on your face
as in the photograph,
your smile's undone.

Among the other things
it could be named
this too is love, the kind
I'm most familiar with—
the weight I claim
I cannot bear and do,
and do.

ROO BORSON

(b. 1952)

Born in Berkeley, California in 1952, Roo Borson studied at the University of California at Santa Barbara and Goddard College in Vermont before completing a MFA in Creative Writing at the University of British Columbia. Since then, she has resided in Australia and New Mexico, but mostly in Canada, where she has conducted poetry workshops and been writer-in-residence at Concordia University. Now living in Toronto with poet-physicist Kim Maltman, she has written the following books: *Landfall* (1977), *In the Smoky Light of the Fields* (1980), *Rain* (1980), *A Sad Device* (1981), *The Whole Night Coming Home* (1984, nominated for the Governor General's Award), a collaboration with Maltman called *The Transparence of November/Snow* (1985), *Intent, or the Weight of the World* (1989), *Night Walk: Selected Poems* (1994) and *Water Memory* (1996). She has also participated with painter Andy Patton and Kim Maltman in a poetry performance group called Pain Not Bread, producing a collaborative anthology called *Introduction to the Introduction to Wang Wei* (2000), devoted to exploring Chinese texts and notions surrounding translation, authorship, originality, and intertextuality.

Borson recommends a certain resistance to poetic theory. As she says to interviewer and editor Peter O'Brien (*So to Speak*, 1987), 'Writing by theory is too much like painting by numbers.' However, she acknowledges that 'there are new regions to articulate. With me, this means changing styles, syntax, cadence. A new way of talking brings in new subjects, or vice versa.' She is particularly eloquent about the music of poetry:

> Music is necessary to all writing, not just poetry. Writing is speech, it's out loud, it makes a noise that's rhythmic or arrhythmic, it forms patterns and breaks them. Whenever I think about rhythm I think of contemporary jazz—Weather Report or Carlos Santana and Alice Coltrane, Jean-Luc Ponty. I had to learn to listen to this kind of music. At first I could only hear a big mass of disorganized sound, unharmonic, crashing, confusing—but then I began to hear individual instruments within the welter and *oh* the pleasure when all the conflicting strains are drawn together into melody again. It's astonishing and fills me with happiness. Coming to a piece of fantastic writing is like that point at which the instruments pull together and everything makes sense—out of the welter of everyday impressions and ups and downs, this clear voice is speaking. It makes the crashing and confusion that preceded it that much more valuable, the contrast is sensual and excruciating and cerebral too. . . . Our rhythms are based on street corners, in poetry, and also on individual temperament. We each have a cadence, or several related cadences.

On the poetic line, Borson says in the same interview:

I think the line still has a role in poetry. If it didn't, we should all be writing prose or prose poetry. Lines can be used in different kinds of ways. They can accentuate a rhythm of a tension or space between images or ideas. Line breaks can be used as punctuation or as transitional areas. You can use them to make the reader stop or keep going. Line breaks can be used to accentuate the medium of written language—that's how Robert Creeley uses them—or to minimize that and emphasize a natural chanting speech, as W.S. Merwin uses them (his father was a minister). John Newlove is another master of the line. I'm not saying there's only one way, or three ways, to make line-breaks; they're one of the components of voice, and everyone's voice is a little different. The most individual voices can be identified by their rhythms, their way of moving.

Borson is not averse, personally or poetically, to taking a political stand, but insists that

The thought that poetry, or any other art, has a predetermined moral role is abhorrent to me. Look what happened to the arts in China: fine arts were replaced by bizarre forms of folk-art, fascinating culturally, but also a loss. That is, I don't believe that art has a duty, of any sort, to society. To say that it has played a role, in retrospect, is another thing. Does the rose bloom for the bee? No, but their lives are bound together and they coincidentally, felicitously, serve one another. . . . the best reason for becoming a doctor or a mathematician or a poet is an overwhelming love of the occupation. At their best I think artists are motivated by unsentimental love and by curiosity.

Many readers have responded to the strong sense of physical space, or place, in Borson's poems. 'There's a mood in every place,' she says.

Partly it's the landscape, partly the people, the ways they live. I've never done travelogue or documentary poems, so, for me, the mood of a place comes out more in emotional nuance, in syntax and music. With California, there was restlessness and lushness. . . . In Vancouver it was rain, rain, rain. The quick, beautiful passing away of things. In Toronto there's the incredible vitality of people packed close together, and outside the city there's all that mute, overfarmed countryside, lovely and calm and in decline. For me, the landscape is not separable from our life. Lives are not separable from the apartments and farmhouses they take place in. Societies are not separable from the land.

When pressed to talk about her relationship with the natural world, and the so-called 'city/nature' split, Borson resolutely refused to have her poetry pigeonholed:

You and I, or the reader and the writer, approach the poems from opposite ends of the process of writing. You, as a reader and critic, might draw certain conclusions from my work, but I, as the writer, am not thinking of conclusions at all. All I'm doing is trying to share what I see while making a beautiful sound at the same time. I don't intentionally code messages into my poems; if I had a concrete message I would probably write an essay. I write about the city and about nature because those, combined, are my environment. I write what I see (and hear and smell, etc.) and what I'm thinking/feeling in response to what I see. . . . Poems have minds of their own and you can engage in a dialogue with them. I do write intensely sometimes about nature because I experience it intensely; that's all.

When she penned 'Poetry as Knowing' (*Poetry and Knowing*, 1995, edited by Tim

Lilburn), Borson concluded that poetic knowing has something to do with music. 'Poetry is made of words, yet it is exactly as articulate as music, and as distinct from ordinary speech. . . . What listens is only an ear: the sort of ear that is meant when we say someone has an "ear" for music. It listens for bird calls and the trickle of water, the slamming of a door.' She finds poet Robert Creeley's work rooted in the breath, the limbs, the nervous system: 'A mind, reverent, elemental, readily dumbfounded, native yet not naïve—sensation and recollection lurching elegantly through the line. Not passive, but actively thought. And scrupulously self-conscious, never claiming to know more than can really be known.' To speak, she says, 'as though someone might hear, and hear aright': 'Writing is dreaming. Its logic is biological; it is beautifully cantabile. It says that if you love, and don't follow what you love, you're lost.'

TALK

The shops, the streets are full of old men
who can't think of a thing to say anymore.
Sometimes, looking at a girl, it
almost occurs to them, but they can't make it out,
they go pawing toward it through the fog.

The young men are still jostling shoulders
as they walk along, tussling at one another with words.
They're excited by talk, they can still see the danger.

The old women, thrifty with words,
haggling for oranges, their mouths
take bites out of the air. They know the value of oranges.
They had to learn everything
on their own.

The young women are the worst off, no one has bothered
to show them things.
You can see their minds on their faces,
they are like little lakes before a storm.
They don't know it's confusion that makes them sad.
It's lucky in a way though, because the young men take
a look of confusion for inscrutability, and this
excites them and makes them want to own
this face they don't understand,
something to be tinkered with at their leisure.

WATERFRONT

The women's bodies lying in the sand are curved like shells.
The men can't take their eyes off them.
The seawater spangles like a drink of champagne,
but the fishermen don't see it that way,
they have their clothes on, they don't care about girls.
They only care about fish. They yell to one another down the beach
as if this were their ocean. Meanwhile,
ignorant, the smelts plod into the nets.
Seated on benches, middle-aged women
in magenta travel dresses, going nowhere,
dressed too warmly for the weather,
delve into the sunlight with their eyes closed and pretend
they are dissolving, like a tablet in water.
Only the babies pushed along in carriages
seem to enjoy themselves, twisting their faces
into vast expressions. Their skin
is still translucent. They haven't yet finished
materializing into the world.

FLOWERS

The sunset, a huge flower, wilts on the horizon.
Robbed of perfume, a raw smell
wanders the hills, an embarrassing smell,
of nudity, of awkward hours on earth.
If a big man stands softly, his wide arms
gentled at his sides, women dissolve. It is the access
to easy violence that excites them.

The hills are knobbed with hay,
as if they were full of drawers about to be opened.
What could be inside but darkness?
The ground invisible, the toes feel the way,
bumping against unknown objects
like moths in a jar, like moths
stubbing themselves out on a lamp.

The women sit in their slips,
scattered upstairs through the houses
like silken buds.
They look in the mirror,
they wish they were other than they are.
Into a few of the rooms go a few of the men,
bringing their mushroomy smell.

The other men loll against the outsides of buildings,
looking up at the stars,
inconsequential.

One of them bends down to smell a flower.
There are holes in his face.

A Sad Device

A rat, his eyes like glycerine,
like galleries of landscape paintings,
genitals like a small bell, he,
siphon of smells,
mortician gathering in the gauzy corpses,
construes the world.
The grey warehouse of gothic stars,
the gleaming artillery of water,
the flowerbeds like Arabic scrolls,
all of it.

I think my heart is a sad device,
like can-openers.
Sometimes I would rather step between slices
of dark rye and be taken in
by some larger beast.
Men dreaming of billboards,
cars barrelling on and on in the night marooned,
zeroed in on an immense target.
Now I believe the frozen mammoths
in the laundry room
came of their own accord,
not through coercion

by the Sears appliance man.
Not even he
has a cozy life.

Tiny lions in the zookeeper's hair
keep him busily asleep,
but some of us wake too soon,
when our lover is still a dismantled thing
blue with streetlight.

This rat and I
have more in common than most,
having met once.
Now we go to separate nests
and presumably to dawn
with its crossfire of light
meeting in all the other eyes.

SPRING

The hills plunge through mist as if their contours
romped, but they're dead-still, made in those shapes
long ago. From early morning
the black and white cows have walked
straight through walls and columns of mist as if
their eyes could only see three feet in front of them anyway.

The hills in the morning: a green so delicate and wild
it almost shimmers backwards out of existence.
The cows stand sideways
on the hill gazing three feet in front of them
into empty air or they move in that slow
stumbling shuffle over the dirt clods. They could walk
straight through outer space not blinking an eye.

The fault opens up five feet wide in some places.
The small earthquake in the middle of the night:
the world swaying so hard it almost falls
out of orbit,
with only the sound of glasses
chattering in the cupboard.

Beside the run-off line: the skeleton
of one of last year's cows.
The other cows just walk around it
as if it weren't there.
Or maybe somewhere in those eyes
like bells too far away to hear
they already know.

At sunset the farmer
comes out of his white house on top of the hill
and watches his cows as if
he wished they belonged to him,
as if their four legs didn't move in their own time.
If they knew a little more
they could just walk off and leave him.

Always the hills and mist are making their mute gestures.
People get the feel of it, that's all they ever get.

The sheep stand around like errant clouds.
The lambs just sit in the grass, brand-new,
they haven't been here long enough to dirty their fur.
They rest awhile, looking around
as if they don't quite know how to behave.
Then they heave up on those scrawny legs
unfolded for the first time in the world.
And right away they get it:
the feel of being alive.
They want to romp
over every corner of those green hills.

BEAUTY

On these leaden days of early spring even one stray tentacle of shadowy sun
makes the ground steam. There is a slate-green dust which frosts the backsides
of certain trees, away from the wind, which three young girls have just
discovered. They go from trunk to trunk finding the brighter shades, streaking
it above their eyes, posing for one another. A few of last summer's blackberries
are left hanging like lanterns in the storm of brambles, too deep for the birds

and too high for things that crawl the ground at night. Still the half-fermented
juice is good for staining the lips. The girls are just learning about beauty.

One day they'll be shown what their own beauty or lack of it will do to
them. Not one day, but many nights, nights they'll lie alone sifting through
incidents, certain instances which are the only analogue of those steeply
lengthening bones, the breasts filling calmly, immutably as lakes taking in all
that stormy and random rain.

INTERMITTENT RAIN

Rain hitting the shovel
leaned against the house,
rain eating the edges
of the metal in tiny bites,
bloating the handle,
cracking it.
The rain quits and starts again.

There are people who go into that room in the house
where the piano is and close the door.
They play to get at that thing
on the tip of the tongue,
the thing they think of first and never say.
They would leave it out in the rain if they could.

The heart is a shovel leaning against a house somewhere
among the other forgotten tools.
The heart, it's always digging up old ground,
always wanting to give things a decent burial.

But so much stays fugitive,
inside,
where it can't be reached.

The piano is a way of practising
speech when you have no mouth.
When the heart is a shovel that would bury itself.
Still we can go up casually to a piano
and sit down and start playing
the way the rain felt in someone else's bones
a hundred years ago,

before we were born,
before we were even one cell,
when the world was clean,
when there were no hearts or people,
the way it sounded
a billion years ago, pattering
into unknown ground. Rain

hitting the shovel leaned against the house,
eating the edges of the metal.
It quits,
        and starts again.

CITY LIGHTS

To board the train for Toronto and glance over at the other
tracks as that train starts rolling and the woman there,
opposite, dozing, opens her eyes.
To look into eyes and know there are many directions.
To have it all at once: cinnamon buns
from the Harbord Bakery and the late poems of Wang Wei.
To step out, bringing traffic to a halt.
To bemoan with total strangers the state of the lettuce,
to be queried concerning the uses of star fruit,
and expostulate thereon.
To guide an unsteady gentleman across the street
and refuse payment in eternity.
To happen on the long light down certain streets as the sun is setting,
to pass by all that tempts others without a thought.
For cigar smoke and Sony Walkmans and random belligerence,
the overall sense of delighted industry
which is composed of idle hatred, inane self-interest,
compassion, and helplessness, when looked at closely.
To wait in queues, anonymous as the price code in a supermarket.
To board a bus where everyone is talking at once.
and count eight distinct languages and not know any.
For the Chinese proprietress of the Bagel Paradise Restaurant,
who is known to her customers as the joyful
otter is known to the clear salt water of Monterey Bay.

To know that everyone who isn't reading, daydreaming,
or on a first date is either full of plans or
playing Sherlock Holmes on the subway.
For eerie cloudlit nights, and skyscrapers,
and raccoons, jolly as bees.
For the joy of walking out the front door and becoming
instantly, and resolutely, lost.
To fall, when one is falling,
into a safety net, and find one's friends.
To be one among many.
To be many.

SUMMER CLOUD

Hello little buntings, if that's what you are—
you look as though you should be reading the stock reports,
keeping up your options on soybeans, gold, and millet.
I married a man once who said the strangest things.
Years later at an airport he knelt down to pray
and the *Playboy* magazines spilled out of his briefcase.
How is it people can go on to become anything at all?
The incomprehensible crystals in the government vault
by which we measure space and time.
The body is impossible. You can hack off every limb
and still it goes on thinking it's whole. It dies,
only to feel it's walking around fully dressed.
Are you in the forest?
One day the grass turns green, and all
the merry little bands of boys
call out to one another in the high, gruff,
sulky voices of robber kings. And no wonder.
This world is only a template for the world,
all painted with a whitewash called Summer Cloud.

GEORGE BOWERING

Somebody at the next table was eating oysters, somebody else was eating clams, and George, beside me, whom I'd only just met, said he couldn't bring himself to eat oysters or clams or any other creature whose *whole body* lies in front of you, no matter how small or ugly. I ordered a Caesar salad, and after dinner we all went over to the reading, where George read a wonderful poem about his father and a bowl of tomato soup. When I told him I loved the poem he said everyone has memories of a father eating something, even if not tomato soup: that is, the poem could be lovable only if people made their own substitutions . . . whereupon deep inside me a miniature person stood up and shouted *No!*—not so loud as to disturb anyone, mind you, but *No!*—because love won't abide substitutions, and what the poem made me love was *his* father, not to mention tomato soup. At the reception afterwards, everyone had gotten their drinks and we were standing around eyeing the arrangements of crackers, when George—apparently failing, in the face of the onrushing sentence, to locate the word 'crustaceans'—referred to the shrimp (keeled over, peeled and cooked on their little platter) as 'Etruscans', and all of us standing around the end table began to laugh, to laugh and eat (except for George, of course) as if in homage to the ancestors, and the agile minds they passed down between us.

WATER MEMORY

Water does not remember, it moves
among reeds, nudges the little boat
(a little), effloresces a shadowy fog
which forgets for us the way home
though the warm dry rooms are
in us. (Stretched on the examining table we
feel it when the unfamiliar hand
presses just there.) Water,
on its own, would not remember,
but herd follows herd, and memory is a shepherd
of the gentlest wants. Not even blood
can recall, though the live
kidney shipped in its special box
wakes up one day in someone new.
No one made this world, there's no need
to feel ashamed. Be water,
find a lower place, go there.

WHUFF

Cousin to the slug, this flesh, fish-bait excess
I love you with
now that I'm not young or slim or lucky
except in love. If luck it is
to lie beside you, sleepless,
hour on hour, moonlight in the room—
not knowledge or luck or love
but breathable stone. And you do,
you breathe it in. You *whuff*, you snort—
and all the pebbles, all the sands
are raked against my eardrums . . .
this your nightly catechism, only catechism,
that I know you'll never learn,
charmed, asleep, yourself—
as I am young again beside you,
and flesh, and wakeful.

DIONNE BRAND

(b. 1953)

Dionne Brand was born and raised in Trinidad, but has lived in Canada, mainly Toronto, since 1970. She has been a strong advocate of human rights, making films and writing about politics, racism, and disadvantaged women from a variety of cultural backgrounds. Her non-fiction works include *Rivers Have Sources, Trees Have Roots: Speaking of Racism* (with Krisantha Sri Bhaggiyadatta, 1986), *No Burden to Carry: narratives of black working women in Ontario 1920s–1950s* (1991), *We're Rooted Here, They Can't Pull Us Up* (with five other writers, 1994), *Bread Out of Stone: recollections sex recognitions race dreaming politics* (1994), and the anthology *Grammar of Dissent: Poetry and Prose of Claire Harris, M. Nourbese Philip and Carroll Morrell* (1994).

Although she published *'Fore Day Morning* (1978), *Earth Magic* (1980/1993), *Winter Epigrams and Epigrams to Ernesto Cardenal in Defense of Claudia* (1983), *Primitive Offensive* (1983), and *Chronicles of the Hostile Sun* (1984), Brand's first major book of poems was *No Language Is Neutral* (1990), which was shortlisted for the Governor General's Award; her next, *Land to Light On* (1997), won that award. She has also published *Sans Souci and Other Stories* (1988/1994) and two novels, *In Another Place, Not Here* (1996) and *At the Full and Change of the Moon* (1999).

Brand's interest in Black women's history and in the task of finding a language that will render that history both credible and compelling has driven her to experiment with poetic form, particularly the serial-poem or poem-sequence. As she says in a note for Sharon Thesen's *The New Long Poem Anthology,*

> What I try to do in *No Language Is Neutral* is to make the poems sound like a constant and full humming. I intended it to be felt as a sustained rhythm and to engage itself in itself, using some of what Henry Louis Gates calls 'Black rhetorical tropes . . . "marking", "loud talking", "specifying", "testifying", "calling out" (of one's name), "sounding". . . .' Therefore I've tried to make the world over in the poems, spoken in what my grandmother used to call 'womanish language'. The structure of the lines came out of the need to say the thing. I wanted to fill every silence with a word and every word with a silence. Since there are so many silences to fill and so many words to silence, the poem continues.

For the National Film Board Brand directed a documentary film called *Listening for Something: Adrienne Rich and Dionne Brand in Conversation*, which contains many images and comments that are useful in understanding both her poetry and her social and political background. 'I write for the people,' she says, 'believing in something other than the nation state in order to be sane. . . . A writer needs earth, soil, not air. . . something in the bone, remembered, not quite known.' When Adrienne Rich expressed disagreement with Virginia

Woolf's comment that she did not need a nation because she was a citizen of the world, Brand replied: 'I feel that, in fact, she may be right, that the word "nation" is no longer useful, that it has been so corrupted by the way in which the states we live in are organized.' She dismisses not only nationalism, as a construction that favours those with power and consists mainly of *leaving out* various groups, but also the Canadian 'myth of wilderness', which does not correspond at all to the experience of most immigrants.

Brand expresses her 'complete antipathy' for what Canada has done to its minorities and for how it has either participated in, or not spoken out strongly against, international acts of bullying and suppression in Vietnam, Chile, Nicaragua, Granada, and Iraq. Her passionate rejection might surprise Canadians who have never looked closely at the history of racism in their own country, or who have bought into the myth of Canada as an international peace-keeper. One has only to think of the horrific treatment of First Nations people, the incarceration of Japanese-Canadians during World War II, the Head Tax on Chinese immigrants, and the turning away of the *Komogatu Maru* with its cargo of South Asian immigrants in the first decade of the twentieth century, which was matched by the refusal, several decades later, of a shipload of Jewish refugees from the Holocaust. Brand's indictment ought to come as a welcome reminder that, as Herschel Hardin says in *A Nation Unaware*, 'creating a simulacrum of innocence [personal or tribal] is only one way colonials have of avoiding their condition'.

Although she insists that when she writes poetry she concentrates on speaking to Black people, those who have shared her history of exile, slavery, and racism, Brand is delighted when others hear and find something in those crafted lines that speaks to their own oppression by institutions, ideologies and individual ignorance. Amazingly, her poetry escapes the stigma of mere rhetoric or propaganda by transmuting these feelings into image, voice and music, as is evident from the work she chose to read and from her final comment in the film: 'I just always had a real love for the sound of things, that's the simplest way I could tell it.'

HARD AGAINST THE SOUL/I

this is you girl, this cut of road up
to Blanchicheuse, this every turn a piece
of blue and earth carrying on, beating, rock and
ocean this wearing away, smoothing the insides
pearl of shell and coral

this is you girl, this is you all sides of me
hill road and dip through the coconut at Manzanilla
this sea breeze shaped forest of sand and lanky palm
this wanting to fall, hanging, greening
quenching the road

this is you girl, even though you never see it
the drop before Timberline, that daub of black shine

sea on bush smoke land, that pulse of the heart
that stretches up to Maracas, La Fillete bay never know
you but you make it wash up from the rocks

this is you girl, that bit of lagoon, alligator
long abandoned, this stone of my youngness
hesitating to walk right, turning to Schoener's road
turning to duenne and spirit, to the sea wall and sea
breaking hard against things, turning to burning reason

this is you girl, this is the poem no woman
ever write for a woman because she 'fraid to touch
this river boiling like a woman in she sleep
that smell of fresh thighs and warm sweat
sheets of her like the mitan rolling into the Atlantic

this is you girl, something never waning or forgetting
something hard against the soul
this is where you make sense, that the sight becomes
tender, the night air human, the dull silence full
chattering, volcanoes cease, and to be awake is
more lovely than dreams

BLUES SPIRITUAL FOR MAMMY PRATER

*On looking at 'the photograph of Mammy Prater an ex-slave,
115 years old when her photograph was taken'*

she waited for her century to turn
she waited until she was one hundred and fifteen
years old to take a photograph
to take a photograph and to put those eyes in it
she waited until the technique of photography was
suitably developed
to make sure the picture would be clear
to make sure no crude daguerreotype would lose
her image
would lose her lines and most of all her eyes
and her hands
she knew the patience of one hundred and fifteen years

she knew that if she had the patience,
to avoid killing a white man
that I would see this photograph
she waited until it suited her
to take this photograph and to put those eyes in it.

in the hundred and fifteen years which it took her to
wait for this photograph she perfected this pose
she sculpted it over a shoulder of pain,
a thing like despair which she never called
this name for she would not have lasted
the fields, the ones she ploughed
on the days that she was a mule, left
their etching on the gait of her legs
deliberately and unintentionally
she waited, not always silently, not always patiently,
for this self portrait
by the time she sat in her black dress, white collar,
white handkerchief, her feet had turned to marble,
her heart burnished red,
and her eyes.

NO LANGUAGE IS NEUTRAL

No language is neutral. I used to haunt the beach at
Guaya, two rivers sentinel the country sand, not
backra white but nigger brown sand, one river dead
and teeming from waste and alligators, the other
rumbling to the ocean in a tumult, the swift undertow
blocking the crossing of little girls except on the tied
up dress hips of big women, then, the taste of leaving
was already on my tongue and cut deep into my
skinny pigeon toed way, language here was strict
description and teeth edging truth. Here was beauty
and here was nowhere. The smell of hurrying passed
my nostrils with the smell of sea water and fresh fish
wind, there was history which had taught my eyes to
look for escape even beneath the almond leaves fat
as women, the conch shell tiny as sand, the rock

stone old like water. I learned to read this from a
woman whose hand trembled at the past, then even
being born to her was temporary, wet and thrown half
dressed among the dozens of brown legs itching to
run. It was as if a signal burning like a fer de lance's
sting turned my eyes against the water even as love
for this nigger beach became resolute.

There it was anyway, some damn memory half-eaten
and half hungry. To hate this, they must have been
dragged through the Manzinilla spitting out the last
spun syllables for cruelty, new sound forming,
pushing toward lips made to bubble blood. This road
could match that. Hard-bitten on mangrove and wild
bush, the sea wind heaving any remnants of
consonant curses into choking aspirate. No
language is neutral seared in the spine's unravelling.
Here is history too. A backbone bending and
unbending without a word, heat, bellowing these
lungs spongy, exhaled in humming, the ocean, a
way out and not anything of beauty, tipping turquoise
and scandalous. The malicious horizon made us the
essential thinkers of technology. How to fly gravity,
how to balance basket and prose reaching for
murder. Silence done curse god and beauty here,
people does hear things in this heliconia peace
a morphology of rolling chain and copper gong
now shape this twang, falsettos of whip and air
rudiment this grammar. Take what I tell you. When
these barracks held slaves between their stone
halters, talking was left for night and hush was idiom
and hot core.

When Liney reach here is up to the time I hear about.
Why I always have to go back to that old woman who
wasn't even from here but from another barracoon. I
never understand but deeply as if is something that
have no end. Even she daughter didn't know but only
leave me she life like a brown stone to see. I in the
middle of a plane ride now a good century from their
living or imagination, around me is a people I will

only understand as full of ugliness that make me
weep full past my own tears and before hers. Liney,
when she live through two man, is so the second one
bring she here on his penultimate hope and she
come and sweep sand into my eye. So is there I meet
she in a recollection through Ben, son, now ninety,
ex-saga boy and image, perhaps eyes of my mama,
Liney daughter. I beg him to recall something of my
mama, something of his mama. The ninety year old
water of his eyes swell like the river he remember
and he say, *she was a sugar cake, sweet sweet*
sweet. Yuh muma! that girl was a sugar cake!

This time Liney done see vision in this green guava
season, fly skinless and turn into river flesh, dream
sheself, praise god, without sex and womb when sex
is hell and womb is she to pay. So dancing an old
man the castilian around this christmas living room
my little sister and me get Ben to tell we any story he
remember, and in between his own trail of conquests
and pretty clothes, in between his never sleeping with
a woman who wasn't clean because he was a
scornful man, in between our absent query were they
scornful women too, Liney smiled on his gold teeth.
The castilian out of breath, the dampness of his
shrunken skin reminding us. Oh god! laughing,
sister! we will kill uncle dancing!

In between, Liney, in between, as if your life could
never see itself, blooded and coarsened on this
island as mine, driven over places too hard to know
in their easy terror. As if your life could never hear
itself as still some years, god, ages, have passed
without your autobiography now between my stories
and the time I have to remember and the passages
that I too take out of liking, between me and history
we have made a patch of it, a verse still missing you
at the subject, a chapter yellowed and moth eaten at
the end. I could never save a cactus leaf between
pages, Liney, those other girls could make them root
undisturbed in the steam of unread books, not me,

admiring their devotion, still I peered too often at my
leaf, eyeing the creeping death out of it and giving up.
That hovel in the cocoa near the sweet oil factory I'll
never see, Liney, each time I go I stand at the road
arguing with myself. Sidelong looks are my specialty.
That saddle of children given you by one man then
another, the bear and darn and mend of your vagina
she like to walk about plenty, Ben said, *she was a*
small woman, small small. I chase Ben's romance as
it mumbles to a close, then, the rum and coconut
water of his eyes as he prepares to lie gently for his
own redemption. *I was she favourite, oh yes.*
The ric rac running of your story remains braided in
other wars, Liney, no one is interested in telling the
truth. History will only hear you if you give birth to a
woman who smoothes starched linen in the wardrobe
drawer, trembles when she walks and who gives birth
to another woman who cries near a river and
vanishes and who gives birth to a woman who is a
poet, and, even then.

Pilate was that river I never crossed as a child. A
woman, my mother, was weeping on its banks,
weeping for the sufferer she would become, she a too
black woman weeping, those little girls trailing her
footsteps reluctantly and without love for this shaking
woman blood and salt in her mouth, weeping, that
river gushed past her feet blocked her flight . . . and go
where, lady, weeping and go where, turning back to
face herself now only the oblique shape of something
without expectation, her body composed in doubt
then she'd come to bend her back, to dissemble, then
to stand on anger like a ledge, a tilting house, the
crazy curtain blazing at her teeth. A woman who
thought she was human but got the message, female
and black and somehow those who gave it to her
were like family, mother and brother, spitting woman
at her, somehow they were the only place to return to
and this gushing river had already swallowed most of
her, the little girls drowned on its indifferent bank, the
river hardened like the centre of her, spinning chalk

stone on its frill, burden in their slow feet, they
weeping, she, *go on home*, in futility. There were
dry-eyed cirri tracing the blue air that day. Pilate was
that river I ran from leaving that woman, my mother,
standing over its brutal green meaning and it was
over by now and had become so ordinary as if not to
see it any more, that constant veil over the eyes, the
blood-stained blind of race and sex.

Leaving this standing, heart and eyes fixed to a
skyscraper and a concrete eternity not knowing then
only running away from something that breaks the
heart open and nowhere to live. Five hundred dollars
and a passport full of sand and winking water, is how
I reach here, a girl's face shimmering from a little
photograph, her hair between hot comb and afro, feet
posing in high heel shoes, never to pass her eyes on
the red-green threads of a hummingbird's twitching
back, the blood warm quickened water colours of a
sea bed, not the rain forest tangled in smoke-wet,
well there it was. I did read a book once about a
prairie in Alberta since my waving canefield wasn't
enough, too much cutlass and too much cut foot, but
romance only happen in romance novel, the concrete
building just overpower me, block my eyesight and
send the sky back, back where it more redolent

Is steady trembling I trembling when they ask me my
name and say I too black for it. Is steady hurt I feeling
when old talk bleed, the sea don't have branch you
know darling. Nothing is a joke no more and I right
there with them, running for the train until I get to find
out my big sister just like to run and nobody wouldn't
vex if you miss the train, calling Spadina *Spadeena*
until I listen good for what white people call it, saying I
coming just to holiday to the immigration officer when
me and the son-of-a-bitch know I have labourer mark
all over my face. It don't have nothing call beauty
here but this is a place, a gasp of water from a
hundred lakes, fierce bright windows screaming with
goods, a constant drizzle of brown brick cutting

dolorous prisons into every green uprising of bush.
No wilderness self, is shards, shards, shards,
shards of raw glass, a debris of people you pick your way
through returning to your worse self, you the thin
mixture of just come and don't exist.

I walk Bathurst Street until it come like home
Pearl was near Dupont, upstairs a store one
Christmas where we pretend as if nothing change we,
make rum punch and sing, with bottle and spoon,
song we weself never even sing but only hear when
we was children. Pearl, squeezing her big Point
Fortin self along the narrow hall singing *Drink a rum
and a* . . . Pearl, working nights, cleaning, Pearl beating
books at her age, Pearl dying back home in a car
crash twenty years after everything was squeezed in,
a trip to Europe, a condominium, a man she suckled
like a baby. Pearl coaxing this living room with a
voice half lie and half memory, a voice no room
nowhere could believe was sincere. Pearl hoping this
room would catch fire above this frozen street. Our
singing parched, drying in the silence after the
chicken and ham and sweet bread effort to taste like
home, the slim red earnest sound of long ago with the
blinds drawn and the finally snow for Christmas and
the mood that rum in a cold place takes. Well, even
our nostalgia was a lie, skittish as the truth these
bundle of years.

But wait, this must come out then. A hidden verb
takes inventory of those small years like a person
waiting at a corner, counting and growing thin
through life as cloth and as water, hush . . . Look I
hated something, policemen, bankers, slavetraders,
shhh . . . still do and even more these days. This city,
mourning the smell of flowers and dirt, cannot tell
me what to say even if it chokes me. Not a single
word drops from my lips for twenty years about living
here. Dumbfounded I walk as if these sidewalks are a
place I'm visiting. Like a holy ghost, I package the

smell of zinnias and lady of the night, I horde the taste
of star apples and granadilla. I return to that once
grammar struck in disbelief. Twenty years. Ignoring
my own money thrown on the counter, the race
conscious landlords and their jim crow flats, oh yes!
here! the work nobody else wants to do . . . it's good
work I'm not complaining! but they make it taste bad,
bitter like peas. You can't smile here, is a sin, you
can't play music, it too loud. There was a time I could
tell if rain was coming, it used to make me sad the
yearly fasting of trees here, I felt some pity for the
ground turned hot and cold. All that time taken up
with circling this city in a fever. I remember then, and
it's hard to remember waiting so long to live . . . anyway
it's fiction what I remember, only mornings took a long
time to come, I became more secretive, language
seemed to split in two, one branch fell silent, the other
argued hotly for going home.

This is the part that is always difficult, the walk each
night across the dark school yard, biting my tongue
on new english, reading biology, stumbling over
unworded white faces. But I am only here for a
moment. The new stink of wet wool, driving my legs
across snow, ice, counting the winters that I do not
skid and fall on, a job sorting cards, the smell of an
office full of hatred each morning, no simple hatred,
not for me only, but for the hated fact of an office, an
elevator stuffed with the anger of elevator at 8 a.m.
and 5 p.m., my voice on the telephone after nine
months of office and elevator saying, I have to spend
time on my dancing. Yes, I'm a dancer, it's my new
career. Alone in the room after the phone crying at
the weakness in my stomach. Dancer. This romance
begins in a conversation off the top of my head, the
kitchen at Grace Hospital is where it ends. Then the
post office, here is escape at least from femininity,
but not from the envy of colony, education, the list of
insults is for this, better than, brighter than, richer
than, beginning with this slender walk against the

mountainous school. Each night, the black crowd of
us parts in the cold darkness, smiling.

The truth is, well, truth is not important at one end of a
hemisphere where a bird dives close to you in an
ocean for a mouth full of fish, an ocean you come to
swim in every two years, you, a slave to your leaping
retina, capture the look of it. It is like saying you are
dead. This place so full of your absence, this place
you come to swim like habit, to taste like habit, this
place where you are a woman and your breasts need
armour to walk. Here. Nerve endings of steady light
pinpoint all. That little light trembling the water again,
that gray blue night pearl of the sea, the swirl of the
earth that dash water back and always forth, that
always fear of a woman watching the world from an
evening beach with her sister, the courage between
them to drink a beer and assume their presence
against the coral chuckle of male voices. In
another place, not here, a woman might . . . Our
nostalgia was a lie and the passage on that six hour
flight to ourselves is wide and like another world, and
then another one inside and is so separate and fast
to the skin but voiceless, never born, or born and
stilled . . . hush.

In another place, not here, a woman might touch
something between beauty and nowhere, back there
and here, might pass hand over hand her own
trembling life, but I have tried to imagine a sea not
bleeding, a girl's glance full as a verse, a woman
growing old and never crying to a radio hissing of a
black boy's murder. I have tried to keep my throat
gurgling like a bird's. I have listened to the hard
gossip of race that inhabits this road. Even in this I
have tried to hum mud and feathers and sit peacefully
in this foliage of bones and rain. I have chewed a few
votive leaves here, their taste already disenchanting
my mothers. I have tried to write this thing calmly
even as its lines burn to a close. I have come to know

something simple. Each sentence realised or
dreamed jumps like a pulse with history and takes a
side. What I say in any language is told in faultless
knowledge of skin, in drunkenness and weeping,
told as a woman without matches and tinder, not in
words and in words and in words learned by heart,
told in secret and not in secret, and listen, does not
burn out or waste and is plenty and pitiless and loves.

ROBYN SARAH

(b. 1949)

Robyn Sarah was born in New York to Canadian parents and studied at McGill University and the Quebec Conservatory of Music. Her poems have appeared widely in magazines and anthologies, won and been shortlisted for various awards, and have been enthusiastically received by reviewers. According to *University of Toronto Quarterly*, her work is notable for its 'tone, its flawless cadences, an imagination rooted in natural things. . . . Each word and image seems set miraculously and simply right.' Her books of poetry include *Shadowplay* (1978), *The Space Between Sleep and Waking* (1981), *Anyone Skating on that Middle Ground* (1984), *Becoming Light* (1987), *The Touchstone: Poems New & Selected* (1992), and *Questions About the Stars* (1998). She has also published two collections of short stories, *A Nice Gazebo* (1992) and *A Promise of Shelter* (1997). She lives in Montreal, where she co-founded (with Fred Louder) Villeneuve Editions and taught at Champlain Regional College.

'People sometimes ask what poets have influenced me,' Sarah says in an unpublished interview with Louise Schrier, 'I think that my poetry has actually been more influenced by two prose writers—Katherine Mansfield and James Agee—who are very, very conscious of sound in their work. You feel, reading them, that every syllable, every punctuation mark, is exactly right. I'm jarred by bad sound, by the sound of a bad sentence. I think that has to do with my exposure to music.' In addition to sound,

her work, like Agee's fiction, pays loving attention to objects in our daily lives, not so much objects in nature as man-made objects and our palpable relations with those objects. Poems such as 'Maintenance' and 'A Meditation Between Claims' reveal a quiet, engaging intelligence that is alert to the intersection of differing realities, the point at the window 'where hot meets cold', and to the celebration of ordinary, perhaps worn, surfaces, where the attentive observer may discover 'always a / small surprise'.

Sarah's poems express a 'delight in the weathered' and a 'respect for tenancy, its wear and tear, its fixed terms'. In the same interview, she discusses this dimension of her work: 'I don't find cracks in plaster or worn floor boards depressing or dismal. I'm moved by the signs of life in these things, the signs that this floor has been walked on, this house has been lived in, people have been here, people have tried to repair things and they've fallen apart again . . . it just strikes me as part of the process of the passage of time . . . I write about them because they're part of the fabric of life.' To some readers Sarah's absorption in the nitty-gritty of domestic life will seem characteristic of contemporary writing by women; to others it will recall the almost mystical relationship with the physical world, natural or man-made, to be found in the work of Emily Dickinson and Elizabeth Bishop. 'We need to make room in our lives,' Sarah says, 'for something other than dailiness, for something other than taking care of our physical needs. A poem makes room for the dance, if you like, for moments of grace.'

D.G. Jones praises Sarah's mastery of repetition and variation and what he calls her 'poésie de cuisine', particularly the poem 'Maintenance', which he describes as 'an ironic hymn to dust'. He also finds her work distinctly English-Canadian: 'I have in mind here her domestic relation to space and time, her documentary eye and ear, her delight in catalogue, her sense of the gravity of the ephemeral and the eternity of the quotidian' (*Canadian Literature*, No. 134, Autumn 1992). Cultivating the art of so-called ordinary reality is no easy task, Sarah insists: 'I don't have a good visual memory. I create the illusion of having it by focusing on certain details very intensely and allowing this to suggest the rest of the picture.... I don't like speaking in an abstract way. I find that often an emotion or a mood can

be conveyed better by evoking the physical objects that are present at the time, than by alluding to feelings.'

Although she draws many of her titles and structural metaphors from music and painting, it is the carefully-wrought cadence as much as the concreteness and specificity of her language that invest her poetic world with such vividness and luminosity. In commenting on this dimension of her work, however, she shifts the emphasis away from observation, or vision, and towards sound. As she puts it in an interview with Kathleen O'Donnell (*Arc*, No. 36, Spring 1996): 'And it's true I write with my ear—I will often leave a blank in my rough copy, with a note that I need a word here that *means* such-and-such, but it has to be two syllables, with the accent on the second syllable. I'll go back later to see if I can find one and if I can't, I may feel I have to scrap the whole line, or sentence, and phrase it some other way.'

FUGUE

Women are on their way
to the new country. The men watch
from high office windows
while the women go.
They do not get very far
in a day. You can still see them
from high office windows.

Women are on their way
to the new country. They are taking
it all with them: rugs,
pianos, children. Or they are leaving
it all behind them: cats,
plants, children.
They do not get very far in a day.

Some women travel alone
to the new country. Some
with a child, or children.

Some go in pairs or groups
or in pairs with a child
or children. Some in a group with
cats, plants, children.

They do not get very far in a day.
They must stop to bake bread on the road
to the new country, and to share
bread with other women. Children
outgrow their clothes and shed them
for smaller children. The women too
shed clothes, put on each other's

cats, plants, children, and at full moon
no one remembers the way to the new country
where there will be room for everyone and
it will be summer and children will
shed their clothes and the loaves will
rise without yeast and women will have come
so far that no one can see them, even from

high office windows.

MAINTENANCE

Sometimes the best I can do
is homemade soup, or a patch on the knee
of the baby's overalls.
Things you couldn't call poems.
Things that spread in the head,
that swallow
whole afternoons, weigh down the week
till the elastic's gone right out of it—
so gone
it doesn't even snap when it breaks.
And one spent week's
just like the shapeless bag
of another. Monthsful of them,
with new ones rolling in and
filling up with the same junk: toys

under the bed, eggplant slices sweating
on the breadboard, the washing machine
spewing suds into the toilet, socks
drying on the radiator and falling down
behind it where the dust lies furry and
full of itself . . . The dust!
what I could tell you about
the dust. How it eats things—
pencils, caps from ballpoint pens,
plastic sheep, alphabet blocks.
How it spins cocoons
around them, clumps up and
smothers whatever strays into
its reaches—buttons,
pennies, marbles—and then
how it lifts, all of a piece,
dust-pelts
thick as the best velvet
on the bottom of the mop.

              Sometimes
the best that I can do
is maintenance: the eaten
replaced by the soon-to-be-eaten, the raw
by the cooked, the spilled-on
by the washed and dried, the ripped
by the mended; empty cartons
heaved down the cellar stairs, the
cans stacked on the ledge, debris
sealed up in the monstrous snot-green bags
for the garbage man.

And I'll tell you what
they don't usually tell you: there's no
poetry in it. There's no poetry
in scraping concrete off the high chair tray
with a bent kitchen knife, or fishing
with a broomhandle behind the fridge
for a lodged ball. None in the sink
that's always full, concealing its cargo
of crockery under a head

of greasy suds. Maybe you've heard
that there are compensations? That, too's
a myth. It doesn't work that way.
The planes are separate. Even if there are
moments each day that take you by the heart
and shake the dance back into it, that you lost
the beat of, somewhere years behind—even if
in the clear eye of such a moment you catch
a glimpse of the only thing worth looking for—
to call this compensation, is to demean.
The planes are separate. And it's the
other one, the one called maintenance,
I mostly am shouting about.
I mean the day-to-day,
that bogs the mind, voice, hands
with things you couldn't call poems.
I mean the thread that breaks.
The dust between
typewriter keys.

A MEDITATION BETWEEN CLAIMS

You want to close your hand
on something perfect, you want to say
Aha. Everything moves towards this,
or seems to move, you measure it
in the inches you must let down
on the children's overalls,
tearing the pages off the wall
each month; a friend phones
with news that another friend
has taken Tibetan vows, meanwhile the
kitchen is filling up with the smell
of burnt rice, you remind yourself
to buy postage stamps tomorrow

The mover
and the thing moved, are they two
or one; if two, is the thing moved
within or without, questions

you do not often bother yourself with
though you should; the corner store
is closed for the high holy days,
and though the air has a smell
not far from snow, your reluctance
to strip the garden is understandable

Laundry is piling up
in the back room, Mondays and Thursdays
the trash must be carried out
or it accumulates, each day
things get moved about and
put back in their places
and you accept this, the shape
that it gives a life, though the need
to make room supersedes other needs

If, bidding your guest goodbye,
you stand too long at the open door,
house-heat escapes, and the oil bill
will be higher next month, the toll
continues, wrapping the green tomatoes
in news of the latest assassination.
The mover
and the thing moved, it all
comes down to this: one wants
to sit in the sun like a stone,
one wants to move the stone; which
is better

STUDY IN LATEX SEMI-GLOSS

There is nothing new. Does that matter? Somewhere a woman is painting
her rooms. She has tied up her hair and covered it with a tattered diaper.
Alone, in a flat lit by bare bulbs, she moves from room to room, her sandals
sticking to the spread pages of old Gazettes pooled with paint spills. She is
looking for something, for a screwdriver with a yellow handle, with which
she now pries off the lid of the last can of paint; she is stirring the paint
with a wooden stick, stirring it longer than necessary, as if it were batter.
Now she pours creamy fold upon fold into the crusted tray. The telephone

shrills in another room; it is you, but she won't get there in time to answer. If she did, what could you say that would apply here?

Late into the night bare windows frame her, bending and stretching, wielding the roller on its broomstick. Paint streaks her bare arms and legs; some hairs have escaped the cloth about her head to fall in her eyes, and she pushes them aside with the clean back of her hand. In the alley behind the flat, cats couple with strangled yells. Soon she will shut herself in the tiny bath, blinking at the dazzle which dulls the fixtures to the colour of stained teeth; she will tack a torn towel over the window and drop her clothes—the loose jersey with the sleeves cut off, the frayed corduroy shorts, stiff with spatters of paint, at whose edges bunches of dark thread dangle. The underpants, damp and musky with sweat, will fall limp to her ankles. She will squat in the narrow tub, scrubbing at her skin with washcloth, solvent, fingernails, and after, with the cracked remnant of a bar of green soap which she tries in vain to work into a lather. Rinsing with splashed water, she'll pause and hug her knees, hug in the sag of her tired breasts, then stand, stretch, pat dry with the clean side of a damp towel. On the toilet she'll bend to examine a broken toenail and remain bent, dreaming, staring at the yellowed tiles.

You will have been asleep an hour, by the time she kills the lights and slips naked into a sleeping-bag spread across a bare mattress on the bare floor. The smell of the bag is the smell of woodsmoke and pine, faint, mixed with old sweat. Perhaps it's the smell that makes her smile a little as she feels herself sucked down into the whirlpool of sleep. Somewhere across blocks and blocks of tenements, her children, half-grown, long-limbed, sprawling on foam mats in their father's studio apartment, will stir as a lone car guns its engine in the empty street. She dreams, if she dreams at all, of holes in the plaster, of places where the baseboard is missing, of the bulging and cracking of imperfect surfaces. Dreams the geography of a wall.

There is nothing new. Even what could bloom between you, if you let it, if she let it, goes on as the paint goes on, over old seams, old sutures. Weathers as the paint will weather, flaking along old stress lines. This matters. Think, before you dial again. What have you to do with those children, blinking sleep from their eyes, breakfasting with their father in a booth of the local diner; where will you be when daylight, like cold water, shocks her awake to pull on yesterday's clothes and squat in the kitchen doorway with her mug of instant coffee? Where, when her clear eyes, steady in their purpose, scan the new surface to discover her painter's holidays?

SCRATCH

The tinder words, where are they,
the ones that
jump-start the heart—

>   like mirrors at the bends
>   of tunnels, that withhold
>   your face, but give you
>   what is to come;

>   like the voice at the end
>   of the tunnel, that says
>   'Terminus', almost
>   tenderly—

Little twigs that snap
like gunshot as they
consume themselves, little
dry twigs,

little sparks, little pops, little bursts
at the smoky heart of where it
begins again, o,

tender and sunny love! what, are you gone
so far away?

Come home to me now, my
brightness. Make a small glow.
Make it to move
the heart, that has sat down
in the road

and waits for something
to turn it over . . .

>   The roomy heart,
>   willing to be surprised.

PASSAGES

All day long, upstairs,
a new mother coos to her baby girl,
and the floorboards creak, creak
under her rocking-chair.

And footsteps go back and forth,
back and forth, in the dead of night,
and yellow light from her kitchen window
suddenly floods the snow.

Coo, coo; motherhood has turned her
into a bird. Silently I tell her: I, too,
once woke in the night with hardened breasts,
and soaked the front of my flannel gown with milk.

Now my daughter stands splay-legged at the mirrow
braiding her hair against night-time tangles,
and already her nipples have begun to stand out,
and she crosses her arms over them, shyly.

And upstairs, you read books about infant growth,
with pages of gleaming photographs—
and downstairs, I read books about divorce,
with no photographs at all.

And all day long, snow blows in small showers
from the tree whose branches brush your window.
Bursts of bright powder, glittery in the sun,
fall past my window.

ON CLOSING THE APARTMENT OF MY GRANDPARENTS OF BLESSED MEMORY

And then I stood for the last time in that room.
The key was in my hand. I held my ground,
and listened to the quiet that was like a sound,
and saw how the long sun of winter afternoon
fell slantwise on the floorboards, making bloom

the grain in the blond wood. (All that they owned
was once contained here.) At the window moaned
a splinter of wind. I would be going soon.

I would be going soon; but first I stood,
hearing the years turn in that emptied place
whose fullness echoed. Whose familiar smell,
of a tranquil life, lived simply, clung like a mood
or a long-loved melody there. A lingering grace.
Then I locked up, and rang the janitor's bell.

THE CUP HALF EMPTY

Happens a woman is tired of her clothes.
November, dark early and raining,
a letter shoved through the slot—it's a
tax reassessment, over a hundred owing.

Happens a woman is tired of mulling over
what to fix for dinner—thinking, *we're
out of eggs again. There's no spaghetti.*
Happens a woman is tired of cooking.

Happens the last leaves hang like wrung rags
encased in sleet. Happens the stereo's broken.
There's nothing in her closet remotely pretty.
Nothing happening, or about to happen.

What is there but the everyday? The scoffers
say what we all know, in our bones and coffers.

ERIN MOURÉ

(b. 1955)

Erin Mouré was born in Calgary. She worked for the railroad in various capacities while living in Vancouver, then at the head office of CN in Montreal; she now divides her time between freelancing, writing, and consulting. Her books include *Empire, York Street* (1979, nominated for a Governor General's Award), *The Whisky Vigil* (1982), *Wanted Alive* (1983), *Domestic Fuel* (1985), *Furious* (1988, Governor General's Award), *WSW* (*West South West*) (1989), *Sheepish Beauty, Civilian Love* (1992), *The Green Word: Selected Poems* (1994), *Search Procedures* (1996), *A Frame of the Book* (1999), and *Pillage Laud: cauterizations, vocabularies, cantigas, topiary, prose* (1999). Of considerable interest is *Two Women Talking: Correspondence 1985–1987, Erin Mouré and Bronwen Wallace* (1993).

In an interview with Peter O'Brien in *So to Speak* (1987), Mouré describes her own unusual creative processes:

I start to write a poem about how I can't describe my own feelings to my lover, and to give an example of how I feel, I start to talk about fish and fishing and pulling the hooks out of their mouths. Pretty soon the example takes over and starts writing the poem! I don't want to write about fish, and in the end an event emerges that is not straightforward, and it's immaterial that there's nothing about feelings and communication, because curiously the poem is still about that! It's what you feel at the

end—how hard it is to feel and communicate personal/public/animate pain. The poem is about fish too! From the sound of words that mean 'fish' we find out about the difficulty and inexpressible nature of pain. And how pain is not an end.

Insisting that 'words have a life of their own' and that poems have a 'subliminal code', Mouré rejects the notion that she is primarily a storyteller. 'I think my poems are narrative in the sense of co-relation, correspondence, rather than "story". The surfaces go very deep.' Her increasingly non-linear poetry moves steadily from the referentiality and surface politics of everyday life to a deeper relation with both today's language and its potential for engagement and change. In the final section of *Furious*, called 'The Acts', she outlines, in a language and syntax scarcely less evocative and challenging than those of the poems, her preoccupation with compression and intertextuality, as well as her commitment to everyday event as it manifests itself in 'ordinary words in their street clothes'. While maintaining her links with Wordsworth, William Carlos Williams, and those many poets who advocate colloquial speech in poetry, Mouré is anything but a conventional Romantic in her poetics. She rejects the denigration of intellect sometimes taken to be represented by Williams's dictum 'no ideas but in things'. She argues, instead, for 'PURE REASON', which she considers more complex than logic. While a poem, on the level of surface content, may appear to be about animals, 'it is not about animals at all, but about the fantasies of the audience, and this content lies under the flat surface of the poem. So that the *surface content* is actually *a form* for the real emotional "content" of the poem.'

Mouré understands that conventional grammar and syntax may blunt or dull a reader's perceptions, so she is not averse to breaking sentences, jumbling syntax, using repetitions, and letting sound override sense. She argues that 'the opening up of sense perception is an opening of the powers to heal. Referentiality distorts more than it conveys, it injects us with the comfortable. I crave instead images that "act within a context but do not refer to it" (Jerome Rothenberg, *Technicians of the Sacred*).' Mouré's poetics shift from a postmodernist to a feminist critique of language, as this statement indicates: 'What this need for affirmation meant before was having an existence affirmed by men. Knowing how they praise well what affirms their relation. They do not have to put themselves at risk, which women have always had to do, to exist, to speak, to have their existence affirmed by others.'

Her feminist shorthand may require more of a reader's attention, but, as Mouré argues, women are accustomed to listening 'so carefully to each other'. As to the question of 'making sense', she says: 'I want to write these things . . . that can't be torn apart by anybody, anywhere, or in the university. I want the overall sound to be one of making sense, but I don't want the inside of the poem to make sense of anything.' The breaking down of logical connections is something that has concerned poets in the past. One has only to think of Eliot's use of juxtaposition and counterpoint in *The Waste Land*, Pound's use of overlapping grids—what he called 'superposition'—in *The Cantos*, Gertrude Stein's upending of sense and narrative, Berryman's wringing

the neck of grammar, and the growing interest of poets like Adrienne Rich, John Thompson, and Phyllis Webb in imported forms such as the *ghazal*, which enables the poet to embrace discontinuity and illogic in a highly charged and emotionally unified context.

Where Mouré differs is in extending her 'program' to the specifics of grammar: to 'break down the noun/verb opposition wherein the present so-called "power" of the language resides' and to shift this power, if only briefly, to other parts of speech, such as the preposition. Whereas the verb is tied to action, to narrative, and the noun is freighted with signification and potential referentiality, the preposition emphasizes relation and gives a heightened sense of our position in time. 'It isn't that to change the weight and force of English will necessarily make women's speaking possible. But to move the force in any language, create a slippage, *even for a moment* . . . to decentre the "thing", unmask the relation. . . .' Mouré's is a worthy and not entirely surprising project, especially in view of our growing attention to other languages, such as Chinese, where there are no pronouns, no past and future tenses, and where the distinction between things and events is entirely relational.

In 'Poetry, Memory, and the Polis' (*Language in Her Eye: Writing and Gender*, edited by Libby Scheier, Sarah Sheard, and Eleanor Wachtel, 1990), Mouré writes:

In my own work, I thought at one time the simplest line was best. Yet when I wrote anecdotal/conversational poems without reversal (which is to say, without the language confronting itself & its assumptions in the poem), I suppressed both my feelings as a lesbian, and my concerns as a woman. My poetry was supposed to reflect my life, especially my life as a worker, and these things were suppressed in that life. To write the poems, then, perpetuated (unknowingly) my own pain at being invisible, my desire silenced. As if I could belong, by force of will, to that sameness, that anaesthesia.

Another chapter in Moure's ongoing discussion of craft may be found in a useful interview conducted by Montreal poet and reviewer Carmine Starnino (*Matrix, #47*), where she speaks about how the brain processes information and about her interest in 'disrupting conventional notions of reading . . . and how we dramatize our experience . . . language is just a material that's limited by the constructs and suppositions around it. But if you unbalance those a bit, language becomes limitless.' Refracting language, she says, 'breaks down usual reading habits, the usual structures of what can be said. It opens ambiguities, contradictions, paradoxes that allow more information to be present, available.'

POST-MODERN LITERATURE

Less to insist upon, fewer
proofs.
Raw metals pulled from the ground, cheaply.
Or a woman in the televised film shouting: thanks to you
I end up surrounded by violence.
So much gratitude, Saturday nights spent
believing in it.

But the end of a city is still
a field, ordinary persons live there, a frame house, & occasionally—
a woman comes out to hang the washing.
From a certain angle you see her
push a line of wet clothes across a suburb.
It sings in the wind there, against
stucco, lilacs, sunken front porches, windows
where nobody moves.
But carefully.   All of it

made carefully, children in snowsuits
after school, appear in the doorway, carry
their tracks shyly.
& you at the kitchen table—your empty
bowl streaked by the spoon, the meal's
memory, papers, juice in one glass, whisky
in another, unwritten greeting cards,
a watch, applesauce, small white medallions.

As if saying the name fixes.
As if the woman will come out again, & pull down
an entire suburb with her washing.
As if the city *could* end, in a field or
anywhere.
or if the woman on the bright TV could
stop saying *thank you.*
or you, saying 'like this,' & pointing shyly.
Too much paper, the children
in their snowsuits holding doorways, white snow,
parrots, singing smuggled information, the corporation gone to

Guatemala.
Leaving Father, the curling rink, a woman dressed
in grey parka & the nearest boots pulling
stiff clothes away from the weather, the back road, post-modern literature

DIVERGENCES

*'I am of today & of the has-been; but there is some thing in me
that is of tomorrow & of the day-after-tomorrow & of the shall-be.'*

Zarathustra

I am the youngest in a family of boots & shoes
I am the youngest lifting its burnt flag above my head
into the ocean
recoiling a bit at the cold kiss of water
I am part of a long family lifting its boots out of the mud.
The family sighs in front of me, I watch the backs of
a thousand children growing gaunter, beckoning me.
I follow them for years & years, forever
arriving.

I am the youngest child of a family that cries its body to sleep,
all over the world
Its body unçonscious in Argentina after questioning,
shot in Zimbabwe with the shout of joy caught in its mouth,
arrested in Lisbon for *insulting the President,*
gassed in an Afghani hill-town.

Also I am the youngest of a long line of gunners, of proud
trigger-pullers, maintainers of public order,
of supporters of the safety of the state, of the increase
in production: I am the youngest dressed in
white   carrying the Host in cathedrals, singing the glorious anthem,
Singing birth & resurrection for   *those who are*
with us

Friend, are you with us? Do you love your
patron with his feudal beneficence, with his
godly benediction, with his new clothes, his whisky & wine,
his descent into the dead
where he found you? Robber, he robbed you.
He took you out of the dead   into the world where you are now,
stumbling with your ancestors, your predecessors, kissing the
lovers who left you after one night, the passengers of trains—
who walk in front of you in their boots & shoes,
a family.

Family of which you are the youngest, barely born, carrying
the same old flag into the sea.
Your eyes pressed open, a light fills them credulously,
the ocean laps at the dryness in your bones.
Is it true you can't go back now?
Go on, says the flag, its burnt edges singing
at the touch of cold water.
Yes, say the family, *yes*, say the boots & shoes,

Go back, cry the gun-shot wounds, opening—

BEING CARPENTER

Then there is the man you always think of
as being Carpenter.
Your brother mentions him in letters, as living
very far away: 'Carpenter is disillusioned about nearly
              all of it, now.'
He doesn't have a first name, he's *Carpenter*,
he builds a small life of which
you hear little.

'When Carpenter comes home from work now,
he lies on the floor for hours & listens
to the radio, moving only
to prevent the baby from wandering near the stairs.'
This is the latest news.
You remember Carpenter in his muddy boots & sweater
sitting on the edge of the sofa with
his mug of coffee, talking about film,
& try to think
of this same Carpenter lying on the floor in the kitchen
of a townhouse you've never seen,
the radio on, the baby crawling near him.
You always think of him as being Carpenter;
It's hard to imagine any other way.
'Carpenter,' people said &
it was a final kind of name, one you could depend on,
one with shelves of books behind,
a film series & a magazine to edit.

Carpenter always busy, Carpenter driving Banff Avenue in his Volvo,
Carpenter sitting on the sofa in his jeans
& plaid shirt, his beard waggling,
animated, articulate, saying what Carpenter would say.
Still you watch for signs of him in your brother's letters.
You hope he has got up off the floor
& turned the stove on to make coffee.
Carpenter is a married man now, & the baby
is growing up as she crawls off toward the stairs.
Maybe he is sad because
he hears her growing.   & himself getting older.
& the film series ending & starting,
& the control of magazines changing hands,
& the extra work of the staff committee.
Still you can't think of him on the kitchen floor, surrounded
by the mess of late afternoon,
his wife gone off to the studio away from the baby,
who wanders near him.
You wish he would sit up at least, &
go on, being Carpenter, inside of Carpenter's face & clothing,
wearing Carpenter's glasses & beard

TOXICITY

Can acupuncture cure the sadness of organs
Can the liver forget sadness when the needles enter,
its field of memory,
words of politic, the mining this week of the ports
of Nicaragua, Corinto & Puerto Sandino
Nicaragua of the liver & the pancreas,
Nicaragua of the heart,
the small cells of the kidneys teeming
The cords of energy severed in the body,
the body poisoned by underwater mines
In a country never seen, fish boats
pulling drag-nets under water,
risking explosion,
can acupuncture cure the sadness of the liver, now?

What is fucked-up in the body, what is blocked
& carried rolled in the intestine,
what suffocates so badly in the lungs,
adhering, we talk about it, *toxicity*, your body standing
at the sink & turned to me,
near but not near enough, not near enough, Gail
What if the blocked space in the liver is just sadness,
can it be cured then?
Can the brain stop being the brain?
Can the brain be, for a few minutes, some other organ,
any organ, or a gland, a simple gland with its fluids,
its dark edges light never enters, can it let us alone?
When I think of the brain I think
how can something this dark help us
together
to stay here, as close as possible, avoiding underwater minefields,
the ships of trade churning perilously toward us,
the throb of their motors calling the mines up,
as close as our two skins

MISS CHATELAINE

In the movie, the horse almost dies.
A classic for children, where the small girl pushes a thin
knife into the horse's side.
Later I am sitting in brightness with the women
I went to high school with in Calgary,
fifteen years later we are all feminist, talking of the girl
in the film.
The horse who has some parasite & is afraid of the storm,
& the girl who goes out to save him.
We are in a baggage car on VIA Rail around a huge table,
its varnish light & cold,
as if inside the board rooms of the corporation;
the baggage door is open
to the smell of dark prairie,
we are fifteen years older, serious
about women, these images:
the girl running at night between the house & the barn,
& the noise of the horse's fear mixed in with the rain.

Finally there are no men between us.
Finally none of us are passing or failing according to
Miss Chatelaine.
I wish I could tell you how much I love you,
my friends with your odd looks, our odd looks,
our nervousness with each other,
the girl crying out as she runs in the darkness,
our decoration we wore, so many years ago, high school
boys watching from another table.

Finally I can love you.
Wherever you have gone to, in your secret marriages.
When the knife goes so deeply into the horse's side, a
few seconds & the rush of air.
In the morning, the rain is over.
The space between the house & barn is just a space again.
Finally I can meet with you & talk this over.
Finally I can see us meeting, & our true tenderness, emerge.

THE COOKING

Political noise.
What we hear above the cooking cinnamon,
the cook in the brown shirt saying:
the government is trying to finish off the middle classes
in Toronto.

Which makes us guffaw
holding the serving spoon or
standing up & opening the window

It's too funny.
Hurrah, we think.

Or later, sobered, the dishes dry
in the cupboard, thinking
the gap between the rich & poor widens
& no one is in it

In thousands of houses the television flickers.
& in the flicker
The prime minister is smiling.

Choose, we think.
Choose.

2

Or a trussed bird.
Its wings bent back to hold shut
The neck cavity.

The riddle of the chicken we all know.

'Why did,' we begin. That, & the sound
of glasses, chair legs scraping the hardwood
& our legs too, folded & unfolded,
this laughter.
The skin's thin parchment.
Is word, the

word for it, whispered here.

3

If there could be a word for anything
we could be satisfied or
we could sit down peaceably
& eat
the goddam chicken.

Whose goose is cooked, anyhow.

4

I am sick of these poem imitations, said the cook
who knows better
waving the metal spatula & opening
the door
to get the smoke out

before the fire department stops playing cards
& turns off the TV prime ministerial
grin

Let's leave the hose out of this
The horse too
The 'house' for that matter
& the 'hours' we spent

painstaking
our hands wet & the teatowel on our shoulder
picking pinfeathers

5

A poem in which a chicken continually interrupts
the 'democratic process.'
An unspeakable chicken.
The chicken of our bad dream.
The one we woke up from, our mouths dry, & looked out.
In the alley, a television light.
Choose, the prime minister said.
We rolled over.
We thought he said: 'choose.'

FOR MITTERAND'S LIFE, FOR MY LIFE, FOR YOURS

I am drinking history into my mouth. Going down
it makes a sound like 'beauty, beauty'.

The convergences of what we have not seen of what is.

A massive tree growing in the spirit, not catalpa, oak, fir, eucalyptus

scission, inner scission.

2

The president seen in the photograph of the far-right demonstrators
in 1935. Another there who heard their cries said the words were:
'down with the filth of foreigners (Jews)'. But he, he
does not remember.

Is it so hard to remember?
Is it so hard to be the person one once was, de l'assumer sur
les épaules de 'maintenant'?
Is there still a thing: the purity of Frenchness?

3

A massive tree growing in the heart, in the darkness or street
under the curved lamp, in sleep, in the limbs
Where my name is, a tree is growing

Silence is the name of such a tree, its weight chokes, oh oaken beauty, oh elm,
history is such 'beauty'

we dream of:
Bulldozers ripping the grey stones of the dead.
Making a parking lot. The building behind is a video store.
All the brothers are in the hotel at the road, behind immense vehicles,
seeking the white bird
seeking the white animal that vanished into the wheel

4

While I am inside wanting 'sexual love', if that is love
but there are no women in this dream
They are somewhere else sewing tricolor flags
They are waiting to shout their own slogans
I don't want to hear, unless it is 'vulva, vulva'
I don't want to hear it, unless

The roots of the tree pass down into the arms I feel these roots
The roots of the tree shimmer in the hands I feel these hands
The leaves are the surface of an ocean

5

I am drinking this ocean like history into my mouth. Going into the stream
my mouth makes a noise. This is beauty. I want you.
The jets have left us & I have landed near you. *This is beauty.*
This is age. This is presence. This is the book of first laws.
To know this. This is beauty.*

GRIEF
(from *Some Civic Streets*)
rue Jeanne-Mance, 1 May 1992 (for Anna)

Albeit a child has walked into the sea

I am thinking of the motion of the Heimlich manoeuvre

& how in my life I will never invent anything as beautiful
& skilled

as marvellous for the purpose for which it is intended
the jaws of life

---

*If she thinks she can fucking get away with this, she is crazy. Sex is not an escape hatch from
poetic difficulty. There is still a thing, damn it: the purity of Frenchness. Is it so hard to
remember? That we struggled so hard against this scourge to save you? *It is we, the dead, who
were the first readers.*

the impertinence of the possible
jumping up at a meal to reach out for the child or friend

reaching across the fields of incendiary destructiveness
of personal treachery

the renovations of city hall they say are necessary to commemorate
le Sieur de Maisonneuve

such duplicity I can't believe in, in a year when the ribs themselves
are patient & surround the inner organs

the heart & lungs

what else is there of any moral significance

the arms locked from behind around the chest
& upward on the solar plexus

a skill you can carry anywhere so beautiful & easy
when you wake up suddenly you may be able to use it

when you are alone &
there is no use for poetry

* or maybe not

SHARON THESEN

(b. 1946)

Sharon Thesen was born in Tisdale, Saskatchewan and raised in the interior of BC, but has spent most of her life in Vancouver, where she teaches English at Capilano College. She was writer-in-residence at Concordia University in Montreal in 1992. Her books include *Artemis Hates Romance* (1980), *Holding the Pose* (1983), *Confabulations: Poems for Malcolm Lowry* (1984), *The Beginning of the Long Dash* (1987, nominated for a Governor General's Award), *The Pangs of Sunday* (1990), *Aurora* (1995), *News & Smoke: Selected Poems* (1999), and *A Pair of Scissors* (2000). Her poems have appeared in many anthologies, including *Poetry by Canadian Women* (edited by Rosemary Sullivan, 1989) and *20th-Century Poetry & Poetics* (edited by G. Geddes), and her essays on poetry and poetics can be found in *A Mazing Space: Writing Canadian Women Writing* (edited by Shirley Neumann and Smaro Kamboureli, 1986), *The Vancouver Review*, and *Po-It-Tree: a selection of poems and commentary* (published as a pamphlet by Roy Miki at Simon Fraser University, 1992). Thesen is editor of *The New Long Poem Anthology* (1991) and a generous selection of articles on her work appears in *Contemporary Literary Criticism*, 56 (1989). She has also co-edited (with Ralph Maud) *Charles Olson and Frances Boldereff: A Modern Correspondence* (1999).

In an essay entitled 'What Poetry Performs', Thesen identifies with poets who present themselves as 'the servants and not the masters of writing'. 'This is my own experience', she says; 'dictation is the mode

I trust.' A mute taking dictation or a trickster subtly manipulating the text? According to poet Barry McKinnon ('Car and Driver', *Vancouver Review*, Fall/Winter, 1955), Thesen is a risk-taker: 'It is this kind of shift from description . . . to personal declaration that is a key to Thesen's method. She writes so that each poem is only "successful" if it dismantles itself (as self dismantles self), until the tattered truth about her attitude to life at that moment is fully revealed. She leaves herself no time to turn back. No time to invent gewgaws and ornament. No time for fear or courage. The poems triumph because they no longer feel like "poems": they become ways of thinking about living that an attentive reader can immediately share and recognize.'

For the 'lady poet' (her own ironic term), trying to navigate between the Scylla of academia's formalist pretensions and the Charybdis of greeting-card banality can be lonely, if not hazardous. For Thesen, we are drawn to poetry, rather than to other forms, instinctively, because 'what poetry performs are the instincts of the rhythmic body—the body in time, the body as process, rhythm, and death.' Or, in the words she quotes from the translators of Julia Kristeva's *Desire in Language*: 'Poetic language is distinct from language as used for ordinary communication—not because it may involve a departure from a norm; it is almost an otherness of language. It is the language of materiality as opposed to transparency . . . a language in which the writer's effort is less to deal rationally with those objects or concepts words seem to encase than to work, consciously or not, with the sounds and rhythms in transrational fashion . . . effecting . . . semantic displacement.'

Thesen's poetry is well known for its quirkiness and unexpected twists, and its resistance to the informed authorial voice. 'When I am writing and pause to think', Thesen says in an essay entitled 'Writing, Reading, and the Imagined Reader/Lover', 'the words I have already written have no history. They do not constitute the case of a moment ago. They are merely what went before, like the tracks of someone. They are signs, and they float, as it were, in an absolute present—a hall of mirrors in which I search for a true reflection or am amazed by the inventiveness of the distortions. I do not know, in the presence of these words, what I mean. They function, rather, as a momentum, from which I seek its rhythmic extension, and sometimes, at the end of a poem, its cessation.' Here the creative process appears as a kind of improvisation, which poet and critic Rosemary Sullivan compares to 'jazz riffs'.

In 'Imaginations Companion' (*Nothing But Brush Strokes*, 1995) Phyllis Webb quotes from Thesen's essay, 'A Few Notes on Poetry', about the ways in which reality impinges on the creative process: 'By strife, I mean the awareness, during the act of writing, of the field that we are in: the apparent "tradition"; the forces of repression both inside and outside; the freshly-prepared ground of the contemporary (innovation, influence, pleasures, displeasures), and the tone of the culture generally—and these are just for starters.' She celebrates Thesen's lyricism, her commitment to the transforming power of imagination and her precise, elegant steps along the tightrope, in a darkness she shares with Malcolm Lowry, Phyllis Webb, and Michael Ondaatje.

Part of the 'strife' Thesen refers to, of course, relates to the question that concerns many women writers: in her own words, 'how can woman write out of, or into, her own truth when language and syntax support and reproduce the consciousness of patriarchy? How can we sing ourselves, and celebrate ourselves, in a strange land?' Thesen responds to this question in 'Poetry and the Dilemma of Expression' by insisting that she prefers poems to feminist texts: 'What I think I do with language I am really doing with form; word play becomes my game of solitaire.' Female imagery, Thesen insists, is not the answer; nor is the deliberate expression of feminine knowledge and desire any guarantee of breaking new ground. Poetic language, she says, paraphrasing Kristeva,

is outside the grid of symbolic language and inside the rhythms of the semiotic, maternal body. So that the feminine in a woman's poem (as distinguished from the feminist content) will always be there, regardless of intent, because it was written by a woman and because poetry is feminine. But the specifically female trace is likely to practice an iconoclasty whether or not it is revealed, whether or not revelation is the project of the surface or the depths of the writing. Female meaning tends to emerge from the necessarily double-voiced expression of women as a glimpse, a slide, a slip, a dash that holds, momentarily and sometimes for the extended period of the text, *the transformation of the world*.

While waiting for a healing language to emerge, Thesen says, 'echo-location becomes the linguistic procedure in female poetry,' one that can have predictably negative results. Thesen prefers 'to move more in the direction of sound and rhythm, and away from fixed images, as women abandon themselves more and more to a felt truth, rather than writing down what they imagine they have repressed all this time and in the process perpetuating the false validity of a code that assumes divisions. Inside this code, a certain kind of expression is falsely inflated as truth (i.e., the expression of "repression") and can only consign female poetry to the unprivileged or the therapeutic.'

THE LANDLORD'S TIGER LILIES

A lost thing was found
On a shiny day we didn't know
was lost. Airplanes
pull tin foil off the roll of the sky
& a wandering dog
gilds the landlord's tiger lilies.

For the barren reach
of modern desire
there must be better forms
than this—
something cool,
intimate as a restaurant.

If I thought you would answer me
Rilke called to the angels,
if I thought
you would answer me

Even so, he was wrong
not to go to his daughter's wedding
& hurting people's feelings.

ELEGY, THE FERTILITY SPECIALIST

He gave it to me straight
and I had to thank him
for the information, the percentages
that dwindled in his pencil writing
hand. I watched them drop
from 70, to 40, to 20
as all the variables were added in
and even after 20 he made a question mark. I felt
doors closing in swift silent succession
as I passed each checkpoint on the way
to the cold awful ruler, expert astronomer,
charterer of heavenly colonies,
answerer of questions, and this question

Could we have a child? And this answer, No
I don't think so. Oh
of course he could go in there
and have a look if I really wanted,
steer his ship around the fraying edges
of my terrain, peering with his spyglass,
cross-hatching impediments on his diagram
of the uterine pear & its two branching filaments:
he wouldn't recommend it, he would say,
squeezing his spyglass shut and putting it back
in its maroon velvet box. We make the usual
small gestures of disappointment
as if we'd run out of luck in a ticket line
and I say goodbye
and walk past the receptionist
busy at her files and it is
as if something with wings was crushing itself
to my heart, to comfort
or to be comforted I didn't know which
or even what it was, some angel, and
entered the elevator with the gabbing nurses
going down to lunch and a little girl
in a sun-dress, her delicate
golden shoulders stencilled from the straps
of her bathing suit: a perfect white X.

SEPTEMBER, TURNING, THE LONG ROAD DOWN TO LOVE

The turning leaves
turn in a wind that rises
as if something warm,
invisible, and female just got up
from a nap and, half-dreaming,
walked to the kitchen
to make a cup of tea: Orange Pekoe?
Ruby Mist? Earl Grey? Which one
did she choose? How about
Ruby Mist agree the women zipping up
their handbags at the airport
and boarding a propellered plane

from whose window porthole heights
topography is listless & small
lucite lakes gather in the deep corners
of mountains, as if assembled
for a meeting. The lakes speak
to one another over the white heads
of the mountains and this for them is like
dealing with the patriarchy. Ah,
the patriarchy, we sigh, having reached
our destination. We button up
our sweaters as the wind rises
and twirls the drying leaves
like you'd turn a wineglass
to look into the red depths and make
a fine judgement. The long
taproots of these rustling
turning trees that stand as a company of
completed metamorphoses of the human body
(branches for arms, bark for skin)
tap a little more love
for language to replace us with, who talk
among the mountains, and talk
with only ourselves, and history,
and the example of the evening
to blame for our silences.

ANIMALS

When I come out of the bathroom
animals are waiting in the hall
and when I settle down to read
an animal comes between me
and my book and when I put on
a fancy dinner, a few animals
are under the table staring at the guests,
and when I mail a letter
or go to the Safeway there's always
an animal tagging along
or crying left at home and when I get
home from work animals leap joyously

around my old red car so I feel like
an avatar with flowers & presents all over
her body, and when I dance around
the kitchen at night wild & feeling
lovely as Margie Gillis, the animals
try to dance too, they stagger on
back legs and open their mouths, pink
and black and fanged, and I take their paws
in my hands and bend toward them,
happy and full of love.

AFTERNOON WITH LIVER

Sunrise a thin scrap of cellophane
from out in the valley where the blue-
berries grow, I'm wide awake early & kind of
disappointed in homeopathy

Later the ceasing
of the rain and a mildness
extends itself & holds me as I walk
through fragile groups of mourners
at the Gospel Chapel on the way
to the meat market where the butcher's
apprentice hauls a plastic bag of
liver from the cooler

& spills it out onto a wide wooden block
where it unfolds like the universe,
finding its own shape & equilibrium—
a little narrower at one end,
a gloss of winter starlight hugging the rise
at the other end

and with newly practised grace he sliced off
a portion for the display case dark red
& full of vitamins and angled the rest
back into the bag. Boy oh boy, I thought.

My hat was off to that particular cow

VALENTINE

Once out of Yeats I can breathe
and every tatter on its singing branch.

Snipping the shoulder pads
out of everything, a mound
of mute foam forms.

In the front row sits pale Lily
and even paler Grace.

At a certain age one is flattered
by earrings that look like teeth.

When we met we looked sideways.

I was happy to tell him
the story of my hair—a long
story involving an elevator.

What a tale! And what
wolfy eyes you have!

French was still in my tongue,
a slight pressure toward the lips,
a certain esprit in the scarf
at my throat—towers tipping in Pisa,
labyrinths and thick spirals.

It was a lot but I got it
thirty percent off.

I heated milk, bubbled
the espresso pot: life,
life, eternal life!

Until the time came I
wasn't thinking anything except
to extend an acquaintance past dark.

Tequila I replied. But they didn't have any.

There was snow on the ground, I saw
the orange plow go by like an ocean liner
with its head up.

The tremble. It reaches you.

UPON THE FAKE MESA

A new vehicle parked outside—
you look in the window there's the
new odometer, the new lighter, new grey seats—
'Nice,' we say, bending to pet
the dog who's come outside
to blink in light of day.
Tail hanging down,
claws on the sidewalk, silly
houses everywhere, traffic
disgorging as the light changes. And
the moon at night—she sails by
in her caftan flipping a fan
embossed with old camellias.
Maybe she'll pause
to glance into the new thing through tinted windows
or smooth the furrowed brow
of a creature enduring broken rock
& cold bulging roots
beneath four sets of toes,
the new tires big and deeply, blackly
scored to climb and crawl
over moraine descents
& jagged mud pools in a diorama
of time's beginnings among
gigantic houseplants and dragonflies
the size of horses—
this too was once considered
normal as the mannequins of ourselves
posed beside the four-wheel drive,
the barbecue, and the mesa, but only
the violently purple sky

will be of interest, signifying
a Venus comet or something we don't
understand yet or won't see
or can't. Struck down with a mouthful
of cedar tree, old-growth, one webbed tire
in Clayoquot Sound the other squashing a mountain
—could be we heard a faint whistling sound
first, thought it was just a woodpecker
falling out of its hole.

A REALLY DELICIOUS MEAL AT MONTRI'S

and nothing to say, why is poetry
so hard? A story & you could see
that red satin coat in the thrift-shop window
is the equivalent of Chekhov's ashtray
& write a story called 'The Red Coat'

& wonder what size it is & how much it is

(thirty dollars she told me on the phone
the next morning; I drove over &
tried it on).

So here you are having just read
one of those Iowa workshop poems—
that long-suffering place,
the very corncobs are pale, sucked dry by
poets tearing the place apart for some heretofore
undescribed sensation

'I hate poetry,' John Newlove said to me
on the phone that time cancelling out on the reading
we were going to, 'I'd rather watch
the hockey game.'

So I went by myself, had a nice chat
with Christopher Logue, who has since published
a great translation of *The Iliad*

and watched Carolyn Kizer read her work
up on the stage at Harbourfront, we were full

of dinner, wine, and cocktails
and dressed as we thought appropriate

I couldn't help noticing the many silver bangle bracelets
on the right wrist of Andrew Motion, who would go on

to ransack the life of Philip Larkin, some say
rightly, in his scrupulous biography.

Poor old Philip Larkin lovelorn and cranky in his flat
a flush rising in his cheeks as he types out another
scurrilous letter to a friend, nasty sour passages
now ponderous exhibits

while Andrew Motion's silver bangles slide up & down his
forearm as he beckons to the waiter
at the dinner before the reading

'Whither, whither
are we going?' Newlove hasn't written since

that last distracted apology to his readers, and claptrap
like milfoil has colonized the lake of art & strangled
the propellers of the mind

with its emptiness.

So here we are
looking out upon Nanoose Bay with Ron Smith on the sun deck
saying, 'You can't *talk* anymore.'

Every occasion
cut short because you can't talk anymore, which
is exhausting so everyone's in bed by 9:30

though the house is full of screens and laptops
and dopy hubristic fantasies
of the power accruing or you can just
join a chat group, lucky you

pointing & clicking like a
lab mouse working a lever for the sugar
of a human voice

unstrangled, in your ear.

PATRICK FRIESEN

(b. 1946)

Patrick Friesen was born in Manitoba, where he lived and worked until the late '90s. He has written for film, radio, television, and theatre. His books include *The Shunning* (1980), a dramatic long poem about the Mennonite community and its values; *Flicker and Hawk* (1987); *You Don't Get To Be a Saint* (1992); *Blasphemer's Wheel: Selected and New Poems* (1994), which won the McNally-Robinson Manitoba Book of the Year Award; *A Broken Bowl* (1997), shortlisted for the Governor General's Award; *St. Mary at Main* (1998), shortlisted for the Dorothy Livesay Prize; and *Carrying the Shadow* (1999). He lives in Vancouver and teaches at Quantlen College.

Although his poetic beginnings, like Purdy's, were modest, critical praise has mounted for Friesen's later work. Writing about *St. Mary at Main*, Janice Kulyk Keefer says: 'The strength of Friesen's rhythms, the sureness of his vision, the sense that he hears with his very skin the "lost human song" of "a city that sends its blood / pluming toward both coasts"—all these make his readers into citizens not just of Winnipeg, but of the heart, "that restless immigrant / without a passport," that midden the poet sifts, layer by layer, uncovering not just dust but silver bracelets of light.' According to Don McKay, the 'peculiar muscle and urgency' of Friesen's poetry stems from the fact there is 'always a poetry beyond the words, a music the longing lines reach after, overrunning the sentence, a place where grief and celebration aren't separable and

the dead are all ears. Time and again the reader is struck, not just with amazement, but with gratitude.' Robyn Sarah describes the transitory quality of Friesen's works as 'watching landscape stream past train windows under a long summer dusk. We are awake, yet dreaming. The particulars have a familiar gravity. Fleeting images shine like icons, then are gone.' Patrick Lane speaks of 'a new simplicity here, as narrow as ecstasy, as thin as sorrow'.

The familiar chord in all of these accolades has to do with Friesen's shift away from narrative towards a more lyrical voice, not a displaced or disembodied voice but one rooted in the particulars of consciousness, in a mind constantly travelling, rummaging through the scrapyard, the boneshop and the word-hoard of personal and tribal history—in search of meaning, of home. His new work is invested with a sense of the evanescence, the transitoriness, of life and its products, including poetry itself. This gives him a certain freedom from literary convention and its formal expectations, permitting the poems to be light, glancing, tentative rather than shaped, formal, closed; it's not that his new poems are without shape, but that they encourage a shift of focus from image and story as organizing principles towards the kind of tonal unity you might expect to find in stream-of-consciousness fiction, where the twists and turns of thought and feeling matter more than causality or the paths of logic.

'I have no formal poetics,' Friesen admits in *Prairie Fire*. 'I have spoken about poetics, and I have contradicted myself. What seems clear one day, is not on another. I write poems, but I'm not sure I'm a poet, or whether what I write is poetry. . . . It's me speaking. Where I'm from and where I'm going. . . . What I'm interested in is the immediacy of poems. Something approaching improvisation, and yet edited for the page and voice. No explanations needed.' Yet his comments in 'Gathering Bones' (*Poetry and Knowing*) are instructive: 'The physical object alive, not merely technically, not as a vessel, but shot through with light. Not a lamp carrying oil, but a wick on fire.' He emphasizes knowing rather than knowledge (literature as process, not product) and praises the work of Russian poet Anna Akhmatova: 'One notices how many of the poems are fragments. Out of the necessity of her time and place. She, working with snatches of verse, caught images, rags of rhythm. Not the luxury of time or freedom to make them whole. Yet the cumulative effect of a whole poetic vision, a growing, alive voice that never freezes.' Overall, he argues for the glimmer, the half-thought: 'Giving voice. Evoking, invoking. Holding together loosely. Precise. Elusive. A handful of water.'

Some of his most interesting aesthetic pronouncements are to be found in writing about other art forms, particularly dance, which he describes in 'The Dance Floor (Apparitions)' as

a code, a precise, condensed knowing. We see ourselves in the dance. Seeing, without thought, our lost gestures. Not only what vanished when dance was abandoned by religion, but the gestures of life outside history. . . . All I know is that when I experience dance, even as an observer, I am re-attached momentarily to something old and resonant. Something nudging memory. A redemption, I guess. A glimpse of lost gestures. What it has always meant to be fully human in this place, passing through the curtain.

In a fiery essay in *Matrix* #50 called 'Jugular Music,' Friesen lashes out against cliques, schools, and the predominance of literary theory:

A poem does not have to be explained. It speaks for itself. It says exactly what it means. It isn't philosophy, theology, economics, literary theory, or politics in fine clothes. All these things may exist within poems, but they don't explain the poem. The poem has to have an emotional component, a rhythmic component. It must appeal to more than the intellectual aspect of human beings, be more than a page exercise. It doesn't worry about contradictions, has no need to become theory. Poetry gestates. It uses language, with all its resonance, to attempt to understand the whole human in the natural world, in the world humanly created, in the intersections between the two. It explores, reveals, weeps, praises. . . . poetry is always knowing, never knowledge. . . . is life and death stuff. It shifts perceptions, changes lives. Jugular music. . . . Unencumbered. Answering to no authority. Poetry, at its best, brings light.

A burning wick, a handful of water, a nudge, a glimpse, a leap in the dark, a poetics of gesture. Modest? Hardly, and sometimes so striking—once the applause, the rhetoric and the analysis have dissipated—it remains etched on the retina long after the house lights go up.

AN AUDIENCE WITH THE DALAI LAMA
OR, THE OLD-FASHIONED PAS DE DEUX

on the one hand a leaf in the shrub beside you
on the other family and work
I have never seen God I have been empty and filled and empty
    again

what can I say about what I know?
hymns that come easily to my lips while I walk
an ancient anger and the bags I carry filled with hats and shoes

I don't think I know much beyond what I know
my left my right hand a leaf wife and children
and sometimes a stony eye

my room you wouldn't believe the books and clothes all over
    the floor the records and stamps the lamp my smell and the
    typer
nothing much has happened there if you think of it and I have
on the other hand nothing more has happened outside the
    room
I grew up with lilacs there are lilacs outside my window there's
    not much I can make of that
it's like looking at old photographs in a way like catching a
    second wind or an animal in me sniffing out its old grounds

sometimes I think I have a question I want to have a question
    about things that matter
my body used to give me pleasure still does but it's beginning
    to break down maybe there's a question here
my knees my eyes sometimes there's a ringing in my ears and
    who knows what's happening just now in my most hidden
    cell a small detonation
but it seems clear where everything's going
I feel a lot more stupid than I did is this wisdom?

listen my love is someone other than me this must be what I need
she goes on journeys you should see her walk toward the
    clearing trees making way you should see her in her
    wedding dress the hem wet in the grass
you should see her when she drops the armour of her veils

when she's away and it's late when I crawl into bed I find she's
    dressed the emptiness beside me with her gown
all night I'm restless I wake when my hand finds silk my legs
    want to wrap around her
no bed has ever been this empty or so full it feels like god

a man can't say what he is that he needs to rut like a plow knows
    earth that he loves it
that he bends his knee to words he loves this too falls insensible
    sometimes before the beauty of memory and ruin
sir richard manuel died a lousy death hanging there cold as a fish
I can't explain it just listen to any of his songs just listen to how
    pure and sad a man's voice can be when he wants paradise
    but his arms aren't long enough
some voices belong to everyone

the boy in me doesn't like conversations he's busy wants to be
    free a word for what he remembers he could have said
    captured surrounded or surprised
he dreams time before love when he could sing the words
    didn't matter only the voice he was
but the man in me accommodates love and loss contemplates
    smoke and mirrors from a distance
he moves toward religion like prey to the lion a leaf to earth or
    a fish to the hook

does the prey feel ecstasy as it kneels into the lion's need? its
    stem hardening does the leaf desire release?
no I don't look for answers the questions are old and will grow
    older I want something other than rhetoric or ritual maybe
    a gesture
my devotion to the lord is imperfect there's some fight left in
    me I may be hooked I am not landed

what's there is my room my hands on the typer my eyes we
    used to say what's the diff
my children chewing at my knees my wife smiling through the
    window where's she going or is she coming home? she
    loves me she loves me not she loves me
what's there is the usual concoction hubble bubble eye of newt
    babbling tongue the old-fashioned pas de deux me and you

sometimes mother's on the phone do I love her yes I do and I
    still have father's hat
no I haven't seen God I live with angels some fallen
I sing *have thine own way lord* half the time I don't mean it
my wife sloughs her gown my pants at my knees like some clown
my son with his other world eyes you could never know them
    or their danger
or my daughter's prayers at night when everyone's asleep this is
    a way she speaks
and this is what I know what I need to know I want to redeem
    love before it does me in

FROM ANNA

let's say it was 1958 *sail along silvery moon* was on the radio
it was sunday afternoon in july I remember the river and
    swallows swooping low over the water
silver medallions fluttering on their chests the catholic boys ran
    along the springboard and jack-knifed into the seine river
there was something ominous about the muddy water like a
    dream anything could be there venomous snakes weeds
    and roots to clutch at you or simply depth something
    ominous and those lean white bodies of faith disappearing
    with graceful dives

I held my breath each time wondering if this one would
    drown forever and not return how could he possibly rise
    from that darkness of river and overhanging trees how
    could the water give him back to light?
but always each boy exploded into air returning from death
    or dreams flinging wet hair from his eyes shouting defiance
    at the shore and each of us shivering there
and then the sun was so bright dancing in the spray around
    the diver's head so bright on his long arms cleaving water
    you could hardly believe in anything

let's say it was 1958 I was sitting on the fender of father's blue
    dodge and it was sunday and I didn't want to ever leave the
    river again

I was eating a persimmon trying to think of God it didn't
    work my tongue wouldn't let me get away with it
there are no miracles only mirages in the desert and
    disappearances in the river
there's nothing human that isn't betrayed and I know nothing
    but what's human my hands my tongue and my face in a
    mirror

grandmother wouldn't show me her photographs said I'd
    never know what I couldn't would I? her life before me
but I think I remember her in the orchard she was a girl her
    hair was soft and flowing down her back her legs brown
    with sun
she said sometimes there were angels in the orchard she saw
    them among the trees but she wasn't sure and if there were
    what should she do?
sometimes there was a black dog or the neighbour's boy with
    a stick sometimes there was nothing she could remember
    and she was running for her life
this is how she learned to pray she said this is how she
    worked her way out her hands at the clothesline her eyes
    on the sky

I don't love the prayer rug obedience or disobedience nothing
    that absolute I love the babylonian body and the human
    wound I love the surprising word the sinuous approach I
    like the world approximately
the way grandfather smoked a cigarette in the garden his feet
    lost among the potato plants the way he smiled and I
    smelled the drifting smoke his stories hovering among the
    raspberry canes the way he leaned on his hoe forever
I love words in the air balanced between mouths and ears I
    love the way they're smoke before they're stone
but it's true I think there's not much a voice can say there's a
    limit I guess to art there's no end to desire

        *   *   *

—what a coincidence.
—what?
—a coincidence that we met.

—oh.

—reminds me. I heard of a man, somewhere, walking down a street. a baby crawled out a window, fourteenth floor, and fell on the man's head. both survived. a year later, to the day, same man walking down another street. a child leaned against a screen window, fourteenth floor, screen gave way and the child fell on the man's head.

—same man?

—yes.

—same child?

—uh huh. they had moved to a different apartment.

—they lived?

—yes.

—and then?

—and then? that's not enough for you?

—there's always more.

—well, there is. you can imagine the man had problems. his neck was never the same. it wouldn't heal. he visited a chiropractor. thought the receptionist looked familiar.

—it was the child's mother.

—no, no, listen. she looked familiar. he thought he must know her. he approached her and began a conversation. before long they realized they were twins. they had been separated at birth and adopted out. in different cities. let's say their names were bob and linda. well, linda had married a bob and bob had married a linda. they each had two daughters with the same names.

—what about the child?

—the child?

—the one who kept falling on the guy's head.

—oh. well, many years later, the child was a teenager, and the man, bob, was desperately ill and his sister had just died.

—same disease?

—of course. they had both divorced, moved in together, their kids were gone. just brother and sister sharing an apartment, helping each other along. well, she died and he was going fast, so he jumped from a tall building.

—same building where the child fell on him?

—I don't know. he jumped. hit a car stopped at a red light. flew in through the windshield, killed the passenger.

—wait. it was the kid.
—no, the kid was driving. it was the kid's mother.
—you're kidding.
—no.
—could make a person look up now and then.
—that's true. you never know what's going to happen.
—truth is stranger than fiction.
—or life.
—I guess.
—and here we are.
—a coincidence.
—I'm not so sure.
—listen.
—are you adopted by any chance?
—no. listen.
—I knew someone once looked just like you.
—I imagine everyone's got someone looks like them.
—your name, you must have a name.
—I'd rather not.
—let me guess.
—I won't tell you.
—well, then, I'll guess what your name isn't.
—listen, I've got to go.
—george.
—I'm not saying.
—lenny.
—listen.
—albert.
—I'm going.
—emile. frankie. vincent.

A WOMAN FROM JAMAICA

I don't think it's too much to ask that for a moment every
    wound heal and stutter toward silence
I don't think it's too much to ask for a hesitation of the
    highball thundering through our veins
let's say we can halt fear let's say this room is enough that all
    streets and rivers flow here that all gods drink at this bar

I know a woman from jamaica who tells annancy stories she's
    laughing like a mischievous child
I know a woman who could outleg the obeah man and she
    has who could walk water and she will
tonight's her final dream what each of us will dream the
    world loosening and shifting like catastrophe but it's only a
    single death

is the music loud enough can you hear it on your skin?
are the chairs and tables dancing is the dolphin diving in?

a woman is dying when she takes my hand I feel the chill of the
    cold mirror she has held
a woman is dreaming annihilation hands reaching and
    rapacious wicked hands that harass her they want to break
    the mirror she raises it high above them with her thin arms
    she knows what this is this encounter with the end she has
    never stood a longer night
when it's over she says when jehovah's come and the mirror
    whole she'll see what is left her long body in death she'll
    know she was here in this blue place of water and grass

is the dream loud enough can you feel it on your skin?

a dying woman has climbed out of the dark agitation of prayer
    and terror with the ghost in her hands
a woman is walking by the water she leaves her shadow and
    the willow a woman is rowing away
I don't think it's too much to ask that for a moment every
    wound heal and stutter into silence
let's say we can halt fear let's say the music's loud enough we
    can hear it on our skins and the chairs are dancing the
    dolphin's diving in

ELLICE AVENUE

among the used furniture shops italian clubs laundromats and german
    corner groceries two wandering ghosts
my two-year-old daughter riding high on my shoulders her fists clutching
    my hair my hands loosely circle her ankles

1975's sun slanting into my squinting eyes her bare legs brown and round
    with power
my dear it's twenty years done and you're back in this city and it feels like
    I'm on my way gone

it's easy to let nostalgia seep in a man's life disappearing his daughter almost
    his age now
you know what I mean how time differs for them so much faster for him
    than it was so much brighter
the way a photograph fades to brilliance a woman's dark hair flaring to
    white fire around her face
it's so easy to vanish into memory slipping from body into mind into thin
    air into light

it's a still-life those blocks a frozen blur of motion us walking through
    our lives
the body remembers the heat the summer swish of traffic the sounds of
    portuguese and german
the body is a memory of landscapes europe and asia gutturals and sibilant
    whispers of history
an old man with his medals maria at the window her nose flattened to
    the glass

all is flesh and the shadow I used to be sloughed skin on sticks following
    me around
there's eternity a rotten concept if ever the blackbird in the marsh as
    my soul
feathered and small-boned on a cattail and swaying in a slow northern wind
doesn't matter marijke because it's enough to be here in the improbability
    of this world

and we're not long for it no one is maria disappears from her window the
    old man already forgotten
they still sell used furniture they play cards in the clubs but the corner store
    is vietnamese
brides still stand on the top steps of their porches waiting for the cameras
    to flash
my shoulders have rounded since 75 but I still feel your fine ankles in
    my hands

WHAT'S THE STORY NATALYA

it's dark downtown natalya everyone standing around waiting for something
blades and naked children fixed on sugar cardboard windowpanes and a
    door on one hinge
there's nothing but cutlery on the table and television's blue light on
    the wall
someone on the corner playing with a bullet in his pocket and a mirror in
    his hand

it's raw in this city hunger and angry jazz in the veins streetlamps
    without light
walking on reeboks and glass a 24 in a baby carriage evening matins about
    to begin
there's nothing to do no one's working for the body no one's working for
    the soul
it's all broken down there's no tenderness in the alley no tenderness
    on broadway

how to say this it's all crooked it's all turned around how to tell you the
    phone is bugged
people waiting for someone to say *come along with me* people waiting for
    some christ
the street cleaner's caught in the crossfire on main street stocks are shooting
    through the roof
even god's tired and looking for the messiah anything to get him out of here

and baby it's so wonderful your natural tan the lord and the beast in
    the street
how do we make it through the day when there's no heart for it no longing?
not waiting for anything though something's got to happen or something's
    going to give
someone's on the corner playing with a bullet and the mirror's flashing in
    the sun

so what's the story natalya how do we get out of here where do we
    find our shoes?
looks like no one knows where they're standing anymore looks like
    no one cares
let's go for a walk the two of us I think I love you but I'm not sure
    in the rain
I want to ask the man for his bullet but I know what's in the mirror

THE MAN WHO LICKED STONES

the man in the long coat licked stones memorizing the world's
    first fire on his tongue
he didn't have time to speak though he had nothing else he
    hadn't come to words
his slow hands hung from the stillness of his torn sleeves
    reaching only to touch what he might remember
with his hands he carefully brushed dust from stones with his
    tongue revealed their rose or cobalt blue
he walked outside town on gravel roads he walked outside love
    too close to worship to say
around him earth's rubble and striations sign and witness of the
    forge he longed to find
his mouth craving volcanoes the taste of ash and rain his mouth
    ground stones in his sleep
I thought he would vanish one day spellbound in his cellar
    among the coal and roots
I thought in the end he might walk into the river with his heavy
    pockets but there was no such privilege for him
with the years I forgot him or he became a shape I couldn't see
    wandering around town
I don't know if he took form again or if it was time for me to see
    but I saw him emerge like a photograph in its bath
he was walking past the church he reeled suddenly with a
    stiff-legged pivot and fell straight on his back
no one falls like that the body in surrender to gravity no one falls
    as if nothing matters and nothing did
his eyes glistening like wet sapphires in snow his dead eyes
    looked through us seeing their way into stone

BRONWEN WALLACE

(1945–1989)

Bronwen Wallace was born and died in Kingston, Ontario, where she worked in a centre for battered women and children and taught intermittently in the English Department at Queen's University. Her poems were first published jointly with work by Mary Di Michele in *Marrying in the Family* (1980). Subsequent books of poetry are *Signs of the Former Tenant* (1983), *Common Magic* (1985), *The Stubborn Particulars of Grace* (1987) and *Keep That Candle Burning Bright and Other Poems* (1991). She went on to win the National Magazine Award, the Pat Lowther Award, the Du Maurier Award for Poetry and the regional award in the Commonwealth Poetry Competition. She edited books for Quarry Press and collaborated with her husband Chris Whynot on two films: *All You Have To Do* (1982) and *That's Why I'm Talking* (1987). A book of short stories, *People You'd Trust Your Life To*, appeared post-humously to great acclaim in 1990; and a book of essays, *Arguments With the World*, in 1992. *Two Women Talking: Correspondence 1985–1987, Erin Mouré and Bronwen Wallace*, edited by Susan McMaster, was published in 1993.

Wallace is an archaeologist of the emotions. The reader of her poems moves, layer by layer, deeper into the substratum of feelings, back to primal moments of fear, pain, and humiliation. Wallace searches out the 'hidden lives' within us, the small invasions of change and memory that crack open the shells of our ordinary lives. She speaks of

the 'unexpected rituals' and objects that 'may tell the stories of our lives / more accurately than we ourselves could.' Thus the poems are full of maps, dreams, mirrors, the reflections of which produce a sense of infinite regression into the past, where we brush our earliest beginnings and, perhaps, feel 'our own deaths rising within us'.

'My fascination with narrative poetry grows out of my fascination with how we tell the story of our own lives,' she said in a conversation with the present writer. . . .

> The story of my poems is simply 'what happens'; beyond that—or rather through that—is the voice of the narrator moving closer and closer to the discovery of the mystery which lies at the centre of her life and every life. I try to keep the language simple and common-place, the rhythm that of everyday speech. In doing so, I hope to have the poem reflect what I believe: that there is no such thing as ordinary, and that in these common place details the mystery of each life is revealed.

Wallace's work falls squarely into the oral tradition of story-telling, with its asides, digressions, and associative leaps. The process, as she has indicated, is one of 'detours and double-backs, leaps', a constant 're-mapping' and reconstruction of the past by each subsequent retelling. She speaks of 'our terrible need to know everything', which explains not only the force that drives her poems, but also the power these poems have for the reader, whose own life and motives are often opaque and inexplicable. As keeper of the stories, Wallace has mastered the so-called digression, or lateral shift, so common to the tradition of oral storytelling, wherein the narrator appears to have forgotten or abandoned the main story momentarily, but has, in effect, deepened the narrative by bringing new material to bear. These objects, places, sounds, names, and persons—surfacing dream-like in her narratives—serve as signposts and exempla for the reader-pilgrim journeying through her poetic landscapes.

Wallace acknowledges the influence on her work of the poetry of Al Purdy and Galway Kinnell, but says her biggest influence has been the 'kitchen-table conversation', with all its revelations, its codes and formulas, and its meanderings. Her parables, whether direct or self-consciously narrated, draw the reader in by deliberately delaying information at crucial moments and by projecting the image of a narrator who is struggling, humbly and somewhat erratically, to get to the bottom of things in her own life and the lives around her. 'The poem', she says, 'never goes from A to B to C as I thought it would. I discover it as I go. I agree with Flannery O'Connor, too, that if I don't discover something during the writing, my reader won't either.'

In a 1989 interview with Janice Williamson that appeared in *Open Letter* (7, 9, Winter 1991), Wallace discusses her concern with the function of poetry and its role in contemporary society: 'Lao Tsu says that you have to treat every person as if they were wounded. I'm writing to the wounded part of each person, men as well as women. The power of feminism is the power of the victim who has recognized a way to use her damage. There's a great line in an Adrienne Rich poem about knowing that her wound came from the same place as her power. When you get in touch with your damage, recognize and care for it, you also discover the source of your power. We know that abusers, men who batter, or anybody who abuses children, have usually been abused themselves and have denied it. It's the denial of our damage, our limitations, our vulnerability, our mortality, that's got us where we are. The voice I try to speak is speaking to that person. I think we're kidding ourselves if we think there's any form of writing that can't be picked up by monopoly capitalism, and that includes any kind of experimental deconstructive writing. Look what's happening in rock and roll on video, all that is being picked up.'

About the apparently autobiographical content in her work, Wallace told Williamson. 'The first two books are intensely autobiographical as well as confessional. But in *Stubborn Particulars*, a lot is not autobiographical but stuff I've made up or stolen from other people's lives. I'm creating a persona in *Stubbon Particulars*, a persona who is the best or bravest part of me. She does the talking and has more courage to explore things than I do in my everyday self . . . when we tell people intimate things about ourselves we are in some way asking for, if not absolution, at least support, inclusion, something, a healing gesture from the other person. That's why we confess. And so I see that it's part of what I was saying about wounds and damage—it's another way of opening yourself up to the other person. This goes far beyond the confessional as we've understood it in autobiography.'

THE WOMAN IN THIS POEM

The woman in this poem
lives in the suburbs
with her husband and two children
each day she waits for the mail and
once a week receives
a letter from her lover
who lives in another city
writes of roses   warm patches
of sunlight on his bed
Come to me he pleads
I need you and the woman
reaches for the phone
to dial the airport
she will leave this afternoon
her suitcase packed
with a few light clothes

But as she is dialing
the woman in this poem
remembers the pot-roast
and the fact that it is Thursday
she thinks of how her husband's face
will look when he reads her note
his body curling sadly toward
the empty side of the bed

She stops dialing and begins
to chop onions for the pot-roast
but behind her back the phone
shapes itself insistently
the number for airline reservations
chants in her head
in an hour her children will be
home from school and after that
her husband will arrive
to kiss the back of her neck
while she thickens the gravy
and she knows that
all through dinner

her mouth will laugh and chatter
while she walks with her lover
on a beach somewhere

She puts the onions in the pot
and turns toward the phone
but even as she reaches
she is thinking of
her daughter's piano lessons
her son's dental appointment

Her arms fall to her side
and as she stands there
in the middle of her spotless kitchen
we can see her growing
old like this
and wish for something   anything
to happen   we could have her go
mad perhaps and lock herself
in the closet   crouch there
for days her dresses withering
around her like cast-off skins
or maybe she could take
to cruising the streets at night
in her husband's car
picking up teenage boys
and fucking them in the back seat
we can even imagine
finding her body
dumped in a ditch somewhere
on the edge of town

The woman in this poem offends us
with her useless phone and the persistent
smell of onions   we regard her as we do
the poorly calculated overdose
who lies in a bed somewhere
not knowing how her life drips
through her drop by measured drop
we want to think of death
as something sudden

stroke or the leap
that carries us over the railing
of the bridge in one determined arc
the pistol aimed precisely
at the right part of the brain
we want to hate this woman

but mostly we hate knowing
that for us too it is
moments like this
our thoughts   stiff fingers
tear at again and again
when we stop in the middle
of an ordinary day and
like the woman in this poem
begin to feel
our own deaths
rising slow within us

A Simple Poem for Virginia Woolf

This started out as a simple poem
for Virginia Woolf   you know the kind
we women writers write these days
in our own rooms
on our own time
a salute   a gesture of friendship
a psychological debt
paid off
I wanted it simple
and perfectly round
hard as an
egg   I thought
only once I'd said egg
I thought of the smell
of bacon grease and dirty frying-pans
and whether there were enough for breakfast
I couldn't help it
I wanted the poem to be carefree and easy
like children playing in the snow

I didn't mean to mention
the price of snowsuits or
how even on the most expensive ones
the zippers always snag
just when you're late for work
and trying to get the children
off to school on time
a straightforward poem
for Virginia Woolf   that's all
I wanted really
not something tangled in
domestic life the way
Jane Austen's novels tangled
with her knitting her embroidery
whatever it was she hid them under
I didn't mean to go into all that
didn't intend to get confessional
and tell you how
every time I read a good poem
by a woman writer I'm always peeking
behind it trying to see
if she's still married
or has a lover at least
wanted to know what she did
with her kids while she wrote it
or whether she had any
and if she didn't if she'd chosen
not to or if she did did she
choose and why   I didn't mean
to bother with that
and I certainly wasn't going
to tell you about the time
my best friend was sick in intensive care
and I went down to see her
but they wouldn't let me in
because I wasn't her husband
or her father   her mother
I wasn't family
I was just her friend
and the friendship of women
wasn't mentioned

in hospital policy
or how I went out and kicked
a dent in the fender of my car
and sat there crying because
if she died I wouldn't be able
to tell her how much I loved her
(though she didn't and we laugh
about it now) but that's what got me
started I suppose   wanting to write
a gesture of friendship
for a woman for a woman writer
for Virginia Woolf
and thinking I could do it
easily   separating the words
from the lives they come from
that's what a good poem should do
after all and I wasn't going to make excuses
for being a woman   blaming years of silence
for leaving us
so much to say

This started out as a simple poem
for Virginia Woolf
it wasn't going to mention history
or choices or women's lives
the complexities of women's friendships
or the countless gritty details
of an ordinary woman's life
that never appear in poems at all
yet even as I write these words
those ordinary details intervene
between the poem I meant to write
and this one   where the delicate faces
of my children   faces of friends
of women I have never even seen
glow on the blank pages
and deeper than any silence
press around me
waiting their turn

THE HEROES YOU HAD AS A GIRL

The heroes you had as a girl
were always three grades ahead of you
taller than the boys in your own class
taller even than your brothers
and the layers of muscle ripening
under their thin shirts their jeans
made your palms itch
for something you didn't know how to explain
but wanted to   sitting with your girlfriends
in the hot dry grass
at the edge of the parking-lot
where all day Saturday they worked on their cars
hunched over the greasy mysteries of their engines
occasionally raising their heads
their eyes flicking
to where you were included
as part of the landscape

Sundays they practised more dangerous manoeuvres
till your eyes stung with the smell
of oil and burning rubber
and once they built arches of flaming
orange crates   you remember them spinning
through the air when one car missed
remember the screams that burned your throat
before you realized no-one was hurt
your voices fluttering like foolish birds
on the wild currents of their laughter
and now twenty years later the hero
who drove that car returns as unexpectedly
as the memory and just as out of place
you watch him study a display of bathroom fixtures
in the hardware department of Simpsons-Sears
he's grown fat and balding
and you think how easy it would be
to walk right over tap him
on the shoulder say *hello*
remember me   and if he didn't
you could laugh it off

at least you've kept your figure
that's not what stops you now
though something does
and as he walks away
you can feel the dry grass biting
the backs of your legs   the uncomfortable
angle of your knees as you sat just so
practising your own dangerous manoeuvres
not being noticed   not noticing
the other girls   forgetting their names
the shapes of their faces reddening in the sun
(though you remember those burning arches
your throat tightening again around those foolish screams,
you think you could explain it now
and that's what stops you
knowing you want nothing less
than for him to turn
peel off his shirt to show you
burn scars on his chest
and in the sullen landscape of his eyes
you want the faces of those girls
your own among them burning
brighter than any fire

COMMON MAGIC

Your best friend falls in love
and her brain turns to water.
You can watch her lips move,
making the customary sounds,
but you can see they're merely
words, flimsy as bubbles rising
from some golden sea where she
swims sleek and exotic as a mermaid.

It's always like that.
You stop for lunch in a crowded
restaurant and the waitress floats
toward you. You can tell she doesn't care

whether you have the baked or french-fried
and you wonder if your voice comes
in bubbles too.

It's not just women either. Or love
for that matter. The old man
across from you on the bus holds
a young child on his knee; he is singing
to her and his voice is a small boy
turning somersaults in the green
country of his blood.
It's only when the driver calls his stop
that he emerges into this puzzle
of brick and tiny hedges. Only then
you notice his shaking hands, his need
of the child to guide him home.

All over the city
you move in your own seasons
through the season of others: old women, faces
clawed by weather you can't feel
clack dry tongues at passersby
while adolescents seethe
in their glassy atmospheres of anger.

In parks, the children
are alien life-forms, rooted
in the galaxies they've grown through
to get here. Their games weave
the interface and their laughter
tickles that part of your brain where smells
are hidden and the nuzzling textures of things.

It's a wonder that anything gets done
at all: a mechanic flails
at the muffler of your car
through whatever storm he's trapped inside
and the mailman stares at numbers
from the haze of a distant summer.

Yet somehow letters arrive and buses
remember their routes. Banks balance.
Mangoes ripen on the supermarket shelves.
Everyone manages. You gulp the thin air
of this planet as if it were the only
one you knew. Even the earth you're
standing on seems solid enough.
It's always the chance word, unthinking
gesture that unlocks the face before you.
Reveals the intricate countries
deep within the eyes. The hidden
lives, like sudden miracles,
that breathe there.

THINKING WITH THE HEART

For Mary di Michele

*'I work from awkwardness. By that I mean I don't like to arrange things. If I stand
in front of something, instead of arranging it, I arrange myself.'*—Diane Arbus.

'The problem with you women is, you think with your hearts.'—Policeman.

How else to say it
except that the body is a limit
I must learn to love,
that thought is no different from flesh
or the blue pulse that rivers my hands.
How else, except to permit myself
this heart and its seasons,
like the cycles of the moon
which never seem to get me anywhere
but back again, not out.

Thought should be linear.
That's what the policeman means
when I bring the woman to him,
what he has to offer for her bruises, the cut
over her eye: *charge him or we can't help you.*
He's seen it all before anyway. He knows
how the law changes, depending on what you think.

It used to be a man could beat his wife
if he had to; now, sometimes he can't
but she has to charge him
and nine times out of ten
these women who come in here
ready to get the bastard
will be back in a week or so
wanting to drop the whole thing
because they're back together,
which just means a lot of paperwork
and running around for nothing.
It drives him crazy, how a woman
can't make up her mind and stick to it,
get the guy out once and for all.
'Charge him,' he says, 'or we won't help.'

Out of her bed then, her house, her life,
but not her head, no, nor her children,
out from under her skin.
Not out of her heart, which goes on
in its slow, dark way, wanting
whatever it is hearts want
when they think like this;
a change in his, probably,
a way to hold what the heart can't
without breaking: how the man who beats her
is also the man she loves.

I wish I could show you
what a man's anger makes
of a woman's face,
or measure the days it takes
for her to emerge from a map of bruises
the colour of death. I wish there were words
that went deeper than *pain* or *terror*
for the place that woman's eyes can take you
when all you can hear
is the sound the heart makes
with what it knows of itself
and its web of blood.

But right now, the policeman's waiting
for the woman to decide.
That's how he thinks of it; choice
or how you can always get what you want
if you want it badly enough.
Everything else he ignores,
like the grip of his own heart's red
persistent warning that he too is fragile.
He thinks he thinks with his brain
as if it were safe up there
in its helmet of bone
away from all that messy business
of his stomach or his lungs.
And when he thinks like that
he loses himself forever.

But perhaps you think I'm being hard on him,
he's only doing his job after all,
only trying to help.
Or perhaps I'm making too much of the heart,
pear-shaped and muscular, a pump really,
when what you want is an explanation or a reason.
But how else can I say it?
Whatever it is you need
is what you must let go of now
to enter your own body
just as you'd enter the room where the woman sat
after it was all over,
hugging her knees to her chest,
holding herself as she'd hold her husband
or their children, *for dear life*,
feeling the arm's limit, bone and muscle,
like the heart's.
Whatever you hear then
crying through your own four rooms,
what you must name for yourself
before you can love anything at all.

TIM LILBURN

(b. 1950)

Tim Lilburn was born in Regina, Saskatch-ewan and completed his BA there in 1974, after which he spent two years working for CUSO in Africa. Following several years as a Jesuit (1979–87), he served as writer-in-res-idence at the University of Western Ontario (1988) and now lives in Saskatoon, teaching literature and philosophy at St Peter's College in Muenster, Saskatchewan, and conducting poetry workshops at the Sage Hill Writing Experience. His publica-tions include *Names of God* (1986), *From the Great Above She Opened Her Ear to the Great Below* (with Susan Shantz, 1988), *Tourist to Ecstasy* (1989, nominated for a Governor General's Award), *Moosewood Sandhills* (1994), and *To the River* (1999), which won the Saskatchewan Book of the Year Award.

Lilburn's view of the relation of poet to world is best explained in 'How to Be Here?' (*Brick* 49, Summer 1994), where he suggests that 'The physical world cannot be known in the way poetry aspires to know it, intimately, ecstatically, in a way that heals the ache of one's separation from the world, it seems to me, outside the sundering of knowledge which contemplation is. . . . As the mind leans into the darkness of God, the old writ-ers said, it is slendered by awe, reduced to a good confusion: this is knowing. Language, as well, is chastened in contemplation and by being broken it provides a way by which the ineffable may be glimpsed.' Paradoxically, Lilburn argues, 'Language is sundered as one courts ecstasy,' constantly replaced by the objects and creatures of the world.

Language again and again springs at the essence, reaching for clarity, the exact fit between the look of the slow hills, occultly breathing and their feel, then denies each time what it comes up with. . . . Language asserts and cancels itself, names the world then erases the name, and in this restlessness one glimpses the aptness of confusion before the ungraspable diversity of here. Silence. The look goes on. The breaking up of language, language drawn into the reversal of language, is the speech of desire beating against the silence of the confusing land.

This provocative essay might seem, at first glance, to be at odds with both the exu-berance and the excess of Lilburn's poetry prior to *Moosewood Sandhills*, for which it serves as prose gloss and apologia. The poems of *Names of God* and *Tourist to Ecstasy* are characterized by an enormous verbal appetite and a headlong, careening quality that takes the breath away. The emerging poet obviously takes more delight in nam-ing than in silence or contemplation; and his approach to language would appear to be more gymnastic than gnostic. In fact, his immersion in language seems no less intense and erotic than his more recent efforts to forge a deeper relationship with the natural world. Perhaps William Blake's observation that 'the road of excess is the path to wisdom' should be summoned here, for Lilburn's temperament and poetic strategies certainly have their roots in the mystical tradition that includes Blake, Hopkins, Merton, and St John of the Cross.

While the early Lilburn dallies like a libertine in an orgy of sound and exploding vocabularies, jazzy rhythms, word-play, and other technical bebop, his own religious yearnings, not to mention his Jesuitical training and discriminations, are seldom out of sight or mind. The earliest poems, however charged they might be linguistically, strike a dominant note of praise or worship, even exultation, before the spectacle of this world and its creatures. However, since ecstasy, in love, poetry, and, presumably, religion is impossible to sustain, a deeper note must be sounded. As he acknowledges in the essay quoted above,

> We are lonely for where we are. Poetry helps us cope. Poetry is where we go when we want to know the world as lover. You read a poem or write one, guessing at the difficult, oblique interiority of something, but the undertaking ultimately seems incomplete, ersatz. The inevitable disappointment all poems bring motions towards the hard work of standing in helpless awe before things. 'The praise of the psalms is a lament,' the old men and women of the desert used to say. Poetry in its incompleteness awakens a mourning over the easy union with the world that seems lost. Poetry is a knowing to this extent: it brings us to this apposite discomfiting.

The contemplative 'requires a cognitive humility, a mortification of the intellect's will to power,' Lilburn argues in 'Contemplation and Cosmology'. 'You cannot truly see this stone if you believe the world is yours to do with as you will.' This is a radical politics that goes beyond red and green. In 'The Return to the Garden', he insists that 'praise is an assertion of language that erases language. . . . All things in their breathtaking otherness have nothing to do with us, but our deepest desire insists on bending us toward them, stripping us from ourselves,

from language, from a feeling of being masters in our own house.' As poet Maggie Helwig suggests (*Canadian Forum*, April, 1999): 'This is not a philosophical game. It is really a guide to a means of living in the world, one that encompasses the postmodern striving for diversity and moves beyond it, into this always-desired union that is never achieved and never entirely lost. It is, if read carefully, a kind of politics—a politics of what Lilburn calls "courtesy": a sort of radical respect and gentleness, that kind of precise delicacy of love that is all you have left when you have lost everything.'

This 'political' stance is further complicated, too, for the Canadian writer, who must struggle to make his own peace with a stolen land and its original inhabitants. As he says in 'Summoning the Land', notes for an exhibition of paintings by Saskatchewan artist Grant McConnell at the Art Gallery of Swift Current (March and April 1999), 'Europeans, helpless as we may be, have to find our own way of authentically being here, have to learn our own songs for this place. Until we learn our own songs and our own stories. . . . we're not sage around others' songs. What would our songs be? Where would they come from? Keeping quiet and listening is one place. This style of singing, of getting ready to sing, comes naturally to us out of the European contemplative tradition. Having nothing, leaning into what we don't know, hoping it will take us in.' (quoted in a review by Iain Higgins entitled 'Hungering Down, Homing In', written for *Books in Canada*).

These ideas find their fullest expression in *Poetry and Knowing: Speculative Essays & Interviews* (1995), which Lilburn edited and contributes to, and his own *Living in the World As If It Were Home* (1999, with an introduction by Dennis Lee), which won the Saskatchewan Non-Fiction Award. Two valuable sources on Lilburn are Brian Bartlett, 'The Grass Is Epic: Tim Lilburn's *Moosewood Sandhills*' (*Studies in Canadian Literature*, Vol. 20, 1, 1995) and Darryl Whetter's 'Listening with Courtesy: A

Conversation with Tim Lilburn' (*SCL*, Vol. 22, 1, 1997). In the latter, Lilburn says: 'First of all, I don't think of myself chiefly as a writer. That strikes me as an empty category, it's an unfilled room—"writer". I think of myself as someone who looks, or someone who engages in various contem-plative acts. That's my work. The writing is the sort of wake thrown by that ocular and contemplative momentum. . . . How does seeing what I do that way affect my work? The work has no shape before the look. The work is shaped by the contemplative exercise.'

NAMES OF GOD
for William Clarke, S.J.

1. LOVE AT THE CENTRE OF OBJECTS

At the pentecostal core of matter, a fire wind
whirligig, centrifuge of joy,
is You, Love, a lung
pumping light, auric squalls
inflating eyes in my skull's raw coal.

Ssssssst.   My bloodstream and the midpoints of my bone hear fire
gouging the inner face of flame. Which speaks.
'Dress, bride, in your blood's maroon gas,
oxygen feathers tipping each bone blue; on the red knuckle
thread desire's compound carat;
moth skip, heart-kamikaze, and explode
vaster, vaster in the inhaling charismatic glow.'

2. ALLAH OF THE GREEN CIRCUITRY

Salamu, my Lord.   Salamu alaikum.
You are here
for my synapses whip and sparkle
like lightninged willows,
are in tumoured air storm's throbbing,
are wind's ululation to my steel-shod nerves
dancing them as dust-spooked stallions.

Runners of rain trellis fire
to earth.   You ride the hissing flame,
Allah of the Green Circuitry,
to jazz with love juice the chlorophyll current
to flash sunflower, crimson, orange.

You live, ah, You
live to unflex in the crux of a woman's dark ear,
coloured cloud
pressing into mind's white storm.

3. LIGHT'S GOBBLING EYE

O nourishing dark, O blank cloud,
You haul in my debris, compress it
in the stupendous clench of Your Heart
to nothing.

Light whorls toward You, a vanishing point
where perfection absents You; whorls
toward You, screwing
itself into its shadow core,
letting its socket eat it.   O dark gravity, we decry
this cannibalism,
though the shimmering particles stampede
with greased monomania.

I, now, feel the suck, tide
of light raking over bones, unsnarling
from joints of thought and feeling,
until I whistle into what-I-know-not,
ears imploding,
riding the bright shaft of self
into Your infolding, gold-splintered eye.

PUMPKINS

Oompah   Oompah   Oompah, fattening
on the stem, tuba girthed, puffing like perorating parliamentarians,
Boompa   Boompah   Booompah,
earth hogs slurping swill from the sun,
jowels burp fat with photons, bigger, bigger, garden elephants,
mirthed like St Francis, dancing (thud), dancing (thud,
brümpht, thud, brümpht) with the Buddha-bellied sun,
dolphin sweet, theatrical as suburban
children, yahooing a yellow

which whallops air. Pure. They are Socratically
ugly, God's jokes. O jongleurs, O belly laughs
quaking the matted patch, O my blimpish Prussian
generals, O garden sausages, golden zeppelins. How do? How do? How do?

Doo dee doo dee doooo.
What a rabble, some explode,
or sing, in the panic of September
sun, idiot praise for the sun that burns like a grand hotel,
for the sun, monstrous pulp in a groaning rind, flame seeded.
Popeyes, my dears, muscular fruit,
apoplexies of grunted energy flexed from the forearm vine,
self-hefted on the hill and shot
putted in the half-acre.

Carro-caroo.   Are you well,
my sweets, pleasure things, my baubles, my Poohs,
well?
I, weeding farmer, I, Caruso
them at dawn crow in the sun
cymballing mornings
and they Brunhilde back, foghorns, bloated alto notes
baroquely happy.
Not hoe teeth, not Rhotenone, but love,
bruited, busied, blessed these being-ward, barn-big,
bibulous on light, rampantly stolid
as Plato's Ideas, Easter Island
flesh lumps of meaning, rolling heads
in my 6-year-old nightmares,
vegetables on a ball and chain, sun anvils
booming with blows of temperature.

Come, phenomena, gourds of light, teach
your joy esperanto, your intense Archimedean aha
of yellow to me, dung-booted serf, whose unhoed brain,
the garden's brightest fruit, ones
communion with the cowfaced cauliflowers,
cucumbers twinkling like toes, and you,
clown prince,
sun dauphin of the rioting plot.

Touching An Elephant In A Dark Room

Poplars know everything about sleep,
their glossolalia saying even more than the *New Catholic Encyclopedia*,
speaking sleep's endless hexameters as a child syllables til her mouth blurs,
so I'll ask them, rosarying there in the wind, Saskatoons ripe-dopey under
    them,
if they think there's a true world next to ours
that sleep, the animal, visits often because it feels more at home there.
And I'll ask them if they think this shadow-place, sleep's nook in the
    country,
is not a shadow place at all, but the place where the grass elopes to,
or water keeps its money,
or at least where those nostalgic shadows in long grass in July that make us
wish we were born grass come from.
I'll ask if this world which is not a shadow-place but seems to be perhaps
    isn't
the true, flat lap where we sit, asleep or awake, when we hear that well-
    known voice
rushing past us, pure force,
expertly thrown, that ventriloquizes our lives into place and some kind of
    order.
Ah, telos.
All the lovely darknesses in the world growing out from there.
Rain engorged over cut hay, bees fattening over roses.
Where the shadows of light are truth itself.
This is what I want to know.   Is what we are really doing, really doing
with our lives whether we think of it or not,
a beast, or one of those forces that terrified Newton changed into an animal
galloping along in the dark afternoon of that other place, the one, lovely
    home
place, intuiting its way through the grassy savannahs they have there,
thinking out from between its shoulder blades?
If so, then we're completely at home in the real world.
All the lovely darknesses.
I have no doubt the poplars, masters and mandarins of sleep, could give
    them to us
chapter and verse, and tell us of all this together, the world, the whole
seen and unseen, how it's
ingeniously physical, and how it makes sense, not by doing anything,
    not by using

some bloody verb, but just by growing fatter each day with variety
as when magpies pass a song through the trees at 6:00 am like a basketball
at a Harlem Gobetrotters warm-up,
until the world gets into that happy numb state where judgements become
    even more
gorgeously impossible and love gets fluid and doubletake-sleek
as showboat acts fluked off in dream.

IN THE HILLS, WATCHING

Among the nerved grass, thrones,
dominions of grass, in chokecherry dewlapped hills,
hills buffalo-shouldered with shag of pulsed heat, meek hills,
sandhills of rose-hip and aster, in the philanthropic silence
fluxed by the grass, hounded, nervous with its own uncountability, grass
the frail piston of all,
in hill heat, lying down in the nearness of deer.
All knowing darkens as it builds.
The grass is a mirror that clouds as the bright look goes in.
You stay in the night, you squat in the hills in the cave of night. Wait.
Above, luminous rubble, torn webs of radio signals.
Below, stone scrapers, neck bone of a deer, salt beds.
The world is ending.

LEARNING A DEEPER COURTESY OF THE EYE

I

This is what you want.
You go into porcupine hills on a cold afternoon, down an aspen-ruffed path
    on Sam's land behind one low grass-knotted dune, then into real bush.
You will see deer.

Eros has nowhere to go but to become sorrow.
Piss marks on snow, flattenings,
creases where animals rolled, hoof-drag through drifts.
Exhaustion now as you walk toward the world's bright things.
Grass over snow, rose-hips clear and large in winter-killed thicket.
You will never make it all the way up to them.

II

The back fields are beautiful.
Take off your glove, coast
                fingers through oatgrass tips.
Four deer fountain from the poplar circle where
last fall the dog and you lay in old fox beds, breathing.
It hurts to look at deer,
deer under their name.
The light from their bodies makes you ashamed
and you look down.

How To Be Here?

I

Desire never leaves.

Looking at wolf willow bloom,
steaming through plushlands of scent toward the feeling
                                of its yellow,
self breaks up, flaring in stratosphere.
Looking undermines us.
The world and its shining can't hold our evaporating weight.
The world or what is there goes away
as we enter it, goes into halls of grass where torches of
                        darkness burn at noon.
Goes into light's lowest mind.
Leaving us, woo-floated from planet-like names and not quite
in things' shimmering gravity, alone in wide June air.
All-thumbs intensity that feels like virtue or music.

The Form quivers in the deer.
She doesn't see me; I'm lying barely above grass on a plank between fallen
                                poplars.

Hot day, slow wind; I lift on the cam of rhizomes.
The light behind her light is a shell she's just now born out of.
The Form is the doe's ease within herself.
I came from there.

If you dug with small tools into radiant belts round her shoulders
you'd come to a first settlement of the soul, stroke pottery bits, put
                              your tongue on old cinders and remember.
Tears will take you part of the way back but no further.

II

You wake, say, inside a large mosquito net,
you're away from yourself, older, near a desert perhaps,
air cool, dry, cloud of small sand, everything seems far
away, North African, night ancient, hard to read, you
look through the flap and see something bent toward a fire,
sparks low round it, stocky, sitting on its man-calves, force, tiptoed.

It is desire.
Yes, adding stick after stick, it seems,
managing in its naked hands
the reins of occurrence,
charioteering the will—horses of night.

You want to walk in the dark garden of the eye of the deer looking at you.
Want a male goldfinch to gallop you into the heart
                    of the distance which is the oddness of other things.
All would be well.
Desire never leaves.
Mercury's flower, a ghost-hurtling.

A mirror held before the spiritual wind
that blows from behind things,
bodying them out, filling them with the shapes and loves
of themselves.
You want that
and all else that shows in the bright surface polished by the lunge and
                              prowling of your desire.
You don't know what you are doing.

III

Desire tells me to sit in a tree.
I live alone, mentally clothed in the skins of wild things.
Desire sways ascent into me.
I look, I look: bull-necked hill, blue sweetgrass in hollows.

Knowing is a bowing, a covering of your face, before the world.
The tree's white tallness praises through me.
What receives the bow?
I am seduced by the shapeliness
          of the failure of knowledge.
My name in religion is the anonymity of grass.
I practise dying.
Each day, the tutor, old man, eros, repeats the lesson,
          I wrinkle my brow, my tongue protrudes.
Outside the window one chokecherry in the bush,
in a thicket of gooseberries,
adds a weight and compression of darkness under the sun
                    that is perfect.

EVERYTHING IS PROPORTION

Time to talk about cougar light
     of unflexed fields, river turning to straw, light
          curling down from the thinning north, the crane-
coloured paths, about the brown woman
and the star cluster of moles high on her back
and the river.

The sun on the geese-lit flow, city of all
                    that's turned away, the hovering night
lets itself down into the ginger reed water.
I've seen the river in the oldest part of the year,
city of sleep on its back,
the sun in its Egyptian boat,
and it said, look, you are worthless.
And then down through slow valleys of light,
sleeping badly then well in the lost house in bleached sand and old
                    cottonwood trees. And then I've come a little
                              further along.

There are small planets on Huaizhao's back
and her waist is a crane-coloured path,
a hawk-coloured path.

I have leaves in my mouth,
    it is deer light in the dark grass,
      water of near-night moving in the grass and
the cranes are cheadling to one another on islands of stubbled light and
    old bone clay. It's late. There is
the sparrow-coloured woman and the river
and the cougar light of the loose fields.
Small river, eyes lowered,
palomino river, the old world, nothing, a stone
shoulder in the grass.
The crane-coloured paths are as her waist is.
The paths go by the chapped water,
    incompetent and more or less certain.

JAN ZWICKY

(b. 1955)

Jan Zwicky, who was raised in Calgary, Edmonton, and Mayerthorpe, Alberta, has published *Wittgenstein Elegies* (1988), *The New Room*, (1989), *Lyric Philosophy* (1992) *Songs for Relinquishing the Earth* (1998), for which she received the Governor General's Award, and *Twenty-one Small Songs* (2000). She is a professional musician and currently teaches Philosophy at the University of Victoria. She also served as an editor for Brick Books and *The Fiddlehead*. Much of Zwicky's writing is concerned with 'lyric as an essentially non-linguistic mode of thought'. In an extended essay, 'Bringhurst's Presocratics: Lyric and Ecology', which appeared in Tim Lilburn's *Poetry and Knowing*, she has much that is interesting and provocative to say about the lyric impulse. Lyric understanding 'is not postmodern in the same way it is not Romantic; it rejects the primacy of words as bearers of meaning, and locates meaning's roots in the prelinguistic gestures of music and the rhythms of the non-human world.' Not only is the 'wordlessness' which she claims lyric 'desires' selfless, its pursuit could be fundamental to a radical social and environmental vision: 'Lyric longing is born of our constitutional inability to immerse ourselves completely in the living rhythms of the planet. The price of our capacity to manipulate these rhythms for our own short-term ends is our separation from them. / This capacity is concomitant with our capacity for language. The condition of language is the Herakleitean oppo-

site of lyric. That is: they die into one another. / To apprehend the mind as a living integrated complex of all facets of human experience, which is itself continuous with the larger integrated complex of the world as a whole, is to apprehend the mind ecologically.' The stance that mediates between the desire for lyric coherence (oneness with nature) and our capacity for technology (rooted in the separation that comes with language-use), she terms 'domesticity'.

What is most radical here, I believe, is that poetic perception is placed among the foremost means of perceiving and apprehending experience. The dissociated sensibility, in other words, recovers an ancient mode of perception, a channel back to primary experience, however that may be construed. If, as I believe, poetry is our first language, it has its own grammar, which is, rather, a code, not for making things fuzzy or difficult or ornate, but for descrambling reality, by taking away the names and by making our personal and tribal history strange so that we are forced to look at it anew.

Zwicky's interest in Wittgenstein has produced not only a book of poems but also an ongoing exploration of a scarcely describable link between music and philosophy. Summarizing the first section of *Lyric Philosophy*, she writes,

lyric poetry and philosophy are not mutually exclusive pursuits. . . [this claim rests] on a demonstration that we (professional philosophers) have not actually provided a *defence* of the claim that clarity of thought (the erotic pull of which I take to be defining of philosophical activity) can be provided only by systematic analysis. In the absence of such a defence, I have suggested, we must take seriously numerous examples of philosophy pursued according to other lights, and, indeed, must take seriously the possibility that there exist compositions which, owing to their form, have never been considered philosophical but which nonetheless *are*. This view, not surprisingly, turns out to point to an understanding of meaning both deeper and broader than that which can be provided by formal semantics. *How* we say, I argue, is integrally bound up with *what* we mean; and, I suggest, there exists a particular subclass of formally anomalous works, conditioned by a (lyric) demand for coherence *as well as* the (philosophical) demand for clarity—which thus might reasonably be called lyric philosophy. In their contexts, it turns out that one of the tests for truth becomes compositional integrity' (Introduction to 'The Geology of Norway', *The Harvard Review of Philosophy*, VII, 1999, 29–31).

While agreeing with Sigmund Freud that there are two basic ways of processing experience—primary psychical process as evidenced in jokes, dreams, music, and lyric poetry, where paradox and contradiction figure significantly as the organizing principles, and secondary process, which is linear, logical, analytical, and focused on judgment—Zwicky rejects the notion that dreams (or poems) need to be 'interpreted' to be understood. She insists, instead, that primary process is a genuine species of thought, that it is simply structured differently. By insisting that dreams must be interpreted, she argues, Freud delegitimizes them as a species of knowing. She rejects this view and its critical corollary, post-structuralism: '—the blithe nihilism of *il n'y a pas de hors-texte*—that most profoundly exemplifies the exclusion of non-linguistic thought from consideration, and is thus most clearly symptomatic of contemporary intellectual malaise. Lyric poetry, on the other hand, emerges as profoundly subversive: it takes the coin of the realm and turns it into jewellery—braids it in its hair, sews it on its dress, shapes it into teeth' ('Freud's Metapsychology and the Culture of Philosophy').

The lyric poet, she says, does not reject reason, but is driven by 'intuitions of coherence': 'lyric thought is also an attempt to arrive at an integrated perception, a picture or understanding of how something might affect us as beings with bodies and emotions as well as the ability to think logically.' She acknowledges that 'Language is a limited instrument—vast, supple, complex—but limited. / There is an implicit recognition of this fact in the extremity of some lyric figures which undoes linguistic knowing's claim to omniscience.' Further, 'If Western European society is founded on aspirations to immortality and a conviction that human fate is ontologically distinct from (because superior to) the lot of the rest of creation, lyric comprehension will come at the price of unreflective participation in dominant social, political, and economic institutions. That is, at the price, of power.'

HIGH SUMMER

High summer, roads home dusty
as the untouched shelf of childhood.
Fields dissolve to heat, bright arid seas.
Dry by the river, too, the floods
that undercut its banks, unrecoverable
violence. The only water we can bring is salt

and useless. What were
the names of hay? Brome? Timothy?
Those tall grey stalks were never so remote.
Wild rhubarb at the pig-barn
offers nothing, monstrous leaves
flat, poisonous. Unreadable.

Cows raise white heads,
their thoughts mysterious as moons.
Like tides they drift through pastures heedless
of the continent beneath their feet,
the sedimented strata, giant,
ferny, mute, dense, fathomless.

YOUR BODY

Like that couple I heard about later
who hit a snowy owl one night in a storm
                        out of nowhere, huge, impossible
            velvet crunch jack-knifed back into the blizzard, good
            god, stopped somehow, dry-throated, half-knowing, scared
            to look, ashamed not to
                        —so,
it now seems to me, I arrived at the door of your room.

I can imagine them
not saying anything, sitting,
snow swirling in the headlights, wondering
how much blood, how broken, what if
it's still alive, what if it looks

at us. And then
instead, all that whiteness,
the immense plain of its fragility,
how the skin does actually hold the body in,
your arms like snapped lilacs, bruises
pooling at your elbows, ankles, knees,
the excellence of the skull,
its visible perfection, and everything
unclenching irretrievably in that moment so that

they, too, must have stooped,
                         the blue-edged carom of beauty
        erupting through terror's grey prairie as a voice
        floods, choking with praise:
                                 lifts.

OPEN STRINGS

E, laser of the ear, ear's
vinegar, bagpipes
in a tux, the sky's blue, pointed;

A, youngest of the four, cocksure
and vulnerable, the white kid
on the basketball team—immature,
ambitious, charming,
indispensable; apprenticed
to desire;

D is the tailor
who sewed the note 'I shall always love you'
into the hem of the village belle's wedding dress,
a note not discovered until ten years later in New York
where, poor and abandoned, she was ripping up the skirt
for curtains, and he came,
and he married her;

G, cathedral of the breastbone,
oak-light, earth;

it's air they offer us,
but not the cool draught of their half-brothers
the harmonics, no,
a bigger wind, the body
snapped out like a towel, air
like the sky above the foothills,
like the desire to drown,
a place of worship,
a laying down of arms.
                    Open strings
are ambassadors from the republic of silence.
They are the name of that moment when you realize
clearly, for the first time,
you will die. After illness,
the first startled breath.

BILL EVANS: 'HERE'S THAT RAINY DAY'

On a bad day, you come in from the weather
and lean your back against the door.
This time of year it's dark by five.
Your armchair, empty in its pool of light.

That arpeggio lifts, like warmth, from the fifth of B minor,
offers its hand—*let me*
tell you a story . . . But in the same breath,
semitones falling to the tonic:
you must believe and not believe;
that door you came in
you must go out again.

In the forest, the woodcutter's son
sets the stone down from his sack and speaks to it.
And from nothing, a spring wells
falling as it rises, spilling out
across the dark green moss.
There is sadness in the world, it says,
past telling. Learn stillness
if you would run clear.

THE GEOLOGY OF NORWAY

*But when his last night in Norway came, on 10 December, he greeted it with some relief,
writing that it was perfectly possible that he would never return.*

—Ray Monk, *Ludwig Wittgenstein*

I have wanted there to be
no story. I have wanted
only facts. At any given point in time
there cannot be a story: time,
except as now, does not exist.
A given point in space
is the compression of desire. The difference
between this point and some place else
is a matter of degree.
This is what compression is: a geologic epoch
rendered to a slice of rock you hold between
your finger and your thumb.
That is a fact.
Stories are merely theories. Theories
are dreams.
A dream
is a carving knife
and the scar it opens in the world
is history.
The process of compression gives off thought.
I have wanted
the geology of light.

They tell me despair is a sin.
I believe them.
The hand moving is the hand thinking,
and despair says the body does not exist.
Something to do with bellies and fingers
pressing gut to ebony,
thumbs on keys. Even the hand
writing is the hand thinking. I wanted
speech like diamond because I knew
that music meant too much.

And the fact is, the earth is not a perfect sphere.
And the fact is, it is half-liquid.
And the fact is there are gravitational anomalies. The continents
congeal, and crack, and float like scum on cooling custard.
And the fact is,
the fact is,
and you might think the fact is
we will never get to the bottom of it,
but you would be wrong.
There is a solid inner core.
Fifteen hundred miles across, iron alloy,
the pressure on each square inch of its heart
is nearly thirty thousand tons.
That's what I wanted:
words made of that: language
that could bend light.

Evil is not darkness,
it is noise. It crowds out possibility,
which is to say
it crowds out silence.
History is full of it, it says
that no one listens.

The sound of wind in leaves,
that was what puzzled me, it took me years
to understand that it was music.
Into silence, a gesture.
A sentence: that it speaks.
This is the mystery: meaning.
Not that these folds of rock exist
but that their beauty, here,
now, nails us to the sky.

The afternoon blue light in the fjord.
Did I tell you
I can understand the villagers?
Being, I have come to think,
is music; or perhaps
it's silence. I cannot say.
Love, I'm pretty sure,
is light.

You know, it isn't
what I came for, this bewilderment
by beauty. I came
to find a word, the perfect
syllable, to make it reach up,
grab meaning by the throat
and squeeze it till it spoke to me.
How else to anchor
memory? I wanted language
to hold me still, to be a rock,
I wanted to become a rock myself. I thought
if I could find, and say,
the perfect word, I'd nail
mind to the world, and find
release.
The hand moving is the hand thinking:
what I didn't know: even the continents
have no place but earth.

These mountains: once higher
than the Himalayas. Formed in the pucker
of a supercontinental kiss, when Europe
floated south of the equator
and you could hike from Norway
down through Greenland to the peaks
of Appalachia. Before Iceland existed.
Before the Mediterranean
evaporated. Before it filled again.
Before the Rockies were dreamt of.
And before these mountains,
the rock raised in them
chewed by ice that snowed from water
in which no fish had swum. And before that ice,
the almost speechless stretch of the Precambrian:
two billion years, the planet
swathed in air that had no oxygen, the Baltic Shield
older, they think, than life.

So I was wrong.
This doesn't mean
that meaning is a bluff.
History, that's what

confuses us. Time
is not linear, but it's real.
The rock beneath us drifts,
and will, until the slow cacophony of magma
cools and locks the continents in place.
Then weather, light,
and gravity
will be the only things that move.

And will they understand?
Will they have a name for us?—Those
perfect changeless plains,
those deserts,
the beach that was this mountain,
and the tide that rolls for miles across
its vacant slope.

Border Station

There had been flooding all that summer, I recall,
acres of grey-brown footage from the Midwest—
but with reports confined to property, and human interest,
the reasons for the land's incontinence suppressed, those images
had skimmed past, seeming, as usual, not quite real.
The day had been hot, clear,
we'd eaten supper on the porch, and
later, quite late, had turned the radio on upstairs—
some thought of midnight news, perhaps—
I don't remember now.
The signal we pulled in—strongly,
because we weren't far from the border then—
was the last half-hour of a Brewers-Red Sox game.
It was coming from Milwaukee,
top of the ninth, two out, the Brewers leading,
and we hadn't been listening long when the announcer,
between a line out and Hatcher's
coming to the plate, commented on the weather:
there'd been a rain delay, it had been raining heavily before,
but now was easing up, just a light shower falling,
though a lot of lightning was still visible to the east and south.

Raised on the prairies, I
could see it clearly, suddenly
could see the whole scene clearly:
the crowd dwindling, several
umbrellas, the glittering aluminum of vacated seats,
the misted loaf of arc-lit light, the night,
deeper by contrast, thick and wet and brown
around it, flickering.

And at the same time I was struck, too—like
looking out across a huge relief map—by the hundreds of miles
between our bedroom and Milwaukee, by that continental
distance, and was overtaken inexplicably
by sorrow.
                    It was as though
in that moment of deep focus
I had tasted the idea of America.
As though it really might have had
something to do with baseball, and radio, and the beauty
of the storms that can form in the vast light above the plains—or,
no, extremity of some kind—clarity, or tenderness—
as though, that close to the end, levels
already rising on the leveed banks again,
the mistakes might have been human:
not justifiable, but as though
some sort of story might be told, simply,
from defeat, without apology, the way you might describe
the fatal accident—not to make sense of it,
but just to say, too late but still to say,
something had happened:
there was blood, blood everywhere, we hadn't realized,
by the time we noticed, rivers of it,
nothing could be done.

POPPIES

Some days, the wall that separates us from the future
is too thin. Standing in my mother's garden
by the bed of poppies on the northwest slope, wind
in the trees and the five-mile sky billowing over us,

I am caught again by their colour: water-colour,
sheer, like ice or silk, or, we imagine,
freedom. Their petals on the ground
collect in drifts, explosions
of arterial light.
                    Or perhaps it's that we are
that membrane, an instant thick, days
shine right through us as we charge around,
looking for some explanation in what hasn't happened yet
or what will never happen again. Like last night at dinner:
glancing up at the picture, the one that's always hung there,
the sudden clear presentiment that I would live
to walk into that dining room someday, after
the last death, and find it
waiting for me, the entire past
dangling from a finishing nail.

Poppies, what can they teach us?
The windshot light fills them
and they are blind.

PASSING SANGUDO

Sangudo, of the long hill and
the river flats; of the long shadows
in the river valley; Sangudo,
of the early evening, in the summertime,
on the way out Highway 43 after
a day in the city: how ugly
I used to think your name; and how,
unhappy in the car, unhappy
at the prospect of unwelcome dressed as welcome
that awaited us, I believed,
as we all believe, that growing up
meant never having to come back;
how, much though I deplored our town,
I was glad it wasn't you: that much smaller,
that much shabbier, the mud a little deeper,
the store fronts just that much more stark.
It must have rained most days that we drove past

because it rained most days then—or so it seems;
but of course plenty of times it must
have been winter, it being winter most of the year then
—or so it seems. And indeed the one recurring
nightmare of childhood, tobogganing down the river bank
and falling through the ice, with my father for some reason,
as well as my sister, and all of us drowning, silently, the ice
growing rigid over us in jagged chunks—that winter dream
was set outside Sangudo, just where the highway
crosses the Pembina, twenty feet
downstream from the bridge.
So it is mildly surprising—like discovering, at 40,
your handwriting closely resembles your great-uncle's
though you've never met—surprising I should find
that what I remember now
is neither rain nor snow, but long shadows,
early summer twilight, the sweet forgiving
roll of the land, the car's movement through it
steady, a quiet humming, exactly as it should be,
coming from nowhere, destined nowhere, simply moving,
driving past Sangudo, over the dark brown Pembina,
up the long hill, home.

ANNE CARSON

(b. 1950)

Anne Carson was born in Canada and, in addition to writing poetry and essays and painting volcanoes, has taught Classics at McGill and Berkeley. She is the author of *Feminist Spirituality and the Feminine Divine: an annotated bibliography* (1986) and *Goddesses and Wise Women: the literature of feminist spirituality, 1980–1992: an annotated bibliography* (1992). Her literary works include *Short Talks* (1992), *Eros the Bittersweet: An Essay* (1986), *Glass, Irony and God* (1995, with an introduction by Guy Davenport), *Plainwater: Essays and Poetry* (1995), *Autobiography of Red: a novel in verse* (1998), *Wild Workshop* (1997), *Economy of the Unlost: reading Simonides of Keos with Paul Celan* (1999), and *Men in Off Hours* (2000). She is a recipient of the QSPELL A.M. Klein Poetry Prize, the Pushcart Prize, and the prestigious Lannan and McCarthy Prizes.

None of her books list a birthplace and she is decidedly unforthcoming in interviews about herself and her writing. However, what she says of Sappho in *Men in the Off Hours* might well be applied to herself as a writer: 'namely, that she plays havoc with boundaries and defies the rules that keep matter in its place. . . . Sappho is one of the people of whom the more you see the less you know.' While Carson's elusiveness may diminish, or appear to diminish, now that her work has gained wide public acceptance and recognition—with accolades from Guy Davenport and Michael Ondaatje—it remains one of her strengths as a poet that the sites she can inhabit are manifold, not limited by notions of what is either possible or appropriate. She seems equally at home playing both the philosopher and the fool, writing poems that are weighty with ideas or with narrative as well as poems that are casual, slight, and epigrammatic, though it should be noted that her apparently casual work is seldom without depth and, like the volcanoes she admires, capable of unexpected eruptions. So, too, her longer narratives and meditations are infinitely playful at the level of language and idea.

The essay is central to Carson's work. The French noun *essai* comes from the verb *essayer*, meaning *to try*, or in Carson's sense to make a case or argument for a way of viewing reality. Even 'The Glass Essay', a narrative poem containing three plot-lines or levels of argument, is the work of a writer not only steeped in ideas and the minutia of literary history, but also fully attuned to the kind of verbal play and deep-imaging that evoke a sympathetic response in readers. In this sense, she is one of the foremost of a new breed of poets in Canada—including Phyllis Webb, Margaret Atwood, Christopher Dewdney, Robert Bringhurst, and Jan Zwicky—who are neither afraid of nor in thrall to ideas and learning.

Carson's unique way of viewing and talking about poetry is evident in her essay, 'Economy, Its Fragrance' (*The Threepenny Review*, Spring 1997), where she says: 'If I were marketing the poetry/prose distinction as a perfume, I would call it Economy. Not because poetry is the only form of verbal expression that manages its resources thriftily but because this thrift seems essential to poetry. Economic measures allow poetry to practice what I take to be its principal subversion. That is, insofar as it is economic, poetry relies on a gesture which it simultaneously dismantles.' She cites Marilyn Monroe's comment, 'I read poetry to save time,' and insists that poetry buys or saves time through various means of compression, 'subversively, by overflowing its own measures. . . .'

Carson presents poetry as a gift, whose principal grace, or value, is its economy. 'Every gift is a debt, the sociologists tell us,' Carson insists, 'insofar as a gift sets up the idea of a countergift: every gift contains the obligation to repay. And here is where we get entangled in the project of saving time. For obligations take place in that curious interval of time that we call in English "the present", and so long as an obligation is pending, the present can continue to be a gift.' Speaking of the two-line epitaph of Theodoros which appears in the work of fifth-century BC poet Simonides—'Someone rejoices now that I Theodoros am dead. Another over him will rejoice. To Death we are all debts owed'—Carson says: 'The poem that maintains his interest does so by a subversive economic action. That is to say, by thrifty management of its own measures—measures of rhythm, diction, syntax, image, and allusion—the poem secretes a residue, the poem generates a profit, the poem yields surplus value; lifting Theodoros past the termination of his debt into an endless extra space and time on the far side of restitution.' Echoing Jean-Paul Sartre's essay 'Why Write', Carson says: 'We as readers bestow this grace on him in the gift of our attention. In return we get the *charis* of the poem—that is, the grace or charm that makes a poem a poem, lifting it above the value of its paraphrasable content and persuading us to read or reread it however occasionally for two thousand years.'

Closely related to her notion that there are gifts and counter-gifts in literature is Carson's ongoing argument with narrative. As much as she understands and exploits the power of narrative in poetry, she also feels it must be resisted, or at least interrogated. In the introductory remarks to *Short Talks*, the ostensible author speaks of having awakened one morning to find that words were missing. In the process of recovering, or reinventing, the names, she mentions taking notes from three old women working in the fields, recording everything they said. Her comments might well stand as a poetic for Carson's overall project as a writer: 'The marks construct an instant of nature gradually, without the boredom of a story. I emphasize this. I will do anything to avoid boredom. It is the task of a lifetime. You can never know enough, never use the infinitives and particles oddly enough, never impede the movement harshly enough, never leave the mind quickly enough.'

THE GLASS ESSAY

I

I can hear little clicks inside my dream.
Night drips its silver tap
down the back.
At 4 A.M. I wake. Thinking

of the man who
left in September.
His name was Law.

My face in the bathroom mirror
has white streaks down it.
I rinse the face and return to bed.
Tomorrow I am going to visit my mother.

SHE

She lives on a moor in the north.
She lives alone.
Spring opens like a blade there.
I travel all day on trains and bring a lot of books—

some for my mother, some for me
including *The Collected Works Of Emily Brontë*.
This is my favourite author.

Also my main fear, which I mean to confront.
Whenever I visit my mother
I feel I am turning into Emily Brontë,

my lonely life around me like a moor,
my ungainly body stumping over the mud flats with a look of transformation
that dies when I come in the kitchen door.
What meat is it, Emily, we need?

THREE

Three silent women at the kitchen table.
My mother's kitchen is dark and small but out the window
there is the moor, paralyzed with ice.
It extends as far as the eye can see

over flat miles to a solid unlit white sky.
Mother and I are chewing lettuce carefully.
The kitchen wall clock emits a ragged low buzz that jumps

once a minute over the twelve.
I have Emily p. 216 propped open on the sugarbowl
but am covertly watching my mother.

A thousand questions hit my eyes from the inside.
My mother is studying her lettuce.
I turn to p. 217.

'In my flight through the kitchen I knocked over Hareton
who was hanging a litter of puppies
from a chairback in the doorway. . . .'

It is as if we have all been lowered into an atmosphere of glass.
Now and then a remark trails through the glass.
Taxes on the back lot. Not a good melon,

too early for melons.
Hairdresser in town found God, closes shop every Tuesday.
Mice in the teatowel drawer again.
Little pellets. Chew off

the corners of the napkins, if they knew
what paper napkins cost nowadays.
Rain tonight.

Rain tomorrow.
That volcano in the Philippines at it again. What's her name
Anderson died no not Shirley

the opera singer. Negress.
Cancer.
Not eating your garnish, you don't like pimento?

Out the window I can see dead leaves ticking over the flatland
and dregs of snow scarred by pine filth.
At the middle of the moor

where the ground goes down into a depression,
the ice has begun to unclench.
Black open water comes

curdling up like anger. My mother speaks suddenly.
That psychotherapy's not doing you much good is it?
You aren't getting over him.

My mother has a way of summing things up.
She never liked Law much
but she liked the idea of me having a man and getting on with life.

Well he's a taker and you're a giver I hope it works out,
was all she said after she met him.
Give and take were just words to me

at the time. I had not been in love before.
It was like a wheel rolling downhill.
But early this morning while mother slept

and I was downstairs reading the part in *Wuthering Heights*
where Heathcliff clings at the lattice in the storm sobbing
Come in! Come in! to the ghost of his heart's darling,

I fell on my knees on the rug and sobbed too.
She knows how to hang puppies,
that Emily.

It isn't like taking an aspirin you know, I answer feebly.
Dr. Haw says grief is a long process.
She frowns. What does it accomplish

all that raking up the past?
Oh—I spread my hands—
I prevail! I look her in the eye.
She grins. Yes you do.

WHACHER

Whacher,
Emily's habitual spelling of this word,
has caused confusion.
For example

in the first line of the poem printed *Tell me, whether, is it winter?*
in the Shakespeare Head edition.
But whacher is what she wrote.

Whacher is what she was.
She whached God and humans and moor wind and open night.
She whached eyes, stars, inside, outside, actual weather.

She whached the bars of time, which broke.
She whached the poor core of the world,
wide open.

To be a whacher is not a choice.
There is nowhere to get away from it,
no ledge to climb up to—like a swimmer

who walks out of the water at sunset
shaking the drops off, it just flies open.
To be a whacher is not in itself sad or happy,

although she uses these words in her verse
as she uses the emotions of sexual union in her novel,
grazing with euphemism the work of whaching.

But it has no name.
It is transparent.
Sometimes she calls it Thou.

'Emily is in the parlour brushing the carpet,'
records Charlotte in 1828.
Unsociable even at home

and unable to meet the eyes of strangers when she ventured out,
Emily made her awkward way
across days and years whose bareness appalls her biographers.

This sad, stunted life, says one.
Uninteresting, unremarkable, wracked by disappointment
and despair, says another.

She could have been a great navigator if she'd been male,
suggests a third. Meanwhile
Emily continued to brush into the carpet the question,

Why cast the world away.
For someone hooked up to Thou,
the world may have seemed a kind of half-finished sentence.

But in between the neighbour who recalls her
coming in from a walk on the moors
with her face 'lit up by a divine light'

and the sister who tells us
Emily never made a friend in her life,
is a space where the little raw soul

slips through.
It goes skimming the deep keel like a storm petrel,
out of sight.

The little raw soul was caught by no one.
She didn't have friends, children, sex, religion, marriage, success, a salary
or a fear of death. She worked

in total six months of her life (at a school in Halifax)
and died on the sofa at home at 2 P.M. on a winter afternoon
in her thirty-first year. She spent

most of the hours of her life brushing the carpet,
walking the moor
or whaching. She says

it gave her peace.
'All tight and right in which condition it is to be hoped we shall all be
    this day 4 years,'
she wrote in her Diary Paper of 1837.

Yet her poetry from beginning to end is concerned with prisons,
vaults, cages, bars, curbs, bits, bolts, fetters,
locked windows, narrow frames, aching walls.

'Why all the fuss?' asks one critic.
'She wanted liberty. Well didn't she have it?
A reasonably satisfactory homelife,

a most satisfactory dreamlife—why all this beating of wings?
What was this cage, invisible to us,
which she felt herself to be confined in?'

Well there are many ways of being held prisoner,
I am thinking as I stride over the moor.
As a rule after lunch mother has a nap

and I go out to walk.
The bare blue trees and bleached wooden sky of April
carve into me with knives of light.

Something inside it reminds me of childhood—
it is the light of the stalled time after lunch
when clocks tick

and hearts shut
and fathers leave to go back to work
and mothers stand at the kitchen sink pondering

something they never tell.
You remember too much,
my mother said to me recently.

Why hold on to all that? And I said,
Where can I put it down?
She shifted to a question about airports.

Crops of ice are changing to mud all around me
as I push on across the moor
warmed by drifts from the pale blue sun.

On the edge of the moor our pines
dip and coast in breezes
from somewhere else.

Perhaps the hardest thing about losing a lover is
to watch the year repeat its days.
It is as if I could dip my hand down

into time and scoop up
blue and green lozenges of April heat
a year ago in another country.

I can feel that other day running underneath this one
like an old videotape—here we go fast around the last corner
up the hill to his house, shadows

of limes and roses blowing in the car window
and music spraying from the radio and him
singing and touching my left hand to his lips.

Law lived in a high blue room from which he could see the sea.
Time in its transparent loops as it passes beneath me now
still carries the sound of the telephone in that room

and traffic far off and doves under the window
chuckling coolly and his voice saying,
You beauty. I can feel that beauty's

heart beating inside mine as she presses into his arms in the high blue room—
No, I say aloud. I force my arms down
through air which is suddenly cold and heavy as water

and the videotape jerks to a halt
like a glass slide under a drop of blood.
I stop and turn and stand into the wind,

which now plunges towards me over the moor.
When Law left I felt so bad I thought I would die.
This is not uncommon.

I took up the practice of meditation.
Each morning I sat on the floor in front of my sofa
and chanted bits of old Latin prayers.

De profundis clamavi ad te Domine.
Each morning a vision came to me.
Gradually I understood that these were naked glimpses of my soul.

I called them Nudes.
Nude #1. Woman alone on a hill.
She stands into the wind.

It is a hard wind slanting from the north.
Long flaps and shreds of flesh rip off the woman's body and lift
and blow away on the wind, leaving

an exposed column of nerve and blood and muscle
calling mutely through lipless mouth.
It pains me to record this,

I am not a melodramatic person.
But soul is 'hewn in a wild workshop'
as Charlotte Brontë says of *Wuthering Heights.*

Charlotte's preface to *Wuthering Heights* is a publicist's masterpiece.
Like someone carefully not looking at a scorpion
crouched on the arm of the sofa Charlotte

talks firmly and calmly
about the other furniture of Emily's workshop—about
the inexorable spirit ('stronger than a man, simpler than a child'),

the cruel illness ('pain no words can render'),
the autonomous end ('she sank rapidly, she made haste to leave us')
and about Emily's total subjection

to a creative project she could neither understand nor control,
and for which she deserves no more praise nor blame
than if she had opened her mouth

'to breathe lightning.' The scorpion is inching down
the arm of the sofa while Charlotte
continues to speak helpfully about lightning

and other weather we may expect to experience
when we enter Emily's electrical atmosphere.
It is 'a horror of great darkness' that awaits us there

but Emily is not responsible. Emily was in the grip.
'Having formed these beings she did not know what she had done,'
says Charlotte (of Heathcliff and Earnshaw and Catherine).

Well there are many ways of being held prisoner.
The scorpion takes a light spring and lands on our left knee
as Charlotte concludes, 'On herself she had no pity.'

Pitiless too are the Heights, which Emily called Wuthering
because of their 'bracing ventilation'
and 'a north wind over the edge.'

Whaching a north wind grind the moor
that surrounded her father's house on every side,
formed of a kind of rock called millstone grit,

taught Emily all she knew about love and its necessities—
an angry education that shapes the way her characters
use one another. 'My love for Heathcliff,' says Catherine,

'resembles the eternal rocks beneath—
a source of little visible delight, but necessary.'
Necessary? I notice the sun has dimmed

and the afternoon air sharpening.
I turn and start to recross the moor towards home.
What are the imperatives

that hold people like Catherine and Heathcliff
together and apart, like pores blown into hot rock
and then stranded out of reach

of one another when it hardens? What kind of necessity is that?
The last time I saw Law was a black night in September.
Autumn had begun,

my knees were cold inside my clothes.
A chill fragment of moon rose.
He stood in my living room and spoke

without looking at me. Not enough spin on it,
he said of our five years of love.
Inside my chest I felt my heart snap into two pieces

which floated apart. By now I was so cold
it was like burning. I put out my hand
to touch his. He moved back.

I don't want to be sexual with you, he said. Everything gets crazy.
But now he was looking at me.
Yes, I said as I began to remove my clothes.

Everything gets crazy. When nude
I turned my back because he likes the back.
He moved onto me.

Everything I know about love and its necessities
I learned in that one moment
when I found myself

thrusting my little burning red backside like a baboon
at a man who no longer cherished me.
There was no area of my mind

not appalled by this action, no part of my body
that could have done otherwise.
But to talk of mind and body begs the question.

Soul is the place,
stretched like a surface of millstone grit between body and mind,
where such necessity grinds itself out.

Soul is what I kept watch on all that night.
Law stayed with me.
We lay on top of the covers as if it weren't really a night of sleep and time,

caressing and singing to one another in our made-up language
like the children we used to be.
That was a night that centred Heaven and Hell,

as Emily would say. We tried to fuck
but he remained limp, although happy. I came
again and again, each time accumulating lucidity,

until at last I was floating high up near the ceiling looking down
on the two souls clasped there on the bed
with their mortal boundaries

visible around them like lines on a map.
I saw the lines harden.
He left in the morning.

It is very cold
walking into the long scraped April wind.
At this time of year there is no sunset
just some movements inside the light and then a sinking away.

KITCHEN

Kitchen is quiet as a bone when I come in.
No sound from the rest of the house.
I wait a moment
then open the fridge.

Brilliant as a spaceship it exhales cold confusion.
My mother lives alone and eats little but her fridge is always crammed.
After extracting the yogurt container

from beneath a wily arrangement of leftover blocks of Christmas cake
wrapped in foil and prescription medicine bottles
I close the fridge door. Bluish dusk

fills the room like a sea slid back.
I lean against the sink.
White foods taste best to me

and I prefer to eat alone. I don't know why.
Once I heard girls singing a May Day song that went:

> Violante in the pantry
> Gnawing at a mutton bone
> How she gnawed it
> How she clawed it
> When she felt herself alone.

Girls are cruelest to themselves.
Someone like Emily Brontë,
who remained a girl all her life despite her body as a woman,

had cruelty drifted up in all the cracks of her like spring snow.
We can see her ridding herself of it at various times
with a gesture like she used to brush the carpet.

Reason with him and then whip him!
was her instruction (age six) to her father
regarding brother Branwell.

And when she was 14 and bitten by a rabid dog she strode (they say)
in to the kitchen and taking red hot tongs from the back of the stove applied
them directly to her arm.

Cauterization of Heathcliff took longer.
More than thirty years in the time of the novel,
from the April evening when he runs out the back door of the kitchen
and vanishes over the moor

because he overheard half a sentence of Catherine's
('It would degrade me to marry Heathcliff')
until the wild morning

when the servant finds him stark dead and grinning
on his rainsoaked bed upstairs in Wuthering Heights.
Heathcliff is a pain devil.

If he had stayed in the kitchen
long enough to hear the other half of Catherine's sentence
('so he will never know how I love him')

Heathcliff would have been set free.
But Emily knew how to catch a devil.
She put into him in place of a soul

the constant cold departure of Catherine from his nervous system
every time he drew a breath or moved thought.
She broke all his moments in half,

with the kitchen door standing open.
I am not unfamiliar with this half-life.
But there is more to it than that.

Heathcliff's sexual despair
arose out of no such experience in the life of Emily Brontë,
so far as we know. Her question,

which concerns the years of inner cruelty that can twist a person into a
    pain devil,
came to her in a kindly firelit kitchen
('kichin' in Emily's spelling) where she

and Charlotte and Anne peeled potatoes together
and made up stories with the old house dog Keeper at their feet.
There is a fragment

of a poem she wrote in 1839
(about six years before *Wuthering Heights*) that says:

> That iron man was born like me
> And he was once an ardent boy:
> He must have felt in infancy
> The glory of a summer sky.

Who is the iron man?
My mother's voice cuts across me,
from the next room where she is lying on the sofa.

Is that you dear?
Yes Ma.
Why don't you turn on a light in there?

Out the kitchen window I watch the steely April sun
jab its last cold yellow streaks
across a dirty silver sky.
Okay Ma. What's for supper?

LIBERTY

Liberty means different things to different people.
I have never liked lying in bed in the morning.
Law did.
My mother does.

But as soon as the morning light hits my eyes I want to be out in it—
moving along the moor
into the first blue currents and cold navigation of everything awake.

I hear my mother in the next room turn and sigh and sink deeper.
I peel the stale cage of sheets off my legs
and I am free.

Out on the moor all is brilliant and hard after a night of frost.
The light plunges straight up from the ice to a blue hole at the top of the sky.
Frozen mud crunches underfoot. The sound

startles me back into the dream I was having
this morning when I awoke,
one of those nightlong sweet dreams of lying in Law's

arms like a needle in water—it is a physical effort
to pull myself out of his white silk hands
as they slide down my dream hips—I

turn and face into the wind
and begin to run.
Goblins, devils and death stream behind me.

In the days and months after Law left
I felt as if the sky was torn off my life.
I had no home in goodness anymore.

To see the love between Law and me
turn into two animals gnawing and craving through one another
towards some other hunger was terrible.

Perhaps this is what people mean by original sin, I thought.
But what love could be prior to it?
What is prior?

What is love?
My questions were not original.
Nor did I answer them.

Mornings when I meditated
I was presented with a nude glimpse of my lone soul,
not the complex mysteries of love and hate.

But the Nudes are still as clear in my mind
as pieces of laundry that froze on the clothesline overnight.
There were in all thirteen of them.

Nude #2. Woman caught in a cage of thorns.
Big glistening brown thorns with black stains on them
where she twists this way and that way

unable to stand upright.
Nude #3. Woman with a single great thorn implanted in her forehead.
She grips it in both hands

endeavouring to wrench it out.
Nude #4. Woman on a blasted landscape
backlit in red like Hieronymus Bosch.

Covering her head and upper body is a hellish contraption
like the top half of a crab.
With arms crossed as if pulling off a sweater

she works hard at dislodging the crab.
It was about this time
I began telling Dr. Haw

about the Nudes. She said,
When you see these horrible images why do you stay with them?
Why keep watching? Why not

go away? I was amazed.
Go away where? I said.
This still seems to me a good question.

But by now the day is wide open and a strange young April light
is filling the moor with gold milk.
I have reached the middle

where the ground goes down into a depression and fills with swampy water.
It is frozen.
A solid black pane of moor life caught in its own night attitudes.

Certain wild gold arrangements of weed are visible deep in the black.
Four naked alder trunks rise straight up from it
and sway in the blue air. Each trunk

where it enters the ice radiates a map of silver pressures—
thousands of hair-thin cracks catching the white of the light
like a jailed face

catching grins through the bars.
Emily Brontë has a poem about a woman in jail who says

> A messenger of Hope, comes every night to me
> And offers, for short life, eternal Liberty.

I wonder what kind of Liberty this is.
Her critics and commentators say she means death
or a visionary experience that prefigures death.

They understand her prison
as the limitations placed on a clergyman's daughter
by nineteenth-century life in a remote parish on a cold moor

in the north of England.
They grow impatient with the extreme terms in which she figures prison life.
'In so much of Brontë's work

the self-dramatising and posturing of these poems teeters
on the brink of a potentially bathetic melodrama,'
says one. Another

refers to 'the cardboard sublime' of her caught world.
I stopped telling my psychotherapist about the Nudes
when I realized I had no way to answer her question,

Why keep watching?
Some people watch, that's all I can say.
There is nowhere else to go,

no ledge to climb up to.
Perhaps I can explain this to her if I wait for the right moment,
as with a very difficult sister.

'On that mind time and experience alone could work:
to the influence of other intellects it was not amenable,'
wrote Charlotte of Emily.

I wonder what kind of conversation these two had
over breakfast at the parsonage.
'My sister Emily

was not a person of demonstrative character,' Charlotte emphasizes,
'nor one on the recesses of whose mind and feelings,
even those nearest and dearest to her could,

with impunity, intrude unlicensed. . . .' Recesses were many.
One autumn day in 1845 Charlotte
'accidentally lighted on a MS. volume of verse in my sister Emily's
    handwriting.'

It was a small (4 x 6) notebook
with a dark red cover marked 6d.
and contained 44 poems in Emily's minute hand.

Charlotte had known Emily wrote verse
but felt 'more than surprise' at its quality.
'Not at all like the poetry women generally write.'

Further surprise awaited Charlotte when she read Emily's novel,
not least for its foul language.
She gently probes this recess

in her Editor's Preface to *Wuthering Heights*.
'A large class of readers, likewise, will suffer greatly
from the introduction into the pages of this work

of words printed with all their letters,
which it has become the custom to represent by the initial and final letter
       only—a blank
line filling the interval.'

Well, there are different definitions of Liberty.
Love is freedom, Law was fond of saying.
I took this to be more a wish than a thought

and changed the subject.
But blank lines do not say nothing.
As Charlotte puts it,

'The practice of hinting by single letters those expletives
with which profane and violent persons are wont to garnish their discourse,
strikes me as a proceeding which,

however well meant, is weak and futile.
I cannot tell what good it does—what feeling it spares—
what horror it conceals.'

I turn my steps and begin walking back over the moor
towards home and breakfast.
It is a two-way traffic,

the language of the unsaid. My favourite pages
of *The Collected Works Of Emily Brontë*
are the notes at the back

recording small adjustments made by Charlotte
to the text of Emily's verse,
which Charlotte edited for publication after Emily's death.
'*Prison* for *strongest* [in Emily's hand] altered to *lordly* by Charlotte.'

HERO

I can tell by the way my mother chews her toast
whether she had a good night
and is about to say a happy thing
or not.

Not.
She puts her toast down on the side of her plate.
You know you can pull the drapes in that room, she begins.

This is a coded reference to one of our oldest arguments,
from what I call The Rules Of Life series.
My mother always closes her bedroom drapes tight before going to bed
    at night.

I open mine as wide as possible.
I like to see everything, I say.
What's there to see?

Moon. Air. Sunrise.
All that light on your face in the morning. Wakes you up.
I like to wake up.

At this point the drapes argument has reached a delta
and may advance along one of three channels.
There is the What You Need Is A Good Night's Sleep channel,

the Stubborn As Your Father channel
and random channel.
More toast? I interpose strongly, pushing back my chair.

Those women! says my mother with an exasperated rasp.
Mother has chosen random channel.
Women?

Complaining about rape all the time—
I see she is tapping one furious finger on yesterday's newspaper
lying beside the grape jam.

The front page has a small feature
about a rally for International Women's Day—
have you had a look at the Sears Summer Catalogue?

Nope.
Why, it's a disgrace! Those bathing suits—
cut way up to here! (she points) No wonder!

You're saying women deserve to get raped
because Sears bathing suit ads
have high-cut legs? Ma, are you serious?

Well someone has to be responsible.
Why should women be responsible for male desire? My voice is high.
Oh I see you're one of Them.

One of Whom? My voice is very high. Mother vaults it.
And whatever did you do with that little tank suit you had last year the
        green one?
It looked so smart on you.

The frail fact drops on me from a great height
that my mother is afraid.
She will be eighty years old this summer.

Her tiny sharp shoulders hunched in the blue bathrobe
make me think of Emily Brontë's little merlin hawk Hero
that she fed bits of bacon at the kitchen table when Charlotte wasn't around.

So Ma, we'll go—I pop up the toaster
and toss a hot slice of pumpernickel lightly across onto her plate—
visit Dad today? She eyes the kitchen clock with hostility.

Leave at eleven, home again by four? I continue.
She is buttering her toast with jagged strokes.
Silence is assent in our code. I go into the next room to phone the taxi.

My father lives in a hospital for patients who need chronic care
about 50 miles from here.
He suffers from a kind of dementia

characterized by two sorts of pathological change
first recorded in 1907 by Alois Alzheimer.
First, the presence in cerebral tissue

of a spherical formation known as neuritic plaque,
consisting mainly of degenerating brain cells.
Second, neurofibrillary snarlings

in the cerebral cortex and in the hippocampus.
There is no known cause or cure.
Mother visits him by taxi once a week

for the last five years.
Marriage is for better or for worse, she says,
this is the worse.

So about an hour later we are in the taxi
shooting along empty country roads towards town.
The April light is clear as an alarm.

As we pass them it gives a sudden sense of every object
existing in space on its own shadow.
I wish I could carry this clarity with me

into the hospital where distinctions tend to flatten and coalesce.
I wish I had been nicer to him before he got crazy.
These are my two wishes.

It is hard to find the beginning of dementia.
I remember a night about ten years ago
when I was talking to him on the telephone.

It was a Sunday night in winter.
I heard his sentences filling up with fear.
He would start a sentence—about weather, lose his way, start another.
It made me furious to hear him floundering—

my tall proud father, former World War II navigator!
It made me merciless.
I stood on the edge of the conversation,

watching him thrash about for cues,
offering none,
and it came to me like a slow avalanche

that he had no idea who he was talking to.
Much colder today I guess. . . .
his voice pressed into the silence and broke off,

snow falling on it.
There was a long pause while snow covered us both.
Well I won't keep you,

he said with sudden desperate cheer as if sighting land.
I'll say goodnight now,
I won't run up your bill. Goodbye.

Goodbye.
Goodbye. Who are you?
I said into the dial tone.

At the hospital we pass down long pink halls
through a door with a big window
and a combination lock (5–25–3)

to the west wing, for chronic care patients.
Each wing has a name.
the chronic wing is Our Golden Mile

although mother prefers to call it The Last Lap.
Father sits strapped in a chair which is tied to the wall
in a room of other tied people tilting at various angles.

My father tilts least, I am proud of him.
Hi Dad how y'doing?
His face cracks open it could be a grin or rage

and looking past me he issues a stream of vehemence at the air.
My mother lays her hand on his.
Hello love, she says. He jerks his hand away. We sit.

Sunlight flocks through the room.
Mother begins to unpack from her handbag the things she has brought
    for him,
grapes, arrowroot biscuits, humbugs.

He is addressing strenuous remarks to someone in the air between us.
He uses a language known only to himself,
made of snarls and syllables and sudden wild appeals.

Once in a while some old formula floats up through the wash—
You don't say! or Happy birthday to you!—
but no real sentence

for more than three years now.
I notice his front teeth are getting black.
I wonder how you clean the teeth of mad people.

He always took good care of his teeth. My mother looks up.
She and I often think two halves of one thought.
Do you remember that gold-plated toothpick

you sent him from Harrod's the summer you were in London? she asks.
Yes I wonder what happened to it.
Must be in the bathroom somewhere.

She is giving him grapes one by one.
They keep rolling out of his huge stiff fingers.
He used to be a big man, over six feet tall and strong,

but since he came to hospital his body has shrunk to the merest bone house—
except the hands. The hands keep growing.
Each one now as big as a boot in Van Gogh,

they go lumbering after the grapes in his lap.
But now he turns to me with a rush of urgent syllables
that break off on a high note—he waits,

staring into my face. That quizzical look.
One eyebrow at an angle.
I have a photograph taped to my fridge at home.

It shows his World War II air crew posing in front of the plane.
Hands firmly behind backs, legs wide apart,
chins forward.

Dressed in the puffed flying suits
with a wide leather strap pulled tight through the crotch.
They squint into the brilliant winter sun of 1942.

It is dawn.
They are leaving Dover for France.
My father on the far left is the tallest airman,

with his collar up,
one eyebrow at an angle.
The shadowless light makes him look immortal,

for all the world like someone who will not weep again.
He is still staring into my face.
Flaps down! I cry.
His black grin flares once and goes out like a match.

HOT

Hot blue moonlight down the steep sky.
I wake too fast from a cellar of hanged puppies
with my eyes pouring into the dark.
Fumbling

and slowly
consciousness replaces the bars.
Dreamtails and angry liquids

swim back down to the middle of me.
It is generally anger dreams that occupy my nights now.
This is not uncommon after loss of love—

blue and black and red blasting the crater open.
I am interested in anger.
I clamber along to find the source.

My dream was of an old woman lying awake in bed.
She controls the house by a system of light bulbs strung above her on wires.
Each wire has a little black switch.

One by one the switches refuse to turn the bulbs on.
She keeps switching and switching
in rising tides of very hot anger.

Then she creeps out of bed to peer through lattices
at the rooms of the rest of the house.
The rooms are silent and brilliantly lit

and full of huge furniture beneath which crouch
small creatures—not quite cats not quite rats
licking their narrow red jaws

under a load of time.
I want to be beautiful again, she whispers
but the great overlit rooms tick emptily

as a deserted oceanliner and now behind her in the dark
a rustling sound, comes—
My pajamas are soaked.

Anger travels through me, pushes aside everything else in my heart,
pouring up the vents.
Every night I wake to this anger,

the soaked bed,
the hot pain box slamming me each way I move.
I want justice. Slam.

I want an explanation. Slam.
I want to curse the false friend who said I love you forever. Slam.
I reach up and switch on the bedside lamp. Night springs

out the window and is gone over the moor.
I lie listening to the light vibrate in my ears
and thinking about curses.

Emily Brontë was good at cursing.
Falsity and bad love and the deadly pain of alteration are constant topics in
    her verse.

> Well, thou hast paid me back my love!
> But if there be a God above
> Whose arm is strong, whose word is true,
> This hell shall wring thy spirit too!

The curses are elaborate:

> There go, Deceiver, go! My hand is streaming wet;
> My heart's blood flows to buy the blessing—To forget!
> Oh could that lost heart give back, back again to thine,
> One tenth part of the pain that clouds my dark decline!

But they do not bring her peace:

> Vain words, vain frenzied thoughts! No ear can hear me call—
> Lost in the vacant air my frantic curses fall. . . .

> Unconquered in my soul the Tyrant rules me still—
> *Life* bows to my control, but *Love* I cannot kill!

Her anger is a puzzle.
It raises many questions in me,
to see love treated with such cold and knowing contempt

by someone who rarely left home
'except to go to church or take a walk on the hills'
(Charlotte tells us) and who

had no more intercourse with Haworth folk
than 'a nun has
of the country people who sometimes pass her convent gates.'

How did Emily come to lose faith in humans?
She admired their dialects, studied their genealogies,
'but with them she rarely exchanged a word.'

Her introvert nature shrank from shaking hands with someone she met on
    the moor.
What did Emily know of lover's lies or cursive human faith?
Among her biographers

is one who conjectures she bore or aborted a child
during her six-month stay in Halifax,
but there is no evidence at all for such an event

and the more general consensus is that Emily did not touch a man in her
    31 years.
Banal sexism aside,
I find myself tempted

to read *Wuthering Heights* as one thick stacked act of revenge
for all that life withheld from Emily.
But the poetry shows traces of a deeper explanation.

As if anger could be a kind of vocation for some women.
It is a chilly thought.

       The heart is dead since infancy.
       Unwept for let the body go.

Suddenly cold I reach down and pull the blanket back up to my chin.
The vocation of anger is not mine.
I know my source.

It is stunning, it is a moment like no other,
when one's lover comes in and says I do not love you anymore.
I switch off the lamp and lie on my back,

thinking about Emily's cold young soul.
Where does unbelief begin?
When I was young

there were degrees of certainty.
I could say, Yes I know that I have two hands.
Then one day I awakened on a planet of people whose hands occasionally
    disappear—

From the next room I hear my mother shift and sigh and settle
back down under the doorsill of sleep.
Out the window the moon is just a cold bit of silver gristle low on fading
    banks of sky.

> Our guests are darkly lodged, I whispered, gazing through
> The vault . . .

THOU

The question I am left with is the question of her loneliness.
And I prefer to put it off.
It is morning.

Astonished light is washing over the moor from north to east.
I am walking into the light.
One way to put off loneliness is to interpose God.

Emily had a relationship on this level with someone she calls Thou.
She describes Thou as awake like herself all night
and full of strange power.

Thou woos Emily with a voice that comes out of the night wind.
Thou and Emily influence one another in the darkness,
playing near and far at once.

She talks about a sweetness that 'proved us one.'
I am uneasy with the compensatory model of female religious experience
    and yet,
there is no question,

it would be sweet to have a friend to tell things to at night,
without the terrible sex price to pay.
This is a childish idea, I know.

My education, I have to admit, has been gappy.
The basic rules of male-female relations
were imparted atmospherically in our family,

no direct speech allowed.
I remember one Sunday I was sitting in the backseat of the car.
Father in front.

We were waiting in the driveway for mother,
who came around the corner of the house
and got into the passenger side of the car

dressed in a yellow Chanel suit and black high heels.
Father glanced sideways at her.
Showing a good bit of leg today Mother, he said

in a voice which I (age eleven) thought odd.
I stared at the back of her head waiting for what she would say.
Her answer would clear this up.

But she just laughed a strange laugh with ropes all over it.
Later that summer I put this laugh together with another laugh
I overheard as I was going upstairs.

She was talking on the telephone in the kitchen.
Well a woman would be just as happy with a kiss on the cheek
most of the time but YOU KNOW MEN,

she was saying. Laugh.
Not ropes, thorns.
I have arrived at the middle of the moor

where the ground goes down into a low swampy place.
The swamp water is frozen solid.
Bits of gold weed

have etched themselves
on the underside of the ice like messages.

> I'll come when thou art saddest,
> Laid alone in the darkened room;
> When the mad day's mirth has vanished,
> And the smile of joy is banished,
>
> I'll come when the heart's real feeling
> Has entire, unbiased sway,
> And my influence o'er thee stealing
> Grief deepening, joy congealing,
> Shall bear thy soul away.

Listen! 'tis just the hour,
The awful time for thee:
Dost thou not feel upon thy soul
A flood of strange sensations roll,
Forerunners of a sterner power,
Heralds of me?

Very hard to read, the messages that pass
between Thou and Emily.
In this poem she reverses their roles,

speaking not *as* the victim but *to* the victim.
It is chilling to watch Thou move upon thou,
who lies alone in the dark waiting to be mastered.

It is a shock to realize that this low, slow collusion
of master and victim within one voice
is a rationale

for the most awful loneliness of the poet's hour.
She has reversed the roles of thou and Thou
not as a display of power

but to force out of herself some pity
for this soul trapped in glass,
which is her true creation.

Those nights lying alone
are not discontinuous with this cold hectic dawn.
It is who I am.

Is it a vocation of anger?
Why construe silence
as the Real Presence?

Why stoop to kiss this doorstep?
Why be unstrung and pounded flat and pine away
imagining someone vast to whom I may vent the swell of my soul?

Emily was fond of Psalm 130.
'My soul waiteth on Thou more than they that watch for the morning,
I say more than they that watch for the morning.'

I like to believe that for her the act of watching provided a shelter,
that her collusion with Thou gave ease to anger and desire:
'In thou they are quenched as a fire of thorns,' says the psalmist.

But for myself I do not believe this, I am not quenched—
with Thou or without Thou I find no shelter.
I am my own Nude.

And Nudes have a difficult sexual destiny.
I have watched this destiny disclose itself
in its jerky passage from girl to woman to who I am now,

from love to anger to this cold marrow,
from fire to shelter to fire.
What is the opposite of believing in Thou—

merely not believing in Thou? No. That is too simple.
That is to prepare a misunderstanding.
I want to speak more clearly.

Perhaps the Nudes are the best way.
Nude #5. Deck of cards.
Each card is made of flesh.

The living cards are days of a woman's life.
I see a great silver needle go flashing right through the deck once from end
    to end.
Nude #6 I cannot remember.

Nude #7. White room whose walls,
having neither planes nor curves nor angles,
are composed of a continuous satiny white membrane

like the flesh of some interior organ of the moon.
It is a living surface, almost wet.
Lucency breathes in and out.

Rainbows shudder across it.
And around the walls of the room a voice goes whispering,
Be very careful. Be very careful.

Nude #8. Black disc on which the fires of all the winds
are attached in a row.
A woman stands on the disc

amid the winds whose long yellow silk flames
flow and vibrate up through her.
Nude #9. Transparent loam.

Under the loam a woman has dug a long deep trench.
Into the trench she is placing small white forms, I don't know what they are.
Nude #10. Green thorn of the world poking up

alive through the heart of a woman
who lies on her back on the ground.
The thorn is exploding

its green blood above her in the air.
Everything it is it has, the voice says.
Nude #11. Ledge in outer space.

Space is bluish black and glossy as solid water
and moving very fast in all directions,
shrieking past the woman who stands pinned

to nothing by its pressure.
She peers and glances for some way to go, trying to lift her hand but cannot.
Nude #12. Old pole in the wind.

Cold currents are streaming over it
and pulling out
into ragged long horizontal black lines

some shreds of ribbon
attached to the pole.
I cannot see how they are attached—

notches? staples? nails? All of a sudden the wind changes
and all the black shreds rise straight up in the air
and tie themselves into knots,

then untie and float down.
The wind is gone.
It waits.

By this time, midway through winter,
I had become entirely fascinated with my spiritual melodrama.
Then it stopped.

Days passed, months passed and I saw nothing.
I continued to peer and glance, sitting on the rug in front of my sofa
in the curtainless morning

with my nerves open to the air like something skinned.
I saw nothing.
Outside the window spring storms came and went.

April snow folded its huge white paws over doors and porches.
I watched a chunk of it lean over the roof and break off
and fall and I thought,

How slow! as it glided soundlessly past,
but still—nothing. No nudes.
No Thou.

A great icicle formed on the railing of my balcony
so I drew up close to the window and tried peering through the icicle,
hoping to trick myself into some interior vision,

but all I saw
was the man and woman in the room across the street
making their bed and laughing.

I stopped watching.
I forgot about Nudes.
I lived my life,

which felt like a switched-off TV.
Something had gone through me and out and I could not own it.
'No need now to tremble for the hard frost and the keen wind.

Emily does not feel them,'
wrote Charlotte the day after burying her sister.
Emily had shaken free.

A soul can do that.
Whether it goes to join Thou and sit on the porch for all eternity
enjoying jokes and kisses and beautiful cold spring evenings,

you and I will never know. But I can tell you what I saw.
Nude #13 arrived when I was not watching for it.
It came at night.

Very much like Nude #1.
And yet utterly different.
I saw a high hill and on it a form shaped against hard air.

It could have been just a pole with some old cloth attached,
but as I came closer
I saw it was a human body

trying to stand against winds so terrible that the flesh was blowing off
    the bones.
And there was no pain.
The wind

was cleansing the bones.
They stood forth silver and necessary.
It was not my body, not a woman's body, it was the body of us all.
It walked out of the light.

LOUISE BERNICE HALFE

(b. 1953)

Louise Bernice Halfe, whose Cree name is Sky Dancer, was born to the Saddle Lake Reserve in Alberta and sent by government decree at age seven to the Blue Quills Residential School in St Paul, Alberta. She chose to complete her schooling at St Paul regional high school, then went on to earn a Bachelor of Social Work degree from the University of Regina, as well as addiction counselling certificates from the Nechi Institute. Eventually, material from the journals she kept found its way into *Writing the Circle: Native Women Writers of Canada*. In 1993, she was awarded a third prize in the League of Canadian Poets national poetry contest. Her first book, *Bear Bones & Feathers* (1994), won the Milton Acorn Award and was shortlisted for three other prizes. In 1998, she published *Blue Marrow*, a multi-voiced long poem about aunts and grandmothers, in which the painful history of Native-White relations is vividly recalled and imagined. Halfe lives in Saskatoon, Saskatchewan.

In an Afterword entitled 'Comfortable in My Bones', Halfe describes her early impulses to write:

> In the Northern woods of Saskatchewan lies a creek; in the summer, it's a slender, lazy snail. When the spring rains come, it becomes a writhing snake creating turbulent waves, carrying everything before it. I walked the woods, following the creek, cradling paper leaves and talking stick, tobacco and

sweetgrass in my hands. On many occasions, I flew over logs in front of me eager to gain my solitude, eager to unload the discoveries I held close to my heart. My favourite spot overlooked the banks where I leaned against an old log I shared with ants. There, I contemplated something I had read, something I heard on CBC, something I dreamt, a conversation I had with my children or my husband. Sometimes, these discoveries were not pretty. . . . Whatever travelled into my thoughts, I immediately wrote, no matter how absurd or obscure. At times, I did nothing but breathe, listen and sleep, comfortable in my bones. The landscape of the earth and my mind were both simple and complex. I bore feelings that needed song. I often suffered the rash of shame bursting through the thin layers of skin. Yet my spirit demanded the spring of clear blood. I saw no need to run. The land, the Spirit doesn't betray you. I was learning to cry with the Spirit. I was safe to tear, to lick, to strip the stories from my bones and to offer them to the Universe.

With the encouragement of the elders and of friends amongst the tribe of writers, Halfe became more and more committed to her task.

> The map of oral stoytelling had long been laid out for me. I often entertained my children with legends I grew up with or made up on my own through the

images in classical music. Writing was a natural process. The stories inside me demanded face. They became my medicine, creating themselves in the form of poetry. These egg-bones were the voice which I had been addressing. My bare feet had felt the drum of the earth and the heartbeat of my palms. I did not fight these stories, though many times I wanted to run. I became a wolf, sniffing and searching, pawing, muzzling, examining every visible track I made or saw. I became the predator on the scent. I was the master, the slave, beholder and beheld, the voice and the song.

The oral tradition which jump-starts much of Halfe's work takes many forms, at times striving for simplicity, at other times being richly symbolic. So there will be poems not only about the functions of the body, but also about the yearnings and questing of the human spirit, poems that, while using his language, refuse the White Man's conventions. 'I will no longer be a binding sinew of stifling rules,' she insists, 'but rather a sinew of wolf songs, clear as morning air.' The poems of *Bear Bones & Feathers*, aside from their deliberate use of Cree words (with a glossary provided), are largely anecdotal, telling small stories or highlighting significant moments of perception. *Blue Marrow*, however, moves beyond the confines, simplicities, and inevitable distortions of the lyric into the complex, polyphonic territory of the long poem, the epic.

Like the epic, *Blue Marrow* embodies tribal history, lifting private memory to the level of collective song. It contains the typical epic cast of characters and list of antecedents, including Mouse Woman, Connolly Woman, Dodging Horse Woman, Big Swan Woman, all of Halfe's real and adopted relations. Rejoicing in what she calls 'these crumbs of memory', the speaker of *Blue Marrow* appeals to her sources: 'Grandmothers hold me. I must pass all that I possess, / every morsel to my children. These small gifts / to see them through life. Raise my fist. Tell the story. / Tear down barbed-wire fences.' The function of poetry, as Frank Kermode argues, is to 'make history strange', so that we are forced to look at it again and again with new insight, learning as we go. Halfe understands this task completely, as her use of the term *barbed-wire* indicates, for barbed-wire is not only the boundary material that turned the Cree grasslands into private farms, but also a prime ingredient for the imprisonment of human beings and entrapping soldiers, making them prime targets in wartime. While Sky Dancer's lyric outpourings are more immediately accessible, the anarchic, not so easily mediated gestures and strategies of *Blue Marrow* create a more powerful, complex, and enduring music that can only be suggested here in an abbreviated form; it must be read in its entirety.

WAGON RIDE

I lean on the wagon boards
and squint over the horse's head.
Blankets of firefly snow sparkle.

Horse's nostrils
bellow clouds and form
halos around their bending heads.

Their broad bodies move
slowly through unbroken trail.

Swishing tails
they fart
as fresh horse manure
fills the air.

I look back and view
the glazing broken path
as fresh snow covers
tracks.

I peer at the skies,
stick out my tongue
catch tiny diamonds,
cross my eyes to look at
the snowflakes before they
melt on the tip of my nose.

I peep at papa.
He's dressed in his trapping beaver mitts
and fraying hudson's bay coat.
A winchester stands by his side.
His head is tilted. He's listening to
the crackling trees.
Tiny antler icicles hang from his eyelids
and underneath his nose.
His cheeks are apple red.
Still
he puffs on his hand-rolled du maurier.

Today there is no smashing fist
and kicking working boots,
no thunder of an outraged bull,
no snarling of a rabid cat.

Just me and papa
cold bound by the mute,
freezing wind.

BODY POLITICS

Mama said,

Real woman
don't steal
from the sky and wear clouds
on their eyelids.

Real woman
eat rabbit well-done
not left half-raw
on their mouth.

Real woman
have lots of meat
on their bones.
They're not starving,
hobbled horses
with bony, grinding hips.

Real woman caress
with featherstone hands
not with falcon fingernails
that have never worked.

When she was finished talking
she clicked her teeth
lifted her arse
and farted
at the passing
city women.

LIZARD'S CURSE

She came in the form of a slippery lizard
with a feather in her mouth.

She wrapped her shiny flesh
over my woman's hills and crawled my crevice.

My eyes puffed and swelled
hailstones on my face.

My head ached
heavy with rocks.

I sought the healing
mountain
and the ocean's salt.

The soft pounding
of a beating drum
and a woman's chanting song.

The sweet scent of cedar
drifted in the wind

pulling, pulling
the power of the lizard.

The skin stretched,
and my wintering flesh
hung loose against my bones.

This lizard's claws and tattered feather
left its trail of scratches in my womb.

Bled dry of tears
the ocean's coolness
flushed my wound.

The mountain cedar released healing sap
its sacred smoke smudged my temples.
The throb of darkness slipped

with the last shedding of the lizard's curse
and the woman's chant.

HAMILTON'S GRAVEYARD

A seed was planted in the North Bay rain, cries, sweet cries
of night birds nesting in sheets of damp leaves.

The seed grew and swelled in the buried bodies of
my guts.

I wanted refund for my ten dollar IUD. Slanted
my eyes at the touch of the physician's hand. Swore
at the man whose pleasure I carried.

At home I thought of my mother's bitter root that would shred
my growing womb. I heard the voice of the sweetgrass braids.
I though of another baby twisted like a knotted tree, her head
an empty bowl. My hand rested on my swollen belly.

It started with liver sliding into the toilet. Later IV
vodka to still the belt around my waist. Then an incision
traced the equator across my skin and delivered
her into my frozen arms.

She died with a head of wet dark hair shining in the butter
dish. The rain fell down my drying breasts.

PICKING LEFTOVERS

There's men in the cellar shovelling, sweeping with combs and toothbrushes,
probing dental picks, doctors in surgical gloves cradling bones, jaws, teeth,
skulls, brittle arms and legs. Glueing pieces through lenses thicker than god's
eye, given birth dates and pencilled in bibles.

When I was a child, father would stop at sites we called picking leftovers. I've
returned with pitchfork in my hand, hammer against my heart. I've offered
tobacco to earth and raked layers of toilet bowls, tin cans, beer bottles, and
open-mouthed refrigerators. The skin of earth peels leaking pails, stench
buried in ceremony. And over there in marble fields boxes of bones cemented
in white rock. I give them birth dates, carefully record locations and fax the
findings to the ship docked, waiting for hundreds of years, on the eastern shore.

SO SORRY

the pope said i'm sorry
i sent a useless sack of scalped
potatoes.

he said indian agents would
give daddy a roll of twine,
a box of shells and whisky.
the spirits crawled inside
my daddy and never left.

he sent blankets
and my babies died.
he sent wooden sticks
with a dead man to hang
around my neck.

he said if i prayed
to you, geezus,
ate your body, drank
your blood,
threw out my bannock,
lived on my knees
counting stones,

i'd never be without
my family.

FROM BLUE MARROW

Mother leans against the door frame.
She seeks the sun. She folds her hand behind
her back, head covered with a red tam.
The distant weeping wakes agony in her arms.
Burning rice, raisins. She hibernates. Wind
gripes her. She no longer knows if her
asthma is acting up as she wipes her face.

She remembers another doorway, waving.
Cheap stupor burping, she watches
her daughter drive away. Grandchildren's
faces pinched against the car window.

> *They stay away. My life filled with husbands who pawed*
> *my children, slammed fist into their hides, my arms pining,*
> *my tongue mute. I bead moccasins, gather moss for the*
> *cradle board. Still the loon dives into my Lodge. The woodpecker*
> *knocks. Next time I see my Nōsisimak we talk like*
> *squirrel and fox.*

> *My window is a smear of greasy neck bones. Finger my heart.*
> *Tomorrow I offer print, tobacco when the sun comes. Pray.*
> *Sing Morning Song. Pray my daughter comes.*

Four winters we live in a red brick house.
Milk delivered, sometimes receive a package
of pemmican or dried meat. My children and I
inhale. I'd weave stories. Mother jigging.
Mother speaking *Michef*, cleaning berries.
Mother mixing flour paste for cardboard
wall. I'd search for Cree on the radio,
walk the valley with my little ones,
picking chokecherries. I'd crush till
I burst all over my canvas. The train
moves too slow. Baby against my breast.
I hold my little boy's hand.

> *The house echoes. My Nōsisim's out of his moss bag*
> *running in puddles. His lakes filled with ships, jet planes.*
> *Green eyes and straw blond hair shrink from my dark skin.*

At the women's cultural centre
Mother and I build our Lodge,
hold ourselves.

> *Kesic, my great-grandson, is like his grandpa. His eyes bluer.*
> *At the Round Dance he wants no other than his grandmother.*
> *My daughter carries him round to each relative. Lifts him high.*
> *I've long worn out my moccasins. I'll carry these memories*
> *deep in my Bundle.*

She wears her apron eating pork,
neck bones, bannock and lard. She uses
a prying knife, carves every crevice. Sucks
marrow making pucker sounds. She
mixes a pot of day-old porridge, swishes
the bone mix for her dogs. My mother.

Sweet grass lingers on her bedroom walls.
The basement, the smell of many loved, dead
cats. Outside the reserve, dogs, their
constant erections, like their jowls. Always
hungry, their ribs cling. Bones scatter the yard.
A slab of bacon hangs on the clothesline for the
chickadees. Garbage heaped on a platform.

She digs in her fridge where white lard is mixed
with stains of raspberry jam, exposed stew turns
black, a jar of cream withered and mossed.
She expects me soon so she keeps it.

She yearns to eat. Rabbit, deer, moose
nose, porcupine, beaver, muskrat, prairie
chicken. She wants fat. Must have fat.
Dried fat from the insides of cows.
Large gut fat from moose. She will hang
it above her sink after scrubbing the blood
and gristle off. The flies will gather,
feast, and she'll hang a sticky flycatcher.
Trapping. She'll hoard all of it. Walk
the night. Stalk her fridge again and again.

In my freezer I keep fresh neck bones, kidneys.
I buy her thick slices of Italian bread. She
hates it. She hands me her head,
thick sour memories.

In my office her fingers snap,
withdrawing from spotted painted snakes,
green and silver, Aborigine snakes.
I've done this on purpose. She knows.
We laugh.

We are collectors.
The most frail carries a pail
she hangs from her belly,
filled with roots, bark, rock,
insect legs, butterfly wings.
She wears them.
Butterfly wings, stuck with safety pins,
hundreds on a rag blanket.
Roots around her skate blades,
wings flap along the creek.
She plasters cedar, goose grease,
birch bark against her breasts.
Yes, wears them,
insects filing their legs on her tailbone,
siblings crying for her Bundles,
fingers too thin to hold the scrapes
of sunlight she moulded with her spit.

In a buffalo-mildewed lodge
lies a woman plucking,
dancing moons swimming marrow.
Spider babies fill her mouth,
spin on tender willow,
drag her skeleton
torched with red lightning,
green thunder, rain star light.
She sings, and sings.
Bones flush the night.

The old one binds ribs, moose gut,
gristle basket spun for her waist.
In the sugar-beet fields, she chops
rattlesnake heads. She cannot
cast them far enough. Venom lips.
She dances in rags,
scabs flaking, her jesus heavy.
Icicles hang in her words. She is
a hunched bear with golden ears.

We are collectors,
each one of us
picking garbage,

hoarding our treasures.
I find a one-eyed doll,
smiling cracked face, a carriage
where I sit my new baby,
a rubber snake, a halloween spider,
a Chinese butterfly.

Ram Woman, we met for the first time.
You stood on top of graves at White Rabbit,
large eye staring.
My legs wrapped my husband.
Your head thumped those stones.

Ram Woman, I stood naked
beneath the falls.
Your hoofs pounded
in that April rain. I remember
your fist in your mother's womb,
heels kicking her door.
When her lips split
two birds flew
from your mouth. You
lifted your moccasins
in a Ghost Dance.
While the drummers sang
dogs ran after your meat
and bones, pissed at your feet.
You let them in. They left
nickels and dimes.
Ram Woman, always in pursuit
of the laughing sun,
the pregnant moon.
A gorging river, you plunge
heedless into the spring fire.
You drag your laughing, weeping
child in a trail of snares, shutting
out the wind.
Ram Woman, Ram Woman,
in Kootenay Plains you sang,
lured me to your grave,
gave my heart a twist and

sent me flying, gave me
your large eye
for my stepping stone.

She came in a Vision, flipped many faces. Stone-aged wrinkled, creased like a
stretch drum, thin flesh, sharp nose. When the Sun sleeps she takes faded rays,
dresses her gown. She's the burnt rose of autumn, a blue-winged warbler. The
awakened river flanked in every woman, rolling pebbles over and over till stone
eggs are left. I travel with her youth, this Night Mistress. Hair fresh, sweet grass
braided in perfection. Long ago Grandmother danced in glades, women
crushed chokecherries, saved the blood, cleaned porcupine quills, wove them
into birch baskets, chewed sinew. They drummed, danced, lifted their dreams.
Ribboned the Sky. Raw-boned, they left their blood. In these moccasin
gardens I pick my medicines.

I talk to Magpies. Their eyes my Womanhood. How can I mark that? The first
ecstasy of climax? Each squealing baby? When told to cross my legs at
ceremony? When told never to walk over men when I was in Full Moon? Or
was it the first time I gave away all my jeans, sexy dresses and wore tents for
a year?

Did our Grandmothers know we would be scarred by the fists and boots of
men? Our songs taxed, silenced by tongues that speak damnation and burning?
Did they know we would turn woman against woman? Did they know some
of us would follow, take mates of colour and how the boarding of our worlds
would pulse breathing exiles connected to their womb? Did they know only
some would dig roots, few hands calloused from tanning? Did they know only
a few would know the preparation of moose nose, gopher, beaver-tail feasts?
Did they know our memory, our talk would walk on paper, legends told spar-
ingly? Did they know of our struggling hearts?

Each month Grandmother waxes and wanes, pregnant with wolverine and
baying dog. I become heat at Midnight, a yowling cat, fingers stained. Quills.
Mark these songs.

We are Star People. *Wēsākēcāhk* sang to the Water People to bring back Earth
from where we dove. She pinched the mud from the exhausted Muskrat. Blew
Yōtin. Blew *Iskotēw*. *Iskwēw* was born. *Pimātisiwin* fills woman. Man is born.

I return to Moon glade, turn up the sod, lift my songs. Dream. Grandmother
dances at Midnight. Grandmother Moon, my Shadow dreams the dark.

Grandmother, the Woman in Me.

ACKNOWLEDGEMENTS

MARGARET ATWOOD 'The Animals in That Country', 'Progressive Insanities of a Pioneer', 'Death of a Young Son by Drowning', 'Game After Supper', 'Notes Towards a Poem That Can Never Be Written', and 'A Women's Issue' from *Selected Poems 1966–1984* (Toronto: Oxford University Press Canada, 1990). Copyright © Margaret Atwood 1990. Reprinted by permission. 'A Night in the Royal Ontario Museum' from *The Animals in That Country* (Toronto: Oxford University Press Canada, 1968). Reprinted by permission. 'They eat out' from Power Politics copyright © 1971 by Margaret Atwood. Reprinted by permission of Stoddart Publishing Co. Limited. 'Morning in the Burned House' from *Morning in the Burned House* by Margaret Atwood. Copyright © 1995 by Margaret Atwood. Used by permission, McClelland & Stewart, Ltd. *The Canadian Publishers* and Houghton Mifflin Company. All rights reserved. MARGARET AVISON 'Snow', 'The World Still Needs', 'To Professor X, Year Y', 'The Swimmer's Moment', 'Voluptuaries and Others', 'Pace', 'Black-White Under Green: May 18, 1965', 'July Man', 'In a Season of Unemployment', 'Oughtiness Ousted', and 'We the Poor Who Are Always With Us' from *Selected Poems* (Toronto: Oxford University Press Canada, 1991). Copyright © Margaret Avison 1991. Reprinted by permission. 'Word: Russets' from *Not Yet But Still*, originally published in 1997 by Lancelot Press, now available from Brick Books, London, Ont. Reprinted by permission of the author. EARLE BIRNEY 'From the Hazel Bough', 'Anglosaxon Street', 'David', 'Bushed', 'Appeal to a Lady With a Diaper', 'A Walk in Kyoto', and 'The Bear on the Delhi Road' from *The Collected Poems of Earle Birney* by Earle Birney. Used by permission, McClelland & Stewart, Ltd. *The Canadian Publishers*. ROBIN BLASER '4', 'So', 'The Medium', 'Winter Words', 'The Finder', 'Tumble-Weed', 'The Truth Is Laughter 14', 'Dreams, April 1981', 'graffito', 'The Iceberg', 'Home for Boys and Girls', 'Image-Nation 21 (territory)', 'For Barry Clinton, d. 17, June, 1984, of aids', 'Praise to Them, December 30, 1984', and 'Of the Land of Culture' from *The Holy Forest* (Vancouver: Talonbooks, 1993). Copyright © Robin Blaser. Reprinted by permission of Talon Books Ltd. ROO BORSON 'Talk', 'Waterfront', 'Flowers', 'A Sad Device', 'Spring', 'Beauty', 'Intermittent Rain', 'City Lights', and 'Summer Cloud' copyright © Roo Borson. Reprinted by permission of the author. 'George Bowering', 'Water Memory', and 'Whuff' from *Water Memory* by Roo Borson. Used by permission, McClelland & Stewart, Ltd. *The Canadian Publishers*. GEORGE BOWERING Reprinted by permission of the author: 'Grandfather' from *Points on the Grid* (Contact Press, 1964); 'Dobbin' and 'Bones Along Her Body'; 'Summer Solstice' from *The Catch* by George Bowering (Toronto: McClelland & Stewart, 1976); 'Kerrisdale Elegies, One' from *Kerrisdale Elegies* by George Bowering (Toronto: Coach House Press, 1984). Reprinted by permission of Talon Books Ltd: 'Death' from *Urban Snow* by George Bowering (Vancouver: TalonBooks, 1991); 'Musing on Some Poets' from *Blonds on Bikes* (Vancouver: Talonbooks, 1997). Copyright © George Bowering. Reprinted by permission of the author and ECW Press: 'Fall 1983, Oliver' from *His Life: A Poem* by George Bowering (Toronto: ECW Press, 2000). DIONNE BRAND 'Hard Against the

Soul/I', 'No Language is Neutral', and 'Blues Spiritual for Mammy Prater' from *No Language is Neutral* by Dionne Brand. Copyright © 1990 by Dionne Brand. Used by permission of McClelland & Stewart, Ltd. *The Canadian Publishers.* ROBERT BRINGHURST Used by permission, McClelland & Stewart, Ltd. *The Canadian Publishers:* 'The Beauty of Weapons', 'Anecdote of the Squid', 'The Stonecutter's Horses', and 'For the Bones of Josef Mengele, Disinterred June 1985' from *The Calling* by Robert Bringhurst. Copyright © 1995 by Robert Bringhurst; 'These Poems, She Said' and 'Poems Without Voices' from *The Calling: Selected Poems, 1970–1995* by Robert Bringhurst. ANNE CARSON 'The Glass Essay' by Anne Carson, from *Glass, Irony, and God,* copyright © 1995 by Anne Carson. Reprinted by permission of New Directions Publishing Corp. LEONARD COHEN 'Elegy' from *Let Us Compare Mythologies* by Leonard Cohen. 'The Genius', 'Story' and 'Now of Sleeping' from *Selected Poems 1956–1968* by Leonard Cohen. 'I Have Not Lingered in European Monasteries', 'You Have the Lovers', 'As the Mist Leaves No Scar', 'Style', 'The Music Crept by Us', and 'How to Speak Poetry' from *Stranger Music: Selected Poems and Songs* by Leonard Cohen. 'God Is Alive' from *Beautiful Losers* by Leonard Cohen. All poems used by permission, McClelland & Stewart, Ltd. *The Canadian Publishers.* LORNA CROZIER 'A Brief History of the Horse', 'Inventing the Hawk', and 'Small Resurrections' from *Inventing the Hawk* by Lorna Crozier. 'Joe Lawson's Wife' from *A Saving Grace* by Lorna Crozier. 'Packing for the Future: Instructions', 'Watching My Lover', and 'A Kind of Love' from *What the Living Won't Let Go* by Lorna Crozier. All poems used by permission, McClelland & Stewart, Ltd. *The Canadian Publishers.* PATRICK FRIESEN Reprinted by permission of Turnstone Press: 'an audience with the dalai lama or, the old-fashioned pas de deux' from *Flicker and Hawk* copyright © 1987 Patrick Friesen; excerpt from 'Anna' and 'a woman from jamaica' from *You Don't Get to Be a Saint* copyright © 1992 Patrick Friesen. Reprinted by permission of the author and the publisher: 'ellice avenue' and 'what's the story natalya' from *St. Mary at Main* (Winnipeg: The Muses' Company/J. Gordon Shillingford Publishing, 1998); 'the man who licked stones' from *Carrying the Shadow* (Victoria: Beach Holme Publishers, 1999). GARY GEDDES All poems reprinted by permission of the author. RALPH GUSTAFSON ' "S.S.R., Lost at Sea" The Times', 'Now at the Ocean's Verge', 'The Newspaper', 'Wednesday at North Hatley', 'In the Yukon', 'I Think of All Soft Limbs', 'Ramble on What in the World Why', 'The Sun in the Garden', 'The Arrival of Wisdom', 'At the Café at Night', and 'State of Affairs' from *The Moment Is All: Selected Poems, 1944–1983* by Ralph Gustafson. 'Saint Lawrence Roasted on One Side Asked to be Turned Over' from *Winter Prophecies* by Ralph Gustafson. Copyright © 1987 by Ralph Gustafson. All poems used by permission from McClelland & Stewart, Ltd. *The Canadian Publishers.* LOUISE BERNICE HALFE 'Wagon Ride', 'Body Politics', 'Lizard's Curse', 'Hamilton's Graveyard', 'Picking Leftovers', 'So Sorry', and excerpt from *Blue Marrow* reprinted by permission of the author. D.G. JONES Used by permission of the author: 'Portrait of Anne Hébert', 'Beautiful Creatures Brief as These', 'For Françoise Adnet', 'These Trees Are No Forest of Mourners', 'Summer Is a Poem by Ovid', 'The Stream Exposed With All Its Stones', and 'Words from the Aviary' from *A Throw of Particles* (Toronto: Stoddart, 1983); 'The Ship as Navigator' and 'Covering Letter' from

The Floating Garden (Toronto: Coach House Press, 1995). Reprinted by permission of the author and the publisher: 'Stumblesong' from *Wild Asterisks in Cloud* (Montreal: Empyreal Press, 1997). A.M. KLEIN 'Heirloom', 'Autobiographical', 'For the Sisters of the Hotel Dieu', 'Political Meeting', 'Montreal', 'Lone Bather', and 'Portrait of the Poet as Landscape' from *Complete Poems*, Zailig Pollack, ed. (Toronto: University of Toronto Press, 1990). Reprinted by permission of University of Toronto Press Inc. ROBERT KROETSCH 'Poem of Albert Johnson' and 'Meditation on Tom Thomson' copyright © 1975 Robert Kroetsch. 'Seed Catalogue' copyright © Robert Kroetsch 1989. From *Completed Field Notes: The Long Poems of Robert Kroetsch* (originally published by McClelland & Stewart, now available from University of Alberta Press). Reprinted by permission. PATRICK LANE 'Passing into Storm', 'The Bird', 'Elephants', 'Mountain Oysters', 'Unborn Things', 'The Carpenter', 'Stigmata', 'Albino Pheasants', 'Winter 22', and 'Fathers and Sons' are reprinted by permission of the author. 'The Bathroom' from *The Bare Plum of Winter Rain* (Madeira Park, BC: Harbour Publishing, 2000). Reprinted by permission of the author and the publisher. IRVING LAYTON 'Look, the Lambs Are All Around Us', 'The Cold Green Element', 'The Fertile Muck', 'On Seeing the Statuettes of Ezekiel and Jeremiah in the Church of Notre Dame', 'Whatever Else Poetry Is Freedom', 'Berry Picking', 'Keine Lazarovitch 1870–1959', and 'A Tall Man Executes a Jig' from *The Collected Poems of Irving Layton*. Used by permission, McClelland & Stewart, Ltd. *The Canadian Publishers*. TIM LILBURN 'Everything is Proportion' from *To the River* by Tim Lilburn; 'In the Hills, Watching', 'Learning a Deeper Courtesy of the Eye', and 'How To Be Here?' from *Moosewood Sandhills* by Tim Lilburn. Used by permission, McClelland & Stewart, Ltd. *The Canadian Publishers*. 'Names of God', 'Pumpkins', and 'Touching an Elephant in a Dark Room' are reprinted by permission of the author. DOROTHY LIVESAY 'Fire and Reason', 'Going to Sleep', 'Spain', 'First Fisherman (from *Call My People Home*)', 'The Three Emily's', 'Bartok and the Geranium', 'Without Benefit of Tape', and 'The Woman I Am' from Collected Poems: *The Two Seasons* by Dorothy Livesay (Toronto: McGraw-Hill Ryerson, 1972). Reprinted by permission. PAT LOWTHER 'Touch Home', 'Regard to Neruda', and 'Wanting' from *Milk Stone* by Pat Lowther (Ottawa: Borealis Press, 1974). Reprinted by permission. 'Two Babies in Two Years' from *The Difficult Flowring* by Pat Lowther (Vancouver: Very Stone House, 1968). Reprinted by permission. 'Coast Range', 'Octopus', 'Hotline to the Gulf', and 'The Dig' from *A Stone Diary*. Copyright © Oxford University Press Canada 1977. Reprinted by permission. GWENDOLYN MACEWEN 'Poems in Braille', 'Manzini: Escape Artist', 'Poems Improvised Around a First Line', 'The Red Bird You Wait For', 'The Discovery', 'Dark Pines Under Water', 'Memoirs of a Mad Cook', and 'The Child Dancing' from *Magic Animals: Selected Poetry of Gwendolyn MacEwen* (Toronto: Stoddart, 1984). Reprinted by permission of the Estate of Gwendolyn MacEwen. 'Apologies', 'Nitroglycerine Tulips', 'Deraa', 'Ghazala's Foal', 'Tall Tales', and 'Notes from the Dead Land' from *The T.E. Lawrence Poems* by Gwendolyn MacEwen (Oakville: Mosaic Press, 1982). Reprinted by permission of Mosaic Press. DON MCKAY 'The Great Blue Heron', 'Fridge Nocturne', and 'Adagio for a Fallen Sparow' from *Birding or Desire: Poems* by Don McKay (Toronto: McClelland & Stewart, 1983); 'Waking at the Mouth of the Willow River' from *Night Field* by Don McKay (Toronto: McClelland & Stewart, 1991); 'Early Instruments' from *Apparatus* by Don McKay (Toronto: McClelland & Stewart, 1997); 'Nocturnal Migrants', 'Wings of Song', and 'Winter Solstice Moon: An Eclogue' from *Another Gravity* (Toronto: McClelland & Stewart, 2000). All poems reprinted by permission of the author. ELI MANDEL 'Thief Hanging in Baptist Halls', 'The Meaning of the I CHING', 'Houdini', 'Pictures in an Institution', 'From the North Saskatchewan', and 'On the 25th Anniversary of the Liberation of Auschwitz: Memorial Services, Toronto, YMHA, Bloor & Spadina, January 25, 1970', reprinted by permission of the estate of Eli Mandel. DAPHNE MARLATT Reprinted by permission of the author: 'Imagine: A Town' and 'A by-channel; a small backwater' from *Steveston*, Third Edition, by Daphne Marlatt, photographs by Robert Minden (Vancouver: Ronsdale Press, 2000); 'Vacant, Lots' and 'listen' from *Network* (Burnaby, BC: Talonbooks, 1980); 'feeding the pigeons' from *How Hug a Stone* (Winnipeg: Turnstone, 1983); 'booking passage' from *Salvage* (Red Deer: Red Deer College Press, 1991). Reprinted by permission of the author and the publisher: 'Healing' and 'Two women in a birth' from *Two Women in a Birth*. Copyright © 1994 Daphne Marlatt and Guernica Editions Inc. ERIN MOURÉ Reprinted by permission of Stoddart Publishing Co. Limited: 'Postmodern Literature', 'Divergences', 'Being Carpenter', and 'Toxicity' from Wanted Alive. Copyright © Erin Mouré; 'Miss Chatelaine' from Furious. Copyright © Erin Mouré; 'For Mitterand's Life, For My Life, For Yours' and 'Grief' from *Search Procedures*. Copyright © Erin Mouré. 'The Cooking' from *Sheepish Beauty, Civilian Love* (Montreal: Véhicule Press, 1992). Reprinted by permission of the publisher. JOHN NEWLOVE 'Then, If I Cease Desiring', 'Crazy Riel', 'Verigin, Moving In Alone', 'Ride Off Any Horizon', and 'The Pride' from *The Fat Man: Selected Poems 1962–1972* by John Newlove. Used by permission, McClelland & Stewart, Ltd. *The Canadian Publishers*. 'Such Fun, Such Fun' from *Apology for Absence: Selected Poems 1962–1992* (Erin, Ont.: Porcupine's Quill, 1993). Reprinted by permission. bp NICHOL 'Blues', excerpt from 'The Captain Poetry Poems', 'What Is Can Lit?', 'Allegory #6', 'Landscape: I', 'The Mouth', 'old mothers', 'For Caspar', 'St. Anzas VII', 'Monotones XXVII', 'sometimes I hear music', and 'You Too, Nicky' are reprinted by permission of the Estate of bp Nichol. ALDEN NOWLAN 'Beginning', 'Warren Pryor', 'God Sour the Milk of the Knacking Wench', 'For Nicholas of All the Russias', and 'For Claudine Because I Love Her' are reprinted by permission of the Estate of Alden Nowlan. 'And He Wept Aloud, So That the Egyptians Heard It', 'Britain Street', 'July 15', 'The Mysterious Naked Man', 'Ypres: 1915', and 'The Broadcaster's Poem' copyright © 1967, 1969, 1982 by Irwin Publishing Inc. Reprinted by permission of Stoddart Publishing Co. Limited. MICHAEL ONDAATJE 'Early Morning, Kingston to Gananoque', 'The gate in his head', 'Elizabeth', excerpt from *The Collected Works of Billy the Kid*, 'Letters & Other Worlds', 'The Cinnamon Peeler', 'Escarpment', and 'Last Ink' reprinted by permission of the author. P.K. PAGE 'The Stenographers', 'Landlady', 'Stories of Snow', 'Photos of a Salt Mine', 'The Permanent Tourists', 'Arras', and 'Evening Dance of the Grey Flies' from *The Hidden Room: Collected Poems, Volume One*, by P.K. Page, and 'After Rain', 'Brazilian Fazenda', and 'Planet Earth' from *The Hidden Room: Collected Poems,*

Volume Two, by P.K. Page (Erin, Ont.: The Porcupine's Quill, 1997). Reprinted by permission. E.J. PRATT 'Newfoundland', 'The Shark', 'Sea-gulls', 'Erosion', 'The Man and the Machine', 'From Stone to Steel', 'Newfoundland Seamen', and excerpt from 'Titanic' from *E.J. Pratt: Complete Poems*, ed. Sandra Djwa and R.G. Moyles (Toronto: University of Toronto Press, 1989). Reprinted by permission of University of Toronto Press. AL PURDY 'Home-Made Beer', 'A Handful of Earth', and 'Moonspell' from *Rooms for Rent in the Outer Planets* by Al Purdy (Madeira Park, BC: Harbour Publishing, 1996). Reprinted by permission. Used by permission, McClelland & Stewart, Ltd. *The Canadian Publishers*: 'The Country North of Belleville', 'The Cariboo Horses', and 'Wilderness Gothic' from *The Cariboo Horses* (Toronto: McClelland & Stewart, 1972); 'Arctic Rhododendrons' from *North of Summer* (Toronto: McClelland & Stewart, 1967); 'Lament for the Dorsets' and 'The Runners' from *Wild Grape* (Toronto: McClelland & Stewart, 1968). ROBYN SARAH 'Fugue', 'Maintenance', 'A Meditation Between Claims', 'Study in Latex Semi-Gloss', 'Scratch', and 'Passages' from *The Touchstone: New and Selected Poems* copyright © 1992 by Robyn Sarah. Reprinted by permission of Stoddart Publishing Co. Limited. 'On Closing the Apartment of My Grandparents of Blessed Memory' and 'The Cup Half Empty' from *Questions About the Stars* (London, Ont.: Brick Books, 1998). Reprinted by permission of the author. F.R. SCOTT 'Lakeshore', 'Old Song', 'Laurentian Shield', 'Overture', 'Charity', 'W.L.M.K.', 'The Canadian Authors Meet', 'Saturday Sundae', 'Martinigram', 'A Lass in Wonderland', 'Bonne Entente', and 'For Bryan Priestman' from *Collected Poems* by F.R. Scott (Toronto: McClelland & Stewart, 1981). Reprinted with the permission of William Toye, Literary Executor for the Estate of F.R. Scott. RAYMOND SOUSTER 'Young Girls', 'Lagoons, Hanlan's Point', 'Downtown Corner News Stand', 'Study: The Bath', 'Flight of the Roller-Coaster', 'All This Slow Afternoon', 'The Six-Quart Basket', 'The Death of the Grenadiers', 'A Morning in Brussels', 'Night Raider', 'Graveyard Shift', and 'Somalia' from *Collected Poems of Raymond Souster* (Ottawa: Oberon Press, 1980). Reprinted by permission of Oberon Press. ANNE SZUMIGALSKI 'Victim' and 'Girl with a Basket' from *Woman Reading in Bath* (Toronto: Doubleday Canada, 1974). 'Fishhawks' and 'The Lullaby' from *A Game of Angels* (Winnipeg: Turnstone Press, 1980). 'The Arrangement' and 'Shrapnel' from *Dogstones* (Saskatoon: Fifth House, 1986). 'Third Trimester' from *Voice* (Regina, SK: Coteau Books, 1995. 'Halinka' from *Rapture of the Deep* (Regina, SK: Coteau Books, 1991). All poems reprinted by permission of the Literary Executor for the Estate of Anne Szumigalski. SHARON THESEN 'The Landlord's Tiger Lilies', 'Elegy, the Fertility Specialist', 'September, Turning, the Long Road Down to Love', 'Animals', 'Afternoon With Liver', 'Valentine', 'Upon the Fake Mesa', and 'A Really Delicious Meal at Montri's' reprinted by permission of the author. MIRIAM WADDINGTON 'Girls', 'At Midnight', 'My Lessons in the Jail', 'On My Birthday', 'The Mile Runner', 'Ukranian Church', 'Gossip', 'The Survivors', 'How I Spent the Year Listening to the Ten O'Clock News', 'Ten Years and More', and 'Lately I've Been Feeling Very Jewish' from *Collected Poems* (Toronto: Oxford University Press Canada, 1986). Copyright © Miriam Waddington 1986. Reprinted by permission. FRED WAH 'My Horse', 'The Canoe, Too', 'Under and over', 'I'm Going to Keep on Dancing for the Rest of

My Life', 'waiting for saskatchewan', 'Elite' (2, 3, 4), 'The Poem Called Syntax', excerpt from 'Music at the Heart of Thinking' (89–95), and 'Father/Mother Haibun' (#4, #11, #17, and #19) are reprinted by permission of the author. BRONWEN WALLACE 'The Woman in This Poem', 'A Simple Poem for Virginia Woolf', 'The Heroes You Had As a Girl', 'Common Magic', and 'Thinking With the Heart' from *Signs of the Former Tenant* by Bronwen Wallace (Ottawa: Oberon Press, 1983). Reprinted by permission of Oberon Press. PHYLLIS WEBB 'Love Story', 'Sitting', 'A Tall Tale', 'To Friends Who Have Also Considered Suicide', 'Poetics Against the Angel of Death', 'Rilke', 'Eschatology of Spring', 'Prison Report', 'Treblinka Gas Chamber', 'Seeking Shape. Seeking Meaning', 'Cornflowers and Saffron Robes Belittle the Effort', and 'You Have My Approval' from *Selected Poems* (Vancouver: Talonbooks, 1982). Copyright © Phyllis Webb. Reprinted by permission of the author and Talon Books Ltd. JAN ZWICKY 'High Summer' and 'Your Body' from *The New Room* (Toronto: Coach House Press, 1989). 'Open Strings', 'Bill Evans: "Here's That Rainy Day"', 'The Geology of Norway', 'Border Station', 'Poppies', and 'Passing Sangudo' from *Songs for Relinquishing the Earth* (London, Ont.: Brick Books, 1998). All poems reprinted by permission of the author.

PHOTOGRAPH CREDITS

ATWOOD Graeme Gibson. BIRNEY Bruce Cole, Plum Studies. Used by permission. BLASER Kenneth Toronto. BORSON Sue Schenk. Used by permission of McClelland Stewart Ltd, *The Canadian Publishers*. BRAND Stephanie Martin. Used by permission of McClelland & Stewart Ltd, *The Canadian Publishers*. BRINGHURST Anne Tayler. CROZIER Susan Musgrave. Used by permission of McClelland & Stewart Ltd, *The Canadian Publisher*. COHEN Canada Wide Photo. FRIESEN Marijke Friesen. GUSTAFSON Betty Gustafson. JONES Monique Grandmangin. LANE Brenda Pelky. LILBURN Heather Hodgson. LIVESAY Lawrence Eddy, Victoria. LOWTHER *Vancouver Sun*. MacEWEN Sheldon Grimson. MARLATT John Reeves. MOURÉ Kim Fullerton. NEWLOVE Franke E. Brooke. NOWLAN Charles Clark. ONDAATJE Dominic Sansoni. PAGE Kate Williams. PRATT Ashley & Crippen. PURDY Intelligencer photo by Julia Drake. SARAH D.R. Cowles, Montreal. SCOTT William Toye. SOUSTER John Ayris. SZUMIGALSKI Fifth House Publishers. WEBB Betty Fairbank. WADDINGTON Paul Orenstein.

AUTHOR/TITLE INDEX